Stigma:

The Many Faces of Mental Illness

Joy Bruce, M.D.

Published by Starry Night Publishing.Com
Rochester, New York

TABLE OF CONTENTS

Stigma

Mental Illness has many faces…

I hide my face behind the mask…

Of many forms…and many colors…

To not be judged by painful stigma…

But why should I?

All that I have…and all that I am…

Are all that matter…

For I am me

And I am them

I'm not alone….

PREFACE

There is a lot of confusion and misinformation out there about mental illness. Despite a massive effort to diminish the stigma associated with mental illness, strong negative attitudes still persist because people don't know enough, and don't talk enough about it. Many don't realize that mental disorder can affect anyone from any walk of life, and that there are people with mental illness who have made remarkable achievements and who even have become quite famous.

Much of the information in this book, including personal accounts of celebrities and famous persons who have suffered from mood and personality disorders, is derived from valid media outlets and authoritative sources. I have endeavored to provide accurate and scientifically reliable information about the different forms of mental illness, to give the readers a greater understanding and knowledge that have eluded most, and to help remove the stigma that has always beset those who are suffering from the disorder.

If you see yourself anywhere in the discussion or personal accounts, then you are probably one of us. If you recognize any of those symptoms in yourself or in those you know and love, I hope that you will consider seeking some help, instead of denying that they exist. I do not advocate that you deal with mental issues on your own, because self-diagnosis of mental disorder is often misleading and inaccurate. An official diagnosis of mental disorder requires formal assessment by a qualified health professional trained in psychiatric diagnosis and evidence-based treatment.

When well-known personalities with mental disorders speak openly about their illness, they help reduce the mental health stigma and encourage other people to step up and seek help for their own issues.

This book was written with the goal of sharing public information about the various mental illnesses that affect one's mood and mind, breaking down the stigma, and making it less shameful for individuals to admit that they are who they are.

I hope it has achieved its purpose.

My thanks to Genevieve Torres Tiangco for giving me permission to use her photograph for the book cover.

Joy Bruce, M.D.
Miami, Florida
May 2017

THE STIGMA

The first time I told my family that I had been diagnosed with Bipolar Disorder, they could not believe it. One of my sisters was aghast.

"Not you", she said. "You are not like my clients. They are all crazy. Don't take their medicine."

She used to own and operate a home for the mentally disturbed. And she was prejudiced. She only accepted my condition after reading and understanding more about Bipolar Disorder.

-oOo -

Stigma is based on ignorance, extreme prejudice, and judgmental attitude. It is not acceptable in today's society.

People with mood disorders and mental illnesses are often stigmatized. News stories about deranged murderers often describe them as having a long history of bipolar disorder or other mental illness. This leads people to believe that individuals diagnosed with bipolar disorder have all sorts of extreme behavior and will almost always commit violent or criminal acts. When we have the disorder, we lose friends because they do not want to associate with someone who is manic-depressive or mentally ill.

Because of stigma, people may outright call us crazy and weird. Or they may talk behind our back, afraid that we could be dangerous and violent because we are emotionally or mentally unstable.

Because social support is key to our recovery, we are devastated when our family and friends begin to reject us, or when we get discriminated at work or in school because of the stigma that is associated with mood or mental disorder. Such a stigma contributes to the many tragic suicides that occur when those who suffer cannot see a way out of their situation.

Why is there so much lingering stigma about us? Much of the stereotyping is because people still do not know or understand what bipolar disorder and other mental illness are all about. Joking about us, belittling us, or calling us “psycho” can make us feel that we are not welcome and we do not belong. This attitude can be damaging, especially because belonging and feeling accepted is so central to our recovery. People do not realize that bipolar individuals like us are just like everyone else. We are not "crazy". We have a medical illness.

Although we have bipolar moods that go back and forth, there still are many times when we are normal and in control of our emotions. When we are symptom free, we still are able to fully use all of our mental faculties.

Our own belief that we are weak or damaged because of our illness can sometimes be the most difficult kind of stigma to fight. Our self-stigma can make us feel ashamed and can discourage us from getting the help that we need. We don’t want to be called “crazy” and we don’t want be singled out, branded, or degraded when people learn that we are seeing a psychiatrist. So, we refuse to see a mental health specialist and we avoid seeking treatment. We don’t realize that the extent to which we fight stigma can directly influence our recovery and quality of life. We might worry about our own reputation when we talk about bipolar disorder. This kind of attitude prevents us from learning more about our mental problem — and understanding that, like other medical conditions, our illness is treatable. We can’t just make ourselves well or “snap out of it”. Our illness is not contagious. We can’t catch it from someone else or transmit it to others, even though it can run in our family. If treated properly, we can be creative like many highly successful authors, artists and professionals who have been diagnosed with bipolar disorder and still thrived.

If you have a bipolar disorder, you have to realize that you are not your diagnosis. Your illness is not your fault, and it is not a character flaw. You have dreams, aspirations, and feelings just like everyone else. Coping with your bipolar disorder is challenging enough, without having to deal with the perceived shame and mistrust that can go along with it. You should not be blamed or ridiculed; rather, you should be commended if you are open about your illness and you get treatment for your symptoms. Your impulsive, erratic behavior may appear reckless, immature, and irresponsible to people unacquainted with the signs and symptoms of your disorder. The truth is, you can still control what's taking place chemically inside of you, if you get help from mental health professionals and find the right medication that can stabilize your moods. You can also help others who are suffering from the same disorder by listening, understanding, sharing your experiences, and making it clear that you are not alone. You are them.

Don't let stigma create self-doubt and shame on you. Seeking psychological counseling, educating yourself about your condition and connecting with others who are diagnosed with a mental illness can help you gain self-esteem and overcome destructive self-judgment.

If you have a mental illness, you need to learn how to deal with people who mock you out of ignorance. There are many misconceptions surrounding bipolar disorder, and until they are dispelled, the stigma will continue to cause you to suffer alone — hesitant or fearful to admit that you have a mental disorder.

Although knowledge about mental illness has improved, many people still do not fully understand it. The ignorance about the nature of mental or mood disorder can lead to unfair and baseless stigma, preventing people from understanding that it is treatable like other medical conditions.

Don't let the fear of being labeled with a mental illness prevent you from seeking help. Treatment can provide relief by identifying what's wrong and reducing symptoms that interfere with your work and personal life.

We have the power and option to decide whether or not to tell others about our illness. We can always state the facts about our depression or bipolar disorder, and dismantle any myth about our illness. When they learn about our diagnosis, our friends and family should be reminded that we do not fit into the stereotype of a “crazy person.” The stigma associated with bipolar disorder has to be challenged so that people like us who suffer from this illness can cope with our mental symptoms more effectively. If you are not familiar with the symptoms and signs of serious mental illness or mood disorder, it will help to know the facts, spend time with others who have the same disorder, and discuss feelings of self-stigma with others who can understand.

The stigma of bipolar disorder and other mental illnesses needs to be eradicated from our society by fighting against inaccurate information. If you are worried that you might have bipolar disorder or other mental illness, the best thing to do is educate yourself about the different types of disorder and then consult your doctor. Educating the public about mental and mood disorders can decrease the stigma and make it easier for people like us to ask for and receive the help that we need. People may even welcome the chance to learn more about us and our mental disorder.

-o0o-

BIPOLAR DISORDER

After my mom died in November 1994, I convinced my siblings to start a foundation in her memory. I called it NANAY, which was the name I used to call her when she was alive. Within two months after her death, I wrote the Articles and Bylaws, incorporated, and submitted our application for 501(c)(3) tax-exempt nonprofit organization in Florida. On New Year's Day, two and a half months later, I hosted our first event that was attended by more than 200 guests. I coordinated the event, designed the invitation card, created the souvenir program, and planned the program activities including performances for the night. Because I was working full time in the hospital, I spent my evening hours calling my friends, sending emails and writing letters to tell everyone about my new project. I attended two or three social events on weekends to talk about NANAY. I stayed up until 3:00 in the morning working on my project, and woke up at 6:00 am to prepare for my full day's work at the hospital. My goals included building a Center for the elders.

I rented a space at the back of a restaurant, taught the elders how to dance, convinced my friends to showcase them during community events, took them to a cruise and bought them a van. I wrote, designed, published and marketed a monthly magazine called "Current Medical News" containing medical and scientific information that I had translated into layman's term, and I gave copies to the elders and their families.

Seven months after my mom died, we held our first Mother's Day celebration, which later became our signature annual event. We honored the Most Distinguished Mothers of the Year with trophies and sashes. I rented limousines for their families so they could tour the city for a whole day and relax prior to the event. After the gala, I got calls from my friends thanking and congratulating me for what they said was a remarkable celebration.

The next day, I woke up feeling empty and so sad that I started crying. I felt helpless and hopeless, convinced that the previous evening's event was a flop and that I didn't do enough to make it a success. I stayed in bed and cried the whole day. I called in sick. I stopped seeing the elders, kept my door closed, and stayed in my bedroom, refusing to see anybody, or to answer any calls. I felt worthless. I was tired but could not sleep. I lost my appetite. I stayed that way for almost a month before I went back to my normal self. Then, I returned to work and began to see the elders again.

-o0o-.

Everyone, at various times in life, feels sad. This is normal. We experience ups and downs every now and then, when we fail a big test, when we don't get what we want, or when we break up with someone we love. But there is a difference between "normal" feelings of sadness and the depression associated with bipolar disorder. In contrast to the good days and bad days that everyone experiences every now and then, bipolar disorder is characterized by extreme mood swings that are a drastic change from our usual mood and behavior. The up and down moods ranging from high levels of energy to deep despair can be quite debilitating and, unless treated, can significantly increase the risk of suicide.

Bipolar disorder, also known as manic depression, causes serious shifts in mood, energy, thinking, and behavior—from the highs of mania on one extreme, to the lows of depression on the other. More than just a fleeting good or bad mood, the cycles of bipolar disorder last for days, weeks, or months. These mood swings are significant, usually extreme, and typically recur across the person's life span. It affects one's energy level, judgment, memory, concentration, appetite, sleep patterns, sex drive, and self-esteem. Although depression is not always part of the clinical picture, the hallmark symptoms of bipolar disorder are prolonged sadness and elevated, irritable mood that can be experienced at different times or they may be experienced within the same day.

To meet the definition of a manic episode, one must exhibit three or more of the following behaviors: racing thoughts, rapid and excessive speech that jumps from one topic to another, lack of focus, decreased need for sleep, inflated self-esteem, increased goal-oriented activities, impaired judgment, agitation and high-risk behavior such as impulsive sex and gambling one's life savings or mortgage money. A small percentage of bipolar disorder patients may demonstrate heightened productivity or creativity during manic phases. More often than not, the distorted thinking and impaired judgment that are characteristic of manic episodes can lead to dangerous behavior.

Excessive spending is one of the primary examples of risky behavior during manic episodes, but it can also happen during depression. It's an impulsive move to buy hundreds of dollars' worth of art supplies because of a sudden desire to become an artist, gamble your life savings, buy cars or houses that you can't afford, or buy last minute plane tickets to a vacation in Europe even if you are on a limited budget. At the end of a manic episode, you may find that you have spent all your life savings, incurred loans, and filled your credit cards with high debts resulting in a low credit score. You may have to put your retirement on hold, and be forced to work, because you have exhausted your emergency funds, and you need money to survive after you spending spree.

People with mania often have issues with substance abuse due to a combination of thrill-seeking and clouded judgment, or they can experience psychotic delusions or hallucinations that may lead to violent behaviors and immediatc hospitalization.

Some people are naturally talkative. One indication that someone is experiencing a manic episodc is pressured speech or jumping from one subject to another in rapid-fire mode, displaying thought patterns that make little sense to others around them, and rarely being able to follow a train of thought. They will talk rapidly and they will just talk over you if you try to speak.

Manic patients describe the euphoria of bipolar disorder as being "high", feeling very outgoing and unnaturally happy even if the situation does not warrant such behavior. Conversely, they may suddenly become extremely irritable. In mania, the disturbances in mood or behavior can be so damaging, or their sense of reality is so distorted that patients must be hospitalized for their own protection. Sometimes, severe episodes of mania or depression include symptoms of psychosis such as hallucinations and delusions. Psychotic symptoms in bipolar disorder tend to reflect the person's extreme mood state at the time. For example, delusions of grandeur, believing that God is speaking to them, that they are invincible, or that they are extremely wealthy and have special powers, may occur during mania; while unwarranted feelings of guilt, such as believing that they have stolen large amounts of money, that someone is stalking them, that they have committed a felony, that they have killed someone, or that the FBI is after them, may appear during depression. People with bipolar disorder who have these symptoms are sometimes incorrectly diagnosed as having schizophrenia,

Hypomania is the milder form that rarely progresses to full blown manic episodes, does not cause a significant decrease in the individual's ability to socialize or work, and does not require psychiatric hospitalization. All the features reported in mania – except psychotic symptoms – can occur in hypomania but to a less severe degree. In general, insight is preserved, and the person may not feel in need of help. Increased productivity, creativity, and decreased need for sleep can be experienced and can enhance every day functioning. It is also common for people to experience sleep disturbances, change in appetite, and anxiety occurring up to three weeks prior to a full onset of manic or depressive episode.

A depressive episode is characterized by extreme sadness, lack of energy, inability to enjoy normally pleasurable activities, withdrawal from family and friends, significant loss or increase in appetite, drastic weight change, sleep difficulty, lack of concentration, fatigue, feelings of helplessness, hopelessness, worthlessness, and suicidal tendencies. During severe depression, the neurotransmitters that regulate emotion become disturbed, causing bipolar individuals to think only of sad events, or only remember the bad times and the disappointments in life.

Self-injury, often including cutting or self-mutilation or self-harm, is an injurious attempt to cope with overpowering negative emotions such as extreme anger, anxiety, and frustration. Often, people who deliberately injure themselves have survived traumatic events during childhood. Self-injuring behaviors that occur because of difficulty coping with stress are more common with borderline personality disorder, but may happen when certain other mental health problems co-exist with bipolar disorder.

The dramatic mood episodes of bipolar disorder do not follow a set pattern -- depression does not always follow mania and the severity of mood phases can differ from person to person. Some people alternate between extreme episodes of mania and depression, but most are depressed more often than they are manic. Mania may be so mild that it goes unrecognized. People with bipolar disorder can also go for long stretches without symptoms. Both the manic and depressive periods can be brief, from just a few hours to a few days. Or the cycles can be much longer, lasting up to several weeks or even months. Many people may not even be aware that they have the disorder.

Bipolar disorder and symptoms of depression are not as uncommon as people may think. The disorder affects an estimated 1 to 2 percent of Americans, or more than 10 million people in the United States and as many as 60 million people worldwide. The estimated average age for the onset of bipolar disorder is during the early 20s, although there have been reports of the disorder beginning in childhood or adolescence. In fact, bipolar disorder appears before age 20 in about one in five manic individuals. People with bipolar disorder experience depressive symptoms at least three times as often as they do manic symptoms. In addition, recovering from depressive episodes typically takes longer than it does for manic episodes.

During a mixed affective state, both manic symptoms such as grandiose thoughts and depression such as excessive guilt or suicidal tendencies occur simultaneously. Anxiety disorder occurs frequently as a comorbidity in mixed bipolar episodes. They are considered to be high-risk for suicidal behavior since their depressive emotions such as hopelessness are occurring simultaneously with their manic or hypomanic swings so they are unable to control their impulses. Adult bipolar disorder is often accompanied by changes in cognitive processes and abilities, including reduced attention and executive capabilities and impaired memory.

Most marriages involving a partner with bipolar disorder end in divorce. A person may have frequent thoughts of suicide, which is a real risk for people with bipolar disorder. The suicide rate for people with bipolar disorder is 60 times higher than in the general public. That risk is present at each phase of the disease, not just during the depressive state. In fact, people with bipolar disorder are more likely to commit suicide during the manic phase because they have more energy to complete their plan.

Many people with bipolar disorder tend to wait years before disclosing their symptoms. During times of extreme moods, they can convince themselves that nothing is really wrong, although their family or co-worker can notice the change in their behavior. The most obvious indication of an oncoming episode is a change in personality. More often than not, they are unable to recognize that they are ill or that their life is being disrupted, and they might refuse to admit that they need help. It is not uncommon to feel deeply ashamed or humiliated, and lose confidence because of the behavior they have exhibited during one of these episodes. However, it is important that they be treated for this condition so they can manage their emotional state. Ignoring the problem won't make it go away. In fact, it will almost certainly get worse and can lead to problems in everything from their career to their relationships to their health. They are likely to live with the condition for the rest of their life if they are not treated. Since bipolar disorder is a chronic, relapsing illness, it is important to continue treatment even when they are feeling better. Most people with bipolar disorder need to continue treatment to prevent new episodes and stay symptom-free.

-o0o-

CAUSES AND RISK FACTORS

I was seeing my psychiatrist every week, and having psychotherapy sessions every other week for depression. My psychotherapist would ask me about my life experiences to identify possible stressors that could have triggered or caused my depression. I was 50 years old then, working full time as a professor at University of Miami and neuropathologist at Jackson Memorial Hospital, while also working part-time as consultant neuropathologist at Children's Memorial Hospital, and as a consultant to a number of research projects.

I was born to a big family. I was the third of sixteen siblings, and I was the eldest girl. Ever since I could remember, my parents expected me to discipline and take care of my younger siblings. It was a big responsibility that I had to carry on even as an adult. Although I never wanted to be a doctor, I had to take the medical course just to please my parents. I felt guilty when my mother died because I did not get the chance to be with her before she had her stroke. Because I lived in Miami and was busy with my work schedule, I would make excuses whenever she asked me to see her in San Francisco. I told her a couple of times that I could not make the trip because I was hosting a fundraising event for the nonprofit community organization of which I was a president. When I got the news that she was admitted for stroke, I called her and promised to visit her the next weekend. She was already brain dead by the time I saw her at the hospital.

Mostly out of guilt, I formed a nonprofit organization in her memory. When I hosted the first Mother's Day Event honoring the Most Distinguished Mothers of the Year, I placed her portrait prominently in front of the stage so everyone could see her. It was a tremendous success, but instead of celebrating, I woke up the next day in tears and became depressed for at least a month. And then I had another bout of depression after my father died.

My psychotherapist explained that perhaps my depression was triggered by my guilt and sense of loss following my mom's death. This was amplified after the Mother's Day event that was supposed to be held in her honor, because she was not physically there to celebrate with me. The depression that occurred after the death of my dad was most likely because I was torn between leaving and staying in my profession. Having lost both of my parents who were the reason why I became a doctor in the first place, I no longer had the pressure of having to please them and I was free get out of the medical field. But my sense of duty and responsibility for the profession that I had been practicing for more than 25 years were stopping me from leaving my medical practice and pursuing my real interest.

Also, I was living a stressful life, working four jobs, taking care of my family, and running two organizations at the same time.

She said that all these environmental and psycho-social factors were enough to drive me to depression.

I thought everything my psychotherapist was saying made sense. Still, I could not figure out why I would be okay every time I saw her, but would be crying and feeling worse by the time I walked out of her door. And the anti-depressant that I was taking was not helping me at all.

I showed her my collection of poems and the self-affirmations that I used to write every time I felt depressed. She read it and told me that my writings should have helped me get out of my depression.

I stopped seeing my therapist.

-o0o-

No one knows exactly what causes bipolar disorder. Like most mental illnesses, there is not a single cause of bipolar disorder that scientists can pinpoint. Biochemical, genetic and environmental factors may trigger the chemical imbalances in the brain. Genetic factors are likely to account for around 60-80% of the risk for developing bipolar disorder – indicating the key role that heredity plays in this condition. Your risk of developing bipolar disorder is also increased significantly if you have a first-degree relative suffering from this mental state.

It appears that certain people are genetically predisposed to bipolar disorder, yet not everyone with an inherited vulnerability develops the illness, indicating that genes are not the only cause. Genetic factors do not completely predict who will develop bipolar disorder and who will not, although your risk of developing bipolar disorder increases significantly if you have a first-degree relative who suffers from this mental state. More than two-thirds of the people with bipolar disorder have at least one close relative including grandparent or cousin, aunt, or uncle with the disorder or with unipolar major depression, indicating that the disease has a genetic component. Children of persons with bipolar disorder have about one in four chance of developing mood disorder and about one in ten chance of developing bipolar disorder, even if they are raised in the home of parents without the illness. The risk in a child jumps to 30 to 40 percent chance if both parents have bipolar disorder.

The inheritance pattern suggests that more than one gene may be involved in increasing susceptibility to psychiatric illness. There is an increased risk of a twin developing the illness, although this does not always occur. Even if one twin develops bipolar disorder, the other identical twin does not always develop the disorder, even though they share all of the same genes. Non-identical twins, who share only about half their DNA, tend to share bipolar disorder only about 10-20% of the time. They also face approximately twice the risk of developing unipolar major depression, suggesting that the two disorders may share some degree of genetic susceptibility. However, it is important to note that people with a family history of bipolar disorder do not always develop the illness.

Evidence shows that bipolar disorder is primarily due to a malfunction of certain chemical messengers called neurotransmitters that affect certain brain structures related to emotions, behavior, and thinking. These neurotransmitters may be activated on their own or they may be triggered by external factors such as psychological stress and personal relationships. Norepinephrine, serotonin, and dopamine, known as "monoamines", are examples of these neurotransmitters. This is why antidepressants that alter the levels of monoamines can sometimes have side effects on the brain.

Serotonin is the principal neurotransmitter that helps control moods and is involved in sleep, depression and memory; noradrenaline is generally associated with the body's alert and active state; while dopamine has been associated with psychosis and schizophrenia, a mental disorder characterized by distortions in reality and illogical thought patterns and behavior. Dopamine helps control movement in the body and is also linked to motivation, thinking and emotions.

Dopamine transmission has been shown to increase during the manic phase while decreased dopamine transmission is characteristic of the depressive phase.

Stressful life events can trigger bipolar disorder in someone with a genetic vulnerability. Recent life events and interpersonal relationships are also known to contribute to the likelihood of onsets and recurrences of bipolar mood episodes, as they do for onsets and recurrences of unipolar depression. Risk factors may include a family history, temperament, attitude and style of parenting that include parental rejection, hostility, harsh discipline, and child abuse. Like diabetes or asthma, the person has a biological vulnerability to changes in brain chemical, hormonal and immunologic changes. Stressful events and painful life experiences such as physical illness, problems with money, work or relationships, grief, loss of a loved one and physical or emotional abuse can trigger symptoms of bipolar disorder.

If you are living with bipolar disorder, a mixture of genes and a life event probably triggered your disorder. Environmental factors are likely to interact with genetic predispositions and play a significant role in the development and course of your bipolar disorder. Episodes of mania and depression also often follow a seasonal pattern. Manic episodes are more common during summer, and depressive episodes more common during the fall, winter, and spring. Sleep deprivation, acutely stressful life situations and hostility or criticism from the family may trigger depressive or manic episodes in those with an established illness.

There have been repeated findings that 30 to 50% of bipolar adults with traumatic or abusive experiences in childhood have an earlier onset, a higher rate of suicide attempts, and more co-occurring disorders such as Post-Traumatic Stress Disorder (PTSD). Stressful circumstances and difficult life events such as physical illness, problems with money, death in the family, unemployment, recent marriage, marital breakdown or abuse can trigger symptoms of bipolar disorder. These factors place genetically and biologically vulnerable individuals at risk for a more severe course of illness.

Compared to the average population, those with bipolar disorder also have a higher rate of substance abuse that can worsen the illness and interfere with their recovery. Use of alcohol, drugs, or tranquilizers may induce a more severe depressive phase. Likewise, concurrent factors such as social class, lack of social support and self-esteem can precipitate bipolar episodes. Patients with bipolar disorder tend to have a negative self-image, highly variable self-esteem and increased drive even during remission.

Antidepressants can trigger a manic episode if you are susceptible to bipolar disorder. Over the counter medications like appetite suppressants and cold preparations, non-psychiatric medications such as medicine for thyroid problems and corticosteroids like prednisone drugs, illicit drugs such as cocaine, Ecstasy and amphetamines may also cause increased energy, decreased need for sleep and increased talkativeness that resemble a manic episode.

If you have bipolar disorder, you may also have another health condition that is diagnosed before or after your diagnosis of bipolar disorder. Unipolar depression, social and generalized anxiety disorder, post-traumatic stress disorder (PTSD), attention-deficit/hyperactivity disorder (ADHD) and borderline personality disorder have symptoms that overlap with and can be difficult to differentiate from bipolar disorder. More often than not, women with bipolar disorder also experience thyroid disease, obesity, and migraines. Men are more likely to deal with substance abuse alongside their bipolar disorder.

If you are vulnerable to bipolar disorder, stress, frequent use of stimulants or alcohol, and lack of sleep may prompt the onset of your disorder. Certain medications also may set off a depressive or manic episode. If you have a family history of bipolar disorder, you should notify your physician to help avoid the risk of a medication-induced manic episode.

-o0o-

BIPOLAR I

He was in his early 20s when my nephew, a computer consultant, was first diagnosed with bipolar disorder after going through a severe manic episode. Shortly after graduating from college, he was admitted to the hospital. He thought he was there because he was having trouble sleeping and eating. What he had not realized was that he hadn't eaten or slept in over 72 hours

He would go two days without sleeping, then become so frazzled and dependent on his family to carry out his daily chores, like shopping and cleaning. While in the hospital, a long distance phone call from his cousin in Japan helped calm him down: "Please listen to the doctors because they are really doing their best to help you." His trust in his cousin got him to take his first dose of medication.

He resisted the idea that medication was very important in managing his bipolar disorder. He could never come up with anything better than "there has to be a way other than medication to beat this condition!" He would stop the medication without telling his therapist and psychiatrist; His manic episodes came at times that he later recognized as being particularly stressful.

The first episode was after the Sept. 11 terrorist attacks, shortly after his graduation from the University of California in Irvine. He was overcome by feelings that he had to save the world by setting up some sort of charity, and he was eventually hospitalized, while his family had little understanding of what was wrong. He was given Depakote and Risperdal.

Mainly due to self-stigma, he thought that taking his medication was an admission that there was something wrong with him. He thought it was degrading and hindering—even killing—his potential. In hindsight, he realized that he would always stop taking the medication when it was working best; that taking the medication enabled him to reach his potential and push his limits in a healthy way.

Eight years later, the second manic episode came amidst the stress of starting a relationship with a woman he had been infatuated with for 10 years, and a job promotion. He felt that he needed to prove himself worthy of both.

One early morning, at 4 a.m., he woke the woman he was seeing, and asked, "Do you trust me?" When she said that she did, he persuaded her to come with him to Kennedy Airport and fly to Los Angeles, where he would deliver sixteen e-mail messages of support to his former college dance team, which was about to perform in a nationally televised competition. He was convinced, he now recalls, that hand-delivering those messages would have somehow changed the fate of the dance team, and perhaps even the world. There was a sense of urgency.

He was enlightened and felt that what he was doing would be the best Easter present for his friends and for the world."

In an effort to calm him down, his girlfriend took him to a Bikram yoga class, where he would follow his instructor, doing poses in what he described as a "militant, super-focused" way, with robotic intensity. When told to change his clothes, he began taking all his clothes off in the lobby, and when told to put his clothes back on, he went to the bathroom and stayed there for two hours.

When they got him home, he persuaded his girlfriend and his brother to go to the roof and watch the sunrise, but once there, he asked if they wanted him to jump off from the building. They called 911. By the time the police arrived, he was in the bathroom, naked, and washing the wall tiles with water, thinking that he was like John baptizing people with water. They talked him into going peacefully to Beth Israel Hospital, but he was able to persuade the doctor there to let him go. Eventually, his brother and sister tricked him into going back to the hospital and into signing the paperwork to be admitted. They changed his medication to Trilafon, and monitored its dosages based on his moods.

It took more than a year to get him on the right medication dose. He had a lot of break through episodes while trying to get stable.

Two years later, when his girlfriend broke up with him, he went back to New York to try to reconcile with her. While on the plane, he began to have racing thoughts and through the six hours of flight, he kept scribbling jumbled characters on his paper tablet, trying to find a solution to a mathematical problem, which he thought he was able to resolve.

Accompanied by his brother, he took his girlfriend out to talk her into getting back with him. When his brother went to work after dinner, he left the restaurant to go home. While walking through town, he felt that God was guiding his path. He walked for hours trying to find his way, allowing God to tell him whether to cross the street or not. He was looking for Starbucks to go to the bathroom, which he had passed without noticing. After asking a guy for direction, he turned around and saw a hotel that he thought was where God wanted him to go to relieve himself.

Inside a nearby restaurant, he saw a thin break in his heart, and heard his heart beat in his head. He tried to repair it with his mind, and jerked when he felt someone shaking his shoulders to tell him that he was not supposed to sleep in the restaurant.

It took hours before he found his way home. His family was frantic because they knew he had not slept for a day. They took him to the hospital.

In the hospital, he talked to every patient on the psych ward, and told them that he was a robot, observing how humans interact. He began to preach and explained to them how they could find love in their lives. Because he claimed that he was representing Jesus, one of the patients gave him a bible to read. The next day he returned the bible and said that he had read the entire book in one night, which was not true.

One year later, his new girlfriend's son asked him which one came first: the chicken or the egg. This became a trigger, which made him think and try to solve the unsolvable question even as he and his brother were walking on a hiking trail.

He began to watch everyone, wondering what they were thinking about. He would sit in a lotus position, meditating and thinking about the chicken question, while trying to find the solution for all the problems in the world. He began to think that he finally solved the riddle, and that his life would be much better if he gave away all his personal possession. He went to a watch shop, took off his watch and left it on the shelf. Then he tried to give all his cash to the cashier without buying anything and walked out.

Later, the police came to him and asked for his ID, asking him why he left his watch, suspecting that he might be a terrorist. He had muted himself and would only answer with a nod. That was when his brother arrived; explaining to the police about his situation and taking him back to the hospital. There, they gave him Lamictal and Abilify.

After years of denial, he was finally able to accept his diagnosis and then persevere through the process of learning how to both manage and thrive in life despite his condition. He learned to regulate his mood swings through medication, meditation, exercise and careful sleep monitoring.

His family support, dropping everything to help him, was an important factor in the treatment of his disorder. Through family-focused therapy, his brother and sister, as well as the woman he was dating, became critical components in his recovery. He later combined his experience in technology and his personal experience with bipolar disorder to start a company called ThriveStreams that now uses technology to track feelings and behavior as a means to monitor one's mood swings

-o0o-

This type of disorder, that used to be called "manic depression", is the most severe type of bipolar disorder. To qualify as having bipolar I, you must have one or more manic episodes that last at least seven days, or manic symptoms so extreme that you require immediate hospitalization. Usually, depressive episodes occur as well, typically lasting at least 2 weeks, but they are not necessary for the diagnosis. If untreated, your manic episode may last three to six months.

Symptoms of mania may include excessive happiness, excitement, irritability, restlessness, increased energy, less need for sleep, racing thoughts, high sex drive, delusions of grandeur, poorly thought-out decisions, and erratic behaviors that quickly escalate until they are out of control. If you are in manic episodes, you might spend money far beyond your means, have risky sex relationships that you wouldn't otherwise have, or pursue grandiose, unrealistic plans. In severe manic episodes, you might lose touch with reality. You could become delusional and behave bizarrely. People with bipolar disorder often have additional psychiatric problems such as anxiety panic disorder, generalized anxiety disorder (GAD), social anxiety disorder, or personality disorders that may complicate their illness and require additional treatment. Post-traumatic stress disorder and obsessive-compulsive disorder also may be common in people with bipolar disorder. You may experience psychotic symptoms such as delusions and hallucinations like hearing the voice of God or persecutory delusions, depending on your state of mind.

You may have an urge to talk incessantly and your speech may be pressured, faster or louder than usual and difficult for others to interrupt. In severe forms of mania, flight of ideas can render your speech incoherent and impossible to understand. You may find it hard to stay still or remain seated, and other forms of psychomotor restlessness may be apparent, such as excessive use of gestures or fidgeting. In severe cases you may develop psychotic symptoms including grandiose delusions and mood-congruent hallucinations. In the acute stages of mania, you may exhibit classic signs of schizophrenia, with severe psychotic symptoms such as thought disorder, delusions and hallucinations. More pronounced psychotic symptoms, increased suicidal ideation, drug misuse or more disturbed behavior may be symptoms of a later presentation of bipolar disorder and not of a schizophrenia-spectrum disorder. Typically, however, your manic delusions and hallucinations are less stable and more episodic than those in schizophrenia and your psychotic symptoms are in keeping with your mood.

If an episode of the mania is left untreated, it can last from a few days all the way up to several years, but the symptoms more commonly last between a few weeks and a few months. After this manic episode, depression follows, sometimes shortly thereafter while other times not until weeks or even months later. Much like clinical depression, the depressive episodes of bipolar disorder may sometimes lead to thoughts of suicide. These depressive symptoms can be very quick or sometimes last for years at a time. Also, many people with bipolar I disorder experience long periods without symptoms in between episodes. A few of them have rapid-cycling symptoms of mania and depression, occurring four or more times within a year. Episodes of depression with mixed features are also possible, in which manic and depressive symptoms occur simultaneously or may alternate from one extreme to the other within the same day.

Suicide is a major risk with bipolar disorder - women with the condition are 10 times and men are 9 times more likely to kill themselves than the general population. First-degree relatives of people with bipolar disorder type I are seven times more likely to develop the disorder compared to the normal population. Some studies show that as many as 60% also abuse drugs or alcohol and may make bipolar episodes more frequent or so severe that medicines used to treat bipolar disorder usually become less effective. Typically, symptoms of drug abuse dissipate within 7 days after the substance is withdrawn, whereas manic symptoms last much longer.

Patients often describe increased productivity and creativity during the early stages of mania that may feel satisfying and rewarding. However, as the episode worsens, severe distractibility, restlessness, and difficulty concentrating can render the completion of tasks impossible. The mood swings of bipolar disorder can be profoundly destructive. Depression can make you isolate yourself from friends and loved ones, and the roller-coaster ride of emotions can make the condition so challenging that most of marriages involving a partner with bipolar disorder end in break-ups and divorce.

Bipolar disorder is generally found in very bright people with above-average IQ. Although they are not part of the diagnostic criteria, certain features often accompany Bipolar I disorder including impaired memory. Disturbance in judgment and perception typically increases over the course of the illness. Higher degrees of impairment correlate with the number of previous manic episodes and hospitalizations, and with the presence of psychotic symptoms. Manic episodes can take months to develop or they can appear within just a couple of days. Your first ever episode may be extremely difficult to predict and it's really only with the benefit of hindsight that your emotional and behavioral changes will start to mean something. Episodes of mania and depression typically recur across your life span. Between episodes, you may be free of symptoms, or you may have some residual symptoms despite treatment.

Majority of people are in their early 20s when their symptoms of bipolar disorder first appear. By the age of 50, almost everyone who has Bipolar 1 disorder will have fully developed illness. People with an immediate family member who has bipolar disorder are at higher risk. It may take up to 10 or sometimes even 20 years before a person with bipolar disorder can be correctly diagnosed. Although accepted as a very rare disorder in the younger age group, it is possible and appropriate to diagnose bipolar I disorder in both children and adolescents. For a diagnosis of bipolar I disorder to be established in a pre-pubescent child, manic symptoms must be present most of the time for 7 days. Although irritability may be a symptom, it should not be a core diagnostic criterion. Sexual, emotional and physical abuse; previously undiagnosed learning difficulties; and possible drug or alcohol abuse should be included in the differential diagnosis.

Bipolar 1 disorder requires treatment with drugs, such as a mood stabilizer, an antidepressant, or a newer antipsychotic. Hospitalization is usually required especially during manic episodes. This hospital admission may be voluntary or involuntary. Many things may happen once you have been diagnosed with bipolar disorder, starting with a hospitalization visit. Often, you are only diagnosed because you have become suicidal or you have become a danger to yourself and others. Once you are hospitalized, your doctor and a qualified team of nurses and specialists will work together to determine which medications and treatment options are best for you. Having a regular therapy session with a social worker or psychologist can help stabilize your mood, which leads to less hospitalizations and feeling better overall. Also, taking medication on a regular basis will help reduce your manic or depressive episodes.

Insight is lost in mania – you may be unaware that your behavior is abnormal and you may not even consider yourself to be in need of treatment. Mental illness broadly, and bipolar disorder specifically, are usually denied or kept hidden by you or your family because of the stigma associated with it. However, this disorder can be treated, and you can lead full and productive lives even if you have the disorder.

-o0o-

BIPOLAR II

I am an introvert by nature. I am generally shy and introspective. I can spend days on end without talking to anybody. I prefer to sit quietly by the corner, read a book, withdraw from the crowd, spend time alone, work on my computer, and do things without having others around me. But most people who know me will disagree.

I had organized and attended numerous community gatherings, mingled with the local, state and national leaders, participated in group discussions and community forums, made speeches in front of large audiences, given formal presentations, workshops and seminars. I had hosted numerous social events, both private and public, taught elders to dance, hosted numerous fundraising events, and even performed on stage.

After graduating from Medical School in the Philippines at the age of 22, I started teaching in the Medical Technology Department at De Ocampo Memorial School and at the University of Santo Tomas - College of Medicine, while having two medical clinics and taking care of my three children. By the time I immigrated to the U.S. at the age of 28, I had written and published "Histopathologic Techniques" which was later adopted as a textbook in the Philippines. After completing seven years of residency training in Cleveland, I started working as a neuropathologist at Jackson Memorial Hospital and Assistant Professor at the University of Miami – Miller School of Medicine. I later rose in rank to Associate Professor and then to tenured Full Professor of Pathology. I taught pathology residents and medical students, gave lectures and conferences to neurologists and neurosurgeons, and did clinical work as a neuropathologist at Jackson Memorial Hospital for more than twenty years.

I served as Editorial Reviewer for three medical journals, and principal investigator for five research grants. I co-authored several Pathology and Neurology book chapters, gave numerous formal presentations at scientific meetings, and published more than 60 scientific articles in peer-reviewed journals.

In addition to my academic pursuits, I was active in the community. I founded five non-profit organizations, wrote grants, created and organized projects, did fundraising events, made presentations, met with local, state and national leaders, and published my own magazine of medical research advances and health topics.

I was full of energy in spite of sleeping for only 3 or 4 hours a day. I would wake up in the middle of the night full of ideas, would go to my computer, and would finish writing my grant by the next day. I raised significant amounts of money for my projects, including the acquisition and renovation of a two-story building that served as our community center.

I was always multi-tasking. My friend once was amazed at how I could work on my computer while being on the phone, eating my sandwich and talking to him as he sat beside me. And I could accomplish a lot.

Then one day, ten years into my practice, I began to feel like I was nobody. After staying up until 4 o'clock preparing for my conference with the neurosurgeons, I woke up at 6 o'clock feeling lousy. I was used to having 2 or 3 hours of sleep without problem, but that morning was different. I did not feel that I had the energy to go to work. I stood up from my bed but did not feel like showering. I went straight to my closet to change my clothes and put on my white coat to get ready for work. Then all of a sudden, I felt this feeling of foreboding as I was putting on my uniform. I had palpitation in my chest, I felt woozy, and had the sudden urge to cry. I sat on my bed and tried to compose myself. I knew I had to make a case presentation that morning, but I felt my head getting big as I imagined myself in front of my colleagues. All of a sudden, I was afraid. I did not think I could face the surgeons, even if I knew that I had prepared to discuss my cases, and even if I had done so confidently many times in the past. I started to cry.

I called up my office and told them that I was ill. They had to cancel my meeting. And I stayed in bed, crying the whole time, because I felt guilty about missing my own conference. I fell asleep and did not wake up until it was time for dinner, but I did not feel like getting out of bed. I stayed awake the whole night, thinking about all the things I had done wrong, about all the bad decisions I had made in the past, and how I did not feel that I was good enough to be a neuropathologist, let alone be a professor in medicine.

I did not go to work until a week later. I stayed in bed the whole time, hardly eating or fixing myself. When I finally reported to work, I still was not feeling right. I started to doubt myself. I locked the door in my office, and avoided talking to the other faculty or interacting with my residents. I did not want to give any lecture and walked quietly in the corridor, always with my head down. I thought I was a failure and a fake, and that my residents knew a lot more than I did. I felt inadequate and was afraid that my residents and colleagues would discover how little I knew about medicine.

I felt guilty staying in my office at the hospital because I could not do my work at home. And I felt guilty staying at home because I could not do my work at the hospital. One of my colleagues advised me to seek help when she noticed that I had not been myself. When I saw a psychiatrist, he told me that I had signs of depression. He gave me a prescription.

"I don't take drugs," I said.

"This is not a drug. This is medicine for depression. Like something you would take if you had hypertension."

"I am not sick."

"Yes, you are. People with an ulcer can bleed. It's the same with depression. Except that you don't bleed. You cry."

When my youngest sister heard about my condition, she gave me money to go to Europe. I went with my daughter and we stayed in Europe for two weeks. By the time we came back, I was feeling better again. I thought that maybe I really just needed some rest.

Then it happened again. Two years later, I had the same feeling of doom. I would cry for no reason. I could not concentrate at work. When I went back to my psychiatrist, he gave me a different prescription. I got better after a month or so. And I began to write grants again.

Every time I got depressed, I would go to the beach and write poems. I would write affirmations to convince myself that everything was alright and that I was okay. And it helped for a while.

Five years later, I had another major episode. This time, it was worse. I would burst into tears every time I got dressed for work. I would cry every time I got into my car. I would cry every time I passed by the library. I would cry every time I turned my head. I could not figure out why. I lost interest in everything that I was doing. I could not make myself go to work. I took a leave of absence. But I was still publishing my magazine.

I went from one psychic to another. I learned how to read tarot cards. I went through past life regression. I started going to casinos and losing a lot of money. I would drive straight to the casino after work, would play the whole night, and would drive back straight to work the next morning without even a change of clothes. I got divorced. And I lost my house to foreclosure. Not because I could not pay the mortgage, but because I wanted to get rid of it. I just did not want to live in that house any more.

I saw my psychiatrist once a week. Sometimes, I would be crying and upset when I got into his office. I was so anxious that I became fidgety and my hands would shake. I told him that I thought I was given the gift of tongue because I could open my mouth at will and say words that I didn't understand. I even taped myself and asked him if he thought I was speaking Aramaic. He told me to go back to my psychotherapist.

I took time off for a year while seeing my psychiatrist, who kept changing my medications because they were not working. Then one day, I woke up feeling better. The depression seemed to have been lifted off my chest. I could not make myself cry even if I wanted to. I stopped feeling sorry for myself. My psychiatrist could not understand how I could have suddenly felt better after almost a year of being depressed.

I went back to my chairman and asked if I could start working again. I had to get a letter from my psychiatrist saying that I was well enough to go back to work. My chairman agreed to take me back, on the condition that my work would be supervised and that someone would co-sign my report for at least six months, until I can prove that I was well enough to work as a neuropathologist. And I did well. My self-confidence came back. I felt better.

Then, ten years later, it happened again. I dressed up and drove to the hospital like I always did. But as soon as I stepped into my office, I started to cry and I felt like everything in my life was falling apart. I was crying when I went to my director's office and told her that I wanted to retire. When she asked me what was wrong, I told her that I was quitting that day. She could not understand what was happening. When she saw that I was serious, she picked up the phone and set up an appointment for me to see a psychiatrist. She advised me to go home and get some rest. When I left my office, I left everything. And I never came back.

-o0o-

Bipolar II is difficult to diagnose although it is four times more common than bipolar I. The signs are harder for people to see in themselves, and it's often up to friends or loved ones to encourage them to get help. It requires a history of at least one major depressive episode, at least one hypomanic episode that lasts for at least four days, and no history of mania. The course of bipolar II disorder is more chronic and consists of more frequent cycling than in bipolar I disorder. It is associated with a greater risk of suicidal thoughts and behaviors than bipolar I or unipolar depression. With bipolar II, it is common to have coexisting conditions such as generalized anxiety disorder, panic attacks, phobias, social anxiety, conduct disorders, eating disorders or substance abuse.

Many people who have bipolar II disorder become very successful – a positive aspect of having the illness. In some cases, Bipolar II can help people achieve goals that would not have otherwise been possible. Many Bipolar II individuals are extremely motivated, talented, and strong-minded producers, writers, musicians, doctors, lawyers, and investment bankers. Hypomania is a far more productive period that is usually associated with highly successful individuals – those that are highly ambitious overachievers and entrepreneurs.

However, it is important to note that not everyone who is enthusiastic and highly driven and who moves quickly is hypomanic. Just because you need little sleep, are highly creative, and have abundance of energy, it does not always mean that you have Bipolar II disorder. There are many men and women who are superb leaders, brilliant entrepreneurs, and high achievers but who do not have mood swings and who are not Bipolar II.

Most hypomanic people are very self-motivated and have an entrepreneurial personality, with a strong inner drive that motivates them to work harder, be more productive and achieve more. They often harbor racing thoughts on how they will accomplish their next venture. If you are a Bipolar II, your increased creativity are often mistaken for high functioning behavior or simply attributed to your personality, so you may not be aware that you arc having hypomanic symptoms. Often you seek treatment for your depressive episode and your history of hypomania gets undiagnosed.

When a bipolar II patient experiences hypomania, it is not always a pleasurable high, particularly when behaviors include being hot-tempered or argumentative. Compulsive gambling or financial loss, impulsiveness, hyper-sexuality or substance abuses are behaviors commonly found with Bipolar II. There are many undiagnosed Bipolar IIs who are routinely prescribed tranquilizers and sleeping pills by their primary care physicians, instead of being referred to a mood disorder specialist who can make the correct diagnosis and prescribe the correct medication.

A profoundly decreased need for sleep without noticeable fatigue is consistent with the Bipolar II hypomanic state. Many high achievers with Bipolar II are able to capitalize on their extreme hypomanic periods to accomplish a lot. A large number of remarkably creative people are also bipolar. People experiencing hypomanic episodes are often quite pleasant to be around. They can often seem like the "life of the party" -- making jokes, taking an intense interest in other people and activities, and infecting others with their positive mood.

The hypomania of bipolar II disorder may first manifest itself after antidepressant treatment. However, hypomania is not diagnosed when the symptoms are the direct physiologic effects of a general medical condition (such as hyperthyroidism) or a drug (like amphetamine or cocaine abuse). Unlike bipolar1, these patients seem to get over their depression after effective doses of antidepressants. The downside to the bipolar II disorder is that it can also lead to erratic and unhealthy behavior that may lead to long-term unemployment, strain on families, substance abuse, and poor quality of life. Excessive moodiness, sustained state of elevated or irritable mood and impulsive or reckless behavior may be seen in Bipolar II, although the hypomania is less severe than mania. The symptoms last at least four days but do not significantly impact quality of life, do not have psychotic features, and do not require hospitalization.

People in a hypomanic state feel euphoric, energetic, and productive; they are able to carry on with their day-to-day lives; and they never lose touch with reality. To others, it may seem as if people with hypomania are merely in an unusually good mood. Unfortunately, hypomania can also result in bad decisions that harm relationships, careers, and reputations.

The vast majority of people with bipolar II disorder experience more time with depressive than with hypomanic symptoms. Depression can occur soon after hypomania subsides, or much later. Some people cycle back and forth between hypomania and depression, while others have long periods of normal mood in between episodes.

The depressive episodes of bipolar II disorder are often longer lasting and may be even more severe than in bipolar I disorder. Therefore, bipolar II disorder is not simply a "milder" overall form of bipolar disorder. The depressed mood of Bipolar II usually persists most of the day, and is characterized by a feeling of sadness, emptiness, or hopelessness; inappropriate guilt; loss of interest in previously enjoyable activities; sleep disturbances; fatigue or loss of energy; changes in appetite; decreased ability to concentrate, and sometimes, recurrent thoughts of suicide.

Patients usually seek help when they are in a depressed state. Unless specifically asked, they may fail to provide their doctor with all the information needed for an accurate assessment. Hence, they are often misdiagnosed with unipolar depression. Depressive episodes in bipolar II disorder are similar to the usual clinical depression, feeling down, with loss of pleasure, low energy and activity, feelings of guilt or worthlessness, and thoughts of suicide. When compared to bipolar I disorder, type II has more frequent depressive episodes that may last for weeks, months, or rarely years.

It is not uncommon for a patient to see three or four doctors before being finally diagnosed as bipolar II, because many patients are more likely to recognize signs of major depression than the symptoms of mild mania. Persons complaining of depression without mentioning periods of hypomania can easily be misdiagnosed and recklessly medicated. So many times, it is a family member or a close friend who becomes first aware of the Bipolar II patient going too high without complaining of insomnia and with no need to catch up on lost sleep by taking a “power nap”.

Perhaps the most reliable predictor of hypomania is the amount of sleep a person requires. Lack of need for sleep oftentimes initiates the hypomanic phase and is absolutely critical in making the accurate diagnosis of Bipolar II. Some people cycle back and forth between hypomania and depression, while others have long periods of normal mood in between episodes. In between episodes of hypomania and depression, many people with bipolar II disorder typically live normal lives.

One reason why Bipolar II may be tricky to identify is because of the confusion about its nature. It is not necessarily about violent, sudden mood swings that leave people feeling elated one minute and crying the next minute. People with Bipolar II find their moods stuck for days, weeks, or months in extreme emotional highs and depressive lows. Sometimes there are periods of stability between these episodes, which make it easy to think that the extreme moods are not part of a complex cycle of bipolar disorder. During your hypomanic moods, you can convince yourself that nothing is really wrong. But hypomania can become extreme. Words and thoughts become faster and difficult for others to follow, and you want things done immediately, which can lead to your overspending and debt.

When hypomanic, Bipolar II persons tend to overestimate their own abilities and become noncompliant to medication and regular doctor's visits. When the patient's symptoms are misdiagnosed as unipolar depression and they are prescribed an antidepressant alone (without a mood-stabilizing drug), they can suddenly switch from depression into elation, restless agitation and insomnia with racing thoughts. This sudden mood switch is actually antidepressant-induced hypomania, and it usually occurs within the first two weeks of starting antidepressant therapy. Many people with bipolar disorder don't get the treatment they need. Despite the mood extremes, people with bipolar disorder often don't recognize how much their emotional instability disrupts their lives and the lives of their loved ones.

Bipolar IIB is a productive subtype of Bipolar II characterized by one or more depressive episodes accompanied by at least one hypomanic episode with high levels of creativity and intelligence.

While experiencing a hypomanic episode, you often feel inspired, ambitious, and willing to engage in new creative endeavors. Your mood and temperament can make you more creative and original in your thinking, and will allow you to take risks, fuel your ambition, and have more than the usual energy needed to pursue your goals. However, it is important to remember that most creative people do not have a mental illness and most people who have bipolar disorder, are not unusually creative. Rather, there is a disproportionate rate of mood disorders, especially bipolar disorder, in creative individuals.

An episode of hypomania, if untreated, can last anywhere from a few days to several months. Most commonly, symptoms continue for a few weeks to a few months. Hypomania often masquerades as happiness and relentless optimism. When hypomania is not causing unhealthy behavior, it often may go unnoticed and therefore remain untreated. And if you are like some people with bipolar disorder, you may enjoy the feelings of euphoria and cycles of being more productive. Thus, even when your family and friends recognize your mood swings, you will often deny that anything is wrong. However, this euphoria is almost always followed by an emotional crash that can leave you depressed, worn out, and perhaps in financial, legal or relationship trouble.

It is possible to reduce the risk of developing future episodes of hypomania or depression once the bipolar disorder is diagnosed. Because of the nature of the disorder, long-term therapy is the best option and aims to not only control the symptoms but also to maintain sustained remission and prevent relapses from occurring. Regular therapy sessions with a psychologist or social worker, combined with medication, can help stabilize mood, leading to fewer hospitalizations and feeling better overall. Psychotherapy can help people better recognize the warning signs of a developing relapse and can help ensure that prescribed medicines are taken properly before the symptoms become full blown. A combination of self-monitoring, close supervision by a therapist, and faithful adherence to one's medication regimen remains part of the treatment and will help to reduce the risk and prevent the likelihood of a completed suicide.

-o0o-

CYCLOTHYMIA

Burgess Meredith was an American actor, director, producer, and writer in theater, film, and television. He was born in Cleveland from an alcoholic father and a mother who was in a constant state of despair. He described his childhood as being "bleak, grim and incoherent" – where he saw "little except violence and fear". For years he became "a boy who lived almost totally within himself". He was able to escape this environment when he got into music and won various competitions, even receiving a full scholarship with the St. John Choir in New York City as a teenager. He never returned home after that. During his adolescent years, he experienced periods of hypomania with decreased sleep and increased activity fluctuating with periods of depression. He went to college sporadically, though he never graduated. He had a major break into show business when he made his Broadway debut in "Little Ol' Boy", although he experienced feelings of low self- esteem, substance abuse, and repeated relationship difficulties. He was married and divorced three times within the span of 13 years, all while appearing in approximately 20 films and serving in the Air Force during World War II. The next several decades were full of noteworthy performances on stage. He took well-known roles as the arch villain in Twilight Zone, as Penguin in the 1960s TV series "Batman," and as Rocky Balboa's trainer in 1974's "Rocky". He won several Emmys, was the first male actor to win the Saturn Award for Best Supporting Actor twice, and was nominated for two Academy Awards. In Hollywood, he was known for having a volatile personality, and in his 1994 autobiography, "So Far, So Good," he wrote that his violent mood swings were diagnosed as an illness called cyclothymia. He passed away from complications of Alzheimer's disease and melanoma at the age of 89.

-o0o-

Cyclothymia is a form of bipolar disorder that most people haven't heard of. According to the Diagnostic and Statistical Manual of Mental Disorders (DSM-IV), it is "a chronic, fluctuating mood disturbance involving numerous periods of hypomanic symptoms and numerous periods of depressive symptoms." It is recognized by psychiatrists and psychologists by the same pattern of chronic, fluctuating moods, but with symptoms that are not frequent enough or severe enough to be diagnosed as Bipolar II disorder. It is a relatively mild but chronic disorder where moods swing between short periods of mild depression alternating with short periods of mild elation. It is characterized by numerous mood swings, with periods of hypomanic symptoms that do not meet the criteria for a hypomanic episode. Because the low and high mood swings are not as severe as major depressive or full manic episodes, cyclothymia is easy to miss.

It may be very difficult to differentiate Cyclothymia from Bipolar II without monitoring the condition for a long period of time and without gathering information from family members. Cyclothymic people may feel stable at a baseline level but experience a noticeable shift to an emotional high during mild hypomanic episodes that often cycle to emotional lows with moderate depressive symptoms. This alternating pattern of emotional highs and lows would last for at least two years (one year in children and adolescents), during which time the person should not be without the symptoms for more than 2 months at a time. Children or teens with cyclothymia may be described as unreliable, moody, or temperamental because of their unpredictable or irritable moods. After the initial two years, there may be superimposed manic or mixed episodes (in which case both Bipolar I Disorder and Cyclothymic Disorder may be diagnosed at the same time) or major depressive episodes (in which case combined diagnosis of Bipolar II Disorder and Cyclothymic Disorder may be reached).

The diagnosis of cyclothymia is not as frequent as that of bipolar disorder, and is based on the absence of any major depressive episode, manic episode or mixed episode. When your major depressive episode manifests after an initial diagnosis of cyclothymia, you may qualify for a diagnosis of bipolar I or bipolar II disorder. Both men and women are affected and symptoms usually begin in adolescence or young adulthood.

Although the emotional highs and lows of cyclothymia are less extreme than those of bipolar I or II, their symptoms, clinical course, family history and treatment response are consistent with bipolar disorder. People with cyclothymia also tend to have an inflated feeling of self-worth, self-confidence and elation during periodic hypomania, often with rapid speech, racing thoughts, and not much need to sleep. And they may sometimes also be productive for a period of several days at a time. The symptoms are not due to the direct physiological effects of drug or substance abuse, or to a general medical condition like hyperthyroidism.

It is difficult to diagnose cyclothymia because its depressive episode is also a diagnostic feature of many disorders, including adjustment and personality disorders, and it can be triggered or exacerbated by life events and circumstances. Unstable moods frequently disrupt personal and work relationships. People with cyclothymic disorder are also more likely to abuse drugs and alcohol. The symptoms manifested during a hypomanic episode such as increased energy, distractibility, impulsive or risk-seeking behavior and unstable lifestyle are also commonly associated with ADHD. But they can be distinguished by problems with concentration and memory in association with ADHD, and by periods of elevated self-confidence in cyclothymia.

Although the exact cause of cyclothymia is unknown, it often occurs in families with major depression and bipolar disorder, suggesting a genetic component. Cyclothymia is common in the relatives of patients with bipolar disorder, and some individuals with cyclothymia eventually develop bipolar disorder themselves. In most people, the pattern is irregular and unpredictable, and the episodes can last for days or weeks. It may cycle continuously from hypomanic to depressed state or it may have normal moods for more than a month between episodes. When elevated or depressed moods become severe, a person is no longer considered to have cyclothymia, but rather has bipolar disorder. This progression to more severe symptoms can happen, and this is when many people first receive treatment, which often takes the form of individual psychotherapy.

Due to lack of definite diagnostic criteria and clear separation from Bipolar disorder, the occurrence of cyclothymia is still widely contested. The persistence of symptoms in cyclothymia suggests that they are enduring personality traits rather than a psychological disorder. It frequently goes undiagnosed and untreated. Most people's symptoms are mild enough that they do not seek mental health treatment. No medicines are specifically approved for the treatment of cyclothymia, although mood stabilizers such as lithium or lamotrigine are sometimes recommended as a possible strategy to reduce mood fluctuations. Antidepressants alone are not known to improve fluctuations in mood, which are hallmark characteristics of cyclothymic disorder.

-o0o-

RAPID CYCLING

"Vivien would get along fine for a few weeks, a few months – be perfectly normal and friendly and involved in her activities. Then, suddenly, a complete turnaround. Sometimes it would last only a few hours, other times a day or more. But when it happened, we'd see a completely different girl – moody, silent, petulant, rude, and hysterical. None of us understand it, not even the schoolmistress. At first we credited it to longing for her family – they were living out in India, you know. But as we got to know her better, we realized that she was quite happy to be at school and didn't seem to miss her family at all. Knowing what we know today about these things, one would definitely have to say that Vivien was a disturbed girl, disturbed in some way that she had no control over."

Joy Bruce, M.D.

"She was like a female Dr. Jekyll and a Mrs. Hyde. Then, like a spring flower bursting open, she'd emerge the next day like the dearest, most gracious and effervescent personality you could ever imagine."

From: http://vivien-leigh.info/bipolar_disorder/

-o0o-

This type of bipolar disorder causes rapid changes in mood, with four or more episodes of major depression, mania, hypomania, or mixed symptoms within a year. With rapid cycling, mood swings can quickly go from low to high and back again, and can occur with more than one episode in a week, over a few days, within one day, and sometimes even hours. If there are four mood episodes within a month, it is called ultra-rapid cycling, and when several mood switches occur within a day, on several days during one week, it is called ultra-ultra-rapid. The person feels like he or she is on a roller coaster, with mood and energy changes that are out of control and disabling. Sometimes, it is characterized by severe irritability, anger, impulsivity, and uncontrollable outbursts that occur at random. For most people, rapid cycling is a temporary occurrence.

Rapid cycling is more common in people with Bipolar II and in people who have their first episode at a younger age. This type affects more women than men. Some individuals experience rapid cycling at the beginning of their illness, but for the majority, rapid cycling begins gradually. In fact, most bipolar experience shorter and more frequent episodes over time if their illness is not adequately treated. They may experience rapid cycling for a time, and then return to a pattern of longer, less frequent episodes, or, in the best-case scenario, return to a stabilized mood with the help of treatment. Often, early episodes are triggered by actual or anticipated life events such as the death of a loved one, a break up, or an upcoming job interview. A small number of individuals continue in a rapid cycling pattern indefinitely.

It is very important to get immediate treatment for this form of bipolar disorder since the longer someone goes without treatment, the more resistant to treatment the person may become. Rapid cycling bipolar disorder can be a dangerous condition and carries a high risk of severe depression and suicide attempts. Certain antidepressants that are used to treat bipolar disorder can trigger or worsen rapid cycling, which often decreases when the antidepressant medication is stopped. Individuals with rapid cycling mood changes may respond differently to standard and experimental treatments and, with its sudden and unpredictable mood changes may be more difficult to manage than the other types of bipolar disorder. If treated early and aggressively, mild or moderate symptoms can be prevented from progressing into a severe manic or depressive episode. Mood stabilizers are the preferred treatment for rapid cycling bipolar disorder.

-o0o-

MIXED EPISODES

After being depressed and on sick leave for almost a year, my psychiatrist agreed that I should apply for long-term disability. When the insurance agent came to my house to determine my eligibility, he saw all the copies of "Current Medical News" scattered on the floor. When he asked me whose magazines they were, I told him I was writing and publishing them because I needed to take my mind out of my depression. The insurance agency disapproved my disability application because he did not believe that I could be depressed while at the same time able to write and publish my magazine.

-o0o-

A mixed episode refers to the symptoms of opposite mood polarities during manic, hypomanic or depressive episodes occurring simultaneously or in rapid sequence. One may be highly energetic, and sleepless with racing thoughts while at the same time feeling hopeless, in despair, irritable, and suicidal, or a sudden switch from being very sad to being very calm or to being happy. People during a mixed episode could be crying while at the same time announcing that they have never felt better. It may be hard to imagine someone being manic and depressed at the same time, but mania and depression are not mutually exclusive symptoms, and their co-occurrence may be much more common than people realize. During episodes with mixed features, people may be at even higher risk for suicide than during episodes of bipolar depression. Depressive symptoms such as hopelessness are often accompanied by lack of impulse control that can lead to completed suicide. Anxiety disorder also occurs more frequently as a comorbidity in mixed bipolar episodes than in pure bipolar depression or mania.

Mixed episodes are common in those who develop bipolar disorder at a younger age, particularly during adolescence. Half of these people may have at least some manic symptoms during a full episode of depression that are not severe or extensive enough to be classified as bipolar disorder. Mood episodes with mixed features can last from days to weeks or sometimes months and may recur if not treated.

-o0o-

DIAGNOSING BIPOLAR DISORDER

During my last episode, my previous psychiatrist was not available so I had to go to a different psychiatrist. It took more than a week before I could see her. I was still crying when I entered her room.

She asked me what was wrong.

I told her that I felt guilty for leaving my work but I could not stand being in my office even for a moment. I told her how fearful I was just thinking that my residents would soon discover that I did not know anything, and that I was just "faking it". I told her that I had trouble sleeping. I didn't have appetite for food. I lost 5 lbs. in two weeks. I did not feel like doing anything. I had trouble concentrating.

She asked me how my work was.

"Busy. I work in two departments. I have to give lectures even if I don't want to. I have to write reports. I have to do consults. It's stressful to do frozen sections because the neurosurgeons depend on me to decide what to do with their patient in the operating room. Most of the time, I am not even sure if my diagnosis is right or wrong. I was feeling guilty because I had not written a scientific paper for so long although I was supposed to publish as a tenured professor."

She asked me what I did when I was not working in the hospital.

"I have a foundation and a community center that helps old people. But recently I have been avoiding them."

"How long have you been feeling this way?"

"I don't know. It's on and off."

I told her about my previous bouts of depression and sessions with my psychiatrist and my psychotherapist. I told her that ten years ago, I had the same episode, which lasted a year. Then I got better and went back to work.

She asked me how I got out of the depression. I said I did not know.

"I just got better."

"Do you have any relative who has mental or emotional problem?"

"I have a nephew who is manic-depressive."

"Do you have anybody in the family who had tried to commit suicide?"

"One of my cousins hanged himself."

"Have you ever thought of harming yourself?"

"Yes, when I was in medical school. But I did not do it."

"Do you have racing thoughts?"

"Sometimes my brain works so fast I could not keep up with it."

"Do you sleep well?"

"I only need two or three hours of sleep every night."

"Do you hear voices?"

"No."

"What do you do when you are not depressed?"

"I write poems. I write grants. I do fundraising. I organize events."

Then she told me that I had bipolar disorder.

I did not know what to say. I had been seeing my old psychiatrist for almost twenty years with a diagnosis of unipolar disorder. He had given me anti-depressants that didn't work, and made me anxious instead.

"Bipolar II is easy to miss, especially if your doctor does not know about your family history. And if you see your psychiatrist only when you are depressed, he may not know that you have manic episodes."

But he was a psychiatrist. How could he have missed it? Then I realized: he never asked me about my family history. He never asked me if I had any hypomanic episode.

-o0o-

Since no specific test can determine if you have bipolar disorder or not, the diagnosis can be reached only by gathering a comprehensive medical, family, and mental-health information in addition to performing physical assessments. Great care must be given through history-taking to establish whether events such as sleep disturbance or life stress triggered the mood episode, and whether they are symptoms or consequences of your disorder. Early detection of bipolar disorder is important for initiating appropriate management regimen to improve ultimate outcome and minimize harm caused by repeated mood episodes. Individuals are often able to identify precipitating changes in their mood or behavior because each episode starts with a similar pattern of symptoms typical for that individual.

With severe mania, your symptoms are unmistakable. If you have hypomania, which is the milder form of severe mania, you may feel more energized than usual, more confident and full of ideas, and you are able to get by on less sleep. You are more likely to seek help if you're suffering from depression, but your doctor may not have the opportunity to observe your manic side.

Before coming up with your own diagnosis of Bipolar Disorder, you should discuss your symptoms with a properly trained health professional. Bipolar disorder is often under-diagnosed, over-diagnosed, or misdiagnosed because of symptoms that are similar to other mental illnesses. When considering a diagnosis of bipolar disorder, healthcare professionals should take into account that psychotic symptoms, thoughts of suicide, drug abuse, alcoholism, or disturbed behavior may be symptoms of bipolar disorder and not that of schizophrenia. People with bipolar disorder may be mistakenly diagnosed with unipolar depression by their primary care doctor and may be given inappropriate treatment because they often seek professional help only during their down periods and they neglect to mention their manic episodes.

Some individuals who meet the criteria for bipolar disorder have never been diagnosed as such. It takes an average of 10 years for people to get treatment for bipolar disorder after their symptoms begin. This is caused in part by delays in diagnosis. There are many productive and accomplished bipolar people who have chosen not to disclose their condition as a consequence of the mental illness stigma.

Conversely, it may be over-diagnosed in people who don't actually have the condition or they may be over-medicated due to aggressive marketing by companies that produce the drugs used to treat bipolar disorder. People with borderline personality disorder, a condition marked by impulsive behavior and problems relating to other people, are often misdiagnosed as bipolar, and might be treated with medications including atypical antipsychotics that can worsen or increase the risk for other medical conditions like high cholesterol, diabetes, thyroid and kidney problems.

Bipolar disorder can be complicated by coexisting psychiatric conditions including obsessive-compulsive disorder, substance abuse, eating disorders, attention deficit hyperactivity disorder (ADHD), premenstrual syndrome, panic disorder or social phobia. Symptoms of other disorders can also mimic the hallucinations and delusions that are characteristics of schizophrenia or drug abuse, and the diagnosis of bipolar disorder may be missed. Certain symptoms such as problems with concentration and sleep can be present in both depression and bipolar disorder. Unstable behavior, episodes of mania or depression, and lack of impulse control are often seen in people with borderline personality disorder as well as with substance abuse. Many women are diagnosed with major depression after delivering their baby. Yet, an unqualified single diagnosis of postpartum depression can prolong symptoms that may be more accurately linked to Bipolar disorder. Because the treatment approaches for these other disorders are different from the management of bipolar disorder, it is imperative that an accurate diagnosis be identified before starting therapy. If a clinician doesn't delve deep enough into the patient's history, he may come away with the mistaken impression that the patient is suffering from depression rather than bipolar disorder.

The delay in diagnosis and treatment is often longer for young patients because symptoms such as moodiness can sometimes be mistaken by parents and doctors as just part of being a teenager. An MRI, CT scan or an electroencephalogram (EEG) is sometimes ordered in patients who have had a sudden change in thinking, mood, or behavior to assure that a neurological disease is not the underlying cause. Thus far, bipolar disorder remains a clinical diagnosis, and no imaging study or other lab test has yet been established to confirm its diagnosis. Most laboratory tests or imaging tests are not useful in diagnosing bipolar disorder. The most important diagnostic tool may be talking openly with the doctor about your mood swings, behaviors, and lifestyle habits. In addition to patient and family history, administration of a screening instrument like Mood Disorder Questionnaire can be very helpful.

Differentiating mania from the effects of substance misuse can be problematic when someone is actively abusing substances that cause mood swings. It may be virtually impossible to manage co-existing mood symptoms of bipolar disorder. Substance abuse may make bipolar episodes (mania and depression) more frequent or severe, and medicines used to treat bipolar disorder are usually less effective when someone is using alcohol or illicit drugs.

Mental health clinicians are sometimes unable to distinguish the depressed phase of bipolar disorder from other types of depression. Many patients have distressing and disruptive symptoms for many years before they receive proper treatment. Often mistaken for depression, bipolar disorder is a psychiatric condition that is caused by an imbalance of chemicals in the brain. Contrary to public opinion, bipolar disorder is not just a mood swing between being happy and being sad throughout the day. The symptoms of bipolar disorder are much more extreme, and come in cycles that usually last for at least one week. Unipolar depression has no intervals of hypomania while bipolar II does have intervals of hypomania. The most consistent symptom of mania is an extreme increase in energy and positive thoughts, but in some people, it may present as an increase in irritability and anger. A diagnosis of bipolar affective disorder requires the experience of at least two mood episodes, one of which must be manic or hypomanic.

If you are wondering whether you have the condition, it is important to talk with your doctor about all of your emotions, both the good ones and the bad ones, so that you can get the right medication and help with your recovery. Identifying particular stressors that are associated with relapse can prevent the escalation of your symptoms. It can enable your family members and close friends to deal with your situation and to increase the support that you need. It is important to pay attention to how you are feeling so that you can seek help if you are consistently dealing with your sadness or if you continue to feel sad every day for at least two weeks.

Many people have bipolar disorder along with another illness such as anxiety disorder, substance abuse, or an eating disorder. People with bipolar disorder are also at higher risk for thyroid disease, migraine headaches, heart disease, diabetes, and obesity. Some non-psychiatric illnesses, such as thyroid disease, lupus, HIV, and syphilis, may have signs and symptoms that mimic those of bipolar disorder and can pose further challenges in making the diagnosis. People with bipolar disorder often have abnormal thyroid gland function. Because too much or too little thyroid hormone alone can lead to mood and energy changes, it is important that a physician carefully monitors thyroid levels.

People with rapid cycling tend to have co-occurring thyroid problems and may need to take thyroid pills in addition to their medications for bipolar disorder. In this instance, the medical problem must precede the onset of the manic symptoms, which resolve within a week or so of the effective treatment of the underlying medical disorder. Changes in mood or behavior caused by steroid medications like prednisone (used to treat inflammatory diseases such as rheumatoid arthritis and asthma, musculoskeletal injuries, or other medical problems) often resemble mania but reflect causes other than bipolar disorder.

-o0o-

My sister had been seeing her doctor for palpitations and irregular heartbeat. She was 44 when she started developing symptoms. After having a problem with her boss at work, she noticed that she was having some difficulty collecting her thoughts. Her family and friends noticed it too. Her behavior became erratic and she slowly lost contact with reality. Within several months, her condition got worse.

She thought that our brother was president of the United States, and that I had discovered the cure for AIDS. She began to talk to and called her pet bird Gary, a male friend. She thought that her dog was Michael Jackson. She wanted to print 3,000 flyers inviting everyone to a birthday party for our dad at the park, but backed out when she learned how costly it would be to do so.

It got so serious that the family decided to use the Baker Act and file a petition to involuntarily institutionalize her because they thought she was trying to commit suicide. She was admitted to a psychiatric facility where they did an MRI. Following her sisters' request for the doctors to check her thyroid, they did further tests and discovered that she had Graves' disease. Her thyroid levels were ten times higher than normal. She stayed in the hospital for 10 days while waiting for her to be scheduled for radiation to her thyroid. She was discharged the next day after her radiation and continued her group therapy for a month to learn how to deal with stress and manage her time.

Before making a diagnosis of bipolar disorder, healthcare professionals should consider checking alternative explanations for the symptoms, including thyroid disease and antidepressant-induced switching of moods. If a patient is at risk of suicide or severe self-neglect, is a significant risk to others, or has a history of recurrent compulsive hospitalization, a crisis plan should be developed in collaboration with the patient and his family.

-o0o-

BIPOLAR DISORDER IN CHILDHOOD, PREGNANCY AND OLD AGE

Bipolar disorder in children and adolescents is more challenging than it is in adults.

Bipolar disorder occurring in the teenage years is often more severe than in adults. Adolescents with bipolar disorder are at higher risk for suicide. Because symptoms of bipolar disorder include lack of judgment and risky behavior, the results can be deadly. It is typical, particularly among those with earlier onset, for depressive episode to occur first. It tends to last longer, to present with mixed features and to have a higher incidence of rapid cycling compared to late-onset bipolar disorder.

The criteria used to diagnose bipolar disorder in adults are similar to those used in diagnosing children and teenagers. Children and teens may have normal mood in between distinct major depressive, manic or hypomanic episodes, although it is often hard to tell whether these mood episodes result from stress or trauma, or represent signs of a mental health problem other than bipolar disorder.

Bipolar disorder in teens frequently goes undiagnosed and untreated. Symptoms of childhood bipolar may be initially mistaken for normal emotions and behaviors of children and adolescents. Some bipolar symptoms, such as irritable mania, are similar to common childhood anger outbursts, behavioral or conduct disorders and attention deficit hyperactivity disorder (ADHD). The bipolar mood swings in children and adolescents are more extreme and are accompanied by changes in sleep, energy level, and the ability to think clearly. On the other hand, bipolar disorder may also be over-diagnosed in children or younger adolescents who have persistent irritability and severe temper outbursts, mood swings or disruptive behaviors without changes in energy or sleep patterns. With teenagers, it may be hard to tell the difference between "normal" mood swings and bipolar mood swings. Healthy adolescents sometimes are defiant, aggressive, disinterested, have low self-esteem or may retreat into themselves. However, weight changes, drug and alcohol use, extreme tiredness and thoughts of suicide can be signs of depression in teenagers.

In addition to a family history of mood disorders, specific screening questions can be useful in evaluating mood changes, sleep disorders and restlessness in children, to prevent overmedication of children who are incorrectly diagnosed with bipolar disorder. Before prescribing powerful psychiatric drugs that can cause serious side effects, it is very important that a psychiatrist or psychologist with expertise in mood disorder evaluates them to make sure that a child’s symptoms are due to bipolar disorder, rather than to emotional or behavioral issues.

Pre-schoolers who are depressed cry a lot, are not interested in playing and are very anxious. School-aged children who are depressed often lose interest in their leisure activities and can be hostile to others. They can lose their temper, get upset quickly over little things and have low self-esteem. Young kids may have severe temper tantrums that can last for hours and become violent over time. Parents may also notice periods of extreme happiness and absurd moods.

It is possible to diagnose bipolar I disorder in a pre-pubescent child if he exhibits a full blown manic episode and euphoria that occurs most of the time over a seven day period. Although irritability may be a symptom, it is not a core diagnostic criterion for the diagnosis of bipolar disorder. Children with a history of depression and a family history of bipolar disorder should be carefully followed up although bipolar I disorder should not be diagnosed solely on the basis of a major depressive episode and a family history. Children and adolescents should be offered separate individual appointments with a healthcare professional in addition to joint meetings with their family members or caregivers. Immediate hospitalization should be considered for children and adolescents at risk of suicide or other serious injury.

Before diagnosing bipolar I disorder in a child or adolescent, other possible explanations for the behavior and symptoms should be considered, including sexual, emotional and physical abuse; drug and/or alcohol misuse; and organic causes like excited and confused states in children with epilepsy. Video games, including non-violent ones, together with other interactive screen use, such as texting and Internet surfing may contribute to aggression and sleep problems in children. They can have negative effects on behavior and mood, which could be wrongly perceived as bipolar disorder. Most of the children with bipolar disorder also have attention deficit/ hyperactivity disorder (ADHD) and other co-existing conditions that include conduct disorder, panic disorder, generalized anxiety disorder, and obsessive-compulsive disorder.

Some children, teenagers, and young adults may have increased risk of suicidal thoughts and actions when treated with antidepressants, so they should be watched closely for worsening of depression, suicidal thoughts or actions, unusual changes in behavior, agitation, and irritability. Patients, families, and caregivers should pay close attention to children's sudden changes in mood and behavior.

-o0o-

Women may develop major depression after delivery, a condition that is called postpartum depression. Yet, depression alone can prolong symptoms and may be a precursor of Bipolar disorder. It's important to diagnose Bipolar disorder early so that treatment can begin right away. While most women experience some degree of euphoria within the first few weeks of childbirth, bipolar women may experience hypomania from day one as opposed to day three or four, with the hypomanic euphoria or irritable mood lasting for at least three to four days. If they are noticing (or someone else notices) their odd behavior after giving birth, they should not be left alone with the baby. Even if postpartum bipolar disorder is misdiagnosed as postpartum depression, the bipolar disorder is likely to re-emerge within the first year after childbirth.

The risks and benefits of bipolar medication during pregnancy are not clear. Women with bipolar disorder have increased risk of relapse during pregnancy and after delivery, so that they need to be closely followed up by a mental health specialist. If a pregnant woman with bipolar disorder is stable on an antipsychotic and likely to relapse without medication, she should be maintained on the antipsychotic, and monitored for weight gain and diabetes. However, women with bipolar disorder who are considering pregnancy are normally advised to stop taking valproate, carbamazepine, lithium, lamotrigine and other anti-manic medication.

Lithium may be continued after full discussion of the risks, while trying to conceive and throughout the pregnancy, if manic episodes have complicated the woman's previous pregnancies and her symptoms have responded well to lithium. Otherwise, she should gradually stop the medication and restart it in the second trimester if the woman is not planning to breastfeed and her symptoms have responded better to lithium than to other drugs in the past. Serum lithium levels should be monitored every 4 weeks, then weekly from the 36th week, and less than 24 hours after childbirth, and the woman should maintain adequate fluid intake.

Pregnant women with bipolar disorder may consider psychological treatment for moderate depression and medication with structured psychological interventions for severe depression. Women who are prescribed an antidepressant during pregnancy should be informed of the potential, but predominantly short-lived, adverse effects of antidepressants on the newborn.

Babies whose mothers took psychotropic drugs during pregnancy should be monitored in the first few weeks for adverse drug effects, drug toxicity or withdrawal (for example, floppy baby syndrome, irritability, constant crying, shivering, tremor, restlessness, increased tone, feeding and sleeping difficulties and rarely seizures). If the mother was prescribed antidepressants in the last trimester, such symptoms may be a toxicity syndrome rather than withdrawal, and the neonate should be monitored carefully.

-o0o-

Mania or hypomania that first appears after 40 years of age usually follows many years of repeated episodes of unipolar depression or may be secondary to other factors such as steroid medication, infection, neuroendocrine disturbance or neurological problems. Late-onset bipolar disorder is less likely to be associated with a family history of the disorder than if it is earlier-onset. The prognosis for late-life depression is generally poor due to increased mortality rate that is accounted for by physical illness, especially cardiovascular and cerebrovascular disease, rather than suicide.

The later onset of mania has a greater degree of variation in presentation and course, and is usually associated with more neurologic impairment. Substance abuse is less common in older groups; but older individuals may develop new-onset mania associated with vascular changes, or become manic only after recurrent depressive episodes. In the elderly, recognition and treatment of bipolar disorder may be complicated by the presence of dementia or the side effects of medications being taken for other conditions. Although mania is less intense with a higher prevalence of mixed episodes, it also has poor response to treatment.

Because the kidneys of elders do not function as well as younger adults, older patients usually require lower drug doses than younger patients. They may be more susceptible to adverse reactions and to the side effects of the psychotropic drugs. They can develop postural hypotension, gastrointestinal bleeding, sedation, tremor and greater tendency to fall when taking medications for bipolar disorder. They have less tolerance for lithium.

DRUG TREATMENT AND OTHER FORMS OF THERAPY

The times I spent with my first psychiatrist had not been very helpful. I saw him during my first three episodes of depression. After filling out the Psychosocial Questionnaire, he asked me about my symptoms. At first, I was resistant and hesitant to take the medication he was prescribing. I told him "I don't take drugs". I only consented after he explained they were "medicines, not drugs". In the same way that anti-hypertensive drugs treat high blood pressure, or Tylenol helps relieve headaches; the medication he was giving me was intended to help with my depression.

He gave me a prescription for Zoloft, which did not help relieve my depression. Then he gave me Lexapro, and when it did not work either, he changed it to Effexor. I later noticed that Effexor made me anxious and made my hands tremble.

Numerous modifications in my drug dosages did not do much to relieve my depression through the years, I stopped taking my medications, and somehow, I got better without them.

When I saw my new psychiatrist for my last episode, she gave me a different set of medication after diagnosing me with Bipolar II disorder. First, she gave me Seroquel, which helped improve my sleep, but made me "groggy" and clouded my thinking so that I would be watching TV and hearing sounds but not understanding the words. After modifying my dosages, my depression got better but I noticed that I was no longer as productive as I used to be. I missed my "highs", so when I started feeling normal again, she gave me permission to stop taking my meds because I told her I was better and I needed to write grants. I went on a cruise with my sisters. I finished writing and submitted three grants that were later approved to fund the projects for my non-profit organization.

But by the time I saw my psychiatrist one month later, I was completely devastated again, and I could not stop crying. She felt bad for allowing me to stop my medicine, which she then restarted. I refused to take Lithium or get Electroconvulsive Therapy, so she added Lamictal instead to help me control my mood.

I stopped experiencing my hypomanic episodes, but by then I had lost my drive and lost my interest in my usual activities, including writing grants, planning projects, and interacting with the elders at the community center.

She added Lexapro to my Seroquel and my Lamictal to help me with my depression, and she scheduled me for group therapy. It took more than a year before my moods finally became stable.

-o0o-

Medications and psychotherapy are the most commonly prescribed treatment plans for people suffering from bipolar disorder.

Treatment can be frustrating and complicated because each individual responds differently to medications, depending on the severity and phase of the illness.

If you are living with bipolar disorder, your medication will depend on the nature and severity of your symptoms, including likelihood of suicide, and the presence or absence of psychosis. Most of the bipolar medications used during acute treatment can also be used long-term. Your doctor may prescribe one or a combination of these medications for maximum effect. Usually, when you have to change medications due to side effects, your doctor will change only one medication at a time so he can better monitor and identify which one is not working.

The most common medications used to treat this condition include mood stabilizers, antidepressants, anti-psychotics, and drugs that relieve anxiety. Most often, mood stabilizers will be the first course of drug therapy. You may also be prescribed an anticonvulsant for use as a mood stabilizer.

Antidepressants may be prescribed, but only with additional mood stabilizing medication. Most doctors agree that antidepressants should be used with caution in the treatment of bipolar disorder due to the possibility of inducing mania or rapid-cycling. Serotonin reuptake inhibitors (SSRIs), the most commonly prescribed antidepressants, may not be appropriate treatment for bipolar disorder and should be prescribed in conjunction with a mood stabilizer to prevent the switch to mania. SSRIs include *citalopram (Celexa), escitalopram (Lexapro), fluoxetine (Prozac), paroxetine (Paxil)* and *sertraline (Zoloft).* They have not been shown to be as effective for treating depression in bipolar disorder as in unipolar depression, In fact, there is a risk that antidepressants particularly *venlafaxine (Effexor)* can make bipolar disorder worse—triggering mania or hypomania, causing rapid cycling between mood states, or interfering with other mood stabilizing drugs.

After successful treatment for an acute depressive episode, you should not routinely continue on antidepressant treatment long-term.

If you develop an acute manic episode while on antidepressant medication, you should stop taking it. This may be done abruptly or gradually, depending on the antidepressant in question, on your clinical need, and your previous experience of developing withdrawal symptoms.

Benzodiazepines such *alprazolam (Xanax), clonazepam (Klonopin), diazepam (Valium)*, and *lorazepam (Ativan)*, are commonly referred to as minor tranquilizers, and are sometimes used in conjunction with anti-manic agents, for short-term symptomatic control of agitation and insomnia but they do not treat euphoria or depression. When used continuously beyond 4 weeks, they can cause withdrawal symptoms and drug dependence. They can also cause sedation, loss of balance and an increased risk of falls, particularly in the elderly.

Treatment for bipolar disorder often focuses on stabilizing mood to prevent both acute and longer-phase shifts between mania and depression. Mood stabilizers, such as *lithium, valproic acid (Depakote), carbamazepine (Tegretol)* and *lamotrigine (Lamictal)*, will help decrease the rate and intensity of manic episodes. If mood stabilizers are not enough to improve your quality of life, your doctor may prescribe an antipsychotic drug combined with an antidepressant.

Older mood stabilizers, such as *lithium*, are reliable and well-tolerated, and can reduce the risk of suicide in people with bipolar disorder. *Lithium* is usually effective in treating both the depressive and hypomanic symptoms in bipolar II, and as a mood stabilizer, it can be used to decrease the risk of hypomanic switch in patients treated with antidepressants. It can take weeks to work fully, making it better for maintenance treatment than for acute manic episodes. Your doctor will need to monitor the levels of *lithium* in your blood to avoid its side effects.

If you are taking *lithium*, you should not take over-the-counter non-steroidal anti-inflammatory drugs. You should seek medical attention if you develop diarrhea and/or vomiting. You need to maintain your fluid intake, particularly after sweating, after exercise, during hot weather, or if you have a fever. Because a shortage of serotonin may contribute to bipolar disorder, antidepressant drugs that increase serotonin activity in the brain may be prescribed in conjunction with lithium. While *lithium* is often considered a gold standard treatment for mania, it may be less effective when mania and depression occur simultaneously, as in a manic episode with mixed features.

Withdrawal mania is well recognized with *lithium.* A variety of temporary physical and psychological withdrawal symptoms, including movement disorders, have been noted with conventional antipsychotics and after stopping antidepressants. So, unless unavoidable, adjustments should be carried out gradually.

Valproate (Depakote) is an anti-seizure medication that also works for bipolar disorder. It has a more rapid onset of action, often making it more effective for an acute episode of mania than *lithium*. Your doctor may start you off at a very high dose so that you can get significant improvement in mood as early as four to five days. If you develop signs and symptoms of blood and liver disorder, you should seek immediate medical help and the drug should be stopped immediately. *Valproate* should not be prescribed routinely if you are a woman younger than 18 or of child-bearing potential because of the risk of ovarian cyst and unplanned pregnancy. If no effective alternative to valproate can be identified, you should use alternative method of contraception. Some other anti-seizure medications, notably *carbamazepine (Tegretol)* and *lamotrigine (Lamictal)*, can also be used to treat or prevent manias or depressions.

Carbamazepine (Tegretol) is a medication used primarily in the treatment of epilepsy and neuropathic pain, but it can also be as a second line agent in bipolar disorder. It effectively treats manic episodes and rapid-cycling bipolar disorder, but is less effective in preventing relapse than lithium or valproate.

Lamotrigine (Lamictal) is effective in treating severe bipolar depression. It has also been shown to have some benefit in preventing further episodes, and it may decrease the risk of relapse in rapid cycling bipolar II. It appears to be more effective in bipolar II than bipolar I, suggesting that *lamotrigine* more effectively treats depressive rather than manic episodes. Doses ranging from 100–200 mg have been reported to have the most efficacy. Unlike most other drugs for manic depression, *lamotrigine* seems to cause few side effects and is well tolerated by patients. There's no weight gain, no drowsiness, no cognitive slowing, or hormonal changes. And no blood tests are required for continued treatment. However, when starting the drug, you should tell your doctor if you develop a rash because it can cause potentially serious problem. But it can be averted if your doctor starts the drug at extremely low doses and just slowly build it up. If you are taking oral contraceptives, you may have to reduce the dose to half and use alternative methods of contraception because the drug may decrease the effectiveness of the contraceptive.

Antipsychotics may provide greater symptom relief, but also have greater side effects. Traditional antipsychotics (such as *Haldol, Loxapine*, or *Thorazine*) as well as newer antipsychotic drugs -- also called atypical antipsychotics such as *Aripiprazole (Abilify), clozapine (Clozaril), olanzapine (Zyprexa), quetiapine (Seroquel), risperidone (Risperdal)*, and *ziprasidone (Geodon)* are often used for severe manic episodes and for preventive treatment. In choosing between antipsychotics, the newer and more expensive atypical antipsychotics, are preferred over conventional antipsychotics.

Many drugs used in the routine treatment of bipolar disorder are known to cause weight gain, in particular, *olanzapine (Zyprexa), quetiapine (Seroquel), valproate (Depakote)* and *lithium*. Your treatment for bipolar must be ongoing. When you are in a manic or hypomanic phase, you may believe you have no further need of treatment or medications and stop taking them or stop meeting with your doctor. More often than not, you will return to treatment when you are in a depressive state again. But with the proper treatment, your disorder can be controlled and you can lead a healthy and productive life.

Hospitalization is considered an option for emergency situations in bipolar treatment. Be sure to create a plan ahead of time in case hospitalization becomes necessary. If a situation becomes unmanageable or dangerous, you or your family may need to contact the police.

-o0o-

Medication alone is usually not enough to fully control the symptoms of bipolar disorder. The most effective treatment strategy for bipolar disorder involves a combination of medication, therapy, and family or social support.

Psychosocial interventions commonly used for bipolar disorder are psychoeducation, family therapy and cognitive behavioral therapy. They are most efficient in preventing relapse and handling residual depressive symptoms.

Psychotherapy can be useful in coping with the consequences that bipolar disorder has on relationships. In the early stages of psychotherapy, you may benefit from regular weekly sessions, face-to-face meetings, phone conversations or communication via Skype or video-call. During this "talk" therapy, you can discuss feelings, thoughts, and behaviors that cause you problems. Regular therapy sessions with a psychologist or social worker, in combination with medication, can help stabilize your mood, make you feel better overall, and lead to fewer hospitalizations. It can help you better recognize the warning signs of a pending episode before it becomes full-blown, and it can also help to ensure that the medications prescribed for you are being taken properly. The therapist can work with you to devise methods to modify your behavior, and will suggest important self-help techniques to manage and reduce your stress. Psychotherapy focuses on helping you understand your thoughts, behaviors, and relationships, and how they impact your mental health and wellbeing. It can help you and your family members feel that you are in control rather than being victims of the disorder.

Psychoeducation involves teaching people with bipolar disorder about the illness and its treatment, and how to recognize signs of relapse so that early intervention can be sought before a full-blown illness episode occurs. Psychoeducation also may be helpful for family members.

Family therapy uses strategies to reduce the level of distress within the family that may either contribute to or result from the ill person's symptoms. It is especially beneficial when treating children and youth who are suffering from the disorder. A focused family intervention should take place over 6–9 months, and cover psychoeducation about the illness, ways to improve communication and solve problems.

Cognitive behavioral therapy (CBT) is useful in restructuring depressive and self-defeating thoughts that tend to exacerbate depressive episodes. It helps you gain a new outlook on your situation by directly challenging your negative thoughts and fears, and by teaching you to control or get rid of them. During a session, you and your therapist will work together to replace these negative thoughts with more positive or constructive ones. The treatment focuses on identifying your problems and your reactions to them, determining which of these reactions are unhealthy and replacing them with healthier alternatives.

-o0o-

When drug therapy, psychosocial therapy, and the combination of these interventions do not relieve severe symptoms such as psychosis or suicidal tendency, *electroconvulsive therapy* (ECT) may be considered. It is recommended only to achieve rapid and short-term improvement of severe symptoms after an adequate trial of other treatment options have not been effective, and/or when the condition is considered to be potentially life-threatening. *Electroconvulsive therapy* (ECT), known for decades to be able to improve mood, is now considered to be a safe and effective treatment for bipolar disorder. ECT may also be considered to treat acute episodes when medical conditions, including pregnancy, make the use of medications too risky. It is a highly effective treatment for severe depressive, manic, and/or mixed episodes.

It is mainly used against the depressive phase, but can also be used during the manic phase. It is also effective in preventing future episodes. But it is considered more of an emergency or backup treatment rather than a first-line treatment, and is often used when drugs are ineffective or when an episode must be treated immediately.

During the procedure, you'll receive a muscle relaxant to prevent injury, and an anesthetic to make you unconscious. A nurse will then place electrode pads on your head. The electrode pads are connected to an ECT machine that can generate electricity. When you're asleep and your muscles are relaxed, a doctor will send a small amount of electricity through your brain. This causes a minor seizure. The seizure reboots or restarts your brain, leading to more normal function. It is considered safe enough to be used on pregnant women and older patients. However, it may be risky for people with heart problems and must be done by a trained professional.

The possibility of long-lasting memory problems, although a concern in the past, has been significantly reduced with modern ECT techniques. However, the potential benefits and risks of ECT should be carefully reviewed and discussed with you and, where appropriate, with your family or friends, if your doctor is considering this treatment.

-o0o-

Regular sleep routines are key to successful treatment, as sleep disruption or sleep deprivation commonly destabilizes moods in bipolar disorder. A healthy diet and regular exercise may contribute to improved sleep, better mood, and can counteract weight gain associated with some medical treatments of bipolar disorder. Avoiding drug abuse and excessive alcohol also promotes stable moods. Drugs, tobacco or alcohol may appear to ease your symptoms, but they can actually trigger, prolong or worsen depression or mania. If you have a problem with alcohol or other drugs, tell your provider so that both your substance use and bipolar disorder can be treated.

Not much research has been conducted on herbal or natural supplements and how they may affect the course of bipolar disorder.

-o0o-

HOW YOU CAN HELP

I am lucky. I have a very supportive family.

When I told my family that I had bipolar disorder they could not believe it at first. They knew that I had been depressed in the past and that I loved to gamble, but they had not seen enough of my manic episodes to make them get concerned. When they read and learned more about the different types of bipolar disorder, they understood what I had. They listened, they paid attention and they allowed me to express and share my fears and my feelings with them.

Up to now, they still remind me about my medical appointments, and sometimes they schedule my appointments themselves when I fail to do so. Every so often, they go with me to the doctor's office, and patiently wait outside while I am having a session with my psychiatrist. They monitor my medications to make sure that I am taking the right dosages and taking them as directed. They make sure that I eat well and that I have enough sleep.

They take me out and spend quality time with me. When they are away, they call often to make sure I am okay. They are always there when I need them.

I could not have asked them for more.

-o0o-

Living with someone who has bipolar disorder is not easy. If your family member, friend or relative is bipolar, you are not only subject to the usual stress of caring but you are also at a particularly high risk of developing bipolar disorder or unipolar depressive disorder yourself.

Disclosing that someone has a bipolar disorder is a sensitive issue. Everyone has a right to privacy. This means that you need to be cautious about who you tell regarding the person's illness. However, keeping the person's bipolar disorder a secret from close family and friends, due to concerns about stigma, might eliminate potential sources of support and lead to isolation.

If your loved ones won't acknowledge that they have bipolar disorder, don't argue about it. The idea may be frightening to them, so be sensitive. Suggest a routine medical checkup instead, or a doctor's visit for a specific symptom, such as insomnia, irritability, or fatigue (you can call ahead to tell the doctor of their bipolar disorder concerns).

To better support and make a positive difference in the life of someone with bipolar disorder, you need to first educate yourself. Read as much as you can about the disorder. Get on the distribution list of as many mental health organizations as you can that provide information, support and research updates. Talk with trusted friends, colleagues and family. The more you know about bipolar disorder, the more you will understand the symptoms of manic and depressive episodes, and the more you can react appropriately to help your loved one during severe mood changes.

You don't always need to provide answers or advice to be helpful. Simply listening, paying attention and allowing them to express and share the fears and the challenges that they may be facing is one of the best things you can do to help. Give them a chance to talk about their feelings, and share your feelings with them as well. Letting them know that you are there to support and help them can go a long way. Stay calm, and avoid discussing things that might irritate or frustrate them or you. Do not raise your voice at them when they start arguing or shouting. People with bipolar disorder can't control their moods. They can't just snap out of depression or get a hold of themselves during a manic episode.

You don't have to agree with their actions and behaviors, but assuring them that you are on their side can be beneficial and can help them feel more secure. People with bipolar disorder often feel helpless, hopeless, and worthless, so that telling them about their strengths and positive qualities can help them recover from their depressive episodes more easily. While you don't necessarily have to attend their doctor's appointments and therapy sessions, it will help if you can accompany them every once in a while and wait for them in the doctor's office until their session is over. You can offer support and help reduce their anxiety just by being there. Remain patient and optimistic while helping them deal with their emotional ups and downs.

You can help them manage their mood by helping them follow a treatment plan, make lifestyle modifications, and stick to a healthy routine. Emphasize the importance of medication and make sure all prescriptions are being taken as directed. Remind them that abruptly stopping medication is dangerous. It is important to have an emergency plan in place when their depressive mood becomes so severe that they start having suicidal thoughts, or when they get out of control during a manic episode. You can write down your plan and share it with them while they are emotionally stable and calm. Help them establish a healthy daily routine and maintain good habits. Assist them in structuring their other activities by creating a list of daily tasks that they can check off when that task is done. Be sure to set aside enough time for them to rest and relax. It is also useful to keep a calendar and sticky notes to help them stay on track. Take extra care to make sure that they attend all their medical appointments.

Neither depression nor mania can be overcome through self-control, willpower, or reasoning. Telling a person to "stop acting crazy" or "look at the bright side" won't help. When they are feeling depressed, they may not be motivated to do anything. Despite their lack of energy, allowing them to do the things that make them happy can alleviate their depressive symptoms. Encourage but do not force them to do physical activities that they don't want to do. This includes low-to-moderately intense walking, jogging, or biking. Show your support by visiting or chatting with them regularly on the phone.

If they have never gotten a massage before, you may want to consider scheduling them for an appointment at a local spa. Similarly, yoga or meditation may be new to them, but can be beneficial activities to try during their depressive episodes. These activities are known to be relaxing, making it easier for them to cope with any stress or irritability that they may be experiencing.

You can offer to hold their cash or credit cards for them while they are well, to minimize potential financial damage when they become impulsive during their manic phase. Don't take it personally when they start demanding that you give them their credit cards, bank books, or cash. Recognize and understand that they can be hostile. They may express anger and feel betrayed by your attempt to control their finances. Remember that these reactions are caused by the illness and will pass once they receive proper treatment. In the midst of a bipolar episode, people often say or do things that are hurtful or embarrassing. When manic, they may be reckless, cruel, critical, and aggressive. When depressed, they may be irritable, hostile, and moody. It's hard not to take such behaviors personally, but try to remember that they are symptoms of a mental illness, not the result of selfishness or immaturity. When their moods and behaviors become out of control, and things are getting too difficult to handle, be prepared to call their doctor or therapist. Call 911 if they become abusive or threaten to harm themselves or others.

If your child has bipolar disorder, do not be judgmental. Stay calm and be patient. You can help by learning about the illness, keeping track of symptoms, and offering hope and encouragement, Instead of focusing on your child's behavior, try to understand his or her feelings. Share your concern in a loving way, ask your child how he or she is feeling, and make an effort to truly listen—even if you disagree or don't relate to what's being said. Learn how to defuse your anger. Your love and support can make a difference in treatment and recovery. Finding a mental health specialist who can provide the right kind of therapy is highly recommended, especially someone that your child can connect with. Encourage your child to have positive lifestyle habits, such as diet, exercise, and regular sleep. Talk about the dangers of self-medicating with drugs or alcohol. If your child is having suicidal ideation, and if they have plans to act on those thoughts, talking openly and showing genuine concern are key elements in preventing suicide.

As a friend or family member, you may have difficulty determining how close a person may be to attempting suicide. If you sense there is a problem, talk to your loved one and point out behavior patterns that concern you. Oftentimes, individuals with depression will talk with those closest to them about extreme feelings of hopelessness, despair, and self-doubt. When they start taking care of their personal affairs and making preparations for the family's welfare after they are gone, there is a good chance that they are thinking of harming themselves or go, such preparation makes it that much easier for them to carry out their impulsive desire.

People with depression often feel alone and withdrawn. Taking a step back and waiting for them to 'get back to normal' isn't the best way to handle the situation. Make sure they know that you are there for them every step of the way, and won't withdraw your support if things get difficult to handle. Talk to them to let them know they are not alone.

When patients are depressed, they are likely to isolate themselves and avoid social contact even with those who are trying to help them. Since loss of contact with others contributes to depression, you need to actively listen when they attempt to express their feelings. You should be especially careful to avoid being judgmental when they express despair, anger, hostility, or some negative feeling. Above all, it is important not to be condescending and not to respond to them by saying, "Don't worry," or "I'm sure everything will turn out okay." These responses convey a lack of empathy with the patient's suffering and are an unrealistic approach to a problem that is very real.

Physical contact and touching may be misunderstood by depressed patients, and may make them feel uncomfortable. Sometimes, it is better just to sit with them and engage in honest dialogue without physical interaction.

Severely depressed patients usually express a lack of desire for socializing or physical activity. They have feelings of worthlessness, low self-esteem, and thoughts of suicide. In dealing with depressed patients, you must always consider these feelings and try to understand the reasons for their behavior. Only by gradually gaining their attention and pointing out encouraging signs of progress can you help them return to reality and socialize with others.

The most important thing for friends and family to do for depressed loved ones is to help them get appropriate diagnosis and treatment. Encourage them to stay with their treatment until their symptoms are relieved or to seek different treatment if their symptoms remain unchecked. Look into reputable treatment programs and make appointments for them to visit treatment facilities.

If they show warning signs that they are contemplating suicide such as talking about death or dying, risky behavior, giving away possessions, or saying goodbye to people, don’t wait for their symptoms to go away. Take them seriously but stay calm. Don't try to handle the crisis alone or jeopardize your own health or safety. Do not be judgmental or argumentative. Often, people just need someone to listen. Offer reassurance and acknowledge the person's feelings. It is important to reassure them that there's nothing shameful about what they are thinking and feeling. Keep stressing that thoughts of hopelessness, guilt, and even suicide are all symptoms of a treatable, medical condition. Reinforce the good work they've done in keeping with their treatment plan. Simply talking and listening are important, but do not take on the role of therapist. This may create more feelings of rejection for the person, who doesn't want to be told what to do.

Make sure guns, blades, old medications and other potentially harmful items are out of reach. If possible, do not leave them alone until you are sure that they are in the hands of competent professionals. If you have to leave, make sure another friend or family member can stay with them until professional help is available. Call 911 if necessary. Contact the individual's doctor, the police, a crisis intervention team or others who are trained to help. Consider hospitalization as an option for emergency situations. Be sure to create a plan ahead of time in case hospitalization becomes necessary.

Episodes of suicidal thinking are usually temporary, but many depression-related suicides do occur. It is important to have a course of action ready and critical information on hand in case they start showing suicidal tendencies. This includes contact information for their doctor and back-up phone numbers (emergency services, pager and mobile phone); contact information for friends and family; list of medical problems and medications; health insurance information; and contact information for a local suicide hotline. If they start having thoughts of suicide during a depressive episode, call the National Suicide Prevention Lifeline at 1-800-273-8255. There are counselors available 24 hours a day, seven days a week. All calls are anonymous.

Taking care of someone with bipolar disorder can be stressful. You have to cope with the mood swings and sometimes other problems, but don't let it run your life. When you find yourself being stressed out and frustrated, find someone you can talk to about your feelings. Talk with the doctor about support groups for caregivers. Finding a support group and talking to other people who are in a similar situation might help. If you're having relationship or marriage difficulties, you can contact and schedule an appointment with a marriage counselor who can talk things through with you and your partner.

-o0o-

FAMOUS PERSONS WITH BIPOLAR DISORDER

Social stigma, stereotypes, and prejudice often deter individuals from seeking treatment and accepting a diagnosis of bipolar disorder. Although there is a high rate of mania, severe depression, and suicide, there is also a link between the mood swings of bipolar disorder and creativity. Many famous creative artists and highly intelligent individuals, past and present, are notorious for their outbursts, unstable behavior and significant mood swings. By openly talking about their condition and sharing their experiences with others, these successful famous people with bipolar disorder can help dispel the myth, reduce the stigma, and make it more acceptable to be honest about one's illness. Knowing about them can be a reassurance that people with bipolar disorder have the same potential for success as others. It must be noted, however, that a diagnosis of bipolar disorder is not always set in stone. Unipolar depression, borderline personality disorder, social and generalized anxiety disorder, post-traumatic stress disorder (PTSD) and attention-deficit/hyperactivity disorder (ADHD) have symptoms that overlap with and may be difficult to differentiate from bipolar disorder.

-o0o-

HANS CHRISTIAN ANDERSEN

Although a prolific writer of plays, travelogues, novels, and poems, Hans Christian Andersen is best known for his fairy tales. His children's stories such as "*The Steadfast Tin Soldier*", "*The Snow Queen*", "*Thumbelina*" and "*The Little Mermaid*" were translated into 150 different languages, and inspired animated films, motion pictures, plays and ballets. Andersen himself stated that he was depressed during his days at school, and that while staying at the headmaster's house, he was constantly abused. Andersen was reported to snap in and out of depression, and is believed to have suffered bipolar disorder.

-o0o-

LUDWIG VAN BEETHOVEN

Ludwig van Beethoven is known for his brilliant gift of composing amazing music. Despite being deaf at age 28, and suffering intermittently from serious bouts of fever and headaches, he conquered his disability and became one of the greatest musicians of all time. He not only suffered from deafness but also had bipolar disorder which some said fueled his creative power. His depression caused him to have rough relationships because of his unstable arguments and delusions. He composed his most famous works during his depressive episodes and while suffering from psychotic delusions. While he could compose numerous works at once when he was manic, it was during his depressed episodes that many of his most celebrated works were written. He stopped caring about his appearance, he flew into rages during dinner parties and also stopped composing almost completely when depressed. At one point in time, he thought about committing suicide. He had been self-medicating himself with alcohol for decades when he died of liver failure.

-o0o-

NAPOLEON BONAPARTE

Napoleon Bonaparte was a political leader and military officer who rose to fame and respect under the First Republic of France. He was known for his intelligence and strong personality, and was admired by his tutors for his application of mathematics, geography, and history in real life. However, Napoleon was believed to have suffered from bipolar disorder due to his aggressiveness and moodiness, as well as his extreme intelligence. The bipolar was said to be the driving force behind his rule. Some writers often portrayed Napoleon as a hard-hearted person, who does not care about other people but only for his own success.

-o0o-

DREW CAREY

Drew Allison Carey is an American stand-up comedian, game show host, writer and movie star whose popularity grew with the production of his show, *The Drew Carey Show*, which he starred. He has appeared in many movies, television series, music videos and a computer game. He is said to have suffered bipolar disorder and confessed in an interview that he suffered depression for a long time. He also admitted that at the age of 18, he tried to kill himself, and then again at age 20 by taking an overdose of pills. His depression was said to have been caused by the stress of his work and the sudden death of his father when he was still young. He overcome his depression by learning to believe in himself and reading anything that could help, instead of turning to substance abuse and ending up in rehabilitation facilities.

-o0o-

JIM CARREY

James Eugene "Jim" Carrey is an American comedian and actor. He took up roles in many movies that became hits and won awards in the movie industry. He is one of the top 25 actors of all time in terms of box office earnings, with his films averaging just under $100 million in sales. Carrey himself had disclosed that he suffered from depression even at the peak of his success, and that depression was the motivation behind the comedies he produced. Many people attributed his depression to bipolar disorder. He was put on the anti-depressant drug Prozac, which he used for a long time. He later overcame his depression through spirituality, perceptual changes of life, maintaining a sense of purpose, and avoiding drugs and alcohol.

-o0o-

AGATHA CHRISTIE

Agatha Christie was a British writer with over 80 detective novels to her credit, and was listed by the Guinness World Records as the best-selling novelist of all time. Her books have been translated into over 103 different languages. *"And Then There Were None"* is Christie's best-selling novel, with 100 million sales to date, making it the world's best-selling mystery ever. She received numerous honors during her lifetime including the Mystery Writers of America's Grand Master Award and the order of Dame Commander of the British Empire. Christie was believed to have suffered the disorder, which eventually led to her disappearance. On the same year that she released *"The Murder of Roger Ackroyd"*, a novel that was later marked as a genre classic and one of the author's all-time favorites, she developed such severe depression due to the death of her mother and the unfaithfulness of her husband that she disappeared only to be discovered by authorities eleven days later as a guest in a hotel, registered under the name of her husband's mistress.

-o0o-

WINSTON CHURCHILL

British Prime Minister Winston Churchill, one of the great leaders of World War II, had incredible energy and was highly productive when he was not in an intense and prolonged depression which he referred to as his "black dog". His family had a history of mental illness. His daughter died of suicide and his father had psychotic episodes during his life. He was established in history and biography writing, published 43 books during his time as prime minister and was awarded the Nobel Prize in Literature. He was diagnosed with bipolar disorder in middle age. Sometimes his depression was connected with traumatic external events such as his dismissal from the Admiralty after the Dardanelles disaster in WWI. Other times his depressive episodes could not be attributed to outside causes. He was combative and belligerent in his personal relationships, had persistent money troubles due to his extravagance and gambling, had unusual energy, and was a prolific writer. Many found him sarcastic and overbearing, and he was notorious for monologues that could last for up to 4 hours or longer. But he is generally regarded as one of the most important leaders in British and world history.

-o0o-

KURT COBAIN

Kurt Cobain, a famous American singer and guitarist, had Attention Deficit Disorder at a young age and was diagnosed with bipolar disorder as an adult. He began singing when he was two; at four, he started playing the piano; and at 14, he learned to play guitar. Kurt was depressed for much of his life, and would have periods of withdrawal and lethargy. He would cycle between being depressed and being highly productive, either in the studio or song writing at home. When manic, he would demolish stage sets and destroy hotel room furniture – sometimes done in high spirits and sometimes done in a fury. He frequently wrote highly emotional, angry letters to or about people he felt had wronged him. He also struggled with substance abuse, developed a heroin addiction, and committed suicide at age 27 in spite of the success of his Seattle–based band, Nirvana.

-o0o-

ROSEMARY CLOONEY

Rosemary Clooney, George Clooney's aunt, was a gifted singer whose career was disrupted midstream by bipolar disorder. In 1951 she recorded *"Come on-a My House,"* which became a gold record. She played in several films, but none as popular as *"White Christmas"* which became a top grosser. Throughout her career she recorded 25 albums, and received several awards. The pressure of raising five children while pursuing careers as a television, movie, radio, and recording star, plus her failing marriage led her to self-medicate on pain killers and tranquilizers. Following the assassination of Robert F. Kennedy, she suffered a raging manic episode onstage, cursed at her audience, walked off stage, and later announced her retirement while also sobbing uncontrollably. She was hospitalized for psychiatric care, at times in a double-locked ward because she had become so violent. She was diagnosed bipolar and was in therapy for several years thereafter. She died at 74 following a struggle with lung cancer.

-o0o-

PATRICIA CORNWELL

Patricia Carroll Daniels, with Patricia Cornwell as her pen name, is an American writer who is famous for her novels featuring a medical examiner, Dr. Kay Scarpetta. Her novels on crime detection subsequently made her the female best-selling author in America. She is also known for her advocacy on the abolishment of the death penalty and for promoting psychiatric research. She has a family history of mental disorder: her mother was hospitalized and later died from depression. After being overwhelmed by publication and success of her book, she bought five houses, many cars and lots of property. While returning from an outing, she crashed her Mercedes, was convicted of drunk driving, and subsequently spent 28 days in a treatment center. She went through moments of mania alternating with very low moments of depression. She openly acknowledges her diagnosis of bipolar disorder, which, although controlled without medication, played a role in a lawsuit that she filed against her financial advisers, on the premise that they are responsible for her loss of some $40 million dollars over four years.

-o0o-

CHARLES DICKENS

Charles Dickens was said to have been a severely depressed man with a fierce passion, rage and drive. As a youth, he suffered from Post-Traumatic Stress Disorder due to his time at Warren's Shoeblacking Factory and Warehouse. The sad realities involving orphans, destitute children, mistreated workers, and childhood trauma became recurrent themes in his writings. By his own accounts, Dickens suffered consistent bouts of "depression" that would start when he was beginning to write, later developing into a "mania" that would power him to complete his work. He had cycles of deep, debilitating sadness followed by periods of acute manic impulsivity and would rent a spacious summer home, holding sumptuous parties for large numbers of people on a daily basis. He needed to be the center of all attention, and showed extreme shifts in mood. He was obsessed with excessive grooming, a constant need to accomplish mini-goals (i.e. his compulsion to complete tremendous amounts of work within one day), and a penchant for looking at himself in the mirror. His depression worsened with age; he abused and eventually separated from his wife – the mother of his ten children – to live with an 18-year-old actress, while sitting on many committees for people working to restore their self-respect.

-o0o-

PATTY DUKE

Actress Patty Duke is an American actress, singer and a mental health advocate. She had a difficult childhood followed by later challenges with drug addiction, alcoholism, and anorexia. She started her acting career at a very early age and won an American Award for Best Supporting Actress at age 16. She was an accomplished singer and she also appeared on printed advertisements and television commercials. Despite her accomplishments, she was an unhappy woman. She resorted to continuous drug use and alcohol addiction even as a teenager, which almost ruined her career. Her father was an alcoholic and her mother suffered from clinical depression. Her periods of severe depression alternated with her manic episodes which included wild spending sprees; out of character promiscuity; multiple suicide attempts; smashing and throwing things; screaming foul mouthed abuse and delusions like hearing voices and believing in secret plots. After a diagnosis of bipolar disorder, she was given a series of treatments including lithium, which helped her recover. She wrote books on bipolar disorder and became a mental health advocate, sharing her experiences with manic-depression and how she has been able to overcome the disease.

-o0o-

RALPH WALDO EMERSON

Ralph Waldo Emerson was an American poet, writer and philosopher. Through his essays and teachings on the individual and pressures from the society, he formed the Transcendentalism philosophy. He was one of America's most influential thinkers and writers, and considered the best orator of his time. He also published essays, a second book and the all-famous *Self-Reliance* essay which generated a lot of public review but earned him world-wide fame. He established a school in Massachusetts and assisted his brother in running his school for young women, but was believed to have suffered bipolar disorder in his life. He suffered depression when his wife died. He exhibited the depression in the form of many disagreements with the beliefs and policies of the Boston's Second Church. He had a morbid outward look at life and lost hope. He sometimes collapsed into severe depression and recovered after days. His life lost hope and meaning. He suffered another bout of depression when his house caught fire. To relieve his depression, his friends contributed to send him abroad while they raised funds to rebuild his home.

-o0o-

CARRIE FISHER

Carrie Fisher, the daughter of Debbie Reynolds, was an American novelist and an actress known and loved as Princess Leia in *Star Wars.* She attained fame for her illustration of Princess Leia in her book *"The Original Star Wars Trilogy"*. When she told the world during a TV interview about her life with bipolar disorder, she became one of the highest-profile celebrities to speak publicly about her struggles with mental illness. Her father, Eddie Fisher, was also bipolar. The disorder can run in families. She suffered a psychotic break during a deep depression episode, thinking and telling the police that she was a serial killer. Unfortunately, she did not have proper medication and so she ended up spending six days and nights in the hospital, without sleep. She became violent and hallucinated about a light coming out of her head. She struggled with drug and alcohol problems. During one of her manic episodes, she hacked off her hair, got a tattoo, and wanted to convert to Judaism. Thanks to the lithium prescribed by her doctor, she was able to lead a normal life and her behavior became much more predictable.

-o0o-

MEL GIBSON

Mel Gibson is an Australian American actor, screenwriter, producer and film director as well. He is known for his movies, some of which also sparked controversies, and his open defamation of gays caused the Gay and Lesbian Alliance against Defamation to accuse him of homophobia. He also expressed his view on the Catholic religion and why women could not be priests. He earned many awards and honors for his good performance on stage and in films. During a custody battle with his girlfriend, it was discovered that Mel suffers from rage issues. He became addicted to alcohol and planned to kill himself one night during a show. He spent some time in rehabilitation. Gibson has acknowledged in the past that he suffers from bipolar disorder, characterized by unusual or extreme shifts in mood, energy, and activity levels. He also has admitted to a longstanding substance abuse problem, which, on its own, can trigger his mood swings or play a role in worsening his symptoms.

-o0o-

LINDA HAMILTON

Linda Hamilton is an American movie actress, best known for her role as Sarah Connor in *"Terminator"* and *"Terminator 2: Judgment Day"*. She has struggled with depression most of her life and was a compulsive eater as a child. For 20 years, she tried different therapies and treatments in a desperate search for answers. During her manic highs, she didn't need sleep and stayed with four hours sleep a night and still woke up feeling great. But she was fighting with her husband, taking everything on, taking too much on, and overachieving .Her rages and mood swings destroyed her marriages despite her considerable professional success, while self-medicating with drugs and alcohol. She was finally diagnosed with bipolar disorder at the age of 40. Once she got her illness under control, she decided to talk about it because she wanted to destigmatize mental illness. Her father, who died in an auto accident when she was five, was also diagnosed with bipolar disorder.

-o0o-

HARRY, PRINCE OF WALES

Prince Harry (real name: Henry Charlie Albert David) is the son of Charles, Prince of Wales, and Diana, Princess of Wales. His mother once described him as "very artistic and sporty." Despite his parents' increasingly strained marriage, he was known for his happy-go-lucky disposition as a child. He and his brother spent their school holidays dividing their time between their parents after their divorce in 1996. One year later, when he was 12, his mother was killed in a car accident. Struggling with this tremendous loss, Prince Harry suffered from nightmares about his mother's death for a time. He struggled to come to terms with his mother's death by shutting down all of his emotions for 20 years, refusing to think about her. It had a serious effect not only on his personal life but also on his work, and it brought him close to a breakdown on numerous occasions. He faced some academic challenges in school, although he passed his entrance exam with flying colors and, like his older brother, studied at Eton College where he excelled in sports, particularly polo and rugby. He was reportedly engaged in underage drinking and tried smoking marijuana during the summer of 2001 so that his father made him visit a South London rehabilitation center to see firsthand the dangers associated with drug use. He earned a reputation in his youth for being rebellious, leading the tabloid press to label him a "wild child". In 2002, the then 17-year-old had experimented with cannabis on several occasions. He was known as "the playboy prince" in his 20s for partying in glamorous London nightspots. That was a period when he was creating significant buzz as “Crazy Harry," regularly making headlines for smoking pot, getting wild at drunken parties, spending evenings with a series of beautiful young women in revealing outfits, and clashing physically with paparazzi outside nightclubs. In 2005, photos of him wearing a Nazi uniform to a costume party were published in several newspapers, for which he issued an apology. In 2009, he was forced to apologize for using offensive language to describe a Pakistani member of his Army platoon after video footage of the incident emerged. In 2012, his nude photos were leaked to the public, taken with a young woman during a private party in a hotel room in Las Vegas where the prince had been vacationing. At times, he felt "on the verge of punching someone" and had taken up boxing as an outlet for his aggression. He spent some time traveling through Australia, Argentina, and Africa after finishing school in 2003. During his 10 years in the Armed Forces, Captain Wales, as he became known, saw action in Afghanistan twice, most recently in 2012 to 2013 as an Apache helicopter co-pilot and gunner. He became involved in charity work while visiting Lesotho in southern Africa where he worked at a home for orphans of AIDS victims in South Africa and created a documentary called The Forgotten Kingdom: Prince Harry in Lesotho, which helped raise approximately $2 million for the British Red Cross Lesotho Fund. It wasn't until he began speaking with friends and family that he realized that it was his unattended, unresolved grief for losing his mother so young that was possibly crippling him. He finally sought professional counseling at the urging of his brother Prince William. In recent years, counselling helped him recover and deal with his grief. He said that things started to change when he was finally able to finally express his grief and anger for the loss of his mother. He shared his personal story to encourage people "to break the stigma surrounding mental health issues". He, together with his brother and sister-in-law, the Duke and Duchess of Cambridge, launched Heads Together, a campaign to end stigma around mental health. He says he wants to dedicate the rest of his life to working with ex-servicemen fighting mental health problems.

-o0o-

MARIETTE HARTLEY

Mariette Hartley is an Emmy-award winning actress who has appeared on "*Law and Order,*" "*Dirt,*" "*Grey's Anatomy,*" "*Big Love,*" "*Star Trek,*" "*M*A*S*H,*" "*The Incredible Hulk*" and on Polaroid commercials with James Garner. She lost both her father and an uncle to suicide, she lost a cousin who struggled with bipolar disorder, and her mother also attempted to take her own life. She was hypersexual at an early an age, and began drinking at age 14. While she was going through a terrible divorce, she started having suicidal thoughts, and contemplated jumping from the 24th floor of the building. She ended up in the doctor's office. Her doctor immediately assumed she was depressed and gave her a round of anti-depressants, but that caused her to go into a manic state. She was also misdiagnosed with Attention Deficit Disorder before finally getting the correct diagnosis of bipolar disorder. She co-founded the American Foundation for Suicide Prevention and worked with the pharmaceutical company GlaxoSmithKline, manufacturers of a medication recently approved by the FDA for bipolar, to help educate people about the proper diagnosis and treatment of the illness.

-o0o-

ERNEST HEMINGWAY

Ernest Hemingway was an American writer who won the Pulitzer Prize and the Nobel Prize in Literature for his best-known novel *"The Old Man and the Sea"*. His mother was a domineering type who wanted a daughter, not a son, dressing him as a girl and calling him Ernestine. She also had a habit of abusing his quiet father who was a physician, who suffered from diabetes, and who eventually committed suicide. He was a hard-drinking womanizer, big game hunter, deep sea fisherman, aficionado of the bullfight, and a boxer with quick-tempered fists both in and out of the ring. Drinking, insomnia, violent outbursts, a sense of dread, and great guilt over his own roguish behavior--four wives and many liaisons—were integral parts of his personal life. Late in life, Hemingway also developed symptoms of psychosis and paranoia likely related to his underlying affective illness, superimposed alcoholism, and traumatic brain injury. He feared that FBI agents would be after him if Cuba turned to the Russians, that the "Feds" would be checking his bank account, and that they wanted to arrest him for immorality. Ernest Hemingway was able to live a prosperous life until he was at the age of 61. As he was diagnosed with bipolar disorder and insomnia, he became addicted to alcohol. He suffered severe amnesia after an unsuccessful electroconvulsive therapy. The memory loss disrupted his writing career and everyday life. He committed suicide in 1961. Members of his family including his father and his sisters also committed suicide.

-o0o-

CONGRESSMAN PATRICK J. KENNEDY

Congressman Patrick J. Kennedy is a prominent politician who represented Rhode Island's first congressional district in the United States House of Representatives. He spoke bravely of his own struggle with addiction and bipolar disorder and said that public ignorance and the social stigma associated with mental illness heightened the suffering of his relatives who were affected in earlier generations. He added that he was treated for cocaine addiction as a teenager and was addicted to drugs and alcohol while in college. He was also often arrested for traffic offenses, either for over speeding or driving under alcoholic influence. He has vocally and publicly advocated for reform of the American health care system. He persistently called for the inclusion of mental health under health insurance. He has become one of the world's leading innovators on the prevention and treatment of mental illness, addiction, and other brain diseases.

-o0o-

VIVIEN LEIGH

Vivien Leigh was an English actress best known for her iconic Oscar-winning role as Scarlett O'Hara in *"Gone with the Wind"*, and for her marriage to fellow actor Laurence Olivier. However, she suffered from unpredictable behavior, severe depression and mania that eventually ruined her professional reputation. Although it was commonly believed that the onset of Vivien's bipolar disorder was triggered by a miscarriage she had while filming the Gabriel Pascal epic *"Caesar and Cleopatra"*, evidence suggests that she may have been displaying periodic warning signs even earlier. Reports of her unstable behavior during manic episodes included nymphomania and physically attacking people. Like many others with bipolar, Leigh abused alcohol. She suffered two miscarriages and contracted a severe case of tuberculosis. She also developed chronic insomnia and, on a flight to LA, she began to hallucinate and tried to jump out of the plane. She was immediately flown back to England and placed in a psychiatric hospital, where she was given electric shock therapy. She was finally diagnosed with cyclical manic-depression with hallucinations and had to be confined to a nursing home only to recover and return to the screen for her last movie. Her condition became too much for Olivier to bear, and he left her for a younger actress, after 20 years of marriage. She died at the age of 53.

-o0o-

ABRAHAM LINCOLN

Abraham Lincoln was the 16th U.S. President and the one who led Amcrica through the American Civil War, abolishing slavery, and ranked as the greatest of all United States Presidents. He was said to have had bipolar disorder. He was described as having major depression while others argue that Lincoln rather loved to laugh. His depression is believed to have stemmed from the many losses he suffered, first by the death of his mother, by the death of his son and, later, by the death of his wife. Both his mother and numerous members of his father's family exhibited similar symptoms of severe depression, indicating that he was probably biologically susceptible to the illness. Lincoln used humor and story-telling as a method of fighting depression. His friends spoke of his jovial demeanor and his animated expression so that his storytelling often evolved into doubling up with his own enthusiastic belly laughter before he could get to the punch line. Despite extreme poverty, Lincoln became a successful country lawyer, a senator and a member of the United States House of Representatives, all through sheer hard work. Though he faced a lot of opposition, he pushed through his policies, amending legislation and the constitution, to pave the way for a new America that is devoid of slavery. He was the first American president to be assassinated.

-o0o-

DEMI LOVATO

Child actor turned Billboard Top 40 chart-topper Demi Lovato was diagnosed with bipolar disorder at the age of 19. Before her diagnosis, she spent a lot of her life feeling vulnerable, sad and withdrawn. At times she could not even find the strength to get out of bed. She was partying, self-medicating and always stressing out. She was depressed, and harmed herself as her way of taking her own shame and her own guilt out on herself. Then she would have manic episodes, writing seven songs in one night and being up until 5:30 in the morning. After years of abusing her body, self-medicating, cutting, drug addiction and eating disorder, she hit rock bottom and was admitted to an inpatient treatment facility at the insistence of her family. Like many others, she struggled to accept her diagnosis at first, believing that she was not sick and that many people were far worse off than she was. After therapy and drug treatment, she spoke openly about the disorder in a documentary entitled "*Stay Strong*", where she shared her story to help others who are going through the same thing but are afraid to speak up about it.

-o0o-

MARILYN MONROE

Marilyn Monroe was an American singer, model, actress, and sex symbol. She suffered serious bouts of depression, the first time when her mother died, and later for her numerous problems in three marriages, all ending in divorce. She abused drugs and alcohol, and also had numerous abortions resulting from her complicated sexual life, reflective of her impulsive decisions and risky behavior. She had the reputation of being unreliable and difficult to work with--often exploding in anger, being aggressive, self-defensive and cautious of anyone who came around her. She flew to New York for a weekend to sing in the president's birthday ball, resulting in her absence at film shooting and the termination of her movie contract. She would have both manic episode and major depressive episode nearly every day during at least a one-week period, requiring hospitalization. In the set she was observed to be very "high" and appeared very excited despite her numerous absences over the past weeks, claiming to be fatigued and sick. She had a maternal history of manic-depression. Her mother also had schizophrenia and suicidal tendency, while her father, grandfather and great-grandfather were also suspected of having mental illness. She was found dead at age thirty-six from an overdose of barbiturates.

-o0o-

WOLFGANG AMADEUS MOZART

Wolfgang Amadeus Mozart is known to be one of the most brilliant composers of all times, with more than 600 works which became some of the most famous music compositions. When he was 5 years old, he composed for the first time and also performed in front of the European royalty. He acquired proficiency in playing the violin and keyboard from his father. After separating from his father at age 25, he exhibited signs of what might be considered adolescent rebellion. Mozart continued to display a childlike or even adolescent sense of humor, was unable to manage his finances, tended to overindulge in whatever happened to catch his attention at the time, and always needed someone to guide and organize his life. In his later years, he talked about having a depressed mood, constant sadness, tearfulness, and a markedly diminished interest in composing. He also complained of being unable to concentrate, and losing energy along with feelings of excessive guilt. He experienced episodes of hypomania, typically getting up at 6 am and often working until 2 am the next morning, writing letters that at times used inappropriate humor and at other times seemed to be incoherent. He showed a temper outburst many times and he also got into a lot of drinking. It is now accepted as a fact that he did suffer from the mental illness.

-o0o-

ISAAC NEWTON

Sir Isaac Newton was the most famous mathematician who invented calculus, explained gravity, and built telescopes, and who made significant contributions to the development of physics, mathematics, astrology, alchemy and natural philosophy. But he suffered from major up and down mood episodes, combined with psychotic tendencies. He wrote delusional letters, suffered "nervous breakdowns" when he worked five days without any sleep. He went through periods of depression and would have fits of rage towards anyone who disagreed with him. He was known to be aggressive and insecure, often exploding with a violent temper whenever he felt threatened. He was diagnosed with bipolar disorder and had a stutter that persisted throughout his entire life.

-o0o-

FLORENCE NIGHTINGALE

Florence Nightingale, considered to be the mother of modern nursing, said that she heard voices beginning at the age of 17, and that God had called her to work. She experienced periods of severe depression in her teens and early 20s. She earned herself the nickname of "*The Lady with the Lamp*" by caring for sick and wounded British soldiers during the Crimean War, working night and day to improve hygiene and provide better food for the soldiers. After serving in Crimea, she became ill and suffered from extreme fever, fatigue, anorexia, anxiety and severe depression, interspersed with bouts of high productivity. She described herself as "starving, desperate, and diseased", and at the age of 31, she asked God, in a letter, why she couldn't find happiness. Her cycles included frequent expressions of a sense of failure and worthlessness despite all her accomplishments. During her lifelong illness, she established the first modern nursing school, wrote 200 reports and books, including the first nursing textbook, and is credited with inventing the pie chart.

-o0o-

JANE PAULEY

Jane Margaret Pauley is an American television journalist who became a household name for her NBC TV news programs "Today" and "Dateline". She is known for her public acknowledgement of her struggles with bipolar disorder. A community health facility was named after her, to recognize her contributions to health care education. Before then, most of her colleagues didn't know about her illness or that, during a leave from the network, she'd been admitted to a psychiatric clinic. She suffered from recurrent hives, and the steroids used to treat her condition first brought on her manic episodes, but a second treatment left her depressed. Treatment with antidepressants threw her into a manic state. At age 50, a year after her first treatment for hives, she was diagnosed as having bipolar disorder. She said there were times she would shout at the top of her voice at the least provocation. She also became very aggressive and reserved. She was however quick to add that it was the depression that inspired her to be successful. She says treatment with lithium keeps her symptoms under control.

-o0o-

EDGAR ALLAN POE

Edgar Poe was an American poet and literature critic. He was known for his attempts to earn his living by writing alone, which was difficult at that time. Poe wrote and published several books and poems. His popular writings were along the lines of mystery and the macabre. He was also known to be part of the American Romantic Movement. Edgar started and contributed a lot to the detective fiction type of books. He was mischievous as a child, playing practical jokes on classmates and teachers, and had a grandiose view of himself. He was argumentative, untrusting, and lacked self-control. When he was young, he was cut off from his family because of his gambling habits. He started drinking while working for Southern Literacy Messenger, and his drinking intensified when his wife became ill. He expressed his personal feelings through his poetry, short stories, and art. In other words, he spoke of his moods through his art. He was described by coworkers and family as chronically melancholic, acquiring the nickname '*the man who never smiles*'. He disassociated himself from other writers and accused them of plagiarizing his work. He lived an extravagant lifestyle that could not be supported by his means of income resulting in a lot of debt. He rambled and scribbled his composition all day, and he read all night while having little-to-no sleep. He died after collapsing 'drunk and delirious' at the age of 40.

-o0o-

ELIZABETH TAYLOR

Elizabeth Taylor was an Anglo-American actress who was known for her extreme uncommon beauty, her acting style and her performances. She made more than 50 films, won two Oscars, was a grandmother at 39 and was married eight times to seven men. Although she was reportedly diagnosed with bipolar disorder, nothing much has been said about it. She was believed to have been depressed during the breakdown of many of her numerous marriages, and was treated for alcohol addiction. She broke into tears when she saw a statue of her late husband Richard Burton in Buckingham Palace while attending a gala evening. Once when Eddie Fisher who was then her husband threatened to leave, she swallowed an entire bottle of *Seconal*, a barbiturate sedative. She started screaming, got out of bed, totally naked, ran down the stairs, and drove her Cadillac while Eddie Fisher, ran right after her. During her last decade she was largely confined to a wheelchair, rarely venturing out of her mansion where a team of nurses provided round-the-clock care. She died at the age of 79.

-o0o-

LEO TOLSTOY

Leo Tolstoy was a Russian novelist, reformer, and moral thinker, who was renowned for his influence on Russian literature and politics. His literary work, "*War and Peace*" and *"Anna Karenina*" are still considered masterpieces of Russian Literature, while his book, *"A Confession"*, revealed the depth of his clinical depression, hypochondriasis, alcoholism, and drug abuse. As he reached middle age, his depression became worse. He became overly concerned with his success, and started giving his personal possessions away. Despite coming from a wealthy family, being celebrated as an author and being father to 13 children, he seriously considered suicide. Later, he was critical of himself for not having the courage to end his life. His final years were filled and great unhappiness, as he was caught in the strife between his beliefs, his followers, and his family. In one journal entry, he wrote about becoming increasingly suicidal. He went through serious personality changes, questioning virtually everything in his life. At times he debated giving away all of his possessions and becoming celibate. An unhappy compromise was when he assigned to his wife the copyright to all his works before 1881. He died of pneumonia after leaving home in the middle of winter at the age of 82.

-o0o-

MARGARET TRUDEAU

Margaret Trudeau is a Canadian author, actress, photographer, former television talk show hostess, and social advocate for people with bipolar disorder. She became the youngest first lady in Canadian history at the age of 22, after marrying Pierre Elliott Trudeau, who would soon become Canadian prime minister. Her first episode of severe depression manifested a few weeks after the birth of her second child. Her loss of interest in life made her just not want to do anything, not even things that previously gave her great joy. She just wanted to weep, she just wanted to stay in bed, and she started cancelling all her invitations. Her husband Pierre, who was then serving as Canada's 15th prime minister, eventually took her to a psychiatrist, who asserted that her condition was nothing to worry about. She felt better by spring, became interested in life again, and joined her husband on the re-election campaign trail. Then she went into a manic episode, making her feel overcharged like superwoman, racing from one thought after another. She felt restless and went to Montreal on her own; then, on a whim, she went to Paris, but that didn't feel like the place she needed to be either, so she travelled to Greece. It was following this experience that Margaret was placed in hospital for the first time. She continued to experience manic episodes, and once ran away with the Rolling Stones. She eventually separated from her husband. She tried yoga, photography, moving to new locations, changing her friends to try and fix herself, but nothing worked. She later tried Prozac, but this artificially pushed her into mania and resulted in her hospitalization for a few months. She stabilized for a time after her release from a psych ward but became depressed again after the death of her youngest son, and the death of her husband. She used marijuana during the day and alcohol at night to cope. She later developed psychosis. Following an intervention, he was readmitted to the hospital where a combination of medication and years of therapy brought her back from psychosis.

-o0o-

TED TURNER

Ted Turner is an American billionaire, media icon and philanthropist who is best known for founding CNN (Cable News Network) and Turner Classic Movies, and for his $1 billion pledge to the United Nations. His father suffered from mood swings caused by bipolar disorder, vented his anger by physically abusing Ted, and eventually committed suicide. Ted's media empire began with his father's billboard business which he took over at the age of 24 after his father's death. As an adult, he also suffered from bipolar disorder with bouts of depression throughout his adult life. His first battle with depression was when he caught his father with a doctor's wife. Over the course of his successful career in broadcasting, he married and divorced three times. His most famous marriage was his third, to actress and activist Jane Fonda. He suffered another round of depression and contemplated suicide when his marriage with Jane Fonda failed. Now, he takes lithium pills to manage his depression. His battle with manic depression can be read about in the book, "*It Ain't as Easy as it Looks*", written by author, Porter Bibb. Turner has written "*Call Me Ted*", in which he tells about his personal life and career.

-o0o-

JEAN-CLAUDE VAN DAMME

Jean-Claude Van Damme is a Belgian actor, martial artist, screenwriter, film producer, and director, best known for his martial arts action films. The most successful of these films include "*Bloodsport*", "*Sudden Death*", and "*Universal Soldier*". He suffered teenage depression which he compensated for through physical training like doing karate and ballet. He started using cocaine when he went into acting and did not work himself out as much as he used to. While married to his third wife, he had begun an affair with Darcy LaPier, who then became his fourth wife in 1994. Three years later, he got divorced and was charged with drug addiction and spousal abuse. He checked into a month-long rehab program and not long thereafter, he was formally diagnosed with rapid cycling bipolar disorder after becoming suicidal, while also heavily addicted to cocaine. He was treated with sodium valproate, though his condition greatly improved after finishing divorce procedures for his fourth marriage in 1997.

-o0o-

VINCENT VAN GOGH

Vincent Van Gogh was a world-renowned Dutch post-impressionist painter and artist who created more than 2,000 artworks made up of 900 paintings and 1,100 drawings and sketches. He is well known for his eccentricities, moodiness and a tragic history that includes cutting off his part of his ear during a bout of depression. He experienced depression and manic episodes which led him to act hostile and aggressive at times. He was born with a brain lesion, which may have contributed to his depression and which was exacerbated by his use of a drug designed to improve the perception of some bright colors, resulting in epileptic seizures. To relieve his epilepsy and depression, he often drank alcohol, and it was speculated that his bipolar disorder drove him to self-mutilation and was the reason why he was repeatedly confined to the Asylum of Saint Paul at Saint Remi. He was reported to have suffered two distinct episodes of reactive depression, both of which were followed by sustained periods of increasingly high energy and enthusiasm, first as an evangelist and then as an artist. He fluctuated between extreme mania and depression, and he ultimately committed suicide with a self-inflicted gunshot wound at age 37. He also had a family history of the illness, like having a brother with depression and a second brother who committed suicide.

-o0o-

ROBIN WILLIAMS

Robin Williams was an American comedian who rose to fame on account of his role in the "*Mork and Mindy*" TV series as the alien, and later with movies such as "*Mrs. Doubtfire*", "*Dead Poets Society*", "*Awakenings*", and "*Good Will Hunting*", where he won an Oscar for his role as a therapist. He also won a number of Grammy awards and Screen Actors Guild Awards as well as Golden Globes. He was known for his fast-paced, improvisational, intense, utterly manic style of stand-up performance, and could talk "a mile a minute". Throughout Williams' 40-year career, his personal life was marked by extreme swings from cocaine-induced hallucinations to severe depression. He described himself as a quiet and shy child who did not overcome his shyness until he became involved with his high school drama department, while his friends recalled him as being very funny. He pursued acting after high school and was known to improvise during his time in Marin's drama program, putting cast members in hysterics. He could instantly perform in many dialects, including Scottish, Irish, English, Russian, and Italian. He often used free association of ideas while improvising in order to keep audience interest. Partly due to the stress of doing stand-up comedy, he started using drugs and alcohol early in his career but quit after the overdose death of his friend, John Belushi. He relapsed after 20 years of being sober and entered rehab for the first time publicly in 2006. He struggled with addiction for more than two decades and also became involved in several tumultuous romantic relationships. In 2009, he went into depression after undergoing open-heart surgery. He remained sober but battled depression. He committed suicide by hanging. He was 63.

-o0o-

VIRGINIA WOOLF

Adeline Virginia Woolf was an English writer and one of the foremost modernists of the twentieth century. Her best-selling works include the novels *"Mrs. Dalloway", "To the Lighthouse"* and *"Orlando"*. As a young girl, her older stepbrothers sexually molested her. She had a genetic predisposition to the development of mood disorders: her father had signs of cyclothymia; her half-sister was institutionalized for schizophrenia; her grandfather and uncle had depression. She had her first nervous breakdown at age 13, following the death of her mother and later of her half-sister. She had her second nervous breakdown which required hospitalization after the death of her father. She spent significant time at a private nursing facility for women where she was treated with sleep, rest and 'milk therapy" to gain weight. She had a mixed episode characterized by symptoms of depression mingled with unmotivated laughter and mental excitability. Many of the episodes preceded the release of her books, causing her anxiety and self-doubt. She experienced hallucinations and heard the voice of her mother who was not alive or the birds outside the window that were talking in Greek. She saw dead people, ghosts and individuals mocking her. The episodes would start with sleeplessness, progressing to hearing voices. Her mood episodes were usually preceded by insomnia, psychomotor agitation and distress. She was hospitalized several times for suicide attempts. After an argument with her husband, she tried to commit suicide by taking an overdose of barbital. With several suicide attempts throughout her life, she finally managed to kill herself by drowning at age 59.

-o0o-

CATHERINE ZETA-JONES

Academy Award-winning actress Catherine Zeta-Jones first became known to movie audiences in the 1998 film *"The Mask of Zorro"*. The musical film *"Chicago"* won her the Academy and BAFTA Awards for Best Supporting Actress. In 2010, she went through a period of mood swings following an intense period of stress when her husband, Michael Douglas, endured both chemotherapy and radiation for stage IV throat cancer. A year later, she sought treatment for bipolar II disorder, characterized by episodes of hypomanic highs and irritability alternating with depression. She broke down when talking about her husband in front of the 13,000 audience at the Ryder Cup "*Welcome to Wales*" concert where she had been booked months before her husband fell ill to speak at the event, but she had to go to the event solo as he was treated back in New York. She was close to tears at New York's John F. Kennedy airport after she reportedly cut short a visit to the United Kingdom when her husband's conditioned worsened. She flew into a rage at a photographer in London, claiming he hit her as she and Douglas returned to their hotel after dinner. She suffered sleepless nights and tried to cope by chain-smoking and drinking. She checked herself into a mental health facility to help balance her mental health before going back to work. She appeared 'happy' during her stay and apparently joined fellow guests for meals, jogged around the grounds and even joined poker sessions before bed. Since then, she has been very outspoken about managing her disorder and advocating for de-stigmatizing mental illness.

-o0o-

As a person who has lived with bipolar disorder for more than 20 years, I am inspired by these people who have achieved success despite their illness. Bipolar disorder is not something to be ashamed of. Despite their symptoms consistent with a mental illness and with proper treatment, these famous people have shown that they can be productive, and even create a lasting legacy. They have proven that this disorder does not prevent people from leading a normal creative and innovative life. I agree.

-o0o-

REFERENCES

http://alothealth.com/conditions/living-with-bipolar-disorder
http://bipolarwellness.blogspot.com/2008/02/president-abraham-lincoln-and.html
http://blogs.psychcentral.com/bipolar-laid-bare/2016/08/planning-a-life-with-bipolar-disorder-part-i/
http://blogs.psychcentral.com/bipolar-laid-bare/2016/08/planning-a-life-with-bipolar-disorder-
https://en.wikipedia.org/wiki/Bipolar_disorder
https://en.wikipedia.org/wiki/Bipolar_II_disorder
http://healthyplace.com/bipolar-disorder/articles/patty-duke-bipolar-disorders-original-poster-girl/patty-duke-s-bipolar-account/
http://ibpf.org/blog/30-things-not-say-those-bipolar-disorder -Melanie Luxenberg
http://jama.jamanetwork.com/article.aspx?articleid=200415
http://news.stanford.edu/news/2005/november16/med-bipolar-111605.html
http://news.ubc.ca/2014/03/29/taking-the-stigma-out-of-bipolar-disorder/
http://news.yale.edu/2015/05/29/adolescent-brain-develops-differently-bipolar-disorder
http://ozonnews.com/8-silent-signs-of-bipolar-disorder-you-might-be-ignoring/
http://pdfsr.com/pdf/what-are-the-symptoms-of-bipolar-disorder
https://prezi.com/xwln5fcst1dg/marilyn-monroes-bipolar-disorder-i/
http://pro.psychcentral.com/differentiating-borderline-personality-disorder-from-bipolar-disorder/005080.html
http://psychcentral.com/disorders/bipolar/

http://psychcentral.com/disorders/bipolar-disorder-treatment/
http://support4bipolarteens.blogspot.com/2009/09/rosemary-clooney-singer-actress-george.html
https://themighty.com/2016/08/10-years-with-bipolar-disorder/
http://umm.edu/news-and-events/news-releases/2003/florence-nightingale-suffered-from-mental-illness
http://vivandlarry.com/general-discussion/vivien-leigh-and-bipolar-disorder/
http://www.activebeat.co/health-news/10-symptoms-of-bipolar-disorder-are-you-bipolar/
http://www.ajmc.com/journals/supplement/2007/2007-11-vol13-n7Suppl/Nov07-2656pS164-S169
http://www.alexandreloch.com/virginia-woolf-and-the-bipolar-disorder/
http://www.abc.net.au/news/2016-08-06/what-its-like-living-with-bipolar-disorder/7688802
http://www.biography.com/people/prince-harry-9542035
http://www.bipolar.treatmentinfo.com
http://www.bipolardisorderconnect.com/arthritis-articles/272-your-medication-regimen-if-plan-a-didn-t-work
http://www.bipolar-lives.com/
http://www.bipolarworld.net/Bipolar%20Disorder/Articles/art14.htm
http://www.bphope.com/margaret-trudeau-forgiveness-gratitude-wisdom/
http://www.cbsnews.com/news/prince-harry-mental-health-after-mother-princess-diana-death/
http://www.cbsnews.com/pictures/famous-people-celebrities-bipolar/15/
http://www.cnn.com/2017/04/21/health/prince-william-harry-heads-together/index.html
http://www.cnn.com/2014/08/14/opinion/jamison-depression-creativity/index.html
http://www.everydayhealth.com/news/why-bipolar-disorder-is-often-misdiagnosed
http://www.famousbipolarpeople.com/
http://www.hcplive.com/medical-news/shared-traits-of-borderline-personality-disorder-and-bipolar-disorder
http://www.healthcentral.com/bipolar/c/458275/166695/doctor-bipolar-disorder
http://www.healthline.com/health/could-it-be-bipolar-seven-signs-to-look-for?ref=tc#Overview1
http://www.helpguide.org/articles/bipolar-disorder/bipolar-disorder-signs-and-symptoms.htm
http://www.huffingtonpost.com/2013/05/21/catherine-zeta-jones-bipolar-treatment_n_3312701.html
http://www.imdb.com/name/nm0002133/bio
http://www.kevinmd.com/blog/2010/06/children-bipolar-disorder.html
http://www.latuda.com/bpd/what-is-bipolar-depression.html?\
http://www.livestrong.com/article/239135-effects-of-serotonin-on-bipolar-disorder/
http://www.marieclaire.co.uk/uncategorised/vivien-leigh-95137
http://www.mayoclinic.org/diseases-conditions/bipolar-disorder/basics/definition/

http://www.mayoclinic.org/diseases-conditions/bipolar-disorder/basics/symptoms/CON-20027544
http://www.mayoclinic.org/diseases-conditions/bipolar-disorder/expert-answers/bipolar-treatment/
http://www.medicinenet.com/script/main/art.asp?articlekey=2468
http://www.medicinenet.com/bipolar_disorder/article.htm
http://www.msn.com/en-us/heahlth/medical/these-popular-antidepressants-may-lead-to-bipolar-disorder/
http://www.nbcnews.com/news/world/prince-harry-opens-about-metal-health-after-mom-s-death-n747216
http://www.ncbi.nlm.nih.gov/pubmedhealth/PMHT0024571/
http://www.nhs.uk/Conditions/Bipolar-disorder/Pages/Symptoms.aspx
http://www.nimh.nih.gov/health/topics/bipolar-disorder/index.shtml
http://www.npr.org/templates/story/story.php?storyId=90231958
https://www.papermasters.com/virginia-woolf-mental-illness.html
hhttps://www.princehenryofwales.org/
https://www.psychologytoday.com/blog/
https://www.psychologytoday.com/articles/200311/managing-bipolar-disorder
http://www.psycom.net/depression.central.bipolar.html
http://www.salon.com/1999/09/27/fisher/
http://www.thejakartapost.com/life/2016/08/10/understanding-bipolar-disorder.htmlhttps://www.theguardian.com/society/2017/apr/17/prince-harry-grief-revelations-praise-mental-health-expertshttp
http://www.today.com/health/linda-hamilton-says-she-has-bipolar-disorder-2D80555887
http://usatoday.com/story/life/people/2017/02/02/prince-harry-talks-mental-health-afghanistan-servce/97391434
http://www.usmagazine.com/celebrities/prince-harry
https://www.verywell.com/rosemary-clooney-singer-378740
https://www.washingtonpost.com/news/morning-mix/wp/2017/04/17/i-just-didnt-know-what-was-wrong-prince-harry-opens-up-about-his-mental-health/?utm_term=.625f86c4e670
http://www.webmd.com/bipolar-disorder/news/20110306/bipolar-disorder-often-untreated
http://www.webmd.com/bipolar-disorder/news/20160725/bipolar-diagnosis-may-take up to 6 years
http://www.webmd.com/bipolar-disorder/guide/bipolar-disorder-warning-signs
http://www.webmd.com/bipolar-disorder/guide/what-is-bipolar-disorder
http://www.webmd.com/bipolar-disorder/news/20160509/depressive-episode-may-not-always-follow-mania-in-bipolar-disorder
http://www.webmd.com/bipolar-disorder/guide/bipolar-disorder-symptoms-types
http://www.webmd.com/bipolar-disorder/guide/bipolar-disorder-diagnosis-chap
http://www.webmd.com/bipolar-disorder/news/20151215/certain-antidepressants-may-be-linked-to-bipolar-disorder-study
http://www.webmd.com/bipolar-disorder/news/20160512/lithium-beats-newer-meds-for-bipolar-disorder-study-finds

http://www.webmd.com/bipolar-disorder/guide/bipolar-disorder-treatment-care
http://www.webmd.com/bipolar-disorder/guide/bipolar-disorder-living-managing
http://www.webmd.com/bipolar-disorder/news/20110306/bipolar-disorder-often-untreated
http://www.webmd.com/bipolar-disorder/guide/bipolar-2-disorder
http://www.wikihow.com/Diagnose-Postpartum-Bipolar-Disorderhttps://en.wikipedia.org/wiki/Prince_Harry

FURTHER READING

American Psychiatric Association. (1994). *Diagnostic and statistical manual for mental disorders* (4th ed.).

Washington, DC: APA Publishing. American Psychiatric Association. (2000). *Diagnostic and statistical manual of mental disorders* (4th ed., text rev.).

Washington, DC: APA Publishing. American Psychiatric Association. (2013). Bipolar and related disorders. In *Diagnostic and statistical manual of mental disorders (DSM-5®)*.

American Psychiatric Pub. American Psychiatric Association. (2013). *Diagnostic and statistical manual of mental disorders (DSM-5®).*

American Psychiatric Pub. Basco, M.R. (2015). *The bipolar workbook: Tools for controlling your mood swings* (2nd ed.). New York, NY: The Guilford Press.

Goodwin, F.K., & Jamison, K. R. (2007). *Manic–depressive illness: Bipolar disorders and recurrent depression* (2nd. ed.). New York, NY: Oxford University Press.

Leahy, R.L., & Johnson, S.L. (2003). *Psychological treatment of bipolar disorder*. New York, NY: The Guilford Press.

Mondimore, F.M. (2014). *Bipolar disorder: A guide for patients and families* (3rd ed.). Baltimore, MD: Johns Hopkins University Press.

U.S. Department of Health and Human Services, Substance Abuse and Mental Health Services Administration, Center for Mental Health Services, National Institutes of Health, National Institute of Mental Health. (1999). *Mental health: A report of the surgeon general*. Retrieved from https://profiles.nlm.nih.gov/ps/access/NNBBHS.pdf

-o0o-

MAJOR DEPRESSIVE DISORDER (UNIPOLAR DEPRESSION)

For more than twenty years of my life, I have had at least four episodes of depression, for which I was seen and treated by a psychiatrist and a psychotherapist. Every one of my depressive episodes presented with the same symptoms. I would have trouble sleeping. I lost my appetite. I cried uncontrollably. I did not feel like getting out of bed. I got panicky every time I dressed up for work. I felt awful, hopeless, helpless and worthless. I lost confidence in myself. I had trouble concentrating and made mistakes at work because of my indecisiveness. I felt guilty for not spending enough time with my mother while she was alive. I was always afraid that others might discover I was a fake and that I didn't deserve the recognition and honors I was getting for my work in and out of my profession. And each time, I was diagnosed with recurrent major depressive disorder or unipolar disorder.

My psychiatrist kept changing my medications and adjusting my dosages. He gave me Zoloft. Then he gave me Lexapro, and then changed it to Effexor. They were all anti-depressants that did not help relieve my symptoms. Rather, they made me anxious and irritable.

It was only after I saw a different psychiatrist that I discovered I did not have a unipolar disorder. After discussing my depressive symptoms, she went one step further and identified the opposite spectrum of my mood swings. I found out that I was also hypomanic, and that I have Bipolar II disorder.

She changed my medications and started me on Seroquel which is an antipsychotic drug. Then she added Lamictal to stabilize my moods. And finally, she added Lexapro which is an anti-depressant drug.

Bipolar depression can be easily misdiagnosed.

-o0o-

We all experience deep sadness and anxiety when a loved one passes away or when we go through a life challenge, such as a divorce or serious illness. It is normally short-lived and usually goes away within one or two months. Its seriousness is in proportion to the impact of the loss, and often does not lead to suicide. Feeling “down” or "depressed" is not considered a psychological disorder unless it begins to interfere with normal life. Even the feeling of grief resulting from the death of someone close is not itself depression if it does not persist. Situational depression or reactive depression precipitated by a stressful life event or other environmental factor is usually transient, and often goes back to a stable mood once that event is over. Feeling down or sad is a normal response to a loss. Some people are particularly affected by depression during fall and winter months. This kind of depression is referred to as seasonal affective disorder.

Depression is more than just feeling down every now and then. It causes long periods of feeling low, lack of motivation and lack of interest in things that used to be enjoyable. People with episodes of depression may have difficulty socializing, going to work, or feeling happy at all. They often feel tired, hopeless, and unable to concentrate, and they typically experience changes in their weight and sleep cycle.

Episodes of depression are always more or less disabling. About one third of affected people will experience only one episode in their lifetime. However, if a person doesn’t receive appropriate treatment for their depression, there is a risk of recurrent depressive episodes occurring in the future. When the depressive episode recurs, it may last months to years with normal mood phases in between.

People with low self-esteem and who are too dependent, self-critical or pessimistic are more likely to develop depression. Traumatic or stressful events, such as physical or sexual abuse, the death or loss of a loved one, a difficult relationship, or financial problems can trigger a depressive episode. Depression may also be related to childhood trauma; blood relatives with a history of depression; bipolar disorder; alcoholism or suicide; social stigma for being lesbian, gay, bisexual or transgender; abuse of alcohol or illegal drugs; or serious or chronic illness, including cancer, stroke, chronic pain or heart disease. Likewise, other mental health conditions may often co-exist with major depressive disorder, including alcohol and drug abuse, anxiety and panic disorders, obsessive-compulsive disorder, eating disorders, and borderline personality disorder.

Melancholia is a severe form of depression where many of the physical symptoms of depression are present. The essential feature of melancholia is either psychomotor retardation or psychomotor agitation. Psychomotor retardation can fluctuate during the day, but is often worse in the morning. It is characterized by a profound lack of energy, preferring to stay in the same position, doing nothing, and/or thinking nothing for hours instead of getting out of bed in the morning or taking a shower. There is remarkable slowing of thought processes, poor concentration and inattention. Psychomotor agitation or anxiety is often seen as inability to sit down, with pacing and hand-wringing.

Postpartum depression is a moderate to severe depression beginning slowly and sometimes undetectably during the second to third week after delivery, increasing steadily for weeks to months and usually resolving spontaneously within a year. The causes of postpartum depression are often the result of a combination of factors. In the days immediately following birth, they undergo hormonal changes. "Baby blues", feeling stressed out while adjusting to pregnancy and/or a new baby, are common experiences, but are different from depression. Postpartum depression is longer lasting and can affect not only the mother, but also her relationship with her baby, the child's development, the mother's relationship with her partner and with other members of the family. It may also be important to advise women about the risks of severe episodes of mood disorder in relation to the postpartum period, given the particularly high risk of severe postpartum episodes in women with bipolar disorder.

Sometimes people experience psychotic depression and can lose touch with reality. They suffer from hallucinations or delusions. They can also be paranoid, believing that they are being followed or persecuted, that everyone is against them, or that they are the cause of illness or bad events occurring around them.

Dysthymia or chronic depression, sometimes called depressive neurosis, causes a milder and less distinct set of symptoms than a depressive episode or recurrent depression. The person feels completely unmotivated for years, and has little appetite, difficulty sleeping and low-grade fatigue. He feels unhappy and down, but this does not affect his everyday life as much as depression. The symptoms change from day to day and week to week. However, the disorder is persistent, lasting much longer, at least 2 years, and sometimes decades. It affects functioning but is less incapacitating. However, it can be just as distressing because it lasts so long. It is estimated that 10%-25% of those who develop major depressive disorder have previously had dysthymic disorder and have more difficulty with full recovery between the episodes.

Unipolar depression, also called Major Depressive Disorder, is a significant medical condition that impacts mood and behavior as well as various physical functions such as changes in sleeping and eating habits, fatigue, lack of concentration and indecisiveness. The depressed person quickly becomes mentally fatigued when asked to read, study, or solve complicated problems. Other symptoms include irritability and agitation, lack of energy, withdrawal from normal and pleasurable activities, and thoughts of suicide. Marked forgetfulness may be sometimes be mistaken for early senility or dementia. There is usually a marked lowering of self-esteem and self-confidence with increased thoughts of hopelessness, helplessness and worthlessness. In the extreme, the person may feel excessively and unreasonably guilty. The diagnosis of major depressive disorder is made when five or more of these symptoms occur for a minimum of two consecutive weeks, according to the National Institute of Health. The most common and typical form of depression is the depressive episode.

By definition, a major depressive disorder cannot be due to physical illness, alcohol, medication, street drug use; or normal bereavement.

In adults, major depressive disorder affects twice as many women as men. It is likely due to genetic predisposition and fluctuating hormones, particularly during puberty, childbirth, and menopause. Although major depression can occur at any age, the average age for developing the illness is in the early 20s. Individuals who have parents or siblings with Major Depressive Disorder have a 1.5-3 times higher risk of developing this disorder. Children adopted at birth, away from biological parents who have a depressive illness, carry the same high risk as a child who is not adopted, even if they are raised in a family where no depressive illness exists.

About two-thirds of those individuals who have a major depressive episode will recover completely. The other one-third may recover only partially or not at all. People who do not recover completely may have a higher chance of experiencing one or more additional episodes separated by years without symptoms. The more depressive episodes a person experiences, the less time there is between the episodes. Lack of coping skills, recurrent stressful events, chronic diseases, and lack of family support, especially in elderly are common risk factors for developing depression.

Genetics is a prevailing cause of major depressive disorder, with an approximately 3-fold increased risk in the parents, siblings, and offspring of individuals with unipolar disorder versus the general population. Neurotransmitters are naturally occurring brain chemicals that likely play a role in depression. Hormonal changes during pregnancy, after delivery (postpartum), with thyroid problems, and during menopause may also trigger depression. The development of major depressive disorder may be related to certain medical illnesses. As many as 20%-25% of those who have illnesses such as cancer, stroke, diabetes, and previous heart attack are likely to develop major depressive disorder sometime during the presence of their medical illness. Most individuals with Major Depressive Disorder also have anxiety symptoms, panic attacks, phobias, and excessive health concerns. Anxiety in a person with major depression leads to a poorer response to treatment, poorer social and work function, greater likelihood of chronicity and an increased risk of suicidal behavior. Managing or treating a medical condition can be more difficult if a person is also clinically depressed.

Unipolar depression should be distinguished from bipolar depression, which refers to an oscillating state between depression and mania. Unipolar depression means "one pole" or one extreme mood of depression. Typical major depressive states may resemble depressions associated with bipolar disorder, with disturbances of sleep, appetite, energy, and concentration, physical slowing (or agitation), loss of interest, feelings of hopelessness and worthlessness, excessive guilt, profound loss of interest in activities, fatigue, weight loss or gain, and suicidal thoughts. Depression is closely associated with a lack of confidence and self-esteem and with an inability to express strong feelings. Unipolar depression has major depression only, without hypomania or mania. It is less likely to involve irritability, guilt, unpredictable mood swings, and feelings of restlessness. People with unipolar depression also tend to move and speak slowly, sleep a lot, and gain weight. In addition, they are less likely to develop psychotic depression. Mixed episodes (during which time they experience a mixture of both manic and depressive symptoms) may be confusing to the clinician not familiar with bipolar disorder.

Bipolar depression can look like unipolar depression, with the same symptoms that last for at least two weeks. For patients presenting with a first episode of depression, it may not be possible to distinguish between those who will go on to suffer recurrent unipolar depression and those who will develop bipolar disorder. The period of mania, or elevated mood that follows the depression is what differentiates a bipolar diagnosis. Mania is a state of high agitation or pleasurable excitement that does not occur with unipolar depression. Manic features are increased energy, less time on sleep, hyper-sexuality, excessive spending, grandiose delusions (thinking he has more money/ power), and pressured speech. People with bipolar disorder experience alternating phases with extreme mood swings. In one phase they might display all the typical symptoms of depression. In the next phase their mood might be completely the opposite. All of a sudden, they feel that they are on top of the world. They become very irritable, extremely active, and self-confident to the point of becoming delusional. They overflow with ideas, but are scatterbrained and often do not sleep much. During these euphoric ("manic") phases many people lose touch with reality and get into trouble. For instance, they might get involved in risky activities or get into a lot of debt. According to the National Institute of Mental Health, manic periods that come with bipolar disorder are interspersed with deep depressive states.

The lifetime suicide rate for unipolar depression is 9%. In contrast, the suicide rate for bipolar depression is 20%. The Bipolar Depression suicide rate reflects the fact that mixed mania, agitation, anxiety and psychosis, can make a person extremely uncomfortable and desperate, along with being depressed. When a person is in a mixed state (episodes where depression, mania and possibly psychosis occur at the same time), they have more energy and drive to actually try suicide. A family history of bipolar disorder, a prior depressive episode with psychotic symptoms, depression at a young age, or severe depression that doesn't respond to treatment are factors that can influence a person's decision to commit suicide. Drugs and alcohol can also influence people who are feeling suicidal, making them more impulsive and likely to act upon their urges than they would be when they sober.

Many patients with bipolar disorder are misdiagnosed as having major depressive disorder, often for several years - even after having experienced full-blown episodes of hypomania and mania, because they have poor recollection of their hypomanic episodes. Also, a person can experience depressive episodes for several years without experiencing mania or hypomania. The manic side of bipolar disorder isn't always bothersome to people. They have more energy and more motivation to do things. So the mental health professionals don't always hear about it. As a consequence, patients may be given inappropriate treatment. While both illnesses include episodes of extreme sadness and are best treated by a counselor or therapist, the types of medication that are used to treat them are very different. When bipolar disorder is missed, people can be put on medications that actually worsen the manic symptoms. So, people end up waiting much longer to get the stability in their life that they're looking for.

Diagnosis depends on the person having had an episode of mania and, unless observed, this can be difficult to detect. It is not uncommon for people to go for years before receiving an accurate diagnosis of bipolar disorder. If you're experiencing highs and lows, it's helpful to make this clear to your doctor or mental health professional.

Depression can be hard to spot in teens who already seem moody and impulsive. Depressed kids and teens can appear angry, bored, or withdrawn rather than sad and dejected. In children and adolescents, irritability, instead of sadness, can be the major mood state in depression. Because irritability is also often prominent in manic episodes, sorting out mood symptoms in children and young adolescents can be difficult.

Teenagers like to have their own "personal space" and spend plenty of time in their rooms. But those who hardly leave their rooms, who lose interest in spending time with friends, or who drop out of activities, may be showing signs of depression. Also, teenagers typically develop a need to stay up late and sleep later into the day. However, those who start sleeping a lot more or a lot less than usual may be depressed. It can be hard to tell the difference between "normal" mood swings and depression. Healthy young people are sometimes defiant, aggressive, uninterested, have low self-esteem or retreat into themselves. Weight changes, drug and alcohol use, extreme tiredness and thoughts of suicide can be, among other things, a sign of depression in teenagers. These behaviors can happen gradually and may be easily overlooked.

Pre-school and school-aged children probably do not get depressed very often. Those who are depressed usually cry a lot, are not interested in playing and are very anxious. They often lose interest in their leisure activities and can be hostile, while others may try unusually hard to be nice and obedient. Although most kids who suffer from depression don't develop bipolar disorder, those who develop depression early in life still have a higher risk of developing bipolar disorder than people who experience depression at a later age. Separation anxiety may be prominent in children with depression.

Older adults also frequently suffer from clinical depression. Their sad moods, fatigue and withdrawal from social life are often mistaken as a normal part of the aging process. Depression is not a normal part of getting old, and it should never be taken lightly. For many older people, clinical depression is linked to the death of a spouse, admission to a nursing home, prolonged illness, or a major operation, such as heart surgery. It is often difficult to distinguish between early dementia and major depressive disorder in the elderly. Unfortunately, depression often goes undiagnosed and untreated in older adults, and they may feel reluctant to seek help. Symptoms of depression may be different or less obvious in older adults, including memory difficulties or personality changes, physical aches or pain, often wanting to stay at home rather than going out to socialize or doing new things, and suicidal thinking especially in older men.

It is important to make a distinction between unipolar and bipolar disorder because the treatments for the two depressions are very different. Failure to make an accurate diagnosis can result in treatments that are ineffective or that can even make the condition worse. Prescribing antidepressants, the treatment for unipolar depression, may not only prove to be ineffective treatment but may actually worsen the bipolar symptoms by inducing rapid cycling or triggering a switch to a manic/mixed, manic, or hypomanic episode.

Major depression is often easily treatable through a combination of medication and talk therapy. Treatment for unipolar depression will involve taking a prescribed antidepressant, and may also include taking a mood stabilizing or antipsychotic drug. Antidepressant drugs such as *imipramine hydrochloride (Tofranil)* and *amitriptyline (Elavil)* are often used in the treatment of profound depression.

Selective serotonin reuptake inhibitor (SSRI) helps inhibit the breakdown of serotonin in the brain, resulting in higher amounts of this neurotransmitter in the brain. Serotonin is a brain chemical that is believed to be responsible for mood. It may help improve mood and produce healthy sleeping patterns. SSRIs include *fluoxetine (Prozac), paroxetine (Paxil), sertraline (Zoloft), citalopram (Celexa)* and *escitalopram (Lexapro).* They have a relatively low incidence of side effects that most people can tolerate well. Medicines known as atypical antidepressants and tricyclic antidepressants may be used when other drugs have not helped. They can cause several side effects, including weight gain and sleepiness.

Tricyclic antidepressants such as *imipramine (Tofranil), nortriptyline (Pamelor), amitriptyline (Doxepin), trimipramine (Surmontil), desipramine (Norpramin)* and *protriptyline (Vivactil)* can be very effective, but tend to cause more-severe side effects than the newer antidepressants. So they are generally not prescribed unless SSRI's have been tried without improvement.

Monoamine oxidase inhibitors (MAOIs) such as *tranylcypromine (Parnate), phenelzine (Nardil)* and *isocarboxazid (Marplan)* may be prescribed, typically when other medications haven't worked, because they can have serious side effects. MAOIs can have dangerous (or even deadly) interactions with foods such as certain cheeses, pickles and wines, as well as some medications including birth control pills, decongestants and certain herbal supplements.

Atypical antidepressants don't fit into any other antidepressant categories. *Trazodone* and *mirtazapine (Remeron)* are sedating and usually taken in the evening. *Vilazodone* is thought to have a low risk of sexual side effects.

Psychotherapy, also known as talk therapy or psychological therapy, may also be recommended to help people deal with their depression. Interpersonal therapists focus on the individual's disturbed personal relationships that both cause and exacerbate the depression. Cognitive behavioral therapists help the individual change their negative style of thinking and behaviors associated with depression. Often mental health practitioners will encourage lifestyle changes such as avoidance of alcohol and drugs, getting plenty of exercise and dietary changes. Approximately 80% of patients who seek treatment for major depression show improvement within four to six weeks, from medication, psychotherapy, attending support groups, or a combination of these treatments.

In addition to medications and psychotherapy, changes in lifestyle can also improve the symptoms of unipolar disorder. Eating foods that contain omega-3 fatty acids, such as salmon and Brussels sprouts to ease symptoms, and foods that are rich in vitamin B including beans and whole grains, have been shown to help some people with depression. Magnesium found in nuts, seeds, and yogurt may also reduce the symptoms of unipolar depression. Avoiding alcohol is also recommended, as it is a nervous system depressant that can make the symptoms worse. Exercising, especially outdoors and in moderate sunlight, can boost people's mood and make them feel better. It is also vital to get at least six to eight hours of sleep per night.

When antidepressants fail, *electroconvulsive therapy* (ECT) may be used in conjunction with the psychotherapy. In ECT, electrical currents are passed through the brain. This procedure is performed under anesthesia, and is believed to have an impact on the function and effect of neurotransmitters in the brain. It typically offers immediate relief of even severe depression when other treatments don't work. Physical side effects, such as headache, are tolerable. Some people also have memory loss, which is usually temporary. ECT is usually used for people who don't get better with medications, can't take antidepressants for health reasons, or are at high risk of suicide. It is generally avoided, except in extreme circumstances.

-o0o-

FAMOUS PERSONS WITH MAJOR DEPRESSIVE DISORDER

The stigma that surrounds major depressive disorder prevents people who are struggling to come forward and seek professional help. Famous people are not exempt from the feelings of low self-worth, sadness, restlessness, irritability, and apathy associated with depression. Stories of celebrities who suffer from unipolar depression provide insights into a condition that affects millions of Americans every year, and show that even people who seemingly have great and successful lives can go through periods of depression and feel suicidal. When famous, intelligent and successful people come forward and admit dealing with depression, they promote an understanding of the illness and help lessen the social stigma that often comes with the label.

-o0o-

BARBARA BUSH

Barbara Bush is the wife of George H. W. Bush, the 41st President of the United States, and served as First Lady of the United States from 1989 to 1993. She is the mother of George W. Bush, the 43rd President, and Jeb Bush, the 43rd Governor of Florida. She served as the Second Lady of the United States from 1981 to 1989. While First Lady of the United States, she worked to advance the cause of universal literacy, and founded the Barbara Bush Foundation for Family Literacy. The death of her daughter from leukemia in October 1953 led her to support numerous leukemia and cancer research and treatment programs. After her son was diagnosed with dyslexia, she began immersing herself in reading and literacy issues.

In 1976, she became seriously depressed after the Bushes returned from a two-year stint in China, where George Bush was U.S. liaison officer in Beijing and where the couple spent most of their time together. She felt ashamed and hid it from everyone, including her closest friends. But she shared it with her husband. She noted in her book, "Barbara Bush: A Memoir" that night after night her husband held her weeping in his arms while she tried to explain how she felt. She couldn't seem to shake off her sadness. She felt alone and unhappy, and she wallowed in self-pity. She was so depressed that she sometimes stopped her car on highway shoulders for fear that she might deliberately crash it into a tree or an oncoming vehicle. She got more depressed when her husband suggested that she get professional help, because she did not want to burden him. She did not seek psychiatric help or medication for depression. Instead, she tried to "shake it off" by immersing herself in her volunteer work. Although she later regretted that she did not seek professional help, she was determined to deal with depression on her own, delivering speeches with a slide show about her life in China, and volunteering at a hospice, the Washington House, a center for the seriously ill, where she changed bedclothes, washed patients' hair, bathed and fed the dying. She felt better, and her depression eased up after about six months. The former First Lady remains devoted to the Barbara Bush Family Literacy Foundation, which continues to grant awards to community literacy programs more than two decades after its founding. Several schools have been named in her honor. The Barbara Bush Library in Harris County, Texas, and the Barbara Bush Children's Hospital at Maine Medical Center in Portland, Maine, are also named after her.

-o0o-

TERRY BRADSHAW

Terry Paxton Bradshaw is a former American football quarterback Hall of Famer—the famous quarterback who led the Pittsburgh Steelers to eight championships and four Super Bowls. After an injury ended his 13-year career with the Steelers in 1983, he moved on to a career in broadcasting, talking about football for CBS and Fox TV. Although he was not diagnosed with clinical depression until 1999, he had frequent anxiety attacks during his playing career that would wear him out. He would go home after games and cry for no reason. Bradshaw has been married four times, the first three of which had ended in divorce. During a preseason game in 1980 at

Three Rivers Stadium in Pittsburgh, he was served with divorce papers from his second wife. It came as a shock, and emotional turmoil overwhelmed him mid-game. He could not bounce back from his divorce – emotionally. He lost weight, couldn't sleep, couldn't concentrate, and couldn't stop crying. If he wasn't crying, he was angry, bitter, hateful and mean-spirited. When his third wife asked for a divorce in 1999, after 16 years of marriage and two daughters together, he couldn't get out of his depression. His anxiety attacks and crying bouts escalated. He couldn't sleep. He lost weight. He grew angry and dark-tempered, and he began to drink heavily. He called his preacher who sent him to a family counselor. When he did not get better, his last resort was to see a psychiatrist. Since then he has taken the antidepressant Paxil regularly. In addition to dealing with depression, he noticed lately that he couldn't focus and remember things. His problem with memory and bouts of depression made him concerned enough to visit a clinic in Newport Beach, California. A winner of four Super Bowls with the Pittsburgh Steelers during the 1970s, his memory loss was thought to be due to the cumulative effect of multiple concussions during his NFL career. He has used medication and assistance from doctors to combat his difficulties. He chose to speak out about his depression to overcome the stigma associated with it and to urge others to seek help.

-o0o-

BILLY JOEL

William Martin "Billy" Joel is an American singer-songwriter and pianist. Since releasing his first hit song, "Piano Man", in 1973, Joel has become the sixth best-selling recording artist and the third best-selling solo artist in the United States. The talented six-time Grammy winner has gone through some personal struggle, brought on by a career downturn and personal problems. In 1970, he left a suicide note and attempted to end his life by drinking furniture polish. His drummer and band mate rushed him to the hospital where he was put on suicide watch and received treatment for depression. The September 11, 2001 series of four coordinated terrorist attacks by the Islamic terrorist group al-Qaeda on the Twin Towers had a devastating effect on him. He went into a deep depression, losing his faith in humanity and questioning life. The depression was compounded by a break-up he had gone through at the time. He used alcohol as medication for his depression, which led to his reckless driving, resulting in three-car accidents. In 2002, Joel entered Silver Hill Hospital, a substance abuse and psychiatric center in New Canaan, Connecticut. One day, he took a fatal dose of the anesthetic Nembutal and phoned his drummer to apologize for cheating with his drummer's wife. He woke up in the hospital and learned that they had pumped his stomach. Another suicide attempt ended with him checking into a mental health center. In 2005, he entered treatment at the Betty Ford Center, but admitted that the Alcoholics Anonymous did not work for him. His depression turned around when he got inspired by Malala Yousafzai, a Pakistani teen who was shot by the Taliban and later published an autobiography advocating for women's education on a worldwide press tour. But he remained uninspired when it came to recording new music. Joel still enjoys a glass of wine with dinner.

-o0o-

J.K. ROWLING

Joanne "Jo" Rowling, pen names J. K. Rowling and Robert Galbraith, is a British novelist, screenwriter and film producer best known as the author of the Harry Potter fantasy series. She had an unhappy early life, and had a difficult relationship with her father. Her mother was diagnosed with multiple sclerosis when she was 15, and later died when she was 25. She was working as a researcher and bilingual secretary for Amnesty International when she conceived the idea for the Harry Potter series, while on a delayed train from Manchester to London in 1990. The seven-year period that followed saw the birth of her first child, and divorce from her first husband. Her first marriage to a television journalist broke down after two years of domestic abuse.

She hit an all-time low when she convinced herself that something awful was destined to happen to her two-year-old daughter. Alone, with her young daughter, she saw herself as a failure and faced the demons of her mistakes that seemed to haunt her. She had regrets and felt she had made a mess of her life. This devastation along with the death of her beloved mother catapulted her into major depression. She contemplated suicide while a single mother in a cramped apartment after her marriage dissolved. She sought medical assistance, but in spite of needing urgent attention, she was dismissed carelessly by a general practitioner who was substituting for her regular doctor. Fortunately her regular doctor saw the warning signs and understood the seriousness of the issue.

She was diagnosed with clinical depression and acting on her doctor's advice, she started cognitive behavioral therapy. After nine months she overcame her suicidal thoughts and depression. Later, she used her daughter as motivation to rise above grim circumstances and finished the first novel in the series, Harry Potter and the Philosopher's Stone while living on state welfare benefits. At the time she was a penniless single mother, writing the book in cafes while her baby daughter slept beside her. Her books later gained worldwide attention, won multiple awards, sold more than 400 million copies, and became the best-selling book series in history

JK Rowling no longer suffers from this debilitating depression, but she hasn't forgotten how painful that time in her life was. She is now happy in her second marriage to a doctor with whom she has a son and a daughter. She discusses her experiences with depression freely and openly, in an effort to de-stigmatize the disease that affects millions worldwide.

-o0o-

BROOKE SHIELDS

Brooke Shields is an American actress, model and former child star who starred in several dramas including The Blue Lagoon, and Endless Love. Brooke and her husband had tried very hard to conceive a child, going through numerous in-vitro fertilizations. Her first pregnancy resulted in an extremely painful miscarriage in the third month. The second pregnancy was perfect. She didn't have morning sickness. But the delivery was far from ideal. She was induced and after 24 hours, she had an emergency Caesarean section. The umbilical cord had become wrapped around the baby's neck, body and leg. She almost had a hysterectomy when her uterus herniated during the surgery and she lost a lot of blood. Instead of the elation she expected to feel after delivering the child she'd always wanted, she experienced severe sadness almost immediately after she gave birth. She first felt the rage in the delivery room when she saw her husband holding the baby in his arms. Over the five days that she was in the hospital, she was in a bizarre state, experiencing feelings that ranged from embarrassment to stoicism to melancholy to shock. Returning home from the hospital, she found herself completely unable to bond with her baby. She found herself crying hysterically and was overwhelmed with feelings of rage and self-hatred. Her friends and family dismissed her sorrow and disinterest as a case of the "baby blues", but her sadness escalated rapidly into severe depression. She was plagued by feelings of self-doubt and self-harm. At her lowest point, Shields contemplated jumping from the apartment's window, and had visions of seeing her baby thrown against a wall. She continued to think she was having an intense version of the "baby blues" until friends suggested that she was suffering from postpartum depression. She realized that her illness might have been triggered by a traumatic childbirth, the death of her father three weeks earlier, stress from in vitro fertilization, a miscarriage and a family history of depression, as well as the hormones and life changes which were brought on by childbirth. She underwent treatment through a combination of therapy and antidepressant, Paxil, along with plenty of rest and help from family and friends. Gradually, she began to feel better and she finally bonded with her daughter. She began to embrace her role as mother and cherished each milestone with her toddler experiences, including "cozy time" before naps, a first trip to the zoo, and graduating from a crib to a big-girl bed. She now speaks openly about her depression, having thoughts of suicide, and difficulty bonding with her first child. She just finished writing her new book, “Down Came the Rain”, doing what she can to remove this stigma, and is seriously considering having more children.

-o0o-

ROD STEIGER

Rodney Stephen "Rod" Steiger was an American actor, noted for his portrayal of offbeat, often volatile and crazed characters. He starred as Marlon Brando's mobster brother Charlie in “On the Waterfront”, the title character Sol Nazerman in “The Pawnbroker”, and as police chief Bill Gillespie opposite Sidney Poitier in the film “In the Heat of the Night” that won him the Academy Award for Best Actor In 1967. After his open-heart surgery in 1979, he was seriously affected by depression for 8 years. He sank into an even deeper depression when he was not involved in acting, but it bothered him more that his acting career had taken a turn for the worse and was no longer challenging. He was laid so low by depression that he almost quit acting. He feared that he would drown screaming for help. In the depth of his depression, he refused to speak, wash or eat, and spent endless days unable to do anything but gaze out his window at the ocean. He experienced many symptoms of depression, including a persistent sad or "empty" mood, feeling hopeless and pessimistic, losing interest in his activities, having anxiety, disturbances in eating and sleeping, loss of self-esteem, an overwhelming sense of self-pity, and thoughts of suicide. He got very hostile, and had bad thoughts like shooting his loved ones and himself. He thought of going into the water, putting the gun in his mouth and blowing his brains out. The thought of his son and daughter stopped him from carrying out his plan, remembering a remark about suicide being a very selfish act. When he told his agent that he wanted to get help, he was warned that people would think he was crazy. His success as an actor and having enough money enabled him to go around and find the right doctor. He overcame his illness after he was put on an anti-depressant regimen and talk therapy. He also instituted some major life changes and stopped taking alcohol. He later became an advocate for the mentally ill, saying that he had a problem with a chemical imbalance, that he was not insane, that there were thousands of people in the same situation, and that the stigma surrounding mental disease was due to prejudice. Since his recovery during the late '80s, he went on a personal campaign to focus public attention on mental illness, for which he was honored with an Erasing the Stigma award. He died of pneumonia and kidney failure at the age of 77.

-o0o-

MIKE WALLACE

Myron Leon "Mike" Wallace was an American journalist, game show host, actor, and media personality who interviewed a wide range of prominent newsmakers during his sixty-year career. He was one of the original correspondents for CBS' 60 Minutes, which debuted in 1968. Wallace retired as a regular full-time correspondent in 2006, but still appeared occasionally on the series until 2008. For many years, Mike Wallace unknowingly suffered from depression. He would have days when he felt blue and it took more of an effort than usual to get through the things he had to do. It worsened in 1984, after General William Westmoreland filed a $120 million libel lawsuit against him, which was later dropped. During the proceedings, he went into a terrible depression that he had attempted suicide. His symptoms included low self-esteem, negativity, tiredness and moodiness. He was losing his appetite and was taking sleeping pills to offset insomnia. He later left a suicide note, took an overdose of sleeping pills and was rushed to the hospital after being found unconscious. Doctors were able to pump his stomach. Every day, he felt worse; unable to sleep, concentrate, or make simple decisions. He was grouchy, full of anxiety and self-doubt. Every night, he would call his doctor, who dismissed his symptoms as sign of exhaustion. Finally, Wallace checked himself into a psychiatric hospital where he was diagnosed with clinical depression. He recovered after getting a combination of psychotherapy and antidepressants. When Wallace next suffered an episode of depressive illness several years later, the only significant development that preceded it was a fall while playing tennis that resulted in a broken wrist. While he continued to suffer off-and-on depressive episodes throughout the rest of his life, the treatments he received helped him cope with his depression. After he began treatment, he started to speak out regularly about depression as well as the stigma and ignorance that often stand in the way of getting help. He died in 2012 at the age 93.

-o0o-

OWEN WILSON

Owen Cunningham Wilson is a charming and affable American comedic actor, producer and screenwriter, known for his role in "Wedding Crashers," "Starsky and Hutch", "Zoolander," "The Grand Budapest Hotel", and "Drillbit Taylor." He is not only financially wealthy; he also has a very likeable personality. He has had a hugely successful film career, starring in hit comedies such as "Wedding Crashers" (2005) and earning an Academy Award nomination for his work on "The Royal Tennenbaums" screenplay in 2001. On August 26, 2007, police were called to his Santa Monica residence in response to an attempted suicide. He was covered in blood and in a state of confusion when discovered by his brother Luke Wilson. He had tried to take his life by overdosing on pills while simultaneously slitting his wrist. An EMT initially treated him before taking him to St. John's Hospital in Santa Monica and eventually transferred to the Cedars-Sinai Hospital in Beverly Hills where he was treated for major depression and detoxification. His family and friends were totally shocked – as he was the last person they expected to battle depression and try to commit suicide. He was never known for throwing any crazy parties, causing trouble, or misbehaving. Most neighbors described him as being quiet and very likable but they didn't know that he had a history of depression and substance abuse. His attorney later confirmed that he had been taking antidepressants. Although it was believed that his depression was worsened by relationship s stress after a breakup with his ex-girlfriend, he denied that emotional distress from such break up triggered his attempt to end his life. He had admitted that he was struggling with depression for months prior to this attempt. Many of his friends noticed that he was not in high spirits during get-togethers and cookouts. In the months before his apparent suicide attempt, the actor was hooked on heroin and cocaine, struggling with depression and hanging out with the wrong crowd. Apparently he withdrew from social relationships and went missing in action for a period of time. This just demonstrates the fact that even celebrities get depressed and are not immune to mental health problems. After his suicide attempt, he continued to work on his movies, went through a "healing" process, and was back to being "funny, friendly, warm, and happy-go-lucky".

-o0o-

REFERENCES

http://abcnews.go.com/blogs/health/2012/04/09/mike-wallaces-battle-with-depression-and-suicide/

http://articles.orlandosentinel.com/1990-05-23/news/9005230529_1_barbara-bush-depression-bush-speaks

http://articles.latimes.com/2011/apr/15/news/la-heb-concussions-football-bradshaw-04152011

http://emedicine.medscape.com/article/286759

http://emedicine.medscape.com/article/290686 (Dysthymic disorder)

http://emedicine.medscape.com/article/913941 (Dysthymic disorder)

http://emedicine.medscape.com/article/914192 (Teen depression)

http://emedicine.medscape.com/article/271662 (Postpartum depression)

https://en.wikipedia.org/wiki/List_of_people_with_major_depressive_disorder

https://en.wikipedia.org/wiki/Barbara_Bush

https://en.wikipedia.org/wiki/Billy_Joel

https://en.wikipedia.org/wiki/Brooke_Shields

https://en.wikipedia.org/wiki/Buzz_Aldrin

https://en.wikipedia.org/wiki/Ellen_DeGeneres

https://en.wikipedia.org/wiki/Mike_Wallace

https://en.wikipedia.org/wiki/Rod_Steiger

https://en.wikipedia.org/wiki/Terry_Bradshaw

http://helpguide.org/mental/depression_signs_types_diagnosis_treatment.htm

http://helpguide.org/mental/depression_women.htm

http://mentalhealthdaily.com/2014/07/27/owen-wilsons-suicide-attempt-celebrities-can-feel-suicidal-too/

https://psychcentral.com/news/2012/04/10/mike-wallaces-battle-with-depression/37182.html
https://psychcentral.com/blog/archives/2007/05/15/brooke-shields-on-postpartum-depression/
http://reference.medscape.com/drugs/antidepressants-ssris
http://reference.medscape.com/drugs/psychiatrics
http://reference.medscape.com/drug/prozac-sarafem-fluoxetine-342955#1
http://reference.medscape.com/drug/zoloft-sertraline-342962#1
http://reference.medscape.com/drug/luvox-cr-fluvoxamine-342956#1
http://reference.medscape.com/drug/tofranil-pm-imipramine-342941#1
http://reference.medscape.com/drug/norpramin-desipramine-342939#1
http://reference.medscape.com/drug/levate-amitriptyline-342936#1
http://thechart.blogs.cnn.com/2012/04/10/mike-wallaces-public-battle-with-depression
http://www.biography.com/people/mike-wallace-9522454#!
http://www.dailymail.co.uk/news/article-2207319/J-K-Rowling-reveals-hit-rock-Harry-Potter-fame.html
http://www.dailymail.co.uk/news/article-2808870/How-Billy-Joel-love-fortune-lost-problems-drinking-depression.html
http://www.dailymail.co.uk/tvshowbiz/article-127169/A-tribute-Rod-Steiger.html
http://www.depression-guide.com/alcohol-and-depression.htm
http://www.depression-guide.com/celebrities/brooke-shields.htm
http://www.firstladies.org/biographies/firstladies.aspx?biography=42
http://.foxnews.com/story/2008/03/23/jk-rowling-considered-suicide-while-suffering-from-depression-before-writing.html
http://www.foxnews.com/story/2007/08/31/attorney-owen-wilson-taking-anti-depressants-no-other- http://people.com/archive/cover-story-owen-wilson-what-happened-vol-68-no-11/ drugs-before-suicide.html
https://www.guideposts.org/better-living/health-and-wellness/coping-with-illness/mike-wallaces-darkest-hour?nopaging=1
http://www.health.harvard.edu/newsweek/Depression_and_pain.htm
http://www.healthcentral.com/depression/c/84292/79275/forty-years
http://www.healthyplace.com/depression/treatment/best-depression-treatment/menu-id-68/
http://www.huffingtonpost.com/2013/05/26/billy-joel-depression-911_n_3339656.html
http://www.hopetocope.com/terry-bradshaw-quarterback-scramble-3/
http://www.howibeatdepression.com/how-jk-rowling-beat-depression/
http://www.lifetimetv.co.uk/biography/biography-harrison-ford
http://www.mayoclinic.com/health/teen-depression/DS01188
http://www.mayoclinic.com/health/depression-treatment/AN00685
http://www.mayoclinic.com/health/electroconvulsive-therapy/MY00129
http://www.mayoclinic.com/health/atypical-depression/DS01181
http://www.mayoclinic.com/health/depression/DS00175
http://www.mayoclinic.com/health/depression-and-pregnancy/MY00415
http://www.mayoclinic.com/health/depression-and-pregnancy/MY00981

http://www.mayoclinic.com/health/alcohol-and-depression/MY01078
http://www.mayoclinic.com/health/stress-and-depression/MY01649
http://www.mayoclinic.com/health/postpartum-depression/DS00546
https://www.myprivatesearch.com/search?q=brooke%20shields%20depression
http://www.ncbi.nlm.nih.gov/pubmed/20805727
http://www.ncbi.nlm.nih.gov/pubmed/20842989
http://www.ncbi.nlm.nih.gov/pmc/articles/PMC2739676/ doi: 10.1038/mp.2008.57
http://www.ncbi.nlm.nih.gov/pmc/articles/PMC2899788/?tool=pubmed
http://www.newsweek.com/owen-wilson-battling-depression-103931
http://www.nimh.nih.gov/health/publications/depression/complete-index.shtml
http://www.nimh.nih.gov/health/publications/men-and-depression/diagnostic-evaluation-and-treatment.shtml
http://www.nimh.nih.gov/health/publications/suicide-in-the-us-statistics-and-prevention/index.shtml
http://www.nimh.nih.gov/health/publications/depression-in-children-and-adolescents/index.shtml
http://www.notablebiographies.com/news/Ca-Ge/DeGeneres-Ellen.html
http://www.nydailynews.com/life-style/health/mike-wallace-spoke-struggle-depression-suicide-attempt-inspire-not-suffer-silence-article-1.1058601
http://www.oprah.com/oprahshow/Postpartum-Depression
https://www.psychologytoday.com/articles/200105/buzz-aldrin-down-earth
http://www.psychologytoday.com/articles/200308/when-depression-hurts
http://www.sciencedaily.com/releases/2007/10/071023183937.htm
http://www.suicide.org/jk-rowling-considered-suicide.html
http://www.tcm.com/tcmdb/person/183669%7C133815/Rod-Steiger/
http://www.telegraph.co.uk/news/worldnews/northamerica/usa/10080418/Billy-Joel-Depression-caused-by-911-not-alcohol-caused-my-car-accidents.html
https://www.theguardian.com/film/2014/mar/01/ellen-degeneres-us-talkshow-host
http://usatoday30.usatoday.com/life/health/doctor/lhdoc052.htm
http://www.webmd.com/mental-health/mental-health-adjustment-disorder
http://www.webmd.com/depression/guide/atypical-depression
http://www.webmd.com/depression/guide/depresssion-support
http://www.webmd.com/depression/postpartum-depression/features/brooke-shields-depression-struggle#1
http://www.webmd.com/mental-health/mental-health-adjustment-disorder

FURTHER READING:

Depression Guidelines Panel. (1993). *Depression in primary care: Treatment of major depression* (vol. 2, AHCPR Publication No. 93-0550). Rockville, MD: U.S. Department of Health and Human Services Public Health Service Agency for Health Care Policy and Research.

U.S. Department of Health and Human Services, National Institutes of Health. (2013). *Men and depression* (NIH Publication No. QF 11-5300). Retrieved from http://www.nimh.nih.gov/health/publications/men-and-depression/diagnostic-evaluation-and-treatment.shtml

U.S. Department of Health and Human Services, National Institutes of Health. (n.d.). *Depression in women: 5 things you should know* (NIH Publication No. TR 16-4779). Retrieved from https://www.nimh.nih.gov/health/publications/depression-in-women/index.shtml

-o0o-

PERSONALITY DISORDERS

The word 'personality' refers to the pattern of thoughts, feelings and behavior that make us the individuals that we are. Everyone's personality is unique. It affects the way we think, feel and behave towards ourselves and others. Most of us develop our personality as we go through different life experiences, and most of us are flexible enough to learn from past experiences and change our behavior when needed. It is normal. But there is a group of people who develop unique traits that cause them to act in ways that they cannot control, and that often end up causing significant problem for themselves and for others. A large number of bipolar patients, like me, are first misdiagnosed with depression and prescribed antidepressants — which can actually be dangerous since they can induce hypomania and trigger the mania to depression cycle over and over again. At the same time bipolar disorder is often confused with borderline personality disorder in people who have severe difficulties in regulating their emotions, leading to unstable personal relationships. A correct diagnosis is of utmost importance if one is to experience recovery from symptoms of either bipolar disorder or borderline personality disorder. Yet the disorders continue to be mistaken for each other. Education about mental illness can help prevent misdiagnosis, help us know the difference, and enable us to distinguish our conditions for what they truly are.

-o0o-

Personality disorders are enduring, inflexible and inappropriate behavioral and mental traits that significantly differ from how the average person in the culture perceives, thinks, and feels, often disrupting and persistently impairing one's social and personal life. People with a personality disorder are rigid, have an unhealthy pattern of thinking, and have trouble coping personally, socially and at the workplace—potentially leading to problems with others and interfering with interpersonal relationships. They believe that their way of thinking and behaving is completely normal, but tend to have a view of the world that is quite different than others. People with personality disorder often create serious problems in society and cause significant distress or impairment that cannot be attributed to another mental illness, brain damage, drugs, alcohol, medication or medical condition. It has a negative impact on one's way of life and interpersonal relations. People with personality disorder have distorted perceptions and a mode of thinking that deviates markedly from those accepted by the society. They have inappropriate expression of emotions, and problems with impulse control in a wide range of personal and social situations. Their patterns of behavior are typically recognized during childhood and adolescence, continuing until adulthood. Their unacceptable coping skills may lead to personal problems that induce extreme anxiety, distress, or depression. In general, 40–60% of psychiatric patients are diagnosed with personality disorders.

-o0o-

There are 10 specific personality disorders that are grouped into the following three clusters based on descriptive similarities in character traits and symptoms. Many people with one personality disorder also have signs and symptoms of at least one additional personality disorder.

CLUSTER A (Odd or eccentric disorders)

People with Cluster A personality disorder all share an inflexible, long-term pattern of social awkwardness and social withdrawal, punctuated by distorted thinking.

Paranoid personality disorder is characterized by extreme suspiciousness and a pervasive distrust of others, including even friends, family, and partner. Paranoid individuals often think of others as malevolent, manipulative, cunning or dishonest. They appear guarded, defensive, short-tempered, secretive, and excessively critical, because of their unfounded belief that others are trying to harm or deceive them. They easily feel shame and humiliation, and persistently bear grudges. They hesitate to confide in others due to unreasonable fear that others will use the information against them. They become angry or hostile when innocent remarks or nonthreatening situations are perceived as personal insults or attacks. They are generally difficult to work with and are very hard to form relationships with. They have a tendency to hold grudges and usually have unjustified, recurrent suspicion that their spouse or sexual partner is unfaithful.

Schizoid personality disorder is characterized by a lack of interest, indifference, and detachment from social or personal relationships. People with schizoid personalities, mostly men, are emotionally distant, prefer to be alone, and are prone to introspection and fantasy. They are humorless, dull, withdrawn, generally immersed in their own thoughts and have no desire for social or sexual relationships. They are hardly driven and have little ambition, if any. Because they tend not to show emotion, they may appear as though they don't care about what's going on around them.

Schizotypal personality disorder is characterized by distorted perceptions, odd or unusual beliefs, and extreme discomfort in establishing long term relationships. These individuals may have an eccentric way of behaving, speaking, or dressing, and they often have difficulty connecting with others. They also tend to display outlandish, strange and bizarre beliefs, such as believing that they can see the future or travel to other dimensions, or that they can read the thoughts of others. They exhibit peculiar mannerisms and behaviors. They avoid social interaction because they fear others. They have a flat affect and inappropriate emotional responses. For them, there is a blur line between reality and fantasy, and they usually have few, if any, close relationships because they do not see the impact of their behavior on others. They may develop brief psychotic disorder, delusional disorder, or schizophreniform disorder, at the time of diagnosis.

Paranoid, schizoid and, especially schizotypal personality disorders are very common among homeless people and may be observed as premorbid antecedents of delusional disorders or schizophrenia. The risk of developing these disorders is greater if the first-degree relatives also have either schizophrenia or a Cluster A personality disorder. While they share some hallmark symptoms, such as acute discomfort in close relationships, distorted perceptions, and eccentric behavior, those diagnosed with odd-eccentric Cluster A personality disorders are more in touch with reality compared to those diagnosed with schizophrenia. It is important to distinguish their distorted perception of reality from the delusions or hallucinations of schizophrenic people.

-o0o-

CLUSTER B (Dramatic, overly emotional, unpredictable thinking, or erratic disorders)

People with Cluster B personality disorders have marked and persistent impulse control and emotional regulation issues. They are particularly susceptible to problems of substance abuse, impulse control, and suicidal behavior, which may shorten their lives.

Antisocial personality disorder is characterized by little respect for the right of others, disregard for others' needs or feelings, absence of guilt or remorse for their behavior, and recurring problems with the law. People with antisocial, sociopathic or psychopathic personality have aggressive, often violent behavior. They are known to be manipulative, impulsive, irresponsible, and deviant. They lack empathy, and act without due consideration of what their actions can do to others. They can lie, steal, lose aliases or con others without difficulty. They see themselves as independent, and they meet social obligations only when self-serving. They are consistently irresponsible and have no respect for societal customs, rules, and standards. They are also at risk for abusing drugs to relieve their boredom.

Borderline personality disorder (or emotionally unstable personality disorder) is characterized by unstable relationships and a strong fear of abandonment. People with borderline personalities are impulsive, unpredictable, manipulative and unstable. They essentially lack a sense of self, and, as a result, experience feelings of emptiness. They may form an intense personal attachment with someone and then feel disenchanted and end their relationship for no apparent reason, only to be distressed and go into depression when their partner leaves them permanently. Self-mutilation, suicidal gestures or attention-seeking destructive behaviors are not uncommon, for which reason many borderline people frequently come to medical attention. They have a pervasive pattern of abrupt mood swings, often leading to self-harm and impulsivity. Borderline personality disorder is seen in association with mood and anxiety disorders, with impulse control disorders, eating disorders, ADHD, or a substance use disorder. It is sometimes considered as a mild form of bipolar disorder.

Histrionic personality disorder is characterized by persistent attention-seeking behavior that includes inappropriate sexual overtures and excessive emotions. People with histrionic personality see themselves as attractive, charming and seductive, and they have an excessive need to be the center of attention. They display impulsive and risky behavior, such as having unsafe sex, gambling or binge eating. They have a fragile self-image and ongoing feelings of emptiness, as well as unstable and intense relationships. They can be oversensitive about themselves and constantly seek reassurance or approval from others. They overreact to interpersonal stress with intense displays of anger, and minor events easily frustrate them. Disorder is characterized by constant attention-seeking, emotional overreaction, and suggestibility. They are often high-functioning, and their tendency to be overly-dramatic may impair relationships, leading to depression, suicidal behavior or threats of self-injury.

Narcissistic personality disorder is characterized by a grandiose self-image, an inflated sense of their own importance, and a great need for admiration. Individuals with this disorder believe that they are superior to others. They expect constant praise, they are egotistical and arrogant, and they have a false sense of entitlement with little respect for other people's feelings. They exaggerate their achievements and talents, and they tend to exploit others' weaknesses. They are oversensitive to criticism, manipulative, prone to outburst of anger, and often blame others for their failures. They lack empathy, and are preoccupied with fantasies of success, attractiveness, or achievement. But deep inside, they lack self-esteem, and are susceptible to depression and feelings of inferiority.

-o0o-

CLASS C (Anxious or fearful thinking and behavior)

The common factor of Cluster C disorders is a high level of anxiety. People with this personality disorder have a persistent pattern of obsessive and compulsive thoughts and behaviors, feelings of inadequacy, or an inordinate need to be taken care of by others

Avoidant personality disorder is characterized by severe and chronic social withdrawal, feelings of inferiority, over-sensitivity and social withdrawal. Individuals with avoidant personality are constantly fearful of rejection, disapproval, embarrassment and ridicule. They avoid the risk of being disappointed by forming relationships only with people that they trust. They are socially inhibited, timid and isolated, avoid meeting with strangers and new work activities that require interpersonal contact. They have pervasive feelings of social inhibition and inadequacy, and are extremely sensitive to criticism. Avoidant personality disorder is seen with social anxiety disorder.

Dependent personality disorder is characterized by submissiveness, separation anxiety, and an abnormal desire to be nurtured. People with dependent personalities desperately cling to and seek another partner when a close relationship ends. They always seek the approval of others when making decisions. They find it difficult to start or do projects on their own because of their lack of self-confidence. They have a pervasive psychological need to be taken care of by other people and they fear being abandoned or separated from important people in their life. They could not disagree with others and tend to tolerate and stay with poor or abusive relationships, even when other options are available.

Obsessive-compulsive personality disorder is characterized by an excessive and persistent preoccupation with detail, orderliness, perfectionism and strict conformity to rules, at the expense of interpersonal relationships. People with this disorder are rigid, stubborn, restrained, conscientious and demanding of others. They tend to neglect friends and enjoyable activities because of their excessive commitment to work or to a project. They get distressed when they are unable to finish a project that does not meet their own strict standards. They have a strong desire to be in control of people, tasks and situations, and are inflexible about morality, ethics or values. They are unable to discard broken or worthless objects, and have tight control over budgeting and spending money. Obsessive-compulsive personality disorder is not the same as obsessive-compulsive disorder, a type of anxiety disorder.

-o0o-

There are numerous possible causes of mental and personality disorders, including genetic predispositions and adverse experiences in life. Genes can make some individuals vulnerable to developing a personality disorder, while a life situation may trigger its actual development. Child abuse and neglect pose a greater risk of developing personality disorders in adulthood, with the sexually abused group having the most consistently elevated pattern of psychopathic behavior. Children who had experienced such verbal, emotional or physical abuse are much more likely to have borderline, narcissistic, obsessive-compulsive or paranoid personality disorders in adulthood, with physical abuse having a strong correlation with the development of antisocial and impulsive behavior. The levels of the brain chemical (neurotransmitter) dopamine may influence a person's level of novelty-seeking, and serotonin levels may influence aggression among patients with personality disorders who come from families that appear to be stable and healthy, suggesting that these patients are biologically hypersensitive to normal family stress levels.

The diagnosis of personality disorder is complicated by the fact that affected persons rarely seek help unless they are in serious trouble or until their family (or the law) pressures them to get treatment. It is quite common for people with personality disorders to have distorted views of their situations or to be unaware of the impact of their behavior on others. No test can provide a definitive diagnosis of personality disorder, which is based mainly on in-depth psychologic evaluation and information collected over a period of time, and interviews from several sources to determine how long the patient has been having difficulties, how many areas of life are affected, and how severe the dysfunction is caused by job loss, bereavement, or child abuse.

Psychotherapy, or talk therapy, may help in managing personality disorders. Through psychotherapy with a mental health professional, people can learn about their condition and talk about their moods, feelings, thoughts and behaviors. They can learn to cope with stress and manage their disorder. Psychotherapy may be provided in individual sessions, group therapy, or sessions that include family or even friends. However, the management and treatment of personality disorders can be challenging and difficult, because they involve interpersonal issues, the individuals themselves usually deny that they have a mental health problem, or the symptoms are overlapping and difficult to sort out. The majority of people with a personality disorder never come into contact with mental health services, and those who do usually do so in the context of another mental disorder or at a time of crisis, commonly after self-harming or breaking the law. Likewise, there is no distinct or objective boundary between 'normal' and 'abnormal' personalities, and individuals may not consider their personality to be disordered or the cause of problems, because of ignorance or lack of insight into their own condition. People have misconceptions and a negative image of personality disorder, causing substantial social stigma and discrimination related to the diagnosis.

Personality disorders may require fundamentally different approaches and therapies ranging from one extreme of self-harm and self-neglect, to another extreme that ends in violence and crime. Management of cases are also complicated by other factors such as problematic alcohol and substance abuse that can have a negative impact on emotions and interfere with treatment. Clients undergoing therapy may be negative, hostile, rejecting, demanding, aggressive or manipulative. They may meet the criteria for a diagnosis of multiple personality disorder and/or other mental disorders, thus requiring multiple and coordinated approaches to therapy. People with these types of disorders believe that their personality traits are normal, so they can become quite upset when someone suggests that they may have a personality disorder. And they may blame others for the challenges they face. Reassurance, openness and clear communication are usually helpful, and therapy can take several months of sessions until a trusting relationship is developed, and the client's issues are meaningfully addressed. Inpatient treatment is rarely required for patients with personality disorders, except for borderline patients who are threatening suicide or suffering from drug or alcohol withdrawal; and patients with paranoid personality disorder who are having psychotic symptoms.

There aren't any drugs approved for the treatment of personality disorders, per se. However, some prescription medications might help reduce certain symptoms. Antidepressants can help improve a depressed mood, anger, or impulsivity. Mood stabilizers can prevent mood swings and reduce irritability and aggression. Antipsychotic medications may be beneficial for people who often lose touch with reality. Anti-anxiety medications can help relieve anxiety, agitation, and insomnia.

If there is someone close that you suspect might have a personality disorder, you should encourage him or her to seek help. They may get angry or defensive, but it's important to avoid arguing with them. Instead, you should focus on voicing your concerns about their behaviors. Do not hesitate to call 911 if you ever feel that the other person intends to cause harm to themselves or others.

-o0o-

REFERENCES

http://emedicine.medscape.com/article/294307-overview#a6
https://en.wikipedia.org/wiki/Personality_disorder
http://www.psychone.net/list-of-personality-disorders.php
http://www.mayoclinic.org/diseases-conditions/personality-disorders/
https://www.psychologytoday.com/blog/hide-and-seek/201205/the-10-personality-disorders
https://psychcentral.com/personality/
https://medlineplus.gov/personalitydisorders.html
http://www.healthline.com/health/personality-disorders
http://www.emergenceplus.org.uk/what-is-personality-disorder.html
http://www.healthyplace.com/personality-disorders/personality-disorders-information/types-of-personality-disorders/
http://www.patheos.com/blogs/deaconsbench/2013/05/angelina-jolie-and-the-illness-no-one-wants-to-mention/
http://medical-dictionary.thefreedictionary.com/Personality+Disorders
http://www.medicalnewstoday.com/articles/192888.php
http://www.apa.org/topics/personality/disorders-causes.aspx
https://allpsych.com/personalitysynopsis/personality_disorders/
http://au.reachout.com/all-about-personality-disorders
http://www.mind.org.uk/information-support/types-of-mental-health-problems/personality-disorders
http://www.medicaldaily.com/bipolar-vs-borderline-personality-disorder-differences-between-two-and-how-avoid-335314

FURTHER READING

American Psychiatric Association. (2013). Personality disorders. In *Diagnostic and statistical manual of mental disorders (DSM-5®)* (pp. 645-684). American Psychiatric Pub.

World Health Organization (2010). Specific personality disorders. In *International statistical classification of diseases and related health problems (ICD-10)* (10th rev.). Retrieved from http://apps.who.int/classifications/icd10/browse/2010/en#/F60

BORDERLINE PERSONALITY DISORDER

Coming from a big family in the Philippines, Mary Jane did not have fond memories as a child. She could not understand why her younger sister got to be with their Mom while she had to stay with the other siblings in another house. When she was in her second grade of primary school, she would walk for miles just to be with her Mom because she was longing for attention. She felt alone and unloved. She was bullied at school all the way through eighth grade. She remembers stealing money from her older brother during elementary grade so she could buy things for her classmates because she was desperate for friends. She felt that nobody liked her and that everyone was smarter than her until she got to high school.

She was 10 when she came to San Francisco with her family. There, she was made fun of by her classmates because she could not speak English, and she was beaten up in 8th grade. She always felt alone.

Things changed when she moved to Cleveland with her older sister. She was fourteen when she celebrated her first birthday party and started going out with friends. She broke up with her boyfriend in high school but later felt hurt when he, in turn, decided to ignore her. She was in National Honor Society when she graduated from high school, was offered a scholarship in a private college, and later became a Certified Public Accountant. By then, she had fallen in love with a classmate from high school in Cleveland.

They had their wedding scheduled when she moved to Miami. They sent their wedding invitation to their friends and family. She started shopping for flowers and bouquets. During the final preparations, she suddenly changed her mind and decided to break off the engagement. Her fiancée could not understand why and begged her to go through with the wedding, but to no avail. Broken-hearted and disgusted, he left and stopped communicating with her. When she realized that he was gone, she flew back to Cleveland to make amends, but he refused to see her.

She felt rejected and abandoned. She went into deep depression, hardly eating and barely sleeping. She lost weight, and cried a lot, adversely affecting her job although she still managed to go to work. The only thing that stopped her from ending her life was the realization that her niece was looking up to her and would be devastated if she attempted to harm herself.

She began to feel better after she started going out with an office mate who later became her husband. Her marriage was rocky in the beginning but got better after the birth of a daughter and a son whom she treasured and cared for a lot. She nurtured and showered her children with love as they were growing up, although her relationship with her husband was not as happy as she would have wanted it to be. He would make sarcastic remarks and criticize her every time she went shopping after work. Although they never really fought in front of the children, they began to sleep in separate bedrooms. She did not feel that she was getting enough attention, and resented doing all the work at home and in the yard while her husband stayed in the living room, watching TV. She later accepted a job as financial consultant to an out-of-state pharmaceutical company, and would only come home during weekends and holidays. For years she had thought of leaving him, but could not do so while the children were still in school.

Then one day, she learned that her husband was seeing someone else, and was planning to go through a divorce. The feeling of rejection devastated her, and she again went into deep depression. The thought of separation brought her anguish, intense pain and rage at the idea of breaking her family. She felt empty and distraught. Her children were very supportive but were still caught in between. She received tremendous support from her siblings who flew at a moment's notice and stayed with her during her lowest moments, especially at times when they thought she might hurt herself. Every phone conversation and personal interaction with her husband would bring back the feelings of hurt and resentment. She lost weight and could not stop crying.

Because of a strong history of bipolar disorder in the family, she sought help from her therapist who diagnosed her with Borderline Personality Disorder, for which she underwent Cognitive Behavioral Therapy. She was also prescribed Wellbutrin as an adjunct antidepressant.

Going out with someone whom she met at a Meet-Up event, and getting the attention and caring that was missing in her marriage helped a lot to improve her self-esteem and get her out of depression. After almost a year of therapy, she is finally able to accept what is happening without being depressed, and is now negotiating the terms of divorce.

-o0o-

Borderline Personality Disorder, also known as BPD, is a serious psychological and psychosocial disorder where people have extreme difficulties controlling their emotions. The most distinguishing symptoms of BPD are marked sensitivity to rejection or criticism, and an intense fear of possible abandonment. Other symptoms include impulsive behavior, a feeling of emptiness, inappropriate rage, resentment, intense anger, self-injury, low self-esteem, eating disorder, and suicidal tendencies. Seemingly ordinary events may trigger the symptoms, and they may have a stronger reaction to negative statements compared to people who do not have the disorder. It affects an individual's life at home or at work, and interferes with one's ability to maintain normal relationship with co-workers, friends and family members because of unpredictable and impulsive behavior. The unstable pattern of interaction with others usually persists for years, and is closely related to the person's self-image and early childhood. It results in repeated job changes or losses, multiple legal issues, conflict-filled relationships, marital stress or divorce, and frequent hospitalizations.

The lifetime risk of suicide among people with BPD is between 3% and 10%. There is evidence that men diagnosed with BPD are approximately twice as likely to complete suicide as women diagnosed with BPD. Self-harm or suicidal behavior is a common sign in borderline personality disorder. The reported reasons for non-suicidal self-injury differ from the reasons for suicide attempts. Nearly 70% of people with BPD harm themselves by cutting or taking an overdose of medication to express their anger, punish themselves, or distract themselves from emotional pain or difficult circumstances, with no intention of ending their lives. The rate of completed suicide in people with borderline personality disorder is estimated to be approximately 10%.

A person with this disorder can be bright, intelligent, idealistic, competent, warm, and friendly but goes through intense emotions and fear of abandonment when placed in a stressful situation like the breakup of a romantic relationship or the death of a loved one. He or she may feel overwhelmed by negative emotions, experiencing intense grief, shame, humiliation, panic and rage instead of sadness, mild embarrassment, annoyance, and nervousness. The perception of impending separation or rejection can lead to profound changes in self-image, thinking, and behavior. A history of rapid and sudden deterioration when relationships change such as after a breakup or severe mood swings when separated from family is a warning sign. Generally, the severity of symptoms and behavior correlates with the severity of personal and social instability, although some people may still be able to function at very high levels in their careers. The mood often shifts from being vibrant and happy to feeling empty, lonely, depressed, anxious and irritable. In severe cases, a person can have brief episodes of psychosis with bizarre behavior and loss of contact with reality.

Most of the time, signs of the disorder first appear in childhood, but problems often don't start until late adolescence or early adulthood. It affects 1% of the population and is estimated to comprise 15% of patients in psychiatric hospitals. Like most personality disorders, BPD typically will decrease in intensity with age, and many people will experience few of the most extreme symptoms by the time they are in the 40s or 50s. Although the prognosis of borderline personality disorder is relatively good, a minority of people has persistent symptoms until late in life, and it may occasionally be a problem in the elderly.

Women are diagnosed about three times as often as males, and are more likely to develop depressive episodes that bring patients in for treatment. Women are more likely to have eating disorders, mood disorders, anxiety and post-traumatic stress, leading to symptoms of depression and self-cutting that characterize borderline personality disorder. On the other hand, men are more prone to substance abuse and psychopathy, and do not necessarily always seek help from mental health professionals. Although both sexes have similar psychological problems, men are more likely to have an explosive temper, and have anti-social, narcissistic, passive-aggressive or sadistic personality traits.

It may take more time with BPD than others for people to return to a stable emotional baseline following an intense emotional experience. But with treatment, most people with severe symptoms do get better over time. When treated, at least 50% tends to improve within 5 to 10 years after the first diagnosis.

People with BPD are prone to feeling angry at members of their family and alienated from them. On the other hand, family members often feel angry and helpless at how their BPD family members relate to them. In romantic relationships, BPD is linked to increased levels of chronic stress and conflict, decreased satisfaction of romantic partners, abuse, and unwanted pregnancy, although these links may apply to personality disorders in general.

People with BPD can be very sensitive to the way others treat them, feeling intense joy and gratitude at perceived expressions of kindness, and intense sadness or anger at perceived criticism or hurtfulness. Their feelings often shift from admiration or love to anger or dislike after disappointments, a threat of losing someone, or a perceived loss of esteem in the eyes of someone they value.

Symptoms among adolescents that predict the development of BPD in adulthood may include problems with body image, extreme sensitivity to rejection, behavioral problems, non-suicidal self-injury, attempts to find exclusive relationships, and severe shame. Many adolescents experience these symptoms without going on to develop BPD, but they are 9 times as likely as their peers to develop the disorder.

The emotional instability, impulsiveness, erratic and risky behavior may occur in almost anyone at some point in life, but these patterns of inappropriate negative behavior are long lasting in patients with borderline disorder. They are especially sensitive to feelings of rejection, criticism, and perceived failure. They have severe difficulties in regulating their emotions, which often leads to mood swings, impulsiveness, and unstable personal relationships. They go through a pattern of unstable intense relationships, such as idealizing someone one moment and then suddenly believing the person doesn't care enough or is cruel.

CAUSES AND RISK FACTORS

Borderline Personality Disorder is a complex disorder due to a number of genetic, social, biological, families, psychological and environmental factors. It may be associated with structural and functional changes in the brain, especially in the areas that control impulses and emotional regulation. Certain neurotransmitters of brain chemicals that help regulate mood, such as serotonin, may not be functioning properly. Biological risk factors include a family history of bipolar disorder, substance abuse, antisocial personality disorder, impulsivity, or mood instability. A history of childhood trauma, physical or mental abuse, neglect, separation from, loss or the death of a parent increases the risk of developing BPD. The higher incidence in women compared to men may be related to genetic or hormonal influences, as well as to a greater incidence of incestuous experiences during their childhood. Other factors include exposure to hostile and unstable family relationships.

A history of mood disorder and substance abuse in other family members may be important in the development of borderline personality disorder. Problems with both parents are more likely to be the common pathogenic influence rather than problems with either parent alone. The experience of bi-parental neglect and emotional abuse before the age of 18 may be a predictor of borderline personality disorder, although abuse alone is neither necessary nor sufficient for the development of the disorder. It is more likely to be associated with an unstable disrupted family environment, parental rejection, excessive control, unsupportive relationships, neglect, and communication problems between parent and child. Evidence also suggests that BPD may be related in some way to post-traumatic stress disorder (PTSD).

Borderline personality disorder with its origins in early trauma tends to respond better to counseling (psychotherapy), with medications as more of a supplemental treatment.

DIAGNOSIS

Distinguishing bipolar disorder from borderline personality disorder is not easy, and requires extensive questioning, medical history, and information about the person's background and symptoms. It is especially common for people to be misdiagnosed with bipolar disorder when they have borderline personality disorder or vice versa. It is therefore important that a qualified and licensed mental health professional conduct a thorough assessment to determine whether or not a diagnosis of BPD or other mental disorder is warranted, and to help develop treatment options when appropriate. A diagnosis of personality disorder must never be made on the basis of current behavior alone. It requires a longitudinal history from an informant who has known the patient when he or she has not yet developed the affective symptoms, preferably when the patient was an adolescent or younger. For someone with bipolar disorder, a behavior suggestive of BPD might appear while the client is experiencing an episode of major depression, only to disappear once the client's mood has stabilized. For this reason, it is ideal to wait until the client's mood has stabilized before attempting to make a diagnosis.

Clinicians are discouraged from making a diagnosis before the age of 18, due to the normal ups and downs of adolescence that can confuse the issue, although the symptoms can manifest before age 18, in which case the features must have been present and consistent for at least 1 year.

Bipolar disorder and borderline personality disorder are serious medical illnesses that can disrupt a person's ability to live a normal life. Both mental health disorders can involve mood shifts and problems with impulse control — so much so that even doctors in a clinical setting can sometimes have a difficult time telling the two disorders apart when making an initial diagnosis. While both disorders are characterized by unstable moods, relationships and behavior, the length and intensity of these mood swings are different. Bipolar disorder involves a series of manic or depressive "mood episodes," while borderline personality disorder is more about an ongoing pattern of depressive behavior. Bipolar mood shifts are distinguished by manic episodes of elation. In contrast, people with BPD do not have full blown manic episodes even though they may engage in a variety of destructive and impulsive behaviors including self-harm, eating problems or excessive use of alcohol and illicit substances. When people with BPD experience euphoria, it is usually without the racing thoughts and decreased need for sleep that are typical of hypomania, although the symptoms may be associated with chronic sleep disturbances. Their mood shifts are usually a reaction to an environmental stressor such as an argument or conflict within interpersonal relationships while bipolar mood shifts seem to occur out of nowhere. A positive event will not improve the depressed mood caused by bipolar disorder, but will potentially relieve the depressed mood of someone with BPD. Symptoms of personality disorder are pretty consistent and ongoing, while people with bipolar disorder can have normal periods between their extreme mood swings. Mood symptoms in borderline personality disorder tend toward chronic feelings or irritability or anger and sadness or emptiness as well as anxiety. People with BPD also may view themselves as fundamentally bad or unworthy and are more prone to feelings of loneliness, emptiness and a severe fear of abandonment.

When assessing people with suspected bipolar disorder and/or personality disorder, healthcare professionals should consider a diagnosis of bipolar disorder first, before making a diagnosis of personality disorder in a person with mood swings and functional impairment. It is important to establish that patterns of affective instability, impulsivity, and unstable relationships have been consistent over time. Patients with BPD—particularly younger patients—often struggle with feelings of emptiness and worthlessness, difficulties with self-image, and fear of abandonment. These are less common in bipolar disorder, where grandiosity and inflated self-esteem are common, especially during mood episodes. And while both conditions may include a history of chaotic relationships, a patient with BPD may describe relationship difficulties as the only source of his or her suffering, while the bipolar patient may see them as an unfortunate consequence of his or her behavior.

Adolescents go through a period of major developmental transitions— physically, psychologically and socially—while establishing their sense of identity. Consequently, their symptoms may be dismissed or attributed by their families to the typical stresses and strains of adolescence. Young people with borderline personality disorder may also be known to social services due to child protection concerns, and may also live in foster homes, therapeutic foster placements or residential settings. They may be in detention centers or may be in prison as a result of impulsive behaviors that are antisocial or criminal in nature.

Many clinicians are reluctant to diagnose borderline personality disorder during an untreated mood episode, unless the lifetime history supports the presence of a personality disorder. Clinicians may be reluctant to disclose it due to concern about the stigma attached to this condition, but patients and their families often find it helpful to be informed of the diagnosis. Perhaps more importantly, education about mental illness can help people who are experiencing mood swings or depressive symptoms to be on the lookout for specific features of their disorder. Misdiagnosis of borderline personality disorder can delay and/or prevent recovery. Without an accurate diagnosis, people with the disorder may take medications that will not alleviate their symptoms, and may not be treated with the effective and appropriate psychotherapy.

The psychological evaluation includes asking the patient about the beginning and severity of symptoms, as well as other questions about how symptoms impact the patient's quality of life. Issues of particular note are suicidal ideations, experiences with self-harm, and thoughts of harming others. The diagnosis is based both on the person's report of their symptoms and on the clinician's own observations plus the result of physical exam and laboratory tests to rule out other conditions, such as thyroid problem or substance abuse. Clinicians can miss an underlying personality disorder because its symptoms can coexist with other disorders such as depression, post-traumatic stress disorder (PTSD), and bipolar disorder. In contrast with other comorbid conditions, the symptoms of borderline personality disorder are variable and tend to fluctuate over time. Psychotic and paranoid symptoms are not permanent, depressive symptoms change dramatically over a short period, may be intense and unbearable but usually transient. People experience significantly greater impairment in their work, social relationships and leisure compared with those with clinical depression.

Self-injuring behaviors that occur because of difficulty in coping with stress are not symptomatic of bipolar disorder. They are not necessarily required but they often serve as a clue for diagnosing BPD. Suicide threats and attempts may occur along with anger at perceived abandonment. Since BPD can be stigmatized, some survivors of childhood abuse who are diagnosed with BPD are re-traumatized by the negative responses they receive from others.

Manipulative behavior may be a defining characteristic of borderline personality disorder, but it relies upon the assumption that people with BPD who communicate intense pain, or who engage in self-harm and suicidal behavior, do so with the intention of influencing the behavior of others. However, since they lack the ability to successfully manage painful emotions and interpersonal challenges, their frequent expressions of intense pain, self-harming, or suicidal behavior may actually represent an escape mechanism from situations that they feel are unbearable.

People with borderline personality disorder may sometimes also exhibit narcissistic traits and attempt to determine a partner's choice of friends or how a loved one behaves. They might become jealous or possessive, and resort to aggressive behavior to exert control. They might resent a partner who does not focus constant attention on them or cater to their desires.

MANAGEMENT

While they have many similar elements, bipolar disorder and borderline personality disorder are different disorders—and understanding those differences is important in making sure that patients get the right treatment. The most important part of bipolar treatment is medication, followed by psychotherapy. BPD treatment, on the other hand, focuses on psychotherapy or *"talk therapy"*, not medication. Certain drugs may be indicated in BPD, but they should be used only as an adjunct to psychotherapy. The long-term use of a mood stabilizer or atypical antipsychotic drugs should only be reserved for known cases of bipolar disorder.

If you have borderline personality disorder, don't get discouraged. With treatment, the majority of people with BPD can achieve remission, defined as a consistent relief from symptoms for at least two years. Remission rates in BPD can be as high as 85% in 10 years, particularly with effective psychotherapy. It is possible to learn how to manage feelings better and find ways to have healthier and more rewarding relationships. With the help of psychotherapy, one can learn how to reduce impulsive and self-destructive behaviors and understand more about the condition. The therapy may be provided one-on-one, or in a group setting. Long-term psychotherapy is the treatment of choice, and should be based on the needs of the individual, rather than upon the general diagnosis of BPD. Therapists may also switch from one type of psychotherapy to another, or use a combination of techniques to better meet a person's needs.

Cognitive behavioral therapy (CBT) relies on changing people's behaviors and beliefs by identifying and changing core beliefs and/or behaviors that underlie inaccurate perceptions of themselves and others. It is known to reduce some anxiety and mood symptoms as well as reduce suicidal thoughts and self-harming behaviors.

Another type, *Dialectical Behavior Therapy* (DBT) utilizes the concept of mindfulness, or being aware of and attentive to the current situation and moods. It also teaches skills to control intense emotions, reduce self-destructive behaviors, and improve relationships. This type of therapy DBT differs from CBT in that it integrates traditional CBT elements with mindfulness, acceptance, and techniques to improve a person's ability to tolerate stress and control his or her emotions.

Schema-Focused Therapy combines elements of CBT with other forms of psychotherapy that focus on the ways people view themselves. This approach is based on the idea that BPD stems from a dysfunctional self-image—possibly brought on by negative childhood experiences.

Dealing with someone who has personality disorder on a daily basis can be very stressful, and family members may unknowingly act in ways that worsen the patient's symptoms. *Systems Training for Emotional Predictability and Problem Solving* (STEPPS) is a type of group therapy that aims to educate family members about the disorder and helps them develop strategies and skills to better understand and support a relative with BPD. Other therapies focus on the needs of family members and help them understand the obstacles in caring for a loved one with BPD.

While some patients may experience severe symptoms and require intensive inpatient care, short-term hospitalization has not been found to be more effective than community care for improving outcomes or long-term prevention of suicidal behavior. Although some who develop this disorder may improve without any treatment, most people benefit from and improve their quality of life by seeking therapy.

MEDICATIONS

Medications cannot effectively treat the core symptoms of chronic feelings of emptiness, identity disturbance and abandonment, but they may impact isolated symptoms associated with BPD or the symptoms of comorbid conditions. Among the atypical antipsychotics, *aripiprazole (Abilify)* may reduce interpersonal problems and impulsivity, while *olanzapine (Zyprexa)* may decrease affective instability, anger, psychotic paranoid symptoms, and anxiety. Among the mood stabilizers, *valproate (Depakote)* may ameliorate depression, interpersonal problems, and anger. *Lamotrigine (Lamictal)* may reduce impulsivity and anger; *topiramate (Topamax)* may ameliorate interpersonal problems, impulsivity, anxiety, anger, and general psychiatric pathology. Among antidepressants, *amitriptyline (Elavil)* may reduce depression.

Drug therapy should not be used as the primary treatment for BPD. Because of the potentially serious side effects from some of these medications, they should not be used specifically for borderline personality disorder, but it may be considered in the overall treatment of comorbid conditions. Because of the high risk of suicide among people with BPD, health care providers should exercise caution when prescribing medications that may be lethal in the event of an overdose. Approximately half of the individuals who commit suicide meet the criteria for a personality disorder. Borderline personality disorder remains the most commonly personality disorder associated with suicide.

If you are thinking about harming yourself or attempting suicide, tell someone who can help you right away. Call your licensed mental health professional if you are already working with one. If you are not already working with a licensed mental health professional, call your personal physician or go to the nearest hospital emergency room.

If a loved one is considering suicide, do not leave him or her alone. Try to get your loved one to seek immediate help from his or her doctor or the nearest hospital emergency room, or call 911. Remove any access he or she may have to firearms or other potential tools for suicide, including medications, and sharp edges such as knives, ropes, or belts.

-o0o-

FAMOUS PERSONS WITH BORDERLINE PERSONALITY DISORDER

It is not always common knowledge that some celebrities have borderline personality disorder. While it may not be possible to make a definite diagnosis, one can surmise from their behavior that they have symptoms of the disorder. The stigma is so strong against BPD that most famous people would not willingly tell the public that they have it. Hopefully, celebrities with BPD will get treated successfully, recognize the importance of challenging the stigma, and come out. Famous people who admit publicly that they have borderline personality disorder and speak up about their struggles can raise awareness, educate the public, help reduce the stigma and encourage those who suffer from the illness to seek help and feel less alone.

-o0o-

DIANA, PRINCESS OF WALES

Princess Diana was a beautiful, warm-hearted mother dedicated to good works, whom an adulterous husband and the British Royal family unfairly victimized. She is a woman with severe psychological problems (characterized as a “borderline personality”) who never overcame a serious eating disorder and was unable to sustain relationships. She had a difficult childhood due to her parents’ divorce and neglect when she was 7. She was reportedly devastated by the departure of her mother and the emotional withdrawal of her father for several years following the divorce, leaving her with deep feelings of insecurity and unworthiness. Homesick, lonely and somewhat manic at a Swiss boarding school when she was 16, she wrote about 120 letters to her parents in a single month. She grew up as a shy but likable student, and she did not excel in her schooling. After quietly being allowed to drop out of a finishing school at age 16, she worked as a quasi-nanny and baby-sitter. She later developed symptoms that included episodes of depression, fear of rejection and abandonment, sharp mood swings, impulsive behavior, such as binge eating and self-mutilation, and persistent feelings of loneliness, boredom and emptiness. The stress of her marriage to Britain’s Prince Charles, coupled with the stress of her life as a public figure and the strain of her love-hate relationship with the media exacerbated her symptoms. Certain that her husband was having an affair, she retaliated with a series of steamy romances. Her unstable temperament had all the markings of a borderline personality, characterized by insecurity, an unstable self-image; sharp mood swings; fear of rejection and abandonment; an inability to sustain relationships; persistent feelings of loneliness, boredom, and emptiness; depression; and impulsive behavior such as binge eating, self-mutilation and several suicide attempts. At one point, Diana spent an entire day with her head buried in her hands, alternating between bouts of weeping and silence, as a friend tried in vain to console her. She couldn't sustain relationships with friends or lovers alike. As Princess of Wales, she undertook royal duties on behalf of the Queen and represented her at functions overseas. She was celebrated for her charity work and for her support of the International Campaign to Ban Landmines. Her bravery with saving the lives of many people who suffer from bulimia allowed her personal battle with the disorder to become public, which is one reason that she is so beloved and will continue to be influential, even after her death at age 36 in a 1997 car crash in Paris.

-o0o-

PETE DOHERTY

Pete Doherty is an English musician, songwriter, actor, poet, writer, and artist, best known for being the lead singer of two British bands: BabyShambles and the Libertines. He is also known in London for his erratic behavior. He has shocked fans by boasting that he worked as a homosexual prostitute and drug dealer to fuel his drug addictions, before he became famous with his former band. The wild singer once confessed he was so desperate for money to fund his cocaine and heroin habits, that he worked as a rent boy and once robbed a gay client after tying him up at his home. He has been repeatedly arrested for drug offenses, driving under the influence, car theft, and for possession of crack cocaine, heroin, cannabis and ketamine. He exhibited inappropriate anger by assaulting a female reporter and kicking a microphone out of her hand outside the Thames Magistrates court. He has had volatile relationships with a supermodel, Kate Moss, who dumped him, arguing that she “cannot stand his way of life anymore, always worrying about him”. He tried to kill himself in rehab after discovering that Kate Moss was dating a new man, and ended up making himself ill by taking an overdose of pills. He acts rather reserved with others until he knows them well and feels it is safe to be open with them. He tends to cling to people, memories and possessions of personal or sentimental value, and has a strong need for emotional security and sense of belonging. An exhibit of Doherty's paintings titled, "Art of the Albion", at the Paris' Gallerie Chappe in 2008 caused controversy due to artworks made with Doherty's own blood. A graphic footage of the rock star deliberately cutting himself with a broken bottle was featured in a documentary, and were leaked to the national press, raising concerns about his mental health. In 2014, he was admitted to the Hope Rehab Centre in Thailand, and later started a Hope Foundation to help struggling addicts.

-o0o-

ANGELINA JOLIE

Angelina Jolie is an American actress, filmmaker, and humanitarian. She has received an Academy Award, two Screen Actors Guild Awards, and three Golden Globe Awards, and has been cited as Hollywood's highest-paid actress. She made her screen debut as a child alongside her father, Jon Voight, and began her film career a decade later. In addition to her film career, Jolie is noted for her humanitarian efforts, including conservation, education, and women's rights, and is most noted for her advocacy on behalf of refugees. She had a troubled childhood, the result of growing up with an estranged and famous father (Jon Voight) and a mother who rarely gave her care and affection. She has had a lifelong dysfunctional relationship with her father who left the family when she was less than a year old. For the first year or so of her life, she was kept in a white office five floors above her mother's apartment and tended by a number of babysitters. At 14, she was given the master bedroom along with her live-in boyfriend. She also admitted to experiencing obsessive crushes, dependence on other people, and substance abuse. At 14, she used knives to cut and be cut by her live-in boyfriend, and later to cut herself. Later, she contemplated suicide, first by pills, then, more dramatically, by taking a hit out on herself. She voluntarily checked herself into the Neuropsychiatric Institute in the late 1990s due to self-reported suicidal and homicidal ideation. Once diagnosed with BPD, she began to improve and motherhood helped her to adapt to her condition. Before seeking mental health treatment, she has had volatile relationships, was promiscuous, and had admitted to having frequent thoughts of suicide. Psychoanalysts speculate that her unorthodox family situation may have caused the psychological damage, and that she might have experienced profound abandonment, anxiety, and depression. Most of her behavior, like suicidal thoughts, obsessive crushes, drug use, bisexuality, exhibitionism, and perverse tendencies were attributed to her past. During high school, she felt isolated among the children of some of the area's affluent families because her mother survived on a more modest income. She was teased by other students who targeted her for being extremely thin and for wearing glasses and braces. She started dressing in black and wearing studded dog collars, which got her mocked in school, and for a time, she aspired to be a funeral director, taking at-home courses to study embalming. As a teenager, she found it difficult to emotionally connect with other people, and as a result she self-harmed by cutting herself. She also struggled with insomnia and an eating disorder, and she began experimenting with drugs by age 20. She suffered episodes of depression and twice planned to commit suicide—at age 19 and again at 22, when she attempted to hire a hit man to kill her. When she was 24, she experienced a nervous breakdown and was admitted to UCLA Medical Center's psychiatric ward. Two years later, after adopting her first child, Jolie found stability in her life.

-o0o-

LINDSAY LOHAN

Lindsay Dee Lohan is an American actress and singer. Lohan began her career at age three as a child fashion model at the Eileen Ford Agency, and made appearances in over 60 television commercials, including spots for The Gap, Pizza Hut, Wendy's and Jell-O (opposite Bill Cosby). She was later featured on the soap opera Another World for a year when she was 10. At age 11, Lohan made her motion picture debut in Disney's commercially and critically successful remake of The Parent Trap, earning her widespread critical acclaim and a Young Artist award for Best Leading Young Actress in a Feature Film, as well as Blockbuster Entertainment and Young Star award nominations. After appearing in popular movies such as The Parent Trap and Mean Girls, Lindsay began to question her life, and wondered who her real friends were, if she even had any, and wanted to be with her family very badly. The complicated home environment that she had to endure in her younger years was a major factor that shaped her future behavior. Her father was not only abusive to his wife, but when Lindsay was at the young age of four, he was sent to jail for fraudulent trading causing the family to move back to her mother's hometown. She shared that her downward spiral was related to growing up in a "chaotic" household and too much fame too quickly with little supervision. A combination of loneliness, absence of a father, and getting rich led her to use drugs such as cocaine, become bulimic. Her erratic behavior, insecurity, emotional and sexual confusion are signs of an untreated person with BPD. She has dated several people throughout her life, including a girl, and stated that she may be bisexual. She has been arrested multiple times for violating probation on drunk driving charges, and entered rehab at least three different times for her unhealthy addictions. The 24-year-old starlet was taking *Zoloft* (antidepressant), *Trazodone* (antidepressant), *Adderall* (stimulant for ADHD), *Nexium* (acid reflux) and *Dilaudid*, an incredibly dangerous opiate. Psychotherapists who have evaluated her believed she was misdiagnosed with Bipolar Disorder and Attention Deficit Hyperactivity Disorder (ADHD), instead of Borderline Personality Disorder due to a difficult upbringing, and that her manic symptoms were instead due to unnecessary drug medications.

-o0o-

COURTNEY LOVE

Courtney Michelle Love is an American musician, singer, actress, writer, and visual artist whose career has spanned four decades. She rose to prominence as the front woman of the alternative rock band Hole, which she formed in 1989. Love has drawn public attention for her uninhibited live performances and confrontational lyrics, as well as her highly publicized personal life following her marriage to Kurt Cobain. She was abandoned as a child and grew up in -reform school. After her parents' divorce, her father's custody was withdrawn when her mother alleged that he had fed LSD to her as a toddler. Her mother, who was studying to be a psychologist, had her in therapy by the age of two. As a child, she struggled academically and had trouble making friends. At age 9, a psychologist noted that she exhibited signs of autism. She spent her early years living in hippie communes in Oregon and at schools in Europe and New Zealand, under the care of her mother and other family members. At age 14, she was arrested for shoplifting and sent to a juvenile correctional facility. She was then placed in foster care until she became legally emancipated at age sixteen. She traveled throughout Europe, living off of a small trust fund left behind by her grandmother, and eventually returned to the United States to pursue music before making her break into the industry. She supported herself by working illegally as a topless dancer, adopting the surname "Love" to conceal her identity. She said that she learned social skills while frequenting gay clubs, and admitted to struggling with substance abuse problems throughout her life. She is known for her brash erratic behavior and suspected drug problems. Once, she had to go to anger management classes after being arrested for assault and disorderly conduct. On her 40th birthday, she tried to commit suicide at her Manhattan apartment, and was taken to Bellevue Hospital where she was put on a 72-hour watch and later released to a rehab facility. She has had volatile romantic relationships. Her first marriage was short and was annulled after only several months. Her most documented romantic relationship was with legendary Nirvana solo artist Kurt Cobain; with whom she had a daughter born six months after marriage. She was arrested in 2003 for breaking windows in her boyfriend's apartment under the influence of controlled substances and was treated for an accidental overdose of oxycodone. For years she has been publicly shamed in the media for rages of violence, erratic behavior, arrests for defying the law, overdosing on drugs and controlled substances, and for violating probation orders. After losing custody of her daughter, she entered rehab, then violated the terms of her parole and entered house arrest. In 2009, after a physical fight, her grown up estranged daughter, Frances Bean Cobain, filed a petition for a restraining order which was granted in Superior Court. She was obsessed with her allegations of "fraud", complaining to the press that various corrupt lawyers and accountants had cheated her out of $250 million. She also once threatened to jump off a balcony in front of her daughter. She claims that she lost an astonishing 52 pounds over six months with a diet of protein shakes, fish and vegetables—but experts say her emaciated appearance indicates that she might be suffering from an eating disorder.

-o0o-

AMY WINEHOUSE

Amy Jade Winehouse was an English singer and songwriter, known for her deep expressive contralto vocals and her eclectic mix of musical genres, that made her the first British woman to win five Grammy Awards in 2008, Best Contemporary Song in 2007, and three Ivor Novello Awards: in 2004. With a co-dependent husband in jail, exhibitionist parents with questionable judgment, and the paparazzi documenting her emotional and physical distress, she attempted to self-medicate with drugs and alcohol. She had fear of abandonment; intense and unstable interpersonal relationships; impulsivity with drugs, sex and violent behavior toward others; and anger management problems. She was frequently caught on video or even on stage smoking crack, snorting cocaine, smoking various substances and drinking heavily, very often clearly under the influence of drugs and alcohol. Her parents separated when she was 9, and she experienced a traumatic series of abandonments by her parents and other caretakers. At an early age, her behavior was out of control. She consistently defied authority and was expelled from school at the age of 16. She had a low self-image of herself, and she doubted her own talent. She developed bulimia, a serious eating disorder, and had a long history of self-mutilating behavior (especially cutting her legs and arms). Photos showed her tear-stained, with bleeding feet, badly bruised legs, and scars on her arms from a period of self-harm and cutting in her teens. She had been hospitalized for what was reported as an overdose of heroin, ecstasy, cocaine, ketamine and alcohol, following the death of her grandmother, who had a stabilizing influence on her. In various interviews, she admitted to having such problems with self-harm, depression, and eating disorders. She reportedly entered a rehabilitation facility for a two-week treatment program. Her erratic behavior, including an allegation of assault, caused some fears that her drug rehabilitation efforts had been unsuccessful, and she later appeared to have cuts on her legs and arms. She was treated with Librium for alcohol withdrawal and anxiety, and underwent psychological and psychiatric evaluations. Doctors believed she was suffering from borderline personality disorder (BPD), and recommended that she undergo dialectical behavior therapy (DBT), which she refused. She died of alcohol poisoning in 2011 at the age of 27.

-o0o-

INFAMOUS PERSONS WITH BORDERLINE PERSONALITY DISORDER

Impulsive behavior, which includes physical aggression, is one of the symptoms of but not an absolute criterion for borderline personality disorder. Although there is not enough evidence that BPD alone increases violent behavior, there are several reasons why people with the disorder may be more likely to become violent in their relationships. BPD may have associated co-morbidities, including anxiety, antisocial or narcissistic personality disorder, and substance abuse which can increase one's tendency for violence. BPD is more often associated with self-harm, especially cutting, than violence toward others. However, people with BPD often struggle with abandonment issues, and those who are victims of childhood trauma or abuse might somehow learn to externalize their emotions when they become adults, by inflicting harm as a form of retribution on others. Fear of abandonment or rejection after being emotionally intimate with someone else can be overwhelming, and can potentially arouse all the maladaptive defenses in a person with the disorder, resulting in violent behavior and aggression. As much as there are famous people or successful celebrities with borderline personality disorder, there are also documented cases of infamous persons with this personality disorder and unregulated feeling of rage, ending in violence.

-o0o-

JODI ARIAS

On June 4, 2008, salesman Travis Victor Alexander was killed by his ex-girlfriend, Jodi Ann Arias, in his house in Mesa, Arizona. Arias was convicted of first-degree murder and sentenced to life in state prison for brutally murdering her ex-boyfriend, Travis Victor. The diagnosis given to her by mental health experts were mostly circumstantial but nevertheless showed many features characteristic of a Borderline Personality Disorder. In her 20s, she worked at several dead-end jobs and was in and out of unstable and intense relationships. In her diary, she wrote about kicking chairs, her mother and the family dog in a fit of anger. Her relationship with murdered ex-boyfriend showed marked and persistently unstable self-image, playing the submissive partner and doing everything to keep him engaged and interested in him. Taping many sexual conversations with and murdering her ex-boyfriend were frantic efforts to avoid abandonment when he tried to break up with her. She was extremely jealous, following him on a date with his female friend whom she confronted in the women's bathroom during a conference. Her potentially self-damaging impulsiveness was marked by substance abuse, reckless driving and binge-eating. She became increasingly irritable when he started seeing another woman, slicing his tires twice, breaking into his email and sending a threatening email to his new love interest from his phone while he was in the shower. She had recurrent suicidal and self-mutilating behavior like cutting or attempting to slit her wrists. Her moods were directly related to her situation with her boyfriend, feeling well when her relationships were going well, crashing and going into fits of anger when he tried to break it off.

-o0o-

JANE ANDREWS

Jane Andrews, a one-time Royal dresser for Sarah Ferguson, Duchess of York, was convicted of murdering her lover Tom Cressman during a sensational trial in 2001. Throughout her teenage years, she struggled with various psychological problems, including depression, panic attacks and an eating disorder. She had been sexually abused by a close family member as a child. At the age of 15, she attempted suicide by overdose after her mother discovered her truancy. At age 17, she became pregnant and had an abortion, which she stated was a traumatic experience. At age 21, she began working for Sarah, Duchess of York and at Buckingham Palace four days later. The job placed her into a higher status and a new circle of friends. She was reportedly involved with several men whom she met through work. After a short courtship, she married an IBM executive twenty years her senior, and got divorced after five years, citing multiple counts of infidelity on her part. She then went into deep depression following a break up with the son of a Greek shipping magnate, and tried to commit suicide again by taking an overdose of pills, but she survived without seeking medical treatment. After being dismissed from her job as the Duchess' royal dresser, she met a former stockbroker who ran a successful business selling car accessories, and mixed in the upper echelons of London society. Due to her supposed financial hardships at the time, she moved into his flat shortly into their relationship. She alleged that her boyfriend was a dominating individual whose sexual demands—including anal sex, bondage and role-play—she found degrading but acquiesced to. As an insecure woman, she was reportedly expecting him to propose marriage to her but he refused to marry her. The couple got into a heated argument and that night, while he was sleeping, she hit him with a cricket bat and then stabbed him with a kitchen knife in a vengeful rage. Following the bloody attack, she fled the scene but, after having been untraceable for days, police found her overdosed in her car. She once again survived her suicide attempt. After a police interrogation, she was arrested for murder, found guilty and sentenced to life imprisonment. A month later, she was found unconscious in her prison cell, having taken a possible drugs overdose. One year after her incarceration, a psychiatrist diagnosed her with Borderline Personality Disorder.

-o0o-

JEFFREY DAHMER

Jeffrey Lionel Dahmer, also known as the Milwaukee Cannibal, was an American serial killer and sex offender, who committed the rape, murder, and dismemberment of seventeen men and boys between 1978 and 1991. Although doting him when he was a baby and a toddler, his mother was known to be tense, anxious over trivial matters, demanding constant attention, and argumentative with both her husband and her neighbors. He called his early years of family life as being extremely tense, due to constant arguments by his parents. At elementary school, he was described as being reserved and uncommunicative, and his teacher sensed that he felt neglected. At an early age, he collected large insects and dismembered animal carcasses either at home or in the woodland behind the family home. At his request, his father taught him how to cleanse and preserve animal bones. He started abusing alcohol during his freshman year in high school. He discovered he was homosexual when he reached puberty, but did not divulge his sexual orientation to his parents. He committed his first murder when he was 18, following a bitter divorce of his parents, with his mother having custody of his younger brother but leaving him alone in the family home. With his father's urging, he enlisted in the U.S. Army, where he trained as a medical specialist and served as a combat medic. While staying with his grandmother, he frequented gay bars and gay bathhouses, had sexual relations with other men, and was arrested for indecent exposure and masturbating in public. He later killed a man after a sexual encounter, dismembered the body and cut the bones into small pieces. Many of his later murders involved necrophilia, cannibalism, and the permanent preservation of body parts—typically all or part of the skeletal structure. Most of the victims had been rendered unconscious prior to their murder, although some had died as a result of having acid or boiling water injected into their brain. Following his arrest, he underwent multiple psychiatric examinations and was found to have complicated, comorbid psychopathologies, with a tendency to experience recurrent depressive affect, worthlessness, low self-esteem, suicidal ideation and a strong fear of abandonment. He was described as being uncooperative, angry, resistant to change, evasive, manipulative, emotionally unstable, and lacking insight -- traits that are commonly associated with borderline personality disorder. Although diagnosed with borderline personality disorder, schizotypal personality disorder, and a psychotic disorder, he was deemed to be legally sane and was sentenced to sixteen terms of life imprisonment. On November 28, 1994, a fellow inmate at the Columbia Correctional Institution beat Dahmer to death while he was in prison.

-o0o-

KATHERINE MARY KNIGHT

Katherine Mary Knight is the first Australian woman to be sentenced to life imprisonment without parole, convicted for murdering her partner, and currently imprisoned at the Silverwater Women's Correctional Centre in NSW. She was born and raised in an unconventional and dysfunctional family environment. She was the younger twin girl from an alcoholic father who openly used violence and intimidation to rape her mother up to ten times a day. Katherine did not stay at school very long and left it as soon as she could, still almost illiterate. Her brothers sexually abused her on a regular basis, while her parents took turns in beating the kids with anything from an electrical cord to a dog lead until she was 11. She was devastated when her uncle, whom she liked aside from her twin, committed suicide. During high school, she was thought of as a pleasant girl who experienced uncontrollably murderous rages in response to minor upsets. She became a loner and a bully, once assaulting a boy with a weapon, and being injured by a teacher who was found to have acted in self-defense. When not in a rage, she was a model student and often earned awards for her good behavior. As is typical of people with BPD, she had an unending stream of relationships with men. She married a hard-drinking co-worker whom she completely dominated and tried to strangle after he failed to perform up to her sexual expectations, and whom she hit with a frying pan for arriving home late. The husband eventually left her for another woman and went into hiding. The couple had a baby daughter for whom she held little regard, and she was diagnosed with postnatal depression. She was also sent to a psychiatric hospital for assessment due to multiple acts of violence against others. Later, she met a miner who moved in with her and her two daughters. She would throw him out whenever she got jealous, then follow and beg him to return later. After an argument, she hit him in the face with an iron before stabbing him in the stomach with a pair of scissors. He went into hiding. She became pregnant by a former co-worker, but their relationship lasted three years. Just before she broke off the relationship, she vandalized his car and then took an overdose of sleeping pills. She was admitted to a psychiatric hospital for observation once more. She had an affair with someone who had just ended his own marriage. She moved into his house with his two children, although he was well aware of her violent reputation. Following a fight over his refusal to marry her, she stabbed him 37 times with a butcher's knife after having sex with him. She then methodically skinned and decapitated the corpse, then cooked parts of his body, serving up the meat with baked potato and other vegies and gravy at the dinner table for his children. When police discovered his corpse the next day, they found her comatose from taking an assortment of prescription drugs. Following her arrest, she pleaded guilty for the murder and was sentenced to life imprisonment without parole. After psychiatric evaluation, mental health specialists diagnosed her with Borderline Personality Disorder.

-o0o-

DANNY ROLLING

Daniel Harold "Danny" Rolling, also known as the Gainesville Ripper, was an American serial killer who murdered five students in Gainesville, Florida. He later confessed to raping several of his victims, committing an additional triple homicide in Shreveport, Louisiana, and attempting to murder his father during a family argument in which his father lost an eye and ear. His criminal behavior was attributed to his unstable home environment and frequent separation of his parents. He was unwanted from birth and had a difficult upbringing with longstanding verbal and physical abuse from his father, who was a Shreveport police officer. Her mother made repeated attempts to leave her husband but always returned. Since childhood, he was abused, beaten and bullied by an over-bearing and disturbed father. As a teenager and young adult, he was arrested several times for robberies in Georgia and caught spying on a cheerleader getting dressed. As an adult, he had trouble assimilating into society and holding down a steady job. He had a series of failed relationships with women after his wife divorced him, and he had been in and out of prisons in Georgia, Alabama and Mississippi for robbery convictions. He was 36 when he arrived in Gainesville shortly before the fall semester began at the University of Florida, a drifter with a criminal past who pitched a tent in some woods near campus. Over a four-day span, he murdered and mutilated the bodies of five victims in their apartments on the southwest edge of Gainesville, Florida. He decapitated one, and then put the corpses in sexually suggestive positions. He was diagnosed with borderline personality disorder, typified by violent mood swings, unstable relationships, and insecurity, as well as Antisocial Personality Disorder and Paraphilia (intense sexual arousal to atypical objects). He was sentenced to death for the murders and was executed by lethal injection at the age of 52.

-o0o-

AILEEN WUORNOS

Aileen Carol Wuornos, widely believed to be the United States' first female serial killer, never met her schizophrenic father; who was incarcerated at the time of her birth for sex crimes against children and who eventually hung himself in prison. When she was almost four years old, she felt abandoned when her immature and teenage mother left her brother and her with their maternal grandparents, who legally adopted them later. At the age of 11, she began engaging in sexual activities in school in exchange for cigarettes, drugs, and food. She had also engaged in sexual activities with her brother, and claimed that her alcoholic grandfather had sexually assaulted and beaten her when she was a child, forcing her to strip out of her clothes before beating her. She became pregnant at age 14, having been raped by an accomplice of her grandfather. She gave birth to a boy at a home for unwed mothers, and the child was placed for adoption. After her grandmother died of liver failure a few years later, her grandfather threw her out of the house, and she began supporting herself as a prostitute living in the woods near her old home. At age 18, she was arrested for DUI, disorderly conduct, and firing a .22-caliber pistol from a moving vehicle. She later hitchhiked to Florida, where she met and married a 69-year-old yacht club president. She continuously got involved in confrontations at their local bar and eventually went to jail for assault. Their marriage was annulled after nine weeks and she returned to Michigan where she was arrested and charged with assault and disturbing peace. She later moved to Florida where she was arrested multiple times for armed robbery of a convenience store, car theft, resisting arrest, and unlawful possession of firearms. She met a hotel maid with whom she fell in love and whom she supported with her prostitution earnings. She later killed seven men in Florida by shooting them at point-blank range, claiming that her victims had either raped or attempted to rape her while she was working as a prostitute, and that all of the homicides were committed in self-defense. She was convicted and sentenced to death for six of the murders. At her sentencing, psychiatrists for the defense testified that she was mentally unstable and had been diagnosed with borderline personality disorder and antisocial personality disorder. She was executed by lethal injection in 2002.

-o0o-

REFERENCES

http://armchairprofiler.blogspot.com/2013/03/jodi-arias-example-of-borderline-rage.html
http://articles.orlandosentinel.com/1994-03-18/news/9403180387_1_danny-rolling-sadoff-serial-killer
http://bpd.about.com/od/understandingbpd/a/bpdstats.htm
http://bpdfamily.com/bpdresources/nk_a103.htm
https://deathlydames.wordpress.com/2015/01/26/borderline-personality-disorder-pushed-katherine-over-the-borderline/
https://en.wikipedia.org/wiki/Aileen_Wuornos
https://en.wikipedia.org/wiki/Angelina_Jolie
https://en.wikipedia.org/wiki/Bobby_Baker
https://en.wikipedia.org/wiki/Danny_Rolling
https://en.wikipedia.org/wiki/Courtney_Love
https://en.wikipedia.org/wiki/Diana,_Princess_of_Wales
https://en.wikipedia.org/wiki/Jane_Andrews
https://en.wikipedia.org/wiki/Katherine_Knight
https://en.wikipedia.org/wiki/Pete_Doherty
http://gawker.com/5881652/frances-bean-cobain-says-courtney-love-killed-her-pets
http://keirsey.com/4temps/princess_diana.asp
http://mental-health-matters.com/borderline-personality-and-abuse/
http://mentalhealthtreatment.net/blog/was-amy-winehouse-diagnosed-with-borderline-personality-disorder/
http://personalitypsych2011.wikispaces.com/Lindsay+Lohan
http://popdirt.com/britney-spears-has-borderline-personality-disorder/31472/
https://rampages.us/wilderkt/tag/angelina-jolie/
https://rampages.us/wilderkt/tag/lindsay-lohan/http://www.biography.com/people/courtney-love-9542145#!
http://real-life-villains.wikia.com/wiki/Jeffrey_Dahmer
http://research.omicsgroup.org/index.php/Katherine_Knight
http://selectedhealth.org/Famous-People-With-Borderline-Personality-Disorder.html
http://www.biography.com/people/aileen-wuornos-11735792#trial-and-public-impact
http://www.anythingtostopthepain.com/amy-winehouse-and-bpd-borderline/
http://www.anythingtostopthepain.com/angelina-jolie-detailed-possible-bpd-analysis/

http://www.anythingtostopthepain.com/courtney-love-bpd-borderline-eating-disorder/
http://www.anythingtostopthepain.com/lindsay-lohan-possible-bpd-detail/
http://www.anythingtostopthepain.com/why-pete-doherty-has-jumped-to-the-front-of-the-line-for-bpd-celebs/
http://www.anythingtostopthepain.com/update-britney-spears-bpd-borderline-personality-disorder/
https://www.bookdepository.com/Diary-Drawings-Bobby-Baker/9781846683749
http://www.borderlinepersonalitydisorder.com/what-is-bpd/bpd-overview/
https://www.bpdcentral.com/borderline-disorder/bpd-relationships/
http://www.cracked.com/personal-experiences-1528-5-realities-life-people-with-borderline-personalities.html
http://www.crimeandinvestigation.co.uk/crime-files/aileen-wuornos
http://www.crimemuseum.org/crime-library/jeffrey-dahmer/
https://www.datalounge.com/thread/11886752-what-mental-disorder-does-britney-spears-suffer-from-
http://www.healtholino.com/10-famous-celebrities-with-borderline-personality-disorder/
http://www.healthyplace.com/personality-disorders/borderline-personality-disorder/borderline-personality-disorder-treatment/
http://maamodt.asp.radford.edu/Psyc%20405/serial%20killers/Rolling,%20Danny%20-%202004.pdf
http://www.mayoclinic.org/diseases-conditions/borderline-personality-disorder/basics/definition/con-20023204?p=1
http://www.medhealthdaily.com/celebrities-with-borderline-personality-disorder/
http://www.murderpedia.org/male.D/images/dahmer-jeffrey/docs/jeffrey-dahmer-abigail-strubel.pdf
https://www.myprivatesearch.com/search?c=5697&q=lindsay+lohan
http://www.nabpd.org/jodi-arias-has-most-bpd-symptoms/
https://www.nami.org/Learn-More/Mental-Health-Conditions/Borderline-Personality-Disorder
http://www.nationalenquirer.com/celebrity/courtney-love-eating-disorder/
https://www.ncbi.nlm.nih.gov/pubmedhealth/PMH0015300/
http://www.nlm.nih.gov/medlineplus/ency/article/000935.htm
http://www.nimh.nih.gov/health/topics/borderline-personality-disorder/index.shtml
http://www.nydailynews.com/entertainment/gossip/doctors-claim-lindsay-lohan-misdiagnosed-drug-addiction-bipolar-disorder-report-article-1.201755
http://www.nydailynews.com/archives/news/di-struggled-mental-demons-new-biography-reveals-personality-disorder-article-1.842916
http://www.nytimes.com/books/first/s/smith-diana.html
https://www.psychologytoday.com/blog/millennial-media/201308/has-lindsay-lohan-s-next-chapter-truly-begun
https://www.psychologytoday.com/blog/reading-between-the-headlines/201303/does-jodi-arias-have-borderline-personality-disorder

http://www.thedailybeast.com/articles/2010/08/02/angelina-jolies-biography-12-biggest-revelations.html

http://www.thefamouspeople.com/profiles/aileen-wuornos-4113.php

https://www.thefix.com/content/courtney-love-cobain-addictions-e-book8787

https://www.theguardian.com/commentisfree/2009/nov/25/jane-andrews-press-abuse

http://www.thisislondon.co.uk/showbiz/article-22525591-details/Doherty's+blood+paintings/article.do

https://www.verywell.com/amy-winehouses-manic-depressive-life-380564

https://www.verywell.com/borderline-personality-and-violence-425192

http://www.wow.com/wiki/Amy_Winehouse

FURTHER READING

American Psychiatric Association. (1994). *Diagnostic and statistical manual for mental disorders* (4th ed.). Washington, DC: APA Publishing.

Paris, J. (2004). Borderline or bipolar? Distinguishing borderline personality disorder from bipolar spectrum disorders. *Harv Rev Psychiatry, 12*, 140-145

-o0o-

HISTRIONIC PERSONALITY DISORDER

Personality disorders can affect and disrupt a person's life and activities. They comprise a set of enduring behavioral traits that are defined by experiences and behaviors outside of societal norms. The abnormal behavior pattern is enduring, long standing, and not limited to episodes of mental illness; it is pervasive and always appears during childhood or adolescence, continuing into adulthood; causing clinically significant distress or impairment in social, occupational, or other important areas of functioning. Because there is a great deal of overlap between the features of borderline and histrionic personality disorders, it becomes difficult to diagnose and differentiate the two. The same applies to narcissistic and anti-social disorders that are included in the Cluster B disorders of personality. These conditions may co-exist with each other and can even present with similar symptoms causing confusion for many people.

-o0o-

Histrionic personality disorder is one of a group of conditions called "Cluster B" or dramatic personality disorders, which include borderline, narcissistic and antisocial personality disorder. The essential feature of histrionic personality disorder is pervasive and excessive emotionality and attention-seeking behavior. Histrionic people have intense, unstable emotions and distorted self-esteem that depend on the approval of others and do not arise from a true feeling of self-worth. People with histrionic personality disorder cannot rely on their own judgments or ideas, are easily swayed by what other people believe, and basically adopt another's viewpoint as their own without really understanding the reason behind such belief. They have an overwhelming desire to be noticed, and often behave dramatically or inappropriately to get attention. It is a pattern of extreme emotionality and attention seeking behavior that begins by early adulthood and is obvious in different situations. Histrionic individuals are usually overly dramatic, emotional, attention seeking, and uncomfortable in situations where they are not the center of attention. Their interaction with others is often characterized by inappropriate sexually seductive or provocative behavior. As such, they consistently use their physical appearance to draw attention to themselves. They speak to impress, with self-dramatization and exaggerated expression of emotion.

It is sometimes hard to differentiate between borderline personality disorder and histrionic personality disorder. In some instances, it is just a matter of degree. Both include a fear of being alone and a fear of abandonment – with the borderline being frantic and desperate in their efforts to avoid those conditions. Although both are impulsive, the actions of borderline individuals are potentially more dangerous. Histrionic individuals believe that they can do something to avoid abandonment, and they use their sexuality and attention-seeking efforts to secure and maintain their relationships. Borderline individuals see those efforts largely as a failure, become frantic, and may initially turn into rage followed by depression when their relationships are threatened. They have a propensity toward paranoid ideations and severe dissociative symptoms that are usually not present with the histrionic individuals. It is also possible that the two disorders can co-exist, and a dual diagnosis can be made, if appropriate criteria are met for both disorders. It is important to note that a histrionic personality can degenerate into a borderline personality, especially when in crisis and when established defense mechanisms fail. This condition might result in the dual diagnosis of both disorders, and can significantly complicate treatment.

People with borderline personality disorder experience reckless and impulsive behavior, unstable moods and relationships, sometimes accompanied with brief psychotic episodes that change in minutes or hours. In contrast, people with histrionic personality disorder require constant approval from their peers, are inappropriately seductive, dramatic, flirtatious, manipulative and self-indulgent. Their opinions are easily influenced by other people, but are difficult to back up with details, and they almost always blame their failure or disappointments on others. They actively seek an audience because of their constant craving for approval, praise and validation.

Approximately 2 to 3% of the general population suffers from this disorder, although much higher rates of 10 to 15% have been reported in both inpatient and outpatient settings. Between 10 to 15 percent of patients with borderline personality disorder also meet the diagnostic criteria for histrionic personality disorder, due to marked overlap between their symptoms.

Histrionic personality disorder was also known in the past as hysterical personality disorder, and is more commonly diagnosed in women compared to men who are also often diagnosed with narcissistic personality behavior. Histrionic people are actually quite successful and high-functioning individuals that are self-centered and outgoing. They usually have good social skills that they tend to use in order to manipulate others into making them their center of attention. They fall in love easily and become depressed or take it hard when their relationship ends. They may also seek treatment for clinical depression when their relationships die. They may often change jobs as they can quickly become bored and frustrated. They constantly seek reassurance or approval, are overly concerned with their physical appearance, and are extremely sensitive to criticism or disapproval. More than likely, they exaggerate their physical injuries, illnesses and/or weaknesses in an attempt to elicit attention from others. They may falsely threaten to commit suicide to gain sympathy from others, and may engage in risky behaviors such promiscuity, criminal activities and drugs or alcohol abuse to get attention from the opposite sex. They are more likely to seek attention from multiple people, which leads to marital problems due to jealousy and lack of trust from the other party. This makes them more likely to become divorced or separated once married.

The exact cause of histrionic personality disorder is not known, but many mental health professionals believe that both learned and inherited factors play a role in its development. The tendency for histrionic personality disorder to run in families suggests that a genetic susceptibility for the disorder might be inherited. Major character traits may be inherited, while other traits may be due to a combination of genetics and environment, including childhood experiences. The disorder can be caused by emotional, physical or psychological childhood trauma such as death, illness, parental divorce, or loss in the family. They may feel unappreciated or unloved by overly controlling parents, and extreme parental involvement may reduce their ability to care about anyone or anything else. Alternatively, a lack of criticism or punishment as a child, positive reinforcement that is given only when a child completes certain approved behaviors, and inconsistent attention given to a child may lead to confusion about which types of behavior earn parental approval. In addition, some experts believe that sexual predisposition and societal pressure to keep their birth sexual identity may predispose them to this disorder.

Histrionic personality disorder is typically diagnosed by a trained mental health professional, such as a psychologist or psychiatrist. Family physicians and general practitioners are generally not trained or well equipped to make this type of psychological diagnosis. The person's appearance, behavior, and history, along with a psychological evaluation, are usually enough to establish a diagnosis. If signs of this personality disorder are present, a physical exam and laboratory tests (such as neuroimaging studies or blood tests) are also recommended to assure that a physical illness is not causing any of the symptoms that may be present. Because the criteria are subjective and there is no test to confirm this diagnosis, people may be wrongly diagnosed with a different disorder. Most histrionics also have other mental disorders and comorbid conditions including antisocial, borderline, and narcissistic personality disorders, as well as depression, anxiety disorders, panic disorder, anorexia nervosa, and substance use.

Psychotherapy is generally the treatment of choice for histrionic personality disorder. The goal of treatment is to help the individuals uncover the motivations and fears associated with their behavior, and to help them learn to relate to others in a more positive way. In general, people with histrionic personality disorder do not believe they need therapy. They also tend to exaggerate their feelings and to dislike routine, which makes following a treatment plan difficult. However, they might seek help if depression -- possibly associated with a loss or a failed relationship - or another problem caused by their actions causes them distress. Medication may sometimes be used as treatment for other conditions that might also be present with this disorder, such as depression and anxiety.

Although prevention of the histrionic personality disorder might not be possible, treatment can allow a person who is prone to this disorder to learn more productive ways of dealing with situations. As with borderline and other personality disorders, long-term psychotherapy is the most effective way to treat the histrionic personality disorder. The goal of treatment is to help the individual uncover the motivations and fears associated with his or her thoughts and behavior, and to help the person learn to relate to others in a more positive way. Cognitive behavioral therapy is one of the therapies used when dealing with the disorder. In general, people with histrionic personality disorder do not believe they need therapy. However, they might seek help if their depression causes significant distress -- possibly associated with a loss or a failed relationship -- or another problem caused by their actions. But once they arrive at a psychotherapy session, it can be difficult to reach the root of their disorder because of their flamboyant and seductive behaviors. Medication is not indicated unless depression, anxiety, pain or other illness also occurs. In such cases, anti-depressants, anti-anxiety or antipsychotics should be prescribed, but with caution.

-o0o-

FAMOUS PERSONS WITH HISTRIONIC PERSONALITY DISORDER

Although there are a few famous people with symptoms consistent with histrionic and narcissistic personality disorders, they seem to be prevalent among Hollywood celebrities. However, there doesn't seem to be any who publicly has admitted to having the disorder or who is known to have sought treatment for the disorder. It is not uncommon for histrionic, narcissistic and anti-social personalities to occur as co-morbid conditions of borderline personality disorder, since all of them belong to Cluster B group of personality disorder. Signs of mental illness are often insinuated in news articles of persons who have committed crimes, but are overlooked by fans when celebrities, professional athletes, or incredibly powerful and successful persons are involved.

-o0o-

MEGAN FOX

Megan Denise Fox, an American actress and model, is also considered one of the modern female sex symbols. Her parents divorced when she was three years old. She was raised by her mother and her stepfather, who she said were "very strict" and did not allow her to have a boyfriend or invite friends to her house. She began her training in dance and drama at age five, and was involved in Kingston Elementary School's chorus and the Kingston Clipper's swim team. When she was 13 years old, she began modeling after winning several awards at the 1999 American Modeling and Talent Convention in South Carolina. She has spoken extensively of her time in education; that in middle school she was bullied; not because of her looks, but because she had "always gotten along better with boys" and had "rubbed some people the wrong way". She also said that she was never popular and was a "total outcast" in high school because her friends were always guys, and she had a very aggressive personality. At 15, she made her acting debut in the 2001 film Holiday in the Sun, and in the next several years she guest-starred on "What I Like About You" and "Two and a Half Men", as well as being an uncredited extra in "Bad Boys II". She made her film debut in "Confessions of a Teenage Drama Queen", and played the lead female role in the live-action film "Transformers". She got married in 2010, filed for divorce in 2015, and by early 2016, the couple was back together and expecting a third child. She has been open about her feelings on men and socializing, stating that although she had more in common with men, she has a general distrust and dislike for them; and that, despite the public perceiving her as a "wild and crazy sexpot," she is antisocial and has only been sexually intimate with two men her entire life. She alluded to being bisexual, saying that she fell in love with and sought to establish a relationship with a female stripper when she was 18. She admits that she has obsessive–compulsive disorder (OCD), insecurities, self-harming, and has acknowledged that she has low self-esteem. She said that she still speaks in tongues; at times she has to hold back from breaking out in tongues at her current church. She has been featured on "hottest" and "most beautiful woman" lists throughout the years, and was voted the "Sexiest Woman in the World" in 2008. During an interview, she described herself as being very vulnerable, aggressive, hurtful, domineering, selfish, emotionally unpredictable, and a control freak. As a child, she had panic attacks and started seeing a therapist because of her real "emotional problems," but it didn't seem to help. Like many celebrities, she seems to love being the center of attraction and craves for attention. People have labeled her as both a borderline and a histrionic personality. Certainly the two disorders can occur together.

-o0o-

KIM KARDASHIAN

Kimberly Kardashian West (born Kimberly Noel Kardashian) is an American reality television personality, socialite, actress, business-woman and model who first gained media attention as a friend and stylist of Paris Hilton, but received wider notice after the 2007 leak of her sex tape with her former boyfriend. Later that year, she and her family began to appear in the reality television series "Keeping Up with the Kardashians". In 2011, she was engaged to NBA player Kris Humphries, and her marriage coincided with the release of her "wedding fragrance" called "Kim Kardashian Love" and a two-part TV "media blitz" related to the wedding. After 72 days of marriage, she filed for divorce, citing irreconcilable differences. The wedding was believed to be a publicity stunt, to promote the Kardashian family's brand and their subsequent television ventures. In recent years, she has grown an influential online and social media presence, including tens of millions of followers on Twitter and Instagram. In May 2015, she released a portfolio book called 'Selfish', a 325-page collection of self-taken photos of herself. She was included on the Time Magazine's list of 2015's 100 most influential people, and was reported to be the highest-paid reality television personality of 2015. She has posted five-year-old pictures of herself in a bare swimsuit, and seductive bikini swimsuit with her legs slightly spread apart, and another picture of her driving a car bare-skinned. She shows high traits of an attention-seeking disorder, feeling the need to be in the spotlight at all times and being the center of attention at any given cost. Her overly seductive dress, self-made porn video, drama-filled romantic life with rap artist Kanye West, and seemingly insatiable hunger for attention are consistent with a diagnosis of histrionic personality disorder.

-o0o-

MILEY CYRUS

Miley Ray Cyrus (born Destiny Hope Cyrus; November 23, 1992) is an American singer, songwriter, and actress. When she was only eleven years old, she auditioned for the Disney Channel television series Hannah Montana but was instead given the lead role due to her singing and acting abilities. She became a teen idol for her portrayal of the starring character Miley Stewart in 2006; and subsequently signed a recording contract with Hollywood Records. Her debut studio album "Meet Miley Cyrus" was later certified triple-platinum by the Recording Industry Association of America. She released her second album "Breakout" and launched her film career as a voice actress in the animated film "Bolt" in 2008. She starred in the feature film "Hannah Montana: The Movie". Later, she told her mother how she first realized she was sexually attracted to females. She generated considerable media attention after cutting her traditionally long, brown hair in favor of a blonde, pixie-style haircut. As she focused on her acting career with several television and film appearances, her sexually explicit behavior generated widespread controversy. The once wholesome pre-teen star has become an oversexed attention-getter. She regularly appears at public events and personal social gatherings in overtly seductive attire, and often behaves in a manner that can only be seen as desperately attention-seeking. She is loud, obnoxious, rude, and overly dramatic. She talks fast, gestures a lot, and won't let her father get a word without redirecting attention back to herself. She appears to be seeking approval, is self-centered and dresses in a provocative fashion. She wears heavy makeup, enormous jewelry, and ridiculous outfits with bright colors. More recently, her hyper-sexuality, lack of impulse control and boundaries, rapid mood swings, admitted drug use, compulsive tweeting and spending, extreme displays of irritability and argumentative behavior, difficulty sleeping, and hoarding of animals, were all documented on Twitter. Through all these, a Licensed Clinical Professional Counselor, trained to evaluate and diagnose mental illness, has expressed concern over her recent behavior, although not directly implying that she is suffering from mental illness, her behavior suggests that she might have histrionic personality disorder.

-o0o-

KANYE WEST

Kanye Omari West is an American rapper, songwriter, record producer, fashion designer, and entrepreneur. He is among the most critically acclaimed artists of the twenty-first century, receiving praise from music critics, fans, fellow musicians, artists, and wider cultural figures for his work. He began writing poetry when he was five years old, and his mother first noticed his passion for drawing and music when he was in the third grade. Growing up in Chicago, he became deeply involved in hip hop, started rapping in the third grade, and began making musical compositions in the seventh grade. At age thirteen, he wrote a rap song called "Green Eggs and Ham" and persuaded his mother to pay $25 an hour for time in a recording studio. After graduating from high school, he received a scholarship to attend Chicago's American Academy of Art and took painting classes, but dropped out of college to pursue his musical career at age 20. He is the founder and head of the creative content company DONDA. As a fashion designer, he collaborated with Nike, Louis Vuitton, Adidas and A.P.C. on both clothing and footwear. His famous marriage to television personality Kim Kardashian has also been the subject of widespread media coverage. He does not seem to mind if he gets good or bad critiques for his outrageous and entertaining antics, as long as the Internet and media are paying attention and continue to cover him. His outspoken views and controversial conduct in award shows, on social media, and in other public settings have attracted significant mainstream attention. In 2005, he won an impressive 10 Grammy nominations and received an award for Best Rap Album for "The College Dropout", Best Rap Song for "Jesus Walks," and an R&B songwriting Grammy for "You Don't Know." He is known for his off-script denunciation of President George W. Bush during a live 2005 television broadcast for Hurricane Katrina relief. In 2006, when his "Touch the Sky" failed to win Best Video at the MTV Europe Music Awards, he went onto the stage as the award was being presented and argued that he should have won the award instead. In 2009, he made headlines during MTV's Video Music Awards, not for his music but for storming the stage while pop star Taylor Swift was accepting the award for Best Female Video. He later called her to apologize personally and she accepted his apology. In 2010, he told his audience that he once considered suicide. In 2016, soon before abruptly ending a concert, he was persuaded by authorities to be committed to the UCLA Medical Center for depression and paranoia. The episode was initially described as "temporary psychosis" caused by dehydration and sleep deprivation, In November 2016, while on his Saint Pablo Tour, he made headlines again when he interrupted a concert to rant about politics, his support of president-elect Donald Trump, the music industry, Beyoncé and Jay-Z. A few days later, he was late for another concert, performed only two songs and again spoke about politics. Following these incidents, he was hospitalized and treated for exhaustion at the

UCLA Medical Center in Los Angeles and his concert tour was cancelled. He also talks a lot about self-esteem and his ability to influence and inspire young people. Over the course of his career, he has been known to compare himself to various influential figures and entities in art and culture, including Apple founder Steve Jobs, animator Walt Disney, pop artist Andy Warhol, entrepreneur Howard Hughes, singer Michael Jackson, R Leonardo da Vinci, fashion designers Ralph Lauren and Anna Wintour, athletics company Nike, and technology company Google. According to psychologist Rachel Kitson, his antics and drama-laden romantic life appear to fit both narcissistic and histrionic personality disorders.

-o0o-

ANN NICOLE SMITH

Anna Nicole Smith (born Vickie Lynn Hogan) was an American model, actress, and television personality. Smith first gained popularity in Playboy, winning the title of 1993 Playmate of the Year. She modeled for fashion companies including Guess, H&M, and Lane Bryant. She had a difficult life from an early age, after being abandoned by her father when she was just a baby, and later dropping out of high school. She had disastrous incidents with her alcoholic and pedophilic father, and a struggle for custody between her mother and aunt, forcing her to live in a constantly shifting environment. Her life was later marked by unstable interpersonal relationships, low self-image, and marked impulsiveness. Working numerous jobs while growing up, she married at the age of 17, and had a son from her former husband. She did not rise to fame until she was 26, when she met an 89-year old Texas oil tycoon in a club she was working at, nearly 10 years after her first marriage. Only a year after the wedding, her second husband died and she spent years fighting for a share of her late husband's estate. It was also during this time that she began to see her first big break in the porn industry as a playboy model, and the 1993 "Playmate of the Year". She always wanted to show off in sexually seductive ways and dated 80-year-old men just to gain attention in the media. She always worried about what she looked like and often appeared dressed in crazy outfits that many people would not wear. With her sexy image, she attracted a lot of interest from celebrity magazines and tabloids. In 2002, television viewers got an inside look at Smith and her eccentric, bizarre ways with a new reality program, "The Anna Nicole Show". At times, the show was difficult to watch as she seemed disoriented or confused, but the audience continued to tune in to see what she might do or say next. She didn't seem to mind the media scrutiny, and claimed that she loved the paparazzi, wanting to be noticed and always seeking the attention that she didn't get very much while growing up. Her personality disorder apparently became manifest after abusing several kinds of prescription drugs. In 2006, she was pregnant when she was seen at Cedars-Sinai Medical Center and had withdrawal symptoms from the anti-anxiety drug *Xanax* and the pain killer *Methadone*. She discontinued the drugs all at once because she was concerned for the welfare of her expected baby. Her doctor found it difficult to get a medical history because she was "putting on a show" and was deferring questions to her lawyer-boyfriend who was with her at all times. In 2006, she announced that she was pregnant and gave birth to a daughter in Nassau, Bahamas. Although she was thrilled to be a mother again, her happiness was short-lived when her 20-year-old son Daniel died only three days later from an apparent drug overdose. She never fully recovered and she died in 2007, at the age of 39, after being found unconscious in her hotel room at the Seminole Hard Rock Hotel and Casino in Hollywood, Florida. Following her accidental death from drug overdose, the hospital psychiatrist testified in court that medications given to Anna Nicole Smith by a doctor now on trial were "overkill" for the kind of back pain she had been suffering for five years. Another doctor testified that she suffered from chronic pain syndrome all over her body. A doctor who treated her six years before she died also testified that she complained of many physical ailments, but he was unable to diagnose the source of most of her pain. A month after she died, 44 different prescription drugs were gathered from her seaside home in the Bahamas and delivered to a medical examiner in Florida. Many psychologists believe that she is a good example of famous individuals in the whole world that have a histrionic personality disorder.

-o0o-

ELIZABETH DIANE FREDERICKSON DOWNS

Elizabeth Diane Frederickson Downs is an American woman who was convicted in 1983 for the murder of her 7-year old daughter and the attempted murder of her other two children. The eldest, 9-year old daughter suffered a disabling stroke while the youngest, a 4-year boy, was paralyzed from the waist down. Following the shooting, she told police that a stranger had attempted to carjack her and had shot the children. Her eldest, once she recovered her ability to speak, described how her mother shot all three children while parked at the side of the road and then shot herself in the arm. She was convicted in 1984 and sentenced to life in prison. She alleges that her father molested her when she was a child (although both parents denied that any such incidents ever took place, and in the late 1980s she recanted her allegations. Her parents had conservative values, and until the age of 14, she seemed to follow their rules. She became more defiant during her adolescent years as she struggled to fit into the "in" crowd at school. She got rid of her childish hairstyle, opting instead for a trendy, shorter, bleached blond style. She began wearing more stylish clothing that showed off her maturing figure, which attracted boys. She started dating a boy who lived across the street, and with whom she had a sexual relationship by the time she was 16. After high school, she was expelled from a Bible College for promiscuous behavior. She then ran away from her parents' home and married her high school sweetheart. Her marriage was rocky from the start – with fights about money and accusations of infidelities. Her husband had a vasectomy after their second child was born, but it did not stop her from getting pregnant again, which she decided to abort. She began having affairs with some of her male coworkers and again became pregnant and gave birth to a boy whom her husband accepted, even though he knew he was not the father. They decided to get a divorce a year later. She spent the next few years moving in and out with different men, having affairs with married men and at times trying to reconcile with her husband. She decided to become a surrogate mother, but failed two psychiatric exams showing that she was very intelligent but also psychotic—something that she bragged to her friends about. When she got a full-time job as a postal carrier for the U.S. Post Office, her children often stayed with her parents or with her ex-husband. When the children stayed with her, neighbors voiced concerns about their care. Her friends, acquaintances, neighbors, and her surviving daughter attested to her being an unfit parent. The children were often seen poorly dressed for the weather and at times hungry, asking for food. When she went to work, she would leave her then six-year-old Christie in charge of the other siblings. Prosecutors argued that she shot her children to be free of them so she could continue her affair with a fellow postal worker, who she claimed did not want children in his life. Upon arrival at the hospital to visit her children, she called a married man and former co-worker with whom she had been having an extramarital affair. Her lover reported to police that she had stalked him and seemed willing to kill his wife if it meant that she could have him to herself. He was relieved that she had left for Oregon and that he was able to reconcile with his wife. She was convicted on all charges and sentenced to life in prison plus 50 years. The surviving children eventually went to live with, and were later adopted by the lead prosecutor on the case. Psychiatrists diagnosed her with narcissistic, histrionic and antisocial personality disorders.

-o0o-

REFERENCES

http://allpsych.com/disorders/personality/index.html

http://blog.southeastpsych.com/2013/12/02/a-psychologists-perspective-on-kanye-west/

http://cmm.lefora.com/topic/692649/elizabeth-diane-frederickson-downs#

http://crime.about.com/od/female_offenders/a/Diane-Downs.htm

https://en.wikipedia.org/wiki/Anna_Nicole_Smith

https://en.wikipedia.org/wiki/Diane_Downs
https://en.wikipedia.org/wiki/Kim_Kardashian
https://en.wikipedia.org/wiki/Megan_Fox
https://en.wikipedia.org/wiki/Miley_Cyrus
http://healthresearchfunding.org/famous-people-histrionic-personality-disorder/
https://medlineplus.gov/ency/article/001531.htm
http://murderpedia.org/female.D/d/downs-diane.htm
https://prezi.com/ghue-wip-xnp/anna-nicole-smith-and-her-struggle-with-both-histrionic-and/
https://prezi.com/u5c279t5rkd-/kim-kardashian-narcissistic-personality-disorder/
http://www.answers.com/Q/What_is_the_difference_between_histrionic_personality_disorder_and_borderline_personality_disorder
http://www.anythingtostopthepain.com/anna-nicole-smith-celebrities-bpd/
http://www.anythingtostopthepain.com/megan-fox-borderline-personality-disorder-reexamined/
http://www.biography.com/people/kanye-west-362922#recent-projects
http://www.biography.com/people/megan-fox-483434#career-breakthrough
http://www.blisstree.com/2008/02/28/mental-health-well-being/does-miley-cyrus-have-histrionic-personality-disorder-or-is-she-just-plain-annoying-115/
http://www.chicagonow.com/moms-who-drink-and-swear/2013/08/cant-or-wont-stop-is-miley-cyrus-mentally-ill
http://www.dailystormer.com/miley-wants-in-on-bruce-drama-says-all-sex-is-cool-as-long-as-no-animals/
http://www.differencebetween.info/difference-between-borderline-and-histrionic
http://www.disorders.org/narcissistic-histrionic/
http://www.examiner.com/article/website-links-jessica-simpson-with-histrionic-personality-disorder
http://www.foxnews.com/entertainment/2012/08/20/do-kim-kardashian-and-miley-cyrus-have-super-self-confidence-or-personality/
http://www.healthyplace.com/personality-disorders/histrionic-personality-disorder/famous-people-with-histrionic-personality-disorder/
http://www.ibtimes.com/miley-cyrus-recent-behavior-might-be-indication-she-has-mood-personality-disorders-report-1407470
http://www.imdb.com/name/nm1083271/bio?ref_=nm_ov_bio_sm
http://www.medpagetoday.com/CelebrityDiagnosis/33343
http://www.merck.com/mmhe/sec07/ch105/ch105a.html
http://www.minddisorders.com/Flu-Inv/Histrionic-personality-disorder.html
http://www.minddisorders.com/Flu-Inv/Histrionic-personality-disorder.html
https://www.myprivatesearch.com/search?q=kanye+west
https://www.myprivatesearch.com/search?c=5697&q=kim+kardashian
http://www.nlm.nih.gov/medlineplus/ency/article/001531.htm
https://www.revolvy.com/main/index.php?s=Diane%20Downs
https://www.rottentomatoes.com/celebrity/megan_fox/
http://www.shrinktank.com/psychologists-perspective-kanye-west/
http://www.smh.com.au/lifestyle/celebrity/44-drugs-found-emotional-pain-and-anna-nicole-smith-20100811-11z3t.html

http://www.thehealthsite.com/news/are-kim-kardashians-nude-pictures-a-sign-of-mental-illness/

http://www.therapyweb.co.uk/problems/antisocial-borderline-histrionic-and-narcissistic-personality-disorders

https://psychcentral.com/disorders/histrionic-personality-disorder-symptoms/

http://www.psychologytoday.com/conditions/histrionic-personality-disorder

http://www.webmd.com/mental-health/histrionic-personality-disorder#1

FURTHER READING

American Psychiatric Association. (2013). *Diagnostic and statistical manual of mental disorders (DSM-5®)*. American Psychiatric Pub.

Comer, R.J. (1996). *Fundamentals of abnormal psychology*. New York, NY: W.H. Freeman and Company.

Gunderson, J.G. & Choi-Kain, L. (2016). *Personality disorders*. Merck Manual Consumer Version. Retrieved from http://www.merckmanuals.com/home/mental-health-disorders/personality-disorders/personality-disorders

Kaplan, H.I., & Sadoc, B. J. (1996). *Concise textbook of clinical psychiatry*. Baltimore, MD: Williams & Wilkins.

Marshall, W., & Serin, R. (1997). Personality disorders. In S. M. Turner & R. Hersen (Eds.), *Adult psychopathology and diagnosis* (pp. 508–541). Hoboken, NJ: John Wiley & Sons, Inc.

NARCISSISTIC PERSONALITY DISORDER

Narcissistic and histrionic personality disorders, along with antisocial and borderline personality disorders, are part of what the Diagnostic and Statistical Manual of Mental Disorders (DSM-IV) considers as a "Cluster B" dramatic personality disorders, in which afflicted people have very unstable, intense emotions and a distorted image of "self". Because of their overlapping symptoms, they are often mistaken for one another, even though they are distinct disorders with their own set of diagnostic criteria.

Just like with borderline personality disorder, people with histrionic and narcissistic personality disorders have intense fear of abandonment, but they have different responses to potential loss. When borderline individuals are frightened that the person will leave them, they feel helpless and vulnerable. They may lash out and go into offense in order to restore their sense of control, harass the other party by excessive phone calls, emails, or text messages, stay in that dysfunctional relationship or go into deep depression. When narcissists are abandoned, they respond with aggression, which can lead to violence towards the person involved or, in extreme cases, to anyone who resembles the person who left them. Histrionics blow things out of proportion and become over-dramatic about perceived loss or abandonment.

-o0o-

Narcissism is characterized by an exaggerated sense of one's own abilities and achievements, constant need for attention, persistent fantasies about and preoccupation with power and success, a sense of entitlement, envy, lack of empathy, and a feeling of superiority, exploiting other people for personal gain. People with narcissistic personality disorder see themselves, their interests, and their opinions as the only things that truly matter.

Narcissists tend to be cold, show lack of emotion, are incapable of understanding or feeling what another person is experiencing, and have strong self-control. They often are arrogant, put their needs above anybody else's, and cannot appreciate viewpoints outside of their own. Borderlines also tend to lack self-control, but they are capable of understanding other's feelings. Narcissists are generally angered by any suggestion that they are flawed or at fault. Borderlines can be angered by the other person's tone or any perceived sign of abandonment, such as a decrease in attention given to them.

Histrionics long for attention, seek approval at all times, always need the attention of others around them because of their low self-esteem, and try to get people's attention by being provocative or seductive. Narcissists are the opposite of histrionics. They are vain, have an enormous sense of self-importance, a false sense of prestige, or excessive pride for potentials or their achievements. A narcissistic person is in many ways the opposite of a histrionic person. While histrionics seek constant approval and attention from others, narcissists do not seek approval from anyone and are strongly confident that they are the center of attention wherever they go. When challenged with failure or criticism from others they may become aggressive or depressed due to the superior feeling they have about themselves. They believe that they are entitled to what they want and that others are beneath them.

Borderline personality disorder is characterized by self-injury, and threatened or attempted suicide, whereas narcissists are rarely self-harming in this way. Borderline personality disorder may include psychotic breaks, which are uncharacteristic but not unknown with narcissistic personality disorder. The need for constant attention is also found in histrionic personality disorder, but histrionic and borderline persons are both strongly oriented towards relationships, whereas narcissistic persons are aloof and they avoid intimacy. Psychopaths display pathological narcissism, including grandiosity, and are willing to use physical violence in order to get what they want, whereas narcissists rarely commit crimes, although they will occasionally strike out in an impulse of rage.

There is nothing wrong with having a small and reasonable degree of narcissism; because it allows you to be proud of your accomplishment and become self-confident. But as you grow up and mature, you learn that other people's views matter and that you cannot always be the center of attention. In the end, you learn to cope with disappointments and failures without losing your self-esteem. True narcissists do not change. They continue to think of themselves in a grandiose way, and they do not develop the coping skills that are necessary to handle real or perceived criticisms, failure or abandonment.

They have an inflated sense of self- importance and a deep need for admiration. Because they are convinced that they are special, which may or may not be supported by any special talent or actual accomplishment, they limit their associations to equally special people. They manipulate or take advantage of others, become indifferent and show no concern for those around them. They think that everyone is envious of them, and are often also envious of other people's talents, possessions or accomplishments. People with narcissistic personality disorder are typically described as arrogant, conceited, self-centered, and snobbish. Because they imagine themselves as being superior to others, they often insist on possessing items that reflect a successful lifestyle.

There is evidence that narcissistic personality disorder is heritable, and individuals are much more likely to develop it if they have a family history of the disorder. They may inherit the behavior and attitudes of their parents. However the specific genes and gene interactions that contribute to its etiology, and how they may influence the developmental and physiological processes underlying this condition, have yet to be determined. Growing up with abusive, negligent or strict parents may cause them to compensate by isolating themselves from the world, believing that they have some personality defect that makes them unvalued and unwanted. Overprotective and overindulgent parents who spoil their children can also predispose them to the disorder and give them an exaggerated sense of self-worth. They can be controlling, blaming, self-absorbed, intolerant of others' views, unaware of others' needs and the effects of their behavior on others, and they expect others to see them the way they see themselves. Their inability to tolerate setbacks, disagreements or criticism, along with lack of empathy, make it difficult for them to work cooperatively with others or to maintain long-term professional relationships with superiors and colleagues.

Extreme selfishness, exaggerated feelings of self-importance, outward tendency to overemphasize their achievements and lack of empathy do not fully describe the narcissistic personality disorder. Deep within, they swing between having this grandiose view of themselves and their feeling or fear of being completely worthless. Their behavior may be due to an inflated view of themselves, or may be a compensatory mechanism for a feeling of worthlessness. They may exhibit fragile egos, an inability to tolerate criticism, and a tendency to belittle others in an attempt to validate their own superiority. When their own ego is wounded by a real or perceived criticism, their anger can be disproportionate to the situation, but typically, their actions and responses are deliberate and calculated. They use various strategies to protect themselves at the expense of others. They tend to devalue, derogate, insult, blame others and they often respond to threatening feedback with anger and hostility.

Narcissistic personality disorder is thought to be less common than other personality disorders such as borderline personality disorder, antisocial personality disorder, and histrionic personality disorder. About one percent of people are believed to be affected at a certain point in their life. It appears to occur more often in males than females, and affects young people more than older people. Like most personality disorders, narcissistic traits usually decrease in intensity with age, with many people experiencing few of the most extreme symptoms by the time they are in the 40s or 50s.

It is not uncommon for children, teens and highly successful individuals to display some traits similar to narcissistic personality disorder, but these are typically transient without meeting the full criteria for the diagnosis. Children and adolescents may have narcissistic tendency, but this may simply be a reflection of their age and doesn't mean that they'll go on to develop narcissistic personality disorder. True narcissistic symptoms are pervasive, apparent in various situations, and rigid, remaining consistent over time. To make the diagnosis, the symptoms must be severe enough that they significantly impair the individual's ability to develop meaningful relationships with others. The behavior typically begins in early adulthood, and generally impairs an individual's ability to function at work, in school, or in other important settings.

Narcissism may be “overt” or “grandiose”, characterized by arrogance, intense envy, and aggression. On the other hand, “covert" narcissists are characterized by their defensiveness, hypersensitivity, helplessness, emptiness, low self-esteem, and shame. They withdraw and avoid social situations if their expectations and need for approval are not met. There is a high rate of co-morbidity with other mental disorders, including depressive, histrionic, borderline, antisocial, and paranoid personality disorders. Narcissistic rage is a reaction to a perceived threat to one’s self-esteem or self-worth, and can range from mild irritation or annoyance, to serious outbursts, including violent attacks and murder, especially in the presence of other co-morbid personality disorders.

While narcissists are common, malignant narcissists are less common. A notable difference between the two is the feature of sadism, or the gratuitous enjoyment of the pain of others. A narcissist will deliberately damage other people to pursue his own selfish desires, but may show remorse for doing so, while a malignant narcissist will harm others and enjoy doing so, with no empathy or regret for the damage they have caused. Malignant narcissism is the most dangerous of any so-called ‘personality disorders’. It is a psychological syndrome comprising an extreme mix of narcissism, antisocial personality disorder, paranoia, aggression, and sadism. Other symptoms may include an absence of conscience, a psychological need for power, and a sense of importance or grandiosity. Some people believe that malignant narcissism should be considered part of a spectrum of pathological narcissism. It represents a less extreme form of pathological narcissism than psychopathy that is represented by one's ability to internalize his aggression, identify with powerful people, and depend on sadistic but reliable parental images. Malignant narcissists use whatever aggression is necessary to achieve their goals, and have no constraints of conscience. Some psychologists think of pathological narcissism as a spectrum: with psychopaths at the worst end, malignant narcissists in the middle and narcissistic personality disorder as the least severe. Individuals with narcissistic personality disorder, malignant narcissism, and psychopathy all display similar traits associated with impulsivity and aggression, Machiavellianism, persistent criminal behavior, and lack of empathy. Malignant narcissists are different from normal human beings in that they have no conscience, no remorse, no guilt, no ability to feel pity and no compassion for others. Malignant narcissism is highlighted as a key area in the study of mass murders, sexual murders, and serial murders.

The treatment of choice is long-term psychotherapy that can include cognitive behavioral therapy, family therapy, or group therapy. With cognitive behavioral therapy, the therapist helps the client identify negative and distorted thoughts, and become aware of harmful self-serving behavior so that they can be replaced with positive ones based in reality. Family and other group therapies involve encouraging a dialogue between the therapist, the patient, family members and other participants aimed at resolving past conflicts and further developing the client's level of self-awareness.

Therapy is often difficult as people with the disorder frequently do not consider themselves to have a problem. They generally have very positive self-image but poor insight. They fail to recognize that their perception and behavior are inappropriate and problematic. When people with narcissistic personality disorder enter treatment, it is typically because they seek relief from another disorder, such as major depressive disorder, substance use, bipolar disorder, or eating disorder. Hospitalization of patients with severe narcissistic personality may be indicated, but usually due to additional symptoms arising from a co-existing mental disorder.

No medications are indicated for treating narcissistic personality, but they may be used to treat co-occurring mental conditions or symptoms such as anxiety and depression. The newer antidepressant medications like *Prozac®* and others can exacerbate narcissistic personality behaviors and agitate symptoms. Because of this risk, therapists typically prescribe *monoamine oxidase inhibitors* (MAOIs) such as *tranylcypromine (Parnate), phenelzine (Nardil)* and *isocarboxazid (Marplan)* or mood stabilizers, such as *lithium,* for depression. These drugs do not appear to cause any noticeable exacerbation of the narcissistic personality disorder symptoms and behaviors.

-o0o-

FAMOUS PERSONS WITH NARCISSISTIC PERSONALITY DISORDER

It should not be surprising that narcissistic personality disorder is prevalent among the rich and famous. While many actors and entertainers excel in their profession and demonstrate empathy in the roles they play, there are also many celebrities who behave in ways suggesting a narcissistic personality disorder without necessarily coming from a dysfunctional family environment. Well-known individuals who display characteristics of narcissism, if not full-blown narcissistic personality disorder include politicians, celebrities, ministers and business leaders. Some of the more grandiose displays of self-importance come from America's favorite celebrities. While most celebrities pursue careers in acting and entertaining because they have a true love of performing and the arts, there are those who do it specifically as a means to an end, with the end being fame, money, and public adoration. Some successful and famous people acquire narcissistic thinking and behaviors only after they have worked hard to get to where they are, while those who are narcissistic from the beginning tend to seek out opportunities and fields that would satisfy their needs. Most of them show grandiose thinking and exaggerated self-importance, and believe that they need to be admired because they are special.

-o0o-

ALEC BALDWIN

Alexander Rae “Alec” Baldwin III, an American actor, writer, comedian and producer, is well known for his irritability and lack of impulse control. In 2007, he was caught on tape screaming at his then-11-year-old daughter’s voice mail that she was a “rude, thoughtless little pig.” He later admitted that he contemplated suicide over the voicemail that leaked to the public. When he appeared on “The View”, he laid out a chain of excuses as to why he left such a message, and while he apologized to "those who he may have offended", the self-absorbed actor had to be reminded about his daughter--who was the real victim in this sad episode. He also battled with an American Airlines employee who insisted that he power down his cell phone during a flight, and he was eventually removed from the plane. Over the years, Baldwin has engaged in numerous physical and verbal altercations with reporters and paparazzi. He recently launched a scathing attack on NBC - criticizing TV chiefs for giving extra help to other shows at the expense of his own TV comedy. Throwing a 5,000-word, seven-page pity party for himself in the entertainment media he says he abhors, he was mad that countless reporters and photographers dared to cover his little outbursts and violent confrontations over the years, because they ruined his “dreams of running for office at some point in the next five years.” He caused a major uproar in the Philippines when he made a joke that he was interested in buying a Filipina wife, for which he was effectively banned from visiting the Philippines. He said in a 2006 interview with The New York Times that if he did become involved in electoral politics, he would prefer to run for Governor of New York. When asked if he was qualified for the office, Baldwin responded that he considered himself more qualified than California Governor Arnold Schwarzenegger

-o0o-

JUSTIN BIEBER

Justin Drew Bieber is a Canadian singer and songwriter. Throughout his career, Bieber has sold an estimated 100 million records, making him the best-selling male Canadian artist and one of the world's best-selling music artists. He has earned three Grammy nominations (including one win), two Brit awards, four NRJ Music Award nominations (including three wins), thirteen Billboard Music Awards, and numerous fan voted accolades which include eight American Music Awards, twenty Teen Choice Awards and eighteen MTV Europe Music Awards. Aside from his career as a musician, Bieber has ventured into the worlds of business and philanthropy. He has become an angel investor for technology companies and has quietly invested millions of dollars in a dozen of small technology start-ups. In 2013, Bieber launched his online #GiveBackPhilippines campaign to help the victims of Typhoon Haiyan and traveled to Philippines after raising $3 Million. His work for the Philippines earned him a star on the Walk of Fame Philippines. The 19-year-old pop star has repeatedly engaged in reckless behavior with little consideration for those around him, and regularly pairs tank tops with gold chains. When he was arrested for driving under the influence and drag racing, along with resisting arrest, he displayed none of the panic someone his age might show. He signed the visitors' book at Anne Frank's house in Amsterdam with an expression of hope that she would have been a "belieber" if she'd been alive today. He was caught on camera squirting cleaning fluid and shouting expletives at a photograph of former president Bill Clinton. He urinated into a mop bucket used to clean restaurant floors, and got into a Twitter feud with the president of Mexico. He pleaded no contest to a charge of misdemeanor vandalism in his highly-publicized egg throwing barrage on a neighbor's home. Police claimed that they had video footage of him high-fiving friends after the eggs were thrown. With him pleading no contest to the charge, the Los Angeles County Superior Court sentenced him on July 9 to pay US$80,900 in restitution, serve two years' probation, complete twelve weeks of anger management, and do community service for 5 days. He was arrested in Florida on suspicion of DUI, driving with an over six month expired license, and resisting arrest without violence. Police said that he told authorities he had consumed alcohol, smoked marijuana, and taken prescription drugs. The case was settled with a plea bargain pleading guilty to resisting an officer without violence, and a lesser charge of driving without due care and attention. He paid a fine of US$500 and was sentenced to attend both a 12-hour anger management course, and a program that teaches about the impact of drunken driving on victims. As part of the plea bargain, he has made a US$50,000 contribution to Our Kids, a local children's charity. He was arrested and charged with assault and dangerous driving near his hometown after a collision between a minivan and Bieber's all-terrain vehicle. Ontario police said that he then "engaged in a physical altercation" with an occupant of the minivan. He was released shortly and his lawyer blamed the incident on "the unwelcome presence of paparazzi". When he performed in Beijing, people were unimpressed by him and his pictures being carried up the Great Wall on the shoulders of his body guards. As a millennial singer with a huge social media following, who has enough money to crash his Ferrari into a photographer, he is a convincing picture of what makes a person narcissistic.

-o0o-

SIMON COWELL

Simon Phillip Cowell is an English reality television judge and producer, entrepreneur, and philanthropist, most recognized as a judge on the British TV talent competition series Pop Idol, The X Factor, and Britain's Got Talent, and the American TV talent competition shows American Idol, The X Factor, and America's Got Talent. As a judge, Cowell often makes blunt and controversial comments, including insults and wisecracks about contestants and their singing abilities. He is unconcerned with the feelings of hurt and humiliation his derogatory comments provoke in the less talented contestants. The beneficial effect of his scathing criticism on the fate of the contestant is more of a rationalization for him to whom unfiltered commentary seems to be an end in itself, with lack of concern for the audience reaction. He has had an extraordinarily sustained ability to gauge and manipulate public taste. His fervent assertion that he is drawn to "crazy women" elevates the troupe of exes who tend to be flatterers, and to varying degrees financially dependent on him. Dinners at these ladies' favorite restaurants are granted on the proviso that "we'll speak about general matters for the first five minutes and the rest of the time we'll speak about me." One cannot say whether he is a sexual narcissist in the clinical sense, but he talked to some Swiss "scientists" about cryogenically freezing his corpse after death for later reanimation. He has uncontrollable erotic narcissism, claiming that he had fallen for himself. US socialite Lauren Silverman, with whom he has a son, has claimed that she once secretly witnessed the multi-millionaire TV personality giving himself a full 'X-Factor style judgment' of his own body in front of a full-length mirror. He would rub himself down in oil and declare out loud, that 'Simon has serious talent'. He would then tell his own backside that he was 'impressed' and that he was putting it through to 'booty camp'. She discovered that he was seeing himself behind her back, claims the TV producer took himself on secret luxury holidays, 'wined and dined himself' in top London restaurants, and regularly booked himself into single rooms in 5-star hotels for one-in-a-bed romps. He then cruelly ended his relationship with Silverman by telling her "it's not you, it's me".

-o0o-

PARIS HILTON

Paris Hilton is heir-apparent to the vast Hilton hotel and real estate dynasty. Her childhood was spent in palatial dwellings in the priciest neighborhoods on both coasts and featured a brief flirtation with the educational system. Living the glitzy socialite life from a relatively early age, attending exclusive parties, and being covered by the gossip press, she apparently became hooked on obtaining celebrity status. Her lifestyle and rumored short-lived relationships made her a feature of entertainment news and tabloid magazines. Critics and admirers have said that Hilton is famous for being famous, exemplifying the *"celebutante"* - a celebrity not through talent or work, but through inherited wealth and lifestyle. The blonde hotel heiress-turned-amateur porn star, reality TV personality, actress, author, designer, ubiquitous tabloid staple, and now singer, once spent the day prancing and posing in front of the camera while filming a music video for her new album entitled Paris. She is one celebrity socialite who has become famous for her narcissistic personality, notorious for craving the attention of the paparazzi. She is widely scorned for what some see as her narcissism, shallow intellect and materialism, but she seems to be aware of the old saying that there's no such thing as bad publicity. She lives in front of the camera; she has been arrested for DUI, and she appears to lack empathy. She did not acknowledge the danger she put herself and the public in by driving under the influence, nor did she apologize for it. While completing 200 hours of community work as part of her sentence for being caught in possession of cocaine, she showed her self-absorbed ways by claiming that she wanted to focus on helping others, especially the female prisoners that she served with. She was called out by Barbara Walters on "The View" when a clip of her reality TV show portrayed her complaining about her community service and everything from having to mingle with the prisoners to how painting city walls hurts her high heel-clad feet. She buys her own beauty products, she wears a shirt with her face on it, and she thinks the world revolves around her -- qualities that are consistent with a narcissistic personality disorder.

-o0o-

MADONNA

Madonna Louise Ciccone is an American singer, songwriter, actress, and businesswoman. She achieved popularity by pushing the boundaries of lyrical content in mainstream popular music and imagery in her music videos, which became a fixture on MTV.

Music critics have acclaimed her musical productions, which have generated some controversy. Having sold more than 300 million records worldwide, Madonna is recognized as the best-selling female recording artist of all time by Guinness World Records. Her mantra has always been "you can love her or loathe her, but you simply can't ignore her". She once said in an interview that she saw herself in her youth as a "lonely girl who was searching for something. I wasn't rebellious in a certain way. I cared about being good at something. I didn't shave my underarms and I didn't wear make-up like normal girls do. But I studied and I got good grades.... I wanted to be somebody." The anguish of losing her mother at a tender age left her with a certain kind of loneliness and an incredible longing for something. In middle school, she would perform cartwheels and handstands in the hallways between classes, dangle by her knees from the monkey bars during recess, and pull up her skirt during class—all so that the boys could see her underwear. She did not get to the top of her profession by being nice, or by having empathy, or by splashing her cash or even by having much talent. Instead she became a household name by being non-empathic, by using people, by loving and believing in herself above all others and, definitely, because she believed she deserved to be famous. She likes to shock and drum up publicity anyway she can by doing provocative performances, and the sexual imagery that she has always used, has been a tool that benefited her career and catalyzed public discourse on sexuality and feminism. Psychoanalysts maintain that a Madonna–whore complex is the inability to maintain sexual arousal within a committed, loving relationship. She categorizes men as a potential provider, someone to take care of her, or someone to achieve intimacy with. People who have worked for her remember her number one rule: that is, you must always praise her and you can never ever contradict her. At a time in the 80s when it wasn't popular to talk about HIV/AIDS, she stuck her neck out and showed fierce compassion and advocacy. The fact that she didn't become a drug addict helped her stay alive and maintain her enduring success. She has stayed on top for three decades, and was named the top-earning celebrity of 2013. She claims she used Kabbalah fluid (a mystical sect of Judaism) to remove radiation from a Ukrainian lake.

-o0o-

RYAN O'NEAL

Charles Patrick Ryan O'Neal, known professionally as Ryan O'Neal, is an American actor and former boxer. O'Neal trained as an amateur boxer before beginning his career in acting in 1960. In 1964, he landed the role of Rodney Harrington on the ABC nighttime soap opera "Peyton Place". The series was an instant hit and boosted his career. He later found success in films, most notably "Love Story", for which he received Academy Award and Golden Globe nominations as Best Actor. He was described as being very cocky, self-confident, very masculine and gorgeous, and he had every beautiful girl in the world going out with him. For the latter part of his life, although he was never actually married to Farrah Fawcett, he became well-known because of his relationship with her.

In her memoir, Tatum O'Neal, the youngest-ever Academy Award winner, described her father's constant emotional and physical abuse, fueled by his drug use. His daughter walked in on him having sex with her best friend. He confessed to unwittingly "hitting on" estranged daughter Tatum O'Neal at Farrah Fawcett's funeral. An admitted drug user, Ryan has denied stabbing his son with a fireplace poker that same night, but confirmed that he fired a gun at him. His estranged son, also a former addict, claimed his father gave him cocaine at the age of 11, and blasted his "narcissistic" attitude, saying that the "Love Story" star used his own 2001 battle with leukemia to divert attention away from Farrah Fawcett's illness, and only stayed with her to ensure that he would be included in her will. Not only did his ego demand that the public recognize him as the love of Farrah's life, he also needed everyone to know that it was this same intense love that ultimately killed her. His grandiose sense of self would not allow him to play a supporting role in Farrah's cancer fight. A few months after Farrah began her chemotherapy, he became increasingly jealous and resented the 'Charlie's Angels' star for having the terminal illness, and at times, even angry at the outpouring of love and sympathy that she received from all over the world -- not to mention his own children. He was often absent or causing havoc during her illness, resulting in two well-documented arrests and even a restraining order for sexual harassment filed against him by a 20-year old girl who claimed to be "a friend of the family". He blamed his children for Farrah's death and blamed Farrah for the death of his relationship with his children

-o0o-

OPRAH WINFREY

Oprah Gail Winfrey is an American media proprietor, talk show host, actress, producer, and philanthropist. She is best known for her talk show "The Oprah Winfrey Show", which was the highest-rated television program of its kind in history. She has been ranked the richest African-American, the greatest black philanthropist in American history and, currently, North America's first and only multi-billionaire black person. She was born into poverty to a teenage single mother and was later raised in an inner-city neighborhood. She has stated that her cousin, uncle, and a family friend started molesting her when she was nine years old, something she first announced to her viewers on a 1986 episode of her TV show regarding sexual abuse. She now justifies the adoration and exalted mirror image on her altar of self-worship. She is credited with creating a more intimate confessional form of media communication. She is thought to have popularized and revolutionized the tabloid talk show genre which broke 20th century taboos and allowed LGBT people to enter the mainstream. She says that during high school, her poverty was constantly rubbed in her face as she rode the bus to school with fellow African-Americans, some of whom were servants of her classmates' families. She began to steal money from her mother in an effort to keep up with her free-spending peers, to lie to and argue with her mother, and to go out with older boys. She has reinvented her show with a focus on literature, self-improvement, and spirituality. Her image has appeared on every cover of her monthly magazine since it was founded eight years ago. She gives thanks for "the life that I have created." Her giving is always a public production, ultimately about herself and the "good" she is doing. To her, spirituality is not God-centered, but self-centered. She says that spirituality "is about paying attention to your life". She was quoted as saying that she has a church with herself, that the God force lives inside all of us, and once you tap into that, you can do anything. She seems to believe that the public would want to hear about all aspects of her life. She is now devoting entire programs to showing her audience the products she likes to buy. She completely understands how her influence works, and that her power to persuade in a very specific and targeted manner implies that she should be paid attention to. When anyone performs on her stage – a disproportionate number of camera shots during the performance are of her. The power of her opinions and endorsement to influence public opinion, especially consumer purchasing choices, has been dubbed "The Oprah Effect". She has used the power of the media and her personality to change the conversation from one dealing with facts, to one dealing with unsubstantiated "cover-ups" and Hollywood personalities. She will be remembered as an innovator through the landmarks she made, becoming the first female African American to host a television show, and as an icon who paved the way for others to become successful.

-o0o-

INFAMOUS PERSONS WITH MALIGNANT NARCISSISTIC DISORDER

Many dictators and serial killers had or have malignant narcissistic personalities. Many people suffered and many lives were lost from their unfair governance and quest for power. To them, it is all about control. They typically believe that they deserve special recognition for their superior talent or intelligence, giving them the right to exploit, demean, use and control others. They are obsessed with power and authority. They are confident, assertive, and driven to achieve, but they could not empathize nor care about who they hurt. They become more destructive as they gain power simply because they believe that they can get away with it, and that moral rules do not really apply to them. They are sadists who could care less about the collateral damage that they cause out of their single-minded pursuit of their personal goals. Many people throughout history who have or had this type of personality disorder were responsible for unfortunate events that caused irreparable damage to others.

-o0o-

ADOLF HITLER

Adolf Hitler was a German politician, leader of the Nazi Party, Chancellor of Germany, Führer ("Leader") of Nazi Germany, and dictator of the German Reich who initiated World War II in Europe and was central to the ill-fated Holocaust. He frequently denounced international capitalism and communism as being part of a Jewish conspiracy. Under his leadership and racially motivated ideology, the Nazi regime was responsible for the genocide of at least 5.5 million Jews and millions of other victims whom he and his followers deemed "sub-humans" and socially undesirable. He and the Nazi regime were also responsible for the killing of an estimated 19.3 million civilians and prisoners of war. In addition, 29 million soldiers and civilians died as a result of military action in the European Theatre of World War II. He was self- centered, preoccupied with power, control, prestige, and grandiose thinking. Hitler, one of the most infamous men in history, is a prime example of this narcissistic personality disorder. He has often been associated with mental disorders such as hysteria, megalomania or paranoid schizophrenia. He implemented his political goals as a strong dictator, with assertiveness, high readiness to assume risk and unlimited power. He claimed that he was chosen by fate to liberate the German people from their supposedly most dangerous threat -- the Jews. It was argued that he was suffering from hallucinations, hearing voices, paranoia and megalomania. Aside from hysteria, he also demonstrated hypersensitivity, panic attacks, irrational jealousy, omnipotence fantasies, delusions of grandeur, belief in a messianic mission, and extreme paranoia. His alleged psychotic symptoms and paranoid temper tantrums have repeatedly been attributed to possible organic causes, including advanced syphilis and poisoning injury suffered during World War I. Because of the inhumanity of his crimes, he was early on linked with "psychopathy", a severe personality disorder whose main symptoms are a great or complete lack of empathy, social responsibility and conscience. He was described as an immature, self-centered dreamer who did not overcome his childish narcissism. His lust-ridden destructiveness was brought on by the family setting in which he grew up, dominated by the humiliating and degrading treatment and beating that he received from his tyrannical, often brutal father who, as he believed, was of Jewish origin. His mother, whose first three children died at an early age, was barely capable of fostering a warm relationship with her son. It was also pointed out that his mother's sister who lived with the family throughout his entire childhood, possibly suffered from a mental disorder. His family background, his childhood and youth and his behavior as an adult, as a politician and ruler, gave many clues that he had symptoms of a narcissistic personality disorder and of a borderline personality disorder. He was also credited with post-traumatic stress disorder, not only from war trauma but from chronic childhood trauma due to physical and mental abuse by his tyrannical and brutal father, and the parental failure of his depressed mother. His childhood fantasy of becoming European emperor impelled him to start the Second World War in Europe. His convictions on wars of annihilation as the natural order and the Jews as violators of that order resulted in his successive campaigns of mass murder. Because he regularly consumed methamphetamine, barbiturates, amphetamine, opiates and cocaine, his irrational behavior also can be attributed to his excessive drug use.

-o0o-

SADDAM HUSSEIN

While Saddam Hussein, President of Iraq from 1979 to 2003, had been characterized as “the madman of the Middle East”, his psychology can be described in terms of the syndrome of malignant narcissism. He suppressed several movements that sought to overthrow his government or gain independence, and he maintained power during the Iran–Iraq War and the Gulf War. Whereas some in the Arab world lauded Saddam for his opposition to the United States and for attacking Israel—he was widely condemned for the brutality of his dictatorship. He exhibited extreme grandiosity, overconfidence, and self-absorption to a degree that rendered him incapable of empathizing with his adversaries, and insensitive to the pain and suffering of the Iraqi people. He was overly optimistic about his own chances of success. Born to a poor peasant family, his mother rejected him since birth due to her depression. His mother remarried a distant relative when he was 3, and his stepfather continuously abused him, both psychologically and physically until he fled home at the age of 10 to live with his uncle, who became not only his father figure but his political mentor as well. His uncle shaped his world view, ingraining him with a hatred of foreigners. As a leading member of the revolutionary Ba'ath Party, which espoused secular pan-Arabism, economic modernization, and Arab socialism, he played a key role in the 1968 coup that brought his party to long-term power. As president, Saddam maintained power during the Iran–Iraq War from 1980 through 1988, and throughout the Persian Gulf War of 1991. It was not by accident that he had survived for more than two decades as his nation's preeminent leader. While he was driven by dreams of glory, and his political perspective was narrow and distorted, he was a shrewd and patient strategist. His pursuit of power for himself and Iraq was boundless. He genuinely saw himself as one of the great leaders of history. He was a ruthless political calculator who would go to whatever lengths are necessary to achieve his goals. He ruthlessly eliminated any perceived threat to his power and considered criticism as a form of disloyalty. In pursuit of his messianic dreams, there is no evidence that he was restrained by his conscience. His only loyalty is to Saddam Hussein. He used weapons of mass destruction to demonstrate that his army was part of an ongoing race for prestige and authority. For a person with tremendous insecurities, these weapons offered security that could not be matched by any other. He wanted to be seen as a respected world leader, and it was much more of an incentive for him to work with the UN, than for U.S. to do it alone. His unconstrained aggression is instrumental in pursuing his goals, but it is at the same time a defensive aggression, with his grandiose façade masking his underlying insecurity. In 2003, the U.S. and its allies invaded Iraq, eventually deposing him. He was brought to trial under the Iraqi interim government set up by U.S.-led forces, and was sentenced to death by hanging. Saddam was executed in 2006.

-o0o-

JIM JONES

Jim Jones, whose real name was James Warren, was the manipulative and arrogant founder and leader of the People's Temple of the Disciples of Christ, a religious movement which grew rapidly, expanding across the United States with up to 5000 members by the early 1970s. His early separation from his mother may have caused Jim to seek the affirmation of his peers rather than that of his parents. The pain of being alone, of being the outcast, tore him into pieces whether he was visiting his friends or whether he was in school or church. In high school, he was ranked one of the best public speakers who frequently dominated class discussions. For that, he demanded that he be recognized as an intellectual. He once threatened to shoot his best friend who wanted to go home after having dinner with him. In 1956, he began "The People's Temple" and attracted a mixed congregation of African Americans and whites. His feelings of grandiosity and fantasies of power gradually escalated; he denounced the Bible and suggested to his congregation that he was their friend, father, savior, and God. Because of his charm and his talents for preaching, many in the group did not challenge him on his arrogant behavior. He was charismatic, friendly, supportive, and seemed to have "divine" powers to heal the body and soul. He impressed high profile politicians with what he had done with his Peoples Temple, and saw himself as influential and powerful beyond his small group. In 1975, he and a group from the People's Temple flew to Guyana, a town in South Africa, a town that would later be dubbed Jonestown to serve as their Utopia. Believing that he was beyond reproach, he raped women in his group and abused drugs and alcohol, while simultaneously telling his congregation that these things were wrong. He manipulated his followers from the very beginning by convincing them to turn their money and property over to the Temple, demanding of loyalty, and leading rehearsals for the group's mass suicide. The truth became more apparent with beatings, theft, paranoia, drug use, rape, emotional abuse, and virtual imprisonment in his Peoples Temple in Jonestown. The strange behavior of his members later attracted negative attention among journalists, and questions that were raised about misuse and abuse of his position in the group drove him to become even more paranoid about the threat of people leaving. Believing that others were envious of his success, he became hyper-vigilant with the media, outside groups, and government agencies. When U.S. Congressman Leo Ryan went to investigate the People's Temple in Guyana, he found a handful of people who wanted to escape. He offered to take them back to California with him and away from the Jonestown compound. Fearing that the Congressman would pull the group apart, he ordered the shootings at the Guyana airstrip. Not only did he attack those he blamed for the "trouble" and "threats" to his group, but his narcissistic madness drove him to force those in the group to take poison and kill themselves as an act of "revolutionary suicide". He ordered the mass-suicide of around 1000 people which took place at one of their sites known as Jonestown located in Guyana. He died from self-inflicted gunshot wound to his head.

-o0o-

Joy Bruce, M.D.

JOSEF MENGELE

Josef Mengele is a former SS officer in Germany, known as the 'Angel of Death'—the heartless and merciless Nazi doctor who tortured and killed thousands of children in atrocious and involuntary medical experiments at Auschwitz during WWII. He was known for his grandiose ideas, irrational thinking and especially his sadistic exploitation of people. Mengele was suspected to have Narcissistic Personality Disorder because of the immoral acts he committed during the time of Adolph Hitler, seeking more power by killing innocent Jewish children and adults, and deciding who would live or die by detaining them into pressure chambers. He once injected chemicals into children's eyeballs in an attempt to change their color. One goal of his experimentations was to learn to create blond-haired, blue-eyed babies in multiple numbers to increase the German population. He was also hugely fascinated by twins and once sewed Gypsy children together to create Siamese twins. He proceeded to inject chloroform into their hearts, killing them instantly. He then began dissecting and meticulously examining each and every piece of their bodies. His twin research was in part intended to prove the supremacy of heredity over environment and thus bolster the Nazi premise of the superiority of the Aryan race. It was said that his killings and other actions may have been for personal gratification. He was accused of having actively and decisively taken part in selections of prisoners who, through hunger, deprivation, exhaustion, sickness, disease or other reasons, were unfit for work in the camp, or those who had contagious or unsightly illnesses. Those selected were killed either through injections or firing squads or by painful suffocation to death in the gas chambers. He sometimes did the killings himself, without showing any empathy. Yet, he would also treat some prisoners, to emphasize his power over life and death. When a mother fought being separated from her daughter, he shot them both, and then ordered everyone in the transport, including those who had already been selected for work, to the gas chambers. He acknowledged that the Nazi experiment on race had failed but drastic measures still had to be taken to combat what he perceived as the planet's "overpopulation". He was described as sadistic, lacking empathy, showing no remorse, believing the Jews should be eliminated entirely as an inferior and dangerous race. His detachment was described as bordering on the schizoid, narcissism and sadism. Following the war, he suffered from severe depressions, to the point of contemplating suicide. He later fled to South America where he died from drowning while swimming off the Brazilian coast at the age of 67.

-o0o-

JOSEPH STALIN

Joseph Stalin, was secretary-general of the Communist Party of the Soviet Union and premier of the Soviet state who, for a quarter of a century, dictatorially ruled the Soviet Union and transformed it into a major world power. He faced various health issues during his childhood, including smallpox, a deformed arm, and an extremely dysfunctional family. He had a basic inferiority complex, and any sort of criticism became a threat to him. Some historians believed that, as a means of escaping his abusive father, he developed a lust for power borne out of his childhood fantasies about what he would have done if he were in charge of the country. Just before his death, Vladimir Lenin, then Head of the Russian Republic, wrote a testament denouncing Stalin and tried to warn the other Soviet leaders about his ambitions. Yet, Stalin managed to blunt the effect of the testament and still seized power after Lenin's death. He was so preoccupied with having power, control, prestige and vanity that he eliminated political opposition, including Leon Trotsky, once Lenin's heir apparent, whom he felt was a threat. He did not wish to share a historic legacy with anyone, so he ordered the creation of revisionist history that wiped out all mention of Leon Trotsky and actually removed him from existing photographs. He became the chief architect of Soviet totalitarianism; he exercised great political power, industrialized the Union of Soviet Socialist Republics, consolidated his position by intensive police terror, helped to defeat Germany, and extended Soviet controls to include a belt of eastern

European states. He used his communist rhetoric to gain control over Russia, and eventually over the entire Eastern Europe. He considered his switching political and personal alliances, allegiances, mass indoctrination, staged show trials, forced confessions as well as torture and murder of unprecedented proportions as means to his end, which was absolute control. As Secretary General, he launched a campaign of political terror against the very Communist Party members who had brought him to power. He not only "liquidated" veteran semi-independent Bolsheviks but also many party bosses, military leaders, industrial managers, and high government officials totally subservient to himself. His repressive measures resulted in censorship of the arts, literature and cinema, forced exiles of hundreds of thousands and the executions of intellectuals and other potential "enemies of the state". He viewed the human race as instruments with which to accomplish his goals or as obstacles to be eliminated. Among his most heinous crimes was the forced, intentional famine within the Ukraine, meant to force the destruction of the land-owning "kulak" farmers. In a series of paranoid fits of rage, he jailed, tortured and eventually killed his own wife, some of his lifelong friends, colleagues and military leaders. He justified these acts by saying that these people had or were going to betray him and that his actions were taken to protect the state and the revolution, The estimated number of executed political opponents and victims of the famine reached a figure in the order of forty to fifty million men, women and children. It was said that whenever he entered the Soviet Politburo, people would applaud him, sometimes for hours, because everybody was afraid to be the first one to stop. Achieving wide visual promotion through busts, statues, and icons of himself, the dictator became the object of a fanatical cult. Following his death, most of his statues were torn down, and streets and towns named for him were re-named.

-o0o-

REFERENCES

http://archive.azcentral.com/ent/celeb/articles/2009/08/05/20090805ryan-oneal.html
http://askthepsych.com/atp/2007/09/13/narcissism-and-success/
http://blogs.bu.edu/guidedhistory/russia-and-its-empires/rachael-allen/
http://blogcritics.org/culture/article/study-finds-celebrties-to-be-narcissistic
http://blogcritics.org/study-finds-celebrities-to-be-narcissistic/
https://blogs.psychcentral.com/celebrity/2014/07/justin-bieber-is-it-biological/
https://celebsonfire.wordpress.com/2007/07/14/paris-has-narcissistic-personality-disorder/
http://celebnmusic247.com/justin-bieber-release-narsasitic-video/
http://crimefeed.com/2015/06/ted-bundy-grew-thinking-mother-sister-dark-revelations-killers-family/
http://en.citizendium.org/wiki/Josef_Mengele
https://depressionintrospection.wordpress.com/2007/03/04/madonnas-mentally-ill-a-closer-look-at-narcissists/
https://disorderedworld.com/2013/04/01/hitler/
http://emedicine.medscape.com/article/1519417-overview
https://en.wikipedia.org/wiki/Adolf_Hitler
https://en.wikipedia.org/wiki/Alec_Baldwin
https://en.wikipedia.org/wiki/Jim_Jones
https://en.wikipedia.org/wiki/Josef_Mengele
https://en.wikipedia.org/wiki/Joseph_Stalin
https://en.wikipedia.org/wiki/Madonna%E2%80%93whore_complex
https://en.wikipedia.org/wiki/Madonna_%28entertainer%29
https://en.wikipedia.org/wiki/Malignant_narcissism
https://en.wikipedia.org/wiki/Narcissistic_personality_disorder
https://en.wikipedia.org/wiki/Paris_Hilton
https://en.wikipedia.org/wiki/Saddam_Hussein
https://en.wikipedia.org/wiki/Psychopathography_of_Adolf_Hitler
https://en.wikipedia.org/wiki/Ryan_O%27Neal
https://en.wikipedia.org/wiki/Simon_Cowell
https://en.wikipedia.org/wiki/Ted_Bundy
http://flowpsychology.com/ted-bundy-psychological-profile/
http://healthresearchfunding.org/famous-people-narcissistic-personality-disorder/
http://hubpages.com/health/ladygagaandmadonnaandnarcissisticpersonalitydisorder
http://jonestown.sdsu.edu/?page_id=29416
http://jonestown.sdsu.edu/?page_id=40230
https://medlineplus.gov/ency/article/000934.htm
http://narcissisticpersonalitydisorder.org/
http://nypost.com/2014/02/25/alec-baldwin-drama-queen/
https://psychcentral.com/disorders/narcissistic-personality-disorder-symptoms/
https://psychcentral.com/disorders/narcissistic-personality-disorder-treatment/

https://psychcentral.com/blog/archives/2009/06/03/oprah-and-the-power-to-persuade/
https://psychopathyawareness.wordpress.com/category/a-quest-for-power-the-cases-of-hitler-and-stalin/
https://psychopathyawareness.wordpress.com/category/stalin/
http://rffm.typepad.com/republicans_for_fair_medi/2007/04/alec-baldwin-on.html
http://sackwinkie.blogspot.com/2007/05/psychological-profile-of-saddam-hussein.html
http://shelleysargent.blogspot.com/p/antisocial-personality-disorder-ted.html
https://techfeatured.com/1771/ted-bundy-the-boy-next-door
http://thebibliophileblog.blogspot.com/2015/12/jim-jones-life-and-death-of-narcissist-part-two.html
http://thenarcissisticlife.com/famous-people-with-narcissism/
http://thenarcissisticlife.com/malignant-narcissism/
http://twistedminds.creativescapism.com/most-notorious/ted-bundy/
http://www.addictionhope.com/mood-disorder/narcissistic-personality
http://www.arabnews.com/node/226646
http://www.americanthinker.com/articles/2008/09/obama_oprah_and_the_guru_malig_1.html
http://www.au.af.mil/au/awc/awcgate/iraq/saddam_post.htm
http://www.auschwitz.dk/Mengele.htm
http://www.biography.com/people/jim-jones-10367607#murder-and-mass-suicide-
http://www.biography.com/people/oprah-winfrey-9534419#related-video-gallery
https://www.bpdcentral.com/narcissistic-disorder/hallmarks-of-npd/
https://www.britannica.com/biography/Joseph-Stalin
http://www.celebritytypes.com/blog/2011/05/why-simon-cowell-is-istp/
http://www.contactmusic.net/alec-baldwin/news/earl-creator-hits-back-at-narcissist-baldwin_1079531
https://www.crimetraveller.org/2015/07/pathological-narcissism-cult-leader/
http://www.dailymail.co.uk/tvshowbiz/article-2503812/Ryan-ONeal-18-year-relationship-Farrah-Fawcett.html
http://www.decision-making-confidence.com/malignant-narcissism.html
http://www.feelguide.com/2011/06/05/barbara-walters-destroys-narcissist-paris-hilton-on-air-screamfest-with-producers-ensues-backstage/
http://www.foxnews.com/health/2013/11/18/inside-mind-alec-baldwin.html
http://www.halcyon.com/jmashmun/npd/dsm-iv.html
http://www.healthline.com/health/narcissistic-personality-disorder#Coping7
http://www.healthyplace.com/personality-disorders/narcissistic-personality-disorder/what-is-narcissistic-personality-disorder/
http://www.healthyplace.com/personality-disorders/narcissistic-personality-disorder/narcissistic-personality-disorder-treatment/
http://www.healthyplace.com/personality-disorders/narcissistic-personality-disorder/famous-people-with-narcissistic-personality-disorder/
http://history1900s.about.com/od/auschwitz/a/mengeletwins.htm
http://www.huffingtonpost.com/peggy-drexler/-hes-justin-bieber-or-so_b_4662142.html

http://www.icsahome.com/articles/the-violence-of-jim-jones-a-biopsychosocial-explanation
http://www.imdb.com/name/nm0641939/
http://www.imdb.com/name/nm0001856/bio
http://www.imdb.com/name/nm0385296/bio
http://www.imdb.com/name/nm0000285/bio?ref_=nm_ov_bio_sm
http://www.imdb.com/name/nm0821672/bio
https://www.jewishvirtuallibrary.org/josef-mengele
http://www.markedbyteachers.com/as-and-a-level/sociology/ted-bundy-1.html
http://www.mayoclinic.org/diseases-conditions/narcissistic-personality-disorder/basics/definition/CON-20025568
http://www.medicalnewstoday.com/articles/9741.php
http://www.medicinenet.com/narcissistic_personality_disorder/page5.htm
http://www.medicinenet.com/narcissistic_personality_disorder/page2.htm#what_are_causes_and_risk_factors_for_narcissistic_personality_disorder
http://www.mengele.dk/
http://www.mirror.co.uk/news/uk-news/secret-diaries-of-nazi-doctor-josef-144698
http://www.ncbi.nlm.nih.gov/pubmed/18557663
http://www.newsbiscuit.com/2013/08/03/simon-cowell-admits-to-life-long-affair-with-himself/
http://www.newser.com/story/66048/my-dad-constantly-cheated-on-farrah-griffin-oneal.html
http://www.nlm.nih.gov/medlineplus/ency/article/000934.htm
http://www.nydailynews.com/entertainment/gossip/drugs-guns-punch-ups-family-ryan-o-neal-article-1.395909
https://www.oboolo.com/social-studies/psychology/case-study/anti-social-personality-disorder-case-ted-bundy-85012.html
http://www.psychforums.com/narcissistic-personality/topic151507.html
https://www.psychologytoday.com/blog/addiction-in-society/201105/worst-person-in-the-world
https://www.psychologytoday.com/blog/the-athletes-way/201309/the-neuroscience-madonnas-enduring-success
http://www.psychologytoday.com/blog/homo-consumericus/200906/the-narcissism-and-grandiosity-celebrities
https://www.psychologytoday.com/blog/evil-deeds/201412/how-mad-was-hitler
https://www.psychologytoday.com/conditions/narcissistic-personality-disorder
https://www.psychologytoday.com/blog/nurturing-resilience/201310/justin-bieber-little-emperors-and-narcissistic-children
https://www.psychologytoday.com/blog/shadow-boxing/201208/imagining-ted-bundy
http://www.psychopathsguide.com/entry53.html
http://www.salon.com/2009/05/15/oprah_winfrey_health/
http://www.teevee.org/1998/03/narcissistic-talk-show-hosts-next-time-on-oprah.html
https://www.theguardian.com/books/2012/apr/26/sweet-revenge-simon-cowell-review

http://www.themortonreport.com/celebrity/hollywood/exclusive-the-disturbing-truth-about-ryan-oneal-tatum-and-farrah-fawcetts-final-years/

http://www.therichest.com/expensive-lifestyle/9-of-the-most-narcissistic-celebrities/

http://www.tmz.com/person/paris-hilton/

http://uspp.csbsju.edu/Research/Saddam%20profile.html

https://www.verywell.com/what-is-narcissistic-personality-disorder-2795446

http://www.webmd.com/mental-health/narcissistic-personality-disorder#1

http://www.wisegeekhealth.com/what-is-malignant-narcissism.htm#didyouknowout

https://www.yahoo.com/news/why-justin-bieber-perfect-narcissist-141200865.html?ref=gs

FURTHER READING

American Psychiatric Association. (2013). *Diagnostic and statistical manual of mental disorders (DSM-5®)*. American Psychiatric Pub.

Berger, F.K. (2016). Narcissistic personality disorder. *MedlinePlus Medical Encyclopedia*. U.S. National Library of Medicine. Retrieved from https://medlineplus.gov/ency/article/000934.htm

Breedlove, S.M. (2015). *Principles of psychology*. Cary, NC: Oxford University Press.

Caligor, E., Levy, K.N., &Yeomans, F.E. (2015). Narcissistic personality disorder: Diagnostic and clinical challenges. *Am J Psychiatry, 172*(5), 415–422.

-o0o-

ANTISOCIAL PERSONALITY DISORDER

It is sometimes difficult to distinguish between narcissistic personality disorder and antisocial personality disorder. They are often found to co-occur. Both belong to Cluster B personality disorder, which is characterized by highly dramatic, overly emotional thoughts and behaviors. Like other types of personality disorder, antisocial personality disorder is part of a spectrum, which means it can range in severity from occasional bad behavior to repeatedly breaking the law and committing serious crimes. Personality disorders come in many forms, but few, if any, are as deleterious as the antisocial personality disorder. Because people with antisocial personality disorder often break the law, a lot of criminals are found to have the disorder.

-o0o-

Antisocial Personality Disorder and Borderline Personality Disorder are very different from each other, but they are similar in certain ways. Someone has to be at least 18 years old to be diagnosed with Antisocial Personality Disorder or with Borderline Personality Disorder. Because they are both Cluster B personality disorders, people with Borderline Personality Disorder and Antisocial Personality Disorder commonly display impulsive and manipulative behaviors. They both have a tendency to lie and be irritable and aggressive. Treatment strategies for both disorders are also similar. For example, neither one has a medication that specifically treats the personality disorder. The severity of both disorders will also decrease as the sufferer becomes older.

On the other hand, the differences between the two disorders are many. First, their relationships with others are different. People with Antisocial Personality Disorder are more likely to direct their aggression toward others, whereas with Borderline Personality Disorder, this aggression is more self-directed and self-damaging. People with borderline personality also combat depression more often than people with Antisocial Personality Disorder. They are terrified of being abandoned and will take drastic steps to avoid this. They also have an unstable sense of themselves, and, likewise, their relationships and emotions are unstable. In contrast, people with antisocial personality disorder show no remorse for hurting others, have difficulty maintaining close relationships, and will deceive in order to gain profit or some other pleasure. Suicidal or self-mutilating behavior is present among those who suffer from borderline personality disorder, but is typically not a symptom of antisocial personality disorder. Borderline personality disorder tends to affect women more than men, while antisocial personality disorder affects more men than women.

Antisocial personality disorder, sometimes called sociopathic, is a mental condition in which a person consistently shows no regard for right or wrong, and violates the rights and feelings of others. It is a particularly challenging type of personality disorder, characterized by impulsive, irresponsible and often criminal behavior. It is characterized by a pervasive pattern of disregarding morals and social norms, violating the rights of others, breaking laws, and starting fights with no regard for one’s own safety or the safety of others. They are often aggressive and hostile, display an uncontrollable temper, and can lash out violently when provoked. Criminal behavior is a key feature of antisocial personality disorder, and there's a high risk that someone with the disorder will commit crimes and be imprisoned at some point in his or her life. Attachments and emotional bonds are weak, and interpersonal relationships often revolve around the manipulation, exploitation and abuse of others. A core component of antisocial personality disorder is a need to actively look after oneself because of the belief that no one else will do so.

Persons with antisocial personality are often impulsive and reckless, failing to consider or disregarding the consequences of their actions. They can be witty, charming, and fun to be around -- but they also lie and exploit others. They may repeatedly disregard and jeopardize their own safety and the safety of others, and place themselves and others in danger. They are deceptive, impulsive, easily frustrated or aggravated, and may become antagonistic or violent. They disregard the rights and feelings of others, and they take advantage of others for material gain or personal enjoyment, without any feeling of guilt or regret. They see others as weak or vulnerable and often take advantage of this perceived weakness. Serious problems with interpersonal relationships are often seen in those with the disorder. While they generally have no problems in establishing relationships, they may have difficulties in sustaining and maintaining them. They often violate the law and become criminals, justifying their actions by blaming others for things that have gone wrong. Symptoms tend to peak during the late teenage years and early 20s. Many people with antisocial personality disorder experience a decrease in their symptoms by the time they are 50 years old.

Antisocial personality disorder is much more common in men, among those who are in prison, and those who are likely to be alcoholic, have drug-related problems, and be promiscuous or sexually deviant. As with other personality and mental disorders, antisocial personality disorder tends to be the result of a combination of biologic, genetic and environmental factors. Some individuals may be more vulnerable to developing the disorder as a result of their particular genetic background, which is thought to be a factor only when the person is also exposed to adverse life events. While a diagnosis of antisocial personality disorder is rare in people who have no criminal history, not everyone convicted of a criminal offense would meet the criteria for antisocial personality disorder. In the same manner, only 47% of people meeting the criteria for antisocial personality disorder had significant arrest records. A history of aggression, unemployment and promiscuity are more common than serious crimes among people with antisocial personality disorder, suggesting that the relationship between antisocial personality disorder and crime is not that straightforward.

A history of childhood physical, sexual, or emotional abuse; neglect, deprivation, or abandonment; associating with peers who engage in antisocial behavior; or having a parent who is either antisocial or alcoholic are factors that increase the risk of developing antisocial personality disorder. Parental conflict or divorce, and harsh, inconsistent parenting are common, so that social services sometimes become involved with the child's care. It may be associated with co-morbid conditions such as bipolar disorder, borderline personality disorder, narcissistic disorders, substance-related disorders, attention-deficit hyperactivity disorder (ADHD), and reading disorders. People who experience a temporary or permanent brain dysfunction, often called organic brain damage, are also at risk for developing violent or otherwise criminal behaviors. While it has been shown that lower levels of serotonin may be associated with antisocial personality disorder, there has also been evidence that decreased serotonin function is highly correlated with impulsiveness and aggression. Some studies have found a relationship between monoamine oxidase A and antisocial behavior, including conduct disorder and symptoms of adult antisocial personality disorder in maltreated children.

Personality disorders such as antisocial personality disorder are typically diagnosed by a trained mental health professional, such as a psychologist or psychiatrist. Family physicians and general practitioners are generally not trained or well equipped to make this type of psychological diagnosis. Antisocial personality disorder is diagnosed when a person's pattern of antisocial behavior has occurred since age 15 (although only adults 18 years or older can be diagnosed with this disorder). To be diagnosed with antisocial personality disorder, a person must have had emotional and behavioral problems (conduct disorder) during childhood.

Childhood conduct disorder is characterized by a repetitive and persistent pattern of behavior in which the basic rights of others are violated. Children with the disorder are often impulsive, callous and deceitful. They may engage in petty crimes such as stealing, getting into fights with other children and adults, tormenting and torturing animals, bullying and intimidating others, setting fires or vandalizing the property of others, even at an early age. When symptoms manifest before the age of 10 years (childhood onset type), the conduct disorder is often linked to more pervasive behaviors, symptoms of attention deficit hyperactivity disorder (ADHD), more academic problems, increased family dysfunction, and higher likelihood of aggression and violence. Conduct disorder that develops after the age of 10 (adolescent-onset type) is characterized by less severe impairment of cognitive, social and emotional functions, and may resolve or diminish during adulthood.

Psychopathy and sociopathy are different cultural labels applied to the diagnosis of antisocial personality disorder. Although not a formal diagnosis, psychopathy is thought to be a more severe form of antisocial personality disorder. Both psychopaths and sociopaths present risks to society, because they will often try and live a normal life while coping with their disorder. But psychopaths are likely to be more dangerous, because they experience a lot less guilt connected to their actions. In addition to their antisocial behavior, psychopaths do not feel any remorse, tend to be highly suspicious or paranoid, interpret all aggression toward them, justified or not, as being arbitrary and unfair. They show a severe lack of caring for others, a lack of emotion, overconfidence, selfishness and a higher propensity for aggression compared to other people with antisocial personality disorder. While more than 50% of incarcerated individuals have been found to have antisocial personality disorder, only a small percent of those convicted criminals have been shown to have the more severe antisocial personality disorder type of psychopathy. Psychopaths tend to be much more suspicious or paranoid compared to people with antisocial personality disorder. They are arrogant, think lowly and negatively of others, and show no guilt or remorse for their harmful behaviors.

Psychopathy and sociopathy share traits, but may have different origins. A primary psychopathy is an inherited condition. There are specific brain changes resulting in a smaller limbic system and a deficit of emotions such as empathy and fear. When psychologists talk about psychopaths, they refer to people with a distinct set of personality characteristics including ruthlessness, fearlessness, mental toughness, a charismatic personality and lack of conscience and empathy. Compared to “primary” psychopathy, “secondary” psychopathy or sociopathy is created, not inherited, and is associated with greater fear, anxiety, and other negative emotions. An example of a sociopath or secondary psychopath may be someone raised in a gang-infested area.

It is not always easy to spot “cold-hearted” psychopaths because they can be intelligent, charming, and good at mimicking emotions. By contrast, “hot-headed” sociopaths are less able to play along, and make it plain or obvious that they’re not interested in anyone but themselves. They often blame others and have excuses for their behavior, and they act without thinking how others will be affected. Sociopathic traits are developed from environmental and social influences, while psychopaths have genetic predisposition and physical, or biochemical origins.

Psychopaths tend to have narcissistic traits such as selfishness, egocentricity and callousness, in addition to a more antisocial lifestyle with frequent criminal behavior, and tendency to break rules, as well as early and persistent delinquency. In general, they have a hard time forming real emotional attachments with others. Instead, they form artificial, shallow relationships designed to be manipulated in a way that most benefits the psychopath. Some even have families and seemingly loving relationships with a partner. A psychopath’s hurtful actions toward others are often calculated, manipulative and cunning; with no emotion or true empathy for others. They can be deceptively charismatic and charming. By contrast, sociopaths tend to be more impulsive, haphazard, and easily agitated than psychopaths, and can form attachments to others while also disregarding social rules. While most psychopaths also meet criteria for antisocial personality disorder, only about 10% of those with antisocial personality disorder meet the criteria for psychopathy.

In the past, antisocial personality disorder was thought to be a lifelong disorder, but that's not always the case and it can sometimes be managed and treated. However, antisocial personality disorder is one of the most difficult personality disorders to manage. Treatment typically involves stress and anger management plus long-term psychotherapy with a therapist that has experience in treating this kind of personality disorder. In younger people, family or group psychotherapy may help to change destructive patterns of behavior, teach new vocational and relationship skills, and reinforce a person's social support. Psychotherapy also may help a person with this disorder learn to be more sensitive to the feelings of others and encourage new, socially acceptable and productive ways of thinking about one's goals and aims.

Cognitive behavioral therapy is sometimes used to treat antisocial personality disorder. It is a talk therapy that aims to help a person manage their problems by changing the way they think and behave. Teenagers who receive cognitive behavioral psychotherapy to help them change their way of thinking have been found to experience a significant decrease in the incidence of engaging in repeated antisocial and maladaptive behaviors. On the other hand, programs that use a purely reflective (insight-oriented talk therapy) approach to treat depression or eating disorders often worsen rather than improve outcomes in people with antisocial personality disorder.

The most effective intervention is a combination of behavior therapies that emphasize teaching skills to live independently and productively within the rules and limits of society. Family therapy aimed at helping loved ones cope appropriately with the negative behaviors and promote the positive behaviors of the affected person can also be an important part of treatment for this condition. Democratic therapeutic community treatment (DTC) is based upon large and small therapy groups focusing on community issues, and may also be opportunities for educational and vocational work. The recommended length of treatment is 18 months as there needs to be enough time for a person to make changes and put new skills into practice. People who have both antisocial personality disorder and schizophrenia are less likely to comply with treatment programs and are more likely to remain institutionalized in a prison or a hospital.

Medications do not directly treat the behaviors associated with antisocial personality disorder, but they can be useful in addressing depression, anxiety, and mood swings that often co-occur with this condition. Depressed or anxious individuals who also have antisocial personality disorder may benefit from antidepressants like *fluoxetine (Prozac), escitalopram (Lexapro)*, or *duloxetine (Cymbalta)*, and those who exhibit impulsive anger may improve when given mood stabilizers like *lithium, valproate (Depakote)*, or *lamotrigine (Lamictal).*

-o0o-

PERSONS WITH ANTISOCIAL PERSONALITY DISORDER

Most sociopaths can commit vile actions and not feel the least bit of remorse. Sociopaths are great at charming people and know how to make people feel special. They are willing to hurt whomever and whenever, if it means that they will achieve their goals. They understand human weaknesses and can manipulate others to do just about anything they want. They think they are the greatest people in the world, but they have no real friends from high school, college, or any past life. They do as they please and do not care about how it affects others, which is why they become successful in whatever goals they may have. Like con men, they are perfectly comfortable in lying and deceiving people to get what they want. They are always calm and they barely react in dangerous, scary or emotional situations. If you know people who have these traits, be careful. They can blend in so effectively and can easily be a neighbor, a friend, or "the boy next door". People who have this disorder have no regard for right or wrong. However, not all of them are killers.

-o0o-

TED BUNDY

Theodore Robert Bundy (a.k.a. Ted Bundy) was an American serial killer, kidnapper, rapist, burglar, and necrophiliac who assaulted and murdered numerous young women and girls during the 1970s. This infamous serial killer had a number of characteristics of a true psychopath with comorbid narcissistic personality disorder and antisocial personality disorder. In contrast to the general image of a "homicidal maniac", he was attractive, intelligent, and self-assured. By his own account, he had looked at pornographic material and started his fantasy about doing these sexual acts toward women when he was young. Even when he was just in high school, he already started with his crimes that included shoplifting and burglary. He never knew his biological father, but he did remember his grandfather taking his father's place as a male figure in his earliest years as a toddler. In his youth, he was believed to have been exposed to unrelenting cruelty in the hands of his grandfather and open neglect from his mother. He grew up thinking that his mother was his teacher. Adding to his troubled home life, Ted's grandmother received controversial electroshock treatment for severe depression. He idolized his first grade teacher but despised his second grade teacher, possibly for punishing him. His classmates from public school remember him as an intelligent, happy, and popular child with many friends and a good academic record. He lost his confidence and developed a deep sense of insecurity when he was in high school, primarily because of his lack of resources while being surrounded by his wealthy classmates. When his girlfriend broke up with him and left for San Francisco, he was devastated and he dropped out of Stanford. He changed from always being in charge of his emotions to being upset and moody. He later re-entered the University of Washington with a sense of purpose, turning from an average student into an honor student. He excelled in his studies and graduated with a degree in psychology. He became increasingly involved in local politics, continuing to work on and off for political campaigns. He met and began living with his new girlfriend. For unknown reason, he began murdering women in several states –

California, Oregon, Washington, Utah, and Colorado. The women were all single, white, thin, and had striking resemblance to his college sweetheart who broke up with him and caused him to get depressed. His long-time girlfriend reported, in a separate interview, how he started experimenting with various sex moves and methods, and recalled being strangled while she was tied up. Sexual sadism was the primary motive of his criminal behavior and subsequent murder of at least thirty-three young female victims in five years. He knew what he wanted and what to look for. His actions were premeditated and precise. He could work by day and murder by night. He sometimes revisited his secondary crime scenes for hours at a time, grooming and performing sexual acts with the decomposing corpses. His sociopathic tendencies were demonstrated by his total lack of conscience which allowed him to commit heinous crimes without feelings of guilt or remorse. A narcissist up to the end, Bundy was shaken up at the end of his life when his ploy to use confessions to buy time on death row did not work. He died in the electric chair at Raiford Prison in Starke, Florida in 1989.

-o0o-

JOHN GACY

John Wayne Gacy, Jr. was an American homosexual serial killer and rapist who sexually assaulted and murdered at least 33 teenage boys and young men between 1972 and 1978 in Cook County. His victims would typically be lured to his home by force or deception, and murdered mostly by asphyxiation or by strangulation with a tourniquet.

He became known as the “Killer Clown” because of his charitable services at fundraising events, parades, and children's parties, dressed as “Pogo the Clown”. As a child, he was overweight, not athletic, and had a difficult relationship with his father, an alcoholic who was physically abusive to his wife and children. When he was 4, his father beat him with a leather belt for accidentally disarranging car engine components that his father assembled. When he was 6, he was beaten with a belt for stealing a toy truck from a neighborhood store. When he was 7, he was whipped for sexually fondling a young girl. The same year, a family friend molested him as well. Because of a heart condition, he was ordered to avoid all sports at school. He was an average student who had few friends and who was an occasional target for mockery and bullying by neighborhood children and classmates. He was known to assist the school truant officer and volunteer to run errands for teachers and neighbors. Between ages 14 and 18, he began to experience blackouts and seizure, causing him to be hospitalized. His father accused him of faking his illness. As a young adult, he was outgoing and sociable, became a successful building contractor, became a married man and stepfather of two, and opened his own construction business. He later made peace with his father who apologized for the physical and mental abuse he had earlier inflicted upon his son throughout his childhood. He was well known and respected in his suburban Chicago community. His neighbors considered him gregarious and helpful; he was active in his local community and hosted annual summer parties beginning in 1974. He became heavily involved in local politics and was named Jaycee (Junior Chamber of Commerce) "Man of the Year." As a Jaycee, he became involved in wife swapping, prostitution, pornography, and drug use. He regularly cheated on his wife with local prostitutes, and later got divorced. He opened a "club" in his basement, where he allowed employees to drink alcohol and play pool. Although he employed teenagers of both sexes at his restaurants, he socialized only with his male employees. Many were given alcohol before he made sexual advances toward them, which he would laugh off and dismiss as a joke if the teenager rebuffed his advances. In 1967, he committed his first sexual offense when he sodomized a teenage boy. He was convicted and sentenced to 10 years in the State Penitentiary, but was released after 18 months. Following his release, he took a 15-year old to his house, stabbed him to death, buried him in a crawl space, and later covered the body with concrete. By 1975, he had admitted to his wife that he was bisexual. His wife saw him bringing teenage boys into his garage and also found gay pornography inside the house. They divorced by mutual consent after one year. Soon after, he killed 32 more young men after sexually assaulting them. He was caught after a surveillance detective noticed a suspicious smell emanating from a heating duct in his home. The floor boards of his house shook as forensic anthropologists attempted to excavate the twenty-nine bodies buried in the crawl space due to millions of worms that were feeding on the corpses. He was convicted of 33 serial rapes and murders; he spent 14 years on death row and was finally executed by lethal injection in 1994. Unremorseful until the end, his final words before being executed were "Kiss my ass."

-o0o-

CHARLES FREDERICK ALBRIGHT

Charles Frederick Albright is an American killer and diagnosed psychopath from Dallas, Texas, who was convicted of killing one woman and suspected of killing two others in 1991. As a child he was adopted by a very strict and overprotective school teacher. Whenever his aunt was around, she would give him dolls and make him wear dresses. He got his first gun when he was a teenager, and made a pastime of shooting small animals such as squirrels and rabbits, stuffing the animals and using buttons instead of glass eyes. He was convicted of aggravated assault when he was 13, and was found guilty of stealing handguns and petty cash, serving 6 months in prison when he was 17. Following his release, he took pre-med classes, excelling in the subjects that he enjoyed and being a member of several clubs, while holding a number of odd jobs. During his first year in college, he stole some nude photos from a girl's dorm. Once, he cut out the eyes of a girl's photo and pasted them onto another girl's photo as well as on his walls. When he was 19, he manipulated a girl, whom he later married, into giving him keys to the entire college, and was expelled but not persecuted when he was caught stealing. He later falsified a degree, stole documents and forged signatures, giving himself fictitious Bachelor's and Master's degrees. He was frequently arrested for theft, forgery and once for child molestation. After marrying his college girlfriend with whom he had a daughter, he continued to forge checks and was caught while he was teaching at a high school. Following his divorce, he was caught stealing hundreds of dollars' worth of merchandise from a hardware store, for which he received a two-year prison sentence but served less than six months. After his release, he befriended and gained the trust of his neighbors who even asked him to babysit their children. In 1981, he was prosecuted and received probation for sexually molesting the 9-year old daughter of some friends whom he visited. Between 1990 and 1991, there were three separate murders of prostitutes whose eyes were removed after being shot in the head by a .44 caliber handgun. After a number of prostitutes reported that he had assaulted them, and being tipped about him and his obsession with knives and eyes, the police searched his home and found a .44 Magnum revolver, several knives, some books about serial killers, several dolls whose eyes had been removed, and a red condom similar to the ones found on the murder scene. He was convicted of murder and sentenced to life in prison.

-o0o-

KENNETH LEE LAY

Kenneth Lee Lay was a very famous American businessman who, in 1999, was ranked America's highest paid CEO earning around $42.4 million while working at Enron Corp. While running the company, he also led a corruption scandal involving corporate abuse and accounting fraud that eventually led to the downfall of the Enron Corporation. He lacked empathy and sense of personal responsibility for the well-being of the company and its employees, and showed no remorse when his fraudulent actions and deceitful ways caused the company's downfall. People had described him as having a huge ego but always under control and reserved. He was competitive, aggressive, and could come across as greedy in negotiations. But he was almost always also described as a nice guy and good listener, with a reputation of going out of his way to make others at ease. He was at the center of a vast web of friends, colleagues and business associates, and was among the biggest supporters of their charities and political campaigns. He was born to a rural family, but even as a teen, he daydreamed of being like J.P. Morgan and John D. Rockefeller. During high school, he participated in band and several singing groups, was elected to the National Honor Society, named homecoming chairman, and received the American history award. He graduated 10th in a class of 276. He excelled at the University of Missouri, where he became president of the Beta Theta Pi fraternity, known for attracting scholars and intramural athletes. In 1965, he began to work as a senior economist at Humble Oil, later called Enron, a company of international reach with ties to government and lots of promise. He later did a study, which tracked defense spending through different sectors of the economy, was widely hailed in Washington and ultimately adopted by the White House's Council of Economic Advisers. Kinnear, who later retired as a four-star Navy admiral and U.S. representative to NATO, lauded Lay's talents for managing groups and understanding organizations. In 1974, he joined the Florida Gas Company, eventually serving as president of its successor company, Continental Resources Company. In 1981, he left Continental to join Transco Energy Company in Houston, Texas. Three years later, he joined Houston Natural Gas Co. as chairman and CEO. The company merged with InterNorth in 1985, and was later renamed Enron Corp. In 1986, Kenneth Lay was appointed chairman and chief executive officer of Enron. Many benefited from Ken's generosity, including the American Heart Association, Assistance League of Houston, Brookwood Community, The Counsel for Alcohol and Drugs Houston, DIFFA, First United Methodist Church, Horatio Alger Scholarship Fund, Houston Area Women's Center, Houston Food Bank, Houston SPCA, NAACP, Open Door Church, Susan G. Komen Breast Cancer Foundation, Rice University, Salvation Army, Star of Hope, United Negro College Fund, United Way of Texas Gulf Coast, YMCA of Greater Houston, University of Houston, Aspen Institute, Aspen Camp School for the Deaf, Holocaust Museum Houston, Beta Theta Pi Fraternity, Episcopal High School, and Child Advocates Inc. When Enron began to decline, he strongly encouraged his employees to invest in more stocks, promising a rebound for the company, while liquidating over

300 million dollars of his own stock, with completely no regard for the effects that his actions would have on the thousands of people he lied to. Enron went bankrupt in 2001, said to be the biggest bankruptcy in U.S. history. On July 7, 2004, Lay was indicted by a grand jury in Houston, Texas, for his role in the company's failure. He was convicted of conspiracy and fraud, which cost 20,000 employees their jobs and many their life savings, and lost billions for investors. On May 25, 2006, the jury found him guilty on six counts of conspiracy and fraud. In a separate bench trial, he was also found guilty on four additional counts of fraud and making false statements. His sentencing was scheduled for October 23, 2006, but he died of a heart attack on July 25, 2006, while vacationing in Colorado.

-o0o-

HENRY LEE LUCAS

Henry Lee Lucas was a confessed American serial killer. His mother was a prostitute who often would “entertain” clients, known as his “uncles”, in front of his father, his brother and him. He was constantly belittled and mistreated when he was a child. His mother would dress him up as a little girl and send him to school in a dress, with curled hair and barefoot. He was bullied for it by all the other kids, one of whom became his first victim. He experienced a concussion when he was 8, which left him in coma for 3 days, after being beaten by his abusive mother. She killed any animal that her son tried to keep as a pet, and denied him medical attention when he cut his eye with a knife and became infected, leading to its surgical removal and replacement with a glass eye. He was introduced to alcohol by his moonshiner father, and became an alcoholic by the age of 10, while his “Uncle” introduced him to animal torture. His not being able to retaliate against his mom for dressing him as a girl, made him feel like he should take his anger and frustration out on weak and vulnerable animals. He committed his first crime when he was 14 or 15, when he beat, raped, strangled, and buried a 17-year old girl in the woods, for rejecting his advances. The next year, after his first prison sentence for burglary, he went to live with his aunt. When he and his mother got in to a fight, he stabbed his mother to death and claimed self-defense, but he pleaded guilty at his trial. He confessed that he had sexually assaulted his mother's corpse, though he soon recanted. He was convicted of second-degree murder and sent to the state prison in southern Michigan. There, he tried to commit suicide and was transferred to a forensic psychiatric hospital. For his mother's murder, he served only 10 years, but after he was released on parole, he served another 3 and a half years for trying to kidnap two young girls. He got married but his wife left after she accused him of molesting her daughters. He started drifting around, and was later known as the one-eye drifter. He supported himself through odd jobs and met Ottis Toole, a fellow sexual deviant at a soup kitchen. They later became lovers. In 1978, Toole and Lucas moved in with Toole's mother and sister in Jacksonville. Lucas fell in love with Toole's 10-year old female cousin, Frieda "Becky" Powell, whom he eventually adopted and they lived as husband and wife. He and Becky moved to Texas together and lived with an old woman, Kate Rich, whom he worked for. They found a home at a commune called "House of Prayer" after being kicked out by neighbors when they saw them cashing checks written in Rich's name. After a fight with Becky, he drove her hours away, killed her, raped the corpse, and dismembered her body, then scattered them throughout a field. A few weeks later, he killed Kate Rich, raped the corpse, and stuffed her in a drain pipe. He was later arrested on fire arms charges and was charged with Becky's and Kate's murder. Six days before his execution, then-governor George W. Bush pardoned him from a death sentence to life in prison. He died of heart failure on March 13, 2001. There is no solid proof that a genetic disorder might have caused his kind of behavior, but his childhood trauma might have been responsible for his lack of respect for human right and dignity. He claimed that the police treated him with no respect and were always trying to make things worse for him, that everyone treated him negatively, and that he "hated everybody".

-o0o-

OTTIS TOOLE

Ottis Elwood Toole was an American drifter who was convicted of six counts of murder. He had an abusive mother, who would dress him in girls' clothing and call him Susan, while his father was an alcoholic who abandoned him. As a young child, he was a victim of sexual assault and incest at the hands of many close relatives and acquaintances, including his older sister and next-door neighbor. He was forced to have sex with his father's friend when he was five, knew he was gay when he was 10, and claimed to have had sex with a neighborhood boy when he was 12. He claimed that his maternal grandmother was a Satanist who called him "Devil's Child" and exposed him to various satanic rituals, including self-mutilation and grave robbing. He was mildly retarded, with an I.Q. of 75, and suffered from epilepsy. His self-awareness and memory were further impaired by years of consuming commercial and bootleg liquor, along with street drugs, and his mother's "nerve pills". Throughout his childhood, he frequently ran away from home, often slept in abandoned houses, and was sexually aroused by fire at a young age. He dropped out of school in the ninth grade and began visiting gay bars, becoming a male prostitute as a teenager, and was obsessed with gay pornography. He claimed to have committed his first murder at the age of 14, after being propositioned for sex by a traveling salesman. He began drifting around the Southwestern United States, supported himself by prostitution and panhandling, and was suspected of two murders in 1974 - one in Nebraska and one in Colorado. In 1975, he returned to Jacksonville and married an older woman who discovered his homosexuality and left him after 3 days. In 1976, he met Henry Lee Lucas who became his lover. In 1982, he set a boarding house on fire, resulting in the death of a 64 year old man with whom he had a sexual relationship. He was arrested for an unrelated arson, and sentenced to 20 years in prison. In 1983, while imprisoned for two unrelated murders, he confessed to the 1981 murder of 6-year-old Adam Walsh. In 1984, he confessed to two unsolved northwest Florida slayings, and admitted to killing an 18-year-old hitchhiker that he picked up east of

Pensacola, and the kidnapping and murder of a 20-year-old woman who was shot in the head. The psychiatrist testified that he was extremely impulsive and exhibited antisocial personality disorder and that he was a pyromaniac. In 1984, he was found guilty and was sentenced to death for the first-degree murder of Adam Walsh, whom he kidnapped from a Sears mall parking lot, raped, killed and decapitated. Later that year, he was found guilty of the 1983 strangulation murder of a 19-year-old Tallahassee, Florida woman, and received a second death sentence. Both sentences were commuted to life in prison after an appeal. After his incarceration, he pleaded guilty to four more Jacksonville murders and received four more life sentences. While serving his sentence, Toole briefly stayed in the cell adjacent to serial killer Ted Bundy in Florida's Raiford Prison. After his incarceration, Toole pleaded guilty to four more Jacksonville murders in 1991 and received four more life sentences. In prison, he was consistently medicated with *Thorazine* and *Dilantin*, given a regular balanced diet, and punished when he was caught with drugs or jailhouse brew. In 1996, he died in his cell from liver failure at the age of 49.

-o0o-

REFERENCES

https://alchetron.com/Ottis-Toole-802916-W
https://allpsych.com/disorders/personality/antisocial/
http://crimescenedb.com/ottis-toole/
http://criminalminds.wikia.com/wiki/The_Eyeball_Killer
https://en.wikipedia.org/wiki/Category:People_with_antisocial_personality_disorder
https://en.wikipedia.org/wiki/Henry_Lee_Lucas
http://en.wikipedia.org/wiki/John_Wayne_Gacy>.
https://en.wikipedia.org/wiki/Kenneth_Lay
https://en.wikipedia.org/wiki/Ottis_Toole
http://healthresearchfunding.org/famous-people-antisocial-personality-disorder/
http://jeffreydahmer-serialkiller.weebly.com/psychological-analysis.html
http://johngacythekillerclown.weebly.com/psychological-analysis.html
https://prezi.com/6d3xu9g8zb0w/henry-lee-lucas/
http://sociopathology.org/category/sociopath-celebrities/
http://tedbundyproject.weebly.com/psychological-analysis.html

http://theconfessionkiller.weebly.com/psychoanalysis.html
http://whale.to/b/toole1.html
http://www.academia.edu/25731405/John_Wayne_Gacy_A_Psychopath_among_Us
http://www.biography.com/people/henry-lee-lucas-11735804
http://www.biography.com/people/kenneth-lay-234611#criminal-charges-and-convictions
https://www.charlesmanson.com/
http://www.chron.com/business/enron/article/The-rise-of-Ken-Lay-as-dramatic-as-his-fall-1963106.php
https://www.drugs.com/health-guide/antisocial-personality-disorder.html
http://www.fampeople.com/cat-ottis-toolehttp://www.healthyplace.com/personality-disorders/antisocial-personality-disorder/what-is-antisocial-personality-disorder/
http://www.imdb.com/name/nm0524150/bio
http://www.legacy.com/obituaries/houstonchronicle/obituary.aspx?pid=18370951
http://www.mayoclinic.org/diseases-conditions/antisocial-personality-disorder/basics/symptoms/
http://www.med.nyu.edu/content?ChunkIID=96473#causes
https://www.mentalhealth.gov/what-to-look-for/personality-disorders/antisocial-personality-disorder/index.html
http://www.murderpedia.org/male.L/l/lucas-henry-lee.htm
http://mysteriesandmurders.blogspot.com/2016/01/ottis-toole.html
https://www.ncbi.nlm.nih.gov/pubmedhealth/PMHT0024893/
https://www.ncbi.nlm.nih.gov/pubmedhealth/PMH0015230/#ch2.s2
http://www.newhealthadvisor.com/Famous-People-with-Antisocial-Personality-Disorder.html
http://www.nhs.uk/Conditions/antisocial-personality-disorder/Pages/Introduction.aspx
http://www.nlm.nih.gov/medlineplus/ency/article/000921.htm
http://www.nlm.nih.gov/medlineplus/ency/article/000919.htm
http://www.nytimes.com/2006/07/06/business/06lay.html
http://www.nytimes.com/health/guides/disease/antisocial-personality-disorder/overview.html
https://www.psychologytoday.com/blog/wicked-deeds/201405/john-wayne-gacy-the-diabolical-killer-clown
http://www.psychologytoday.com/conditions/antisocial-personality-disorder?tab=Causes
http://www.psyweb.com/mdisord/jsp/anpd.jsp
http://www.telegraph.co.uk/culture/books/10218984/Manson-the-Life-and-Times-ofCharles-Manson-by-Jeff-Guinn-review.html
http://www.webmd.com/mental-health/antisocial-personality-disorder-overview#1
http://www.wow.com/wiki/Ottis_Toole

FURTHER READING

American Psychiatric Association. (2000). *Diagnostic and statistical manual of mental disorders* (4th ed., text rev.). Washington, DC: APA Publishing.

American Psychiatric Association. (2013). *Diagnostic and statistical manual of mental disorders (DSM-5®)*. American Psychiatric Pub.

Blais, M.A., Smallwood, P., Groves, J.E., & Rivas-Vazquez, R.A. (2008). Personality and personality disorders. In T.A. Stern, J.F. Rosenbaum, M. Fava, J. Biederman, & S.L. Rauch (Eds.), *Massachusetts General Hospital comprehensive clinical psychiatry* (1st ed., chap 39). Philadelphia, PA: Elsevier Mosby.

Paris, J., Chenard-Poirier, M.P., & Biskin, R. (2013). Antisocial and borderline personality disorder revisited. *Compr Psychiatry, 54*(4), 321-325.

Semple, D. (2005). *Oxford handbook of psychiatry* (pp. 448-449). New York, NY: Oxford University Press.

PARANOID PERSONALITY DISORDER

The word personality describes deeply ingrained patterns of behavior and the manner in which individuals perceive, relate to, and think about themselves and their world. Personality traits are conspicuous features of personality that are not necessarily pathological, although certain styles of personality traits may cause personal and interpersonal problems. Many people manifest mistrust and suspicion from time to time, but they are not pathological, because they are transient, modifiable and not significantly disruptive. It is fairly normal for everyone to sometimes have some degree of paranoia about certain situations in their lives, like worrying about an impending layoff at work, or worrying about strangers when walking on a poorly lit road at night. In contrast, people with paranoid personality disorder have eccentric and pervasive traits that disrupt virtually every professional and personal relationship that they have.

-o0o-

Paranoid personality disorder, one of "Cluster A" odd or eccentric personality disorders, is characterized by pervasive paranoia and a long-standing, generalized mistrust of others. It is a chronic disorder, which means it tends to last throughout a person's life. Paranoia is a symptom that causes intense feelings of distrust and suspiciousness, and that can sometimes lead to overt or covert hostility in which an individual feels as if the world is "out to get" him or her. Paranoia can also occur as a symptom of other neurological diseases, such as the after-effects of strokes, brain injuries, and various types of dementia, including Alzheimer's disease. When people are paranoid, they feel as if others are always talking about them behind their backs. Persistent and pervasive paranoia is the key component of paranoid personality disorder. Individuals with this personality disorder are reluctant to confide in others or reveal personal information due to a fear that the information will be used against them, and that others have hidden motives, even if there is no evidence to support their assumption. They think that they are in danger, and they read hidden meanings in the innocent remarks or casual looks of others. They have trouble working with others because of their argumentativeness, recurrent complaining, or quiet, apparent aloofness. They become detached, socially isolated, sarcastic, angry and hostile.

They suspect, without sufficient basis, that others are exploiting, harming, or deceiving them, and they are preoccupied with unjustified doubts about the loyalty or trustworthiness of friends or associates. They are always suspicious that their spouses or lovers are being unfaithful, and they may become controlling, cold and distant in their relationships. They cannot see their role in creating problems or conflicts and don't believe that their behavior is abnormal at all. They will often misinterpret harmless comments and behavior from others and may build up and harbor unfounded resentment for an unreasonable amount of time. Their combative and suspicious nature may elicit a hostile response in others, which then serves to confirm their original expectations. Their thinking and behavior interfere with their ability to maintain relationships, as well as their ability to function socially and in work situations. In many cases, individuals with paranoid personality disorder become involved in legal battles, suing people or companies they believe are "out to get them."

This disorder appears to be more common in men than in women. Because personality disorders describe long-standing and enduring patterns of behavior, they are most often diagnosed in adulthood. However, for it to get diagnosed in a child or teen, the features must have been present for at least 1 year. People with paranoid personality features have been associated with histories of both violent and antisocial behavior especially when provoked. Specific unfounded suspicions about the fidelity of intimate partners, commonly seen as a feature of paranoid personality disorder, are associated with an increased risk of threatening and initiating violence against the partner and others. Because they are likely to be both highly suspicious and unforgiving of perceived attacks and past transgressions by others; such tendency to bear grudges may also increase their risk of violence. High levels of delinquency in teenagers have been associated with paranoid features such as feeling mistreated, victimized, betrayed and the target of false rumors.

Researchers believe that a combination of genetic, biological and environmental factors can lead to paranoid personality disorder. It appears to be more common in families with psychotic disorders, such as schizophrenia and delusional disorder, suggesting a genetic link between the two disorders. If a person has this personality disorder, research suggests that there is a slightly increased risk for this disorder to be "passed down" to his or her children. Physical or emotional trauma during early childhood is also suspected to play a role in the development of paranoid personality disorder. It can be triggered by extreme and unfounded parental rage and/or condescending parental influence that cultivate profound childhood insecurities. In addition to violence, paranoid personality features have been associated with other problem behaviors, including stalking, the uttering of threats and frequent abnormal complaining.

Family physicians and general practitioners are generally not trained or well equipped to make this type of psychological diagnosis. If a person has symptoms, the doctor will usually begin an evaluation by performing a complete medical history and physical examination. It is important to find out what drugs, if any, the patient is taking, and to make sure that the patient is not a long-term user of amphetamine or cocaine, since chronic abuse of these stimulants and some prescription medications might cause paranoia as a side effect. Although there are no laboratory tests to specifically diagnose personality disorders, the doctor might use various diagnostic tests to rule out physical illness as the cause of the symptoms. If the primary physician finds no physical reason for the symptoms, the person is referred to a specially trained psychiatrist or psychologist who can use specially designed interview and assessment tools to evaluate a person for a personality disorder. A normal response to unusual circumstances should always be considered as part of the differential diagnosis of a patient with features suggestive of paranoid personality disorder. Schizophrenia and borderline personality disorder are two disorders with symptoms so similar to paranoid personality disorder, that it can be difficult to clearly distinguish one from each other. Paranoid personality disorder generally isn't diagnosed when another psychotic disorder, such as schizophrenia, bipolar or depressive disorder, has already been diagnosed, or if the pattern of suspicious behavior occurs exclusively during the course of schizophrenia or another psychotic disorder.

Paranoid personality disorder is different from psychotic disorders such as paranoid schizophrenia, or persecutory delusional disorder, because it lacks the perceptual distortions (for example, hearing voices) or bizarre delusional thinking (for example, being followed everywhere by the FBI). Patients with paranoid personality disorder remain in touch with reality; and they don't have any of the hallucinations or delusions seen in patients with psychosis. Symptoms of paranoid personality disorder sometimes overlap with symptoms of anxiety disorders such as social phobia, social anxiety, and social withdrawal, because of concerns about how others view them. The crucial distinction is that people with paranoid personality disorder are not merely preoccupied with negative events or potential exposure to public scrutiny, but have a pervasive suspicion that malevolent others are planning to harm them. Delusional disorder also needs to be distinguished from paranoid personality disorder. By definition, people with paranoid personality disorder do not display persistent psychotic symptoms, and can at least entertain the possibility that their suspicions are unfounded or that they are overreacting. In contrast, people with delusional disorder have persistent and firmly held belief that they are being persecuted without any other feature of a psychotic illness.

People with paranoid personality disorder often do not seek treatment on their own because they do not see themselves as the ones having a problem. When individuals are willing to be treated, the treatment of choice usually involves long-term psychotherapy with a therapist that has experience in treating this kind of personality disorder, who can help them cope, communicate with others in social situations, reduce their feelings of paranoia, and improve their self-esteem. However, the mental health professional must first establish trust with them for the treatment to be successful. A strong therapist-client relationship offers the most benefit to people with the disorder, yet is extremely difficult to establish due to the dramatic skepticism of patients with this condition. It is usually up to the therapist alone to overcome a patient's resistance. Not surprisingly, group therapy that includes family members or other psychiatric patients is not useful in the treatment of people with paranoid personality disorder due to the mistrust that they feel towards others. Individual counseling seems to work best but it requires a great deal of patience and skill on the part of the therapist. It is not unusual for patients to leave therapy when they perceive some malicious intent on the therapist's part.

Medications are generally not encouraged, as they may contribute to a heightened sense of suspicion that can ultimately lead to patient withdrawal from therapy. No medication has been proven to effectively relieve the long-term symptoms of the disorder, although the selective serotonin reuptake inhibitors such as *fluoxetine (Prozac)* have been reported to make patients less angry, irritable and suspicious. Antidepressants, *benzodiazepines*, and antipsychotics may be helpful, but only for a limited amount of time, if the person's symptoms are extreme, or if he or she has an associated psychological problem, such as anxiety or depression. Combining medication with talk therapy or psychotherapy can be very successful when the individual is receptive to intervention. Although some people can function fairly well with the disorder and are able to marry and hold jobs, their outcome is often poor, unless they are willing to accept treatment. Their symptoms can be managed with proper care and support, but they must continue treatment throughout their lifetime because there's no cure for paranoid personality disorder. Typically, therapists can trace this pervasive and inflexible pattern of behavior and inner experience back to adolescence or early adulthood. Eventually, paranoid personality disorder leads to considerable distress as it impairs function and success in social and professional settings, but this may not happen until the person reaches his or her 40s or later.

PERSONS WITH PARANOID PERSONALITY DISORDER

Some famous people can have many of the symptoms of paranoid personality disorder, but they cannot be officially diagnosed without a full psychological evaluation. It's difficult to find persons with paranoid personality disorder who publicly admit to their condition, because of the considerable stigma associated with the disorder. Historically, many of the world's most murderous leaders exhibited paranoid personality disorder. For all of these paranoid leaders, the destruction of an enemy was central to their political vision, and they carried out brutal crimes aimed at eradicating their enemy. The difficulties in diagnosing leaders with paranoid personality disorder are the same as the difficulties that we encounter in diagnosing the disorder in our workplace or at home. To us, most of the time, they are normal but just "eccentric and difficult to be with".

-o0o-

SADAM HUSSEIN

Sadaam Hussein was the president of Iraq, or dictator rather, whose unusual and erratic behavior caused much turmoil between him and other countries around the world. Consistent with a person with paranoid personality disorder, he doubted all of his companions, family members, and everyone around him. His fear of being exploited and ruined caused him to make irrational decisions out of anger. He demonstrated this paranoia when, just days after he succeeded former Iraqi president Al-Bakr, he executed "twenty potential rivals, members of the Ba'th Party, and military". He wiretapped leaders who could provide evidence of his paranoia, leading to many executions, including his immediate family. He prohibited political opposition, freedom of speech, freedom of press, and rights of privacy. While he was psychologically in touch with reality, his political view of the world was narrow and distorted. He ruthlessly eliminated perceived threats to his power, and equated criticism with disloyalty. While he was not psychotic, he had a strong paranoid orientation and considered himself to be surrounded by enemies. He killed members of his own government and extended family for political dissent. He was known for torture and free use of the death penalty .All print and broadcast media are controlled by the government that also blocked foreign news broadcasts. He was extremely fearful of losing power. The end of Saddam's rule began with the U.S.-led invasion of Iraqi. After 24 years as the brutal ruler of Iraq and nine months as a fugitive, U.S. soldiers captured Saddam in a raid. In 2006, he was sentenced to death by hanging, after being convicted of crimes against humanity by the Iraqi Special Tribunal.

-o0o-

NICOLAS MADURO

Nicolás Maduro is a Venezuelan politician and labor leader who became the interim president serving the remainder of the term of President Hugo Chávez, who had died from cancer in 2013. Since becoming president, he empowered supporters in the media and surrounded himself with an inner circle of loyal persons who were given positions in the cabinet. Two weeks after the death of President Hugo Chavez from cancer, he increasingly resorted to wild, paranoid, anti-American outbursts. He believed that there was a calculated effort to distract Venezuelan voters from grave violations of the constitutional order. These, including inflation, fiscal deficits, devaluations, crime, and increasing food shortages, have worsened since he took de facto control of the government. Following initial claims that the U.S. or others had killed Chavez, he formed a scientific commission to review the facts surrounding the 58-year-old leader's death. He has accused the United States of intervention in Venezuela several times with his allegations ranging from post-election violence by "neo-Nazi groups", economic difficulties from what he called an "economic war" and various coup plots. He arrested an American citizen for alleged involvement in a "coup conspiracy", and established sanctions on Dick Cheney and

George W. Bush, declaring them "terrorists". He also accused the U.S. government of keeping secret "concentration camps" for children. He ordered all schools in the country to hold an "anti-imperialist day" against the United States with the day's activities including the "collection of the signatures of the students, and teaching, administrative, maintenance and cooking personnel". He blamed capitalism for driving high rates of inflation and creating widespread shortages of staples, and often said that he was fighting an "economic war". He convinced the National Assembly to grant him almost unlimited decision-making powers to revitalize the economy and to stop corruption and money laundering. He enacted economic measures against political opponents that he and loyalists' claims were behind an international economic conspiracy. He also used military equipment from China against protesters during the 2014–15 Venezuelan protests. His lack of trust on those outside his inner circle as well as his continuous quest for common enemies (either against himself or the government's social, economic and political project) have been displayed very vehemently in his discourses and social media strategy.

-o0o-

RICHARD M. NIXON

Richard M. Nixon was the 37th president of the United States who became the only President to resign from office. Based on his behavior and characteristics as a person, he was considered by psychologists to be an example of a person with paranoid personality disorder. In 1972, he became 'frantic' during the presidential campaign against Senator George McGovern, at a time when there seemed little doubt that he would win the election. He sometimes behaved 'irrationally' and in a self-destructive manner, and was crippled by his paranoid distrust of others. After his two Supreme Court nominees were rejected, his plans to attend his daughter's graduation were cancelled because of the potential for an angry confrontation with anti-war demonstrators. Disappointed by the aborted moon voyage of Apollo 13, he ordered the bombing of

Cambodia against the advice of many of his aides. He was a peacemaker who brought about reconciliation with the USSR, with China, and with Vietnam. In addition to gaining and maintaining power by malicious and illegal means, Nixon helped tarnish the reputation of politicians internationally. The stash of recordings that were made public, more than 35 years after he left office in disgrace, included his 1972 election landslide, the Vietnam peace talks, and his "Christmas bombing" campaign. But it also recorded him urging his staff to use all means necessary to discredit opponents, declaring the press and establishment as his enemies. He was also obsessed with his predecessors, instructing his chief of staff to organize a covert raid to uncover information about John F Kennedy, and ordering his staff to remove all pictures of past presidents from the White House. Watergate was a major political scandal that occurred following a break-in at the Democratic National Committee headquarters at the Watergate office complex in Washington, D.C. in 1972 and his administration's attempted cover-up of its involvement. Investigation uncovered an array of clandestine and often illegal activities undertaken by members of his administration. Those activities included such "dirty tricks" as bugging the offices of political opponents and people of whom he was suspicious. He also ordered investigations of activist groups and political figures, using the Federal Bureau of Investigation (FBI), the Central Intelligence Agency (CIA), and the Internal Revenue Service (IRS). Facing virtually certain impeachment in the House of Representatives and equally certain conviction by the Senate, he resigned the presidency in 1974, but was pardoned by his successor, Gerald Ford, on the same year.

-o0o-

DAVID SQUELCH

David Squelch, the man who killed a colleague, James Wallington, in a frenzied knife attack, was diagnosed with paranoid personality disorder by two consultant psychiatrists. The psychiatrists both claimed that he was unable to make a rational judgment nor exercise self-control when he attacked James Wallington. The murder was allegedly due to an accumulation of all the taunting and perceived insults that he received from his victim. He had a pattern of misconception about what were quite innocent things he heard from the victim. He always bore and kept grudges for years against people whom he felt had belittled him, and whom he could not forget and forgive. Once, he suffered a blackout and blamed it on what the murdered victim had been saying and doing. From then on, he began to keep a hunting knife in his bag. He punched Mr. Wallington out of anger when the latter made a comment about the manner in which he had handled his mother's death, suggesting it was time to move on. The two appeared to have made up but he was still angry. A week later, he stabbed Mr. Wallington 17 times at the back with his hunting knife, in the Environment Recycling Center where they worked, claiming that the victim had hurt him emotionally. He then walked into the office, told the foreman what he had done and waited for police to arrive. He was found guilty of murder and was sentenced to life imprisonment.

-o0o-

REFERENCES

http://apt.rcpsych.org/content/15/1/40.full.pdf

http://articles.latimes.com/1991-04-28/opinion/op-1300_1_saddam-hussein

http://counsellingresource.com/lib/distress/personality-disorder/icd-notes/

http://dailysignal.com/2013/03/18/beware-of-venezuelas-paranoid-anti-americanism/

http://emedicine.medscape.com/article/294307-overview

https://en.wikipedia.org/wiki/Nicol%C3%A1s_Maduro

https://en.wikipedia.org/wiki/Richard_Nixon

http://harborlight.hinghamschools.com/1819/news/president-maduro-crazy-or-just-paranoid/

http://healthresearchfunding.org/famous-people-dependent-personality-disorder/

http://healthresearchfunding.org/famous-people-histrionic-personality-disorder/

http://healthresearchfunding.org/famous-people-paranoid-personality-disorder/

http://healthyplace.com/personality-disorders/paranoid-personality-disorder/famous-people-with-paranoid-personality-disorder/

http://historynewsnetwork.org/article/41698

http://my.clevelandclinic.org/disorders/personality_disorders/hic_paranoid_personality_disorder.aspx

http://onlinelibrary.wiley.com/doi/10.1002/pmh.1244/abstract
http://outofthefog.net/Movies.html
http://psychcentral.com/disorders/sx37t.htm>
https://psychcentral.com/disorders/paranoid-personality-disorder-symptoms/
http://psychology.about.com/od/personalitydisorders/a/paranoid.htm
http://psychology.about.com/od/personalitydisorders/a/personalitydis.htm.
http://sites.miis.edu/ccsprofilesofworldleaders/2014/01/13/maduro-traits-of-a-paranoid-personality/
http://umm.edu/health/medical/ency/articles/paranoid-personality-disorder
https://www.allaboutcounseling.com/library/paranoid-personality-disorder/
http://www.apa.org/monitor/mar04/treatment.aspx
http://www.au.af.mil/au/awc/awcgate/iraq/saddam_post.htm
http://www.bbc.com/news/uk-england-kent-35874339
https://www.britannica.com/biography/Nicolas-Maduro
https://www.drugs.com/cg/paranoid-personality-disorder.html
www.dsm5.org/Documents/Personality%20Disorders%20Fact%20Sheet.pdf
http://www.healthline.com/health/paranoid-personality-disorder
http://www.healthyplace.com/personality-disorders/paranoid-personality-disorder/what-is-paranoid-personality-disorder/
http://www.huffingtonpost.co.uk/will-black/richard-nixon-vietnam-politicians-_b_2933866.html
http://www.itv.com/news/meridian/update/2016-03-22/man-jailed-for-life-after-stabbing-colleague-to-death/
http://www.kentonline.co.uk/tunbridge-wells/news/murder-accused-appears-in-court-33389/
http://www.kentonline.co.uk/weald/news/jury-out-murder-trial-david-squelch-93078/
http://www.mayoclinic.org/diseases-conditions/personality-disorders/symptoms-causes/dxc-20247656
https://medlineplus.gov/ency/article/000938.htm
http://www.mentalhelp.net/poc/view_doc.php?type=doc&id=41578&cn=8
http://www.merckmanuals.com/home/mental_health_disorders/personality_disorders/personality_disorders.html
http://www.minddisorders.com/Ob-Ps/Paranoia.html#ixzz4akD79XCc
http://www.minddisorders.com/Ob-Ps/Paranoid-personality-disorder.html
http://my.clevelandclinic.org/health/articles/paranoid-personality-disorder
http://www.mentalhelp.net/poc/view_doc.php?type=doc&id=517
http://www.mentalhelp.net/poc/view_doc.php?type=doc&id=41578&cn=8
http://www.merck.com/pubs/mmanual/section15/chapter191/191a.htm>
https://www.myprivatesearch.com/search?q=paranoid%20personality%20disorder&page 2
http://www.ncbi.nlm.nih.gov/pubmed/22928850.
http://www.ncbi.nlm.nih.gov/pubmedhealth/PMH0001934/
http://www.news-medical.net/health/Differences-between-Paranoid-Personality-Disorder-and-Paranoid-Schizophrenia.aspx
http://www.nlm.nih.gov/medlineplus/ency/article/000938.htm

http://www.nlm.nih.gov/medlineplus/personalitydisorders.html
http://www.nydailynews.com/entertainment/gossip/mental-problem-megan-fox-admits-bouts-mild-schizophrenia-article-1.381064
http://www.nytimes.com/health/guides/disease/paranoid-personality-disorder/overview.html
http://outofthefog.website/personality-disorders-1/2015/12/6/paranoid-personality-disorder-ppd
http://www.patheos.com/blogs/deaconsbench/2013/05/angelina-jolie-and-the-illness-no-one-wants-to-mention/
http://www.personal.umich.edu/~rtanter/F02PS498_Papers/kelley/~kkasisch%20Contents.html
https://www.psychologytoday.com/conditions/paranoid-personality-disorder
http://www.psychologytoday.com/blog/hide-and-seek/201205/the-10-personality-disorders
https://www.quora.com/Who-was-the-most-paranoid-leader-in-the-history-of-mankind
http://www.ralphmag.org/nixon.html
http://www.realclearpolitics.com/articles/2013/03/19/beware_of_venezuelas_paranoid_anti-americanism_117526.html
http://www.sagepub.com/upm-data/15198_Chapter3.pdf
http://www.sane.org.uk/uploads/personality-disorders.pdf
http://www.telegraph.co.uk/news/worldnews/us-politics/9780832/Richard-Nixons-dark-side-has-obscured-his-greatness.html
https://www.theguardian.com/world/2008/dec/03/richard-nixon-tapes
http://www.toad.net/~arcturus/dd/paranoid.htm
https://www.verywell.com/paranoid-personality-disorder-2795448
http://www.villages-news.com/richard-nixons-paranoia/
http://www.webmd.com/mental-health/paranoid-personality-disorder#1

FURTHER READING

American Psychiatric Association. (2000). *Diagnostic and statistical manual of mental disorders* (4th ed., text rev.). Washington, DC: APA Publishing.

American Psychiatric Association. (2013). Paranoid personality disorder. In *Diagnostic and statistical manual of mental disorders (DSM-5®)* (pp. 649-652).

American Psychiatric Pub.Berger, F.K. (2016). Paranoid personality disorder. *MedlinePlus Medical Encyclopedia*. U.S. National Library of Medicine. Retrieved from https://medlineplus.gov/ency/article/000938.htm

Blaney. P. (1999). Paranoid conditions. In T. Millon, P. Blaney, & R.D. Davis, (Eds.), *Oxford textbook of psychopathology*. New York, NY: Oxford University Press.

SCHIZOID PERSONALITY DISORDER

People with personality disorders have long-standing patterns of thinking and acting that differ from what society considers usual or normal. The inflexibility of their personality can cause great distress, and can interfere with many areas of life, including social and work functioning. People with personality disorders generally also have poor coping skills and difficulty forming healthy relationships. Unlike people with anxiety disorders, who know they have a problem but are unable to control it, people with schizoid personality disorder often are not aware that they have a problem and do not believe they have anything to control. Because they often do not believe they have a disorder, people with schizoid personality disorder often do not seek treatment.

-o0o-

Schizoid personality disorder, one of a group of conditions called "Cluster 'A'" or eccentric personality disorders, is characterized by withdrawal or detachment from the outside world, a lack of interest in social relationships, a tendency towards a solitary or sheltered lifestyle, secretiveness, emotional coldness, and apathy. Because they lack meaningful communication with other people, they are not able to develop accurate impressions of how well they get along with others. Because they tend not to show their emotion, they may appear as though they don't care about others or what's going on around them. People with schizoid personality disorder are different from individuals with schizophrenia, schizoaffective disorder, or antisocial personality disorder, because they are able to function fairly well in everyday life, even though they are solitary, aloof, cold, and indifferent to social relationships. They may appear indecisive in their actions, unmotivated, self-absorbed, absentminded and detached from their surroundings. Excessive daydreaming with no goals or direction in life is also often present. They avoid contact with other people, they have difficulty relating to others, and they choose jobs that allow them to work alone.

Because of their lack of social skills and lack of desire for sexual experiences, individuals with this disorder have few friendships, date infrequently, and often do not marry. People with schizoid personality disorder are generally able to function in everyday life, although they have trouble establishing personal relationships or expressing their feelings meaningfully. They may have particular difficulty in expressing anger, even in response to direct provocation, which contributes to the impression that they lack emotion. They are aloof, and they are indifferent to praise or criticism. They can form relationships with others based on intellectual, physical, familial, occupational, or recreational activities as long as their partner places few emotional or intimate demands on them. "Secret schizoids" may sometimes present themselves as socially available, interested, engaged and involved in interacting; yet, in reality, they are simultaneously also emotionally withdrawn and sequestered from the rest of the world.

They can engage in impersonal sexual gratification to ease their feelings of emptiness, as long as there is no emotional attachment. Many feel that masturbation or sexual abstinence is preferable to the emotional closeness they must tolerate when they are having sex. They may appear to be comfortable with regular public speaking engagements, yet experience great difficulty during the breaks when members of the audience try to engage them emotionally.

Like other personality disorders, schizoid personality disorder usually manifests in late adolescence or early adulthood. The disorder affects men more often than women. Co-occurring conditions such as mood disorders, anxiety disorders, and other personality disorders are more common among schizoid individuals than in the general population. Schizoid individuals frequently resort to substance and alcohol abuse, and other addictions as substitutes for human relationships.

Persons with schizoid personality disorder may recognize that they are "different", but unlike depressed people, they generally do not consider themselves inferior to others. They may be down and depressed when all possible connections have been cut off, but as long as there is some relationship or even hope for one, the risk for suicide will be low, and they are not likely to attempt it. People affected with avoidant personality disorder, in general, avoid social interactions due to anxiety or feelings of incompetence even if they are interested in interacting with others. In contrast, schizoid individuals do so because they are not interested and are genuinely indifferent to social relationships. Although schizoid personality disorder may look almost identical to simple-type schizophrenia, the personality disorder is characterized by a pattern that is stable throughout a person's lifetime, while simple schizophrenia deteriorates with time. Although their tone may be flat and not lively, they make sense when they speak and their trend of thought is easy to follow. They are also unlikely to experience paranoia or hallucinations.

Genetic, biological and environmental factors likely play a role in its development. The higher risk for schizoid personality disorder in families with history of schizophrenia, schizoid personality disorder, or schizotypal personality disorder, suggests that a genetic susceptibility for the disorder might be inherited. Environmental factors can cause the symptoms and seem to have the most impact during childhood. Emotionally detached, neglectful, abusive, or excessively perfectionist parenting during early childhood could also play a role in its development. The disorder, characterized by solitariness, poor peer relationships, and underachievement in school may first become apparent in childhood and adolescence. These children may be subject to teasing and bullying because they are "different". There is a very high rate of schizoid and other Cluster A personality disorders among homeless people. It is also more common among introverts.

If symptoms of this personality disorder are present, the doctor usually performs a complete medical history, physical exam, and various diagnostic tests to rule out other conditions that may be causing the symptoms. If no physical illness is identified, their primary care provider may refer them to a mental health professional for further evaluation. Psychiatric assessment will involve filling out questionnaires about their symptoms and thoughts. An interview with the mental health professional will include questions about childhood, relationships, and job history.

People with this schizoid personality disorder rarely seek treatment for their condition unless they have a related problem, such as depression. Because their thoughts and behavior generally do not cause them distress, treatment can be challenging. When treatment is sought, the most often used treatment is psychotherapy. Supportive psychotherapy in an inpatient or outpatient setting by a trained professional focuses on areas such as coping skills, improvement of social skills and social interactions, communication, and self-esteem issues. Educational strategies can help them identify their own positive and negative emotions, and may be effective in creating empathy and allowing them to feel the common emotions with other people with whom they relate. Social skills training also can be an important component of treatment. Group therapy is another option that can help them practice their social skills, and be more comfortable in social situations. The longer-term goal is for patients to understand who and what they are as human beings, and slowly free themselves from the confines of abandonment and depression so that they can uncover their potential. Because trust is an important component of therapy, people with schizoid personality disorder have difficulty forming relationships with others. There is little data on the effectiveness of various treatments for this personality disorder because they are rarely encountered in clinical settings.

Medication is generally not used to treat schizoid personality disorder itself. Drugs might, however, be prescribed if the person also suffers from an associated problem, such as depression. *Bupropion (Wellbutrin),* selective serotonin reuptake inhibitors *(Celexa, Lexapro, Zoloft. Paxil),* tricyclic antidepressants *(Sinequan, Elavil, Tofranil),* monoamine oxidase inhibitors *(Marplan, Nardil)*, low dose *benzodiazepines (Diazepam, Librium, Xanax)*, and beta-blockers *(Metoprolol)* may help allay social anxiety in schizoid individuals. However, social anxiety may not be a main concern for the people who have schizoid personality disorder. Most patients show no additional improvement with the addition of an antidepressant medication, unless they are also suffering from suicidal ideation or a major depressive episode. Medication should be prescribed only for acute symptom relief, and long-term treatment with medication should be avoided.

-o0o-

PERSONS WITH SCHIZOID PERSONALITY DISORDER

People with schizoid personality disorder rarely have the desire to become famous, which is why it is difficult to find verifiable examples of famous people who have the disorder. A number of famous and infamous people have characteristics and behaviors consistent with a schizoid disorder, which cannot be confirmed, either because they are already dead, or because they refuse to submit themselves to a formal psychologic evaluation. Likewise, some people are able to put on an elaborate show at the right times, but never really privately engage with others on any meaningful level. The following famous people have (or had) probable schizoid personality disorder or least exhibited symptoms of schizoid personality disorder, but this is purely speculative.

-o0o-

EMILY DICKINSON

Emily Dickinson, is probably the greatest American poet with a very successful family who had strong connections and influence in their community. She lived much of her life in reclusive isolation while writing several poems that expressed her feelings. Her personality disorder made her different from other people, but it didn't stop her from writing several poems that served as an inspiration for others. She lived in an intensely private world that she felt no one could share or comprehend. Her father was a conservative and overprotective of his wife and children. Her mother was gentle and soft-spoken but was as cold and aloof from her children as her father. She was discouraged from a social life by her father. She was troubled from a young age by the "deepening menace" of death, especially the deaths of those who were close to her. Even in high school, she found herself increasingly isolated from female friends, whose number grew smaller as they left school to marry or graduated to pursue teaching. Male acquaintances also disappeared, and she became increasingly more alone, turning to letters as a form of communicating with friends. She was a voracious reader, but was aloof and skeptical about Civil War issues. She was attracted to strong older men of outstanding intellectual or rhetorical skills who were all unavailable due to marriage or geographic distance. Considered an eccentric by locals, she developed a noted penchant for white clothing and became known for her reluctance to greet guests or, later in life, to even leave her bedroom. Few of the locals, particularly those who exchanged messages with Dickinson during her last fifteen years ever saw her in person. When her father died, she, stayed in her room with the door cracked open, and did not attend her father's memorial service. She never married, and most friendships between her and others were based entirely upon correspondence. Her most productive period occurred while she was largely withdrawn from social life. She died of kidney disease at the age of 55.

-o0o-

BOBBY FISCHER

Bobby Fischer was the greatest American chess player in history and might have been the most talented chess player ever to play the game. His career and legacy were marred by eccentricities that made him an exile from his country of birth. Raised by a single mother, he first learned to play chess at the age of six, and began playing many of his first games against himself, found a book of old chess games which he studied intensely, and spent a lot of time alone, engrossed in his game. When he was 8, he played with a former chess master during a simultaneous exhibition. He lost the game but caught the attention of the Brooklyn Chess Club President, an American chess expert who, together with other grandmasters, became his coaches and mentors. He experienced a "meteoric rise" in his playing strength and became the youngest U.S. Junior Chess Champion at age 13. His interest in chess became more important than schoolwork, to the point that by the time he reached the fourth grade, he'd been in and out of six schools. He dropped out of high school when he turned 16. His first sexual experience during the tournament at age 17 was blamed for his first failure in his competitive career. Afterwards, Fischer said he'd never mix women and chess together, and he kept his promise. He then went on an exhibition tour of sorts from city to city, playing anywhere from 40 to 80 people at a time. In 1968, Fischer began an 18-month-long sabbatical from the game, which included sitting out the '69 American Championship tournament, as he was dissatisfied with the prize money and the tourney format. Failing to compete should have disqualified him from the 1969-72 Championship cycle, but he was able to compete for the world title when an American Grand Master surrendered his own spot for Fischer. He made a large number of demands for the playing conditions at his 1972 World Championship match with Spassky. He became more erratic in his years after losing his World Championship title. Although Fischer's mother was Jewish, Fischer disavowed having Jewish roots. He made numerous anti-Jewish statements and professed a general hatred for Jews since at least the early 1960s when he was 17. He later denounced the United States, and embraced the Cold War rhetoric. While he was never formally diagnosed, there was widespread speculation concerning his psychological condition based on his extreme views and unusual behavior. A psychologist and chess player who met Fischer many times said that some of his behavior was so strange, unpredictable, odd and bizarre that even his most ardent supporters have had a hard time explaining what makes him "tick" and described him as "a troubled human being" with obvious personal problems, but "definitely not schizophrenic". He lived a reclusive life in Iceland, avoiding entrepreneurs and others who approached him with various proposals. In 2008, he died from renal failure at the age of 65.

-o0o-

REFERENCES

http://emilydickinson123.weebly.com/character-traits.htm
https://en.wikipedia.org/wiki/Bobby_Fischer
https://en.wikipedia.org/wiki/Emily_Dickinson
https://en.wikipedia.org/wiki/Schizoid_personality_disorder
https://psychcentral.com/disorders/schizoid-personality-disorder-symptoms/
http://healthresearchfunding.org/famous-people-schizotypal-personality-disorder/
http://healthyplace.com/personality-disorders/schizoid-personality-disorder/schizoid-personality-disorder-treatment/
http://healthyplace.com/personality-disorders/schizoid-personality-disorder/
http://hermitary.com/articles/dickinson.html
https://medlineplus.gov/ency/article/000920.htm
http://mentalfloss.com/article/60401/emily-dickinson-scandalous-spinster
http://outofthefog.website/personality-disorders-1/2015/12/6/schizoid-personality-disorder-spd
http://psychology.wikia.com/wiki/Schizoid_personality_disorder
https://robertchaen.com/2014/07/15/famous-people-with-personality-disorders-about-schizoids-pd-part-2/
http://umm.edu/health/medical/ency/articles/schizoid-personality-disorder
http://www.answers.com/Q/Famous_people_with_schizoid_personality_disorder
http://www.biography.com/people/emily-dickinson-9274190#later-life-and-discovery
http://www.counselling-directory.org.uk/schizoid.html
https://www.drugs.com/mcd/schizoid-personality-disorder
http://www.healthguideinfo.com/personality-disorders/p85166/
http://www.healthline.com/health/schizoid-personality-disorder#Long-TermOutlook6
http://www.healthyplace.com/personality-disorders/schizoid-personality-disorder/famous-people-with--personality-disorder/
http://www.imdb.com/name/nm1648139/bio
http://www.mayoclinic.org/diseases-conditions/schizoid-personality-disorder
http://www.mayoclinic.org/diseases-conditions/schizoid-personality-disorder/basics/definition/con-20029184.
http://www.minddisorders.com/knowledge/Schizoid_personality_disorder.html
http://www.minddisorders.com/Py-Z/Schizoid-personality-disorder.html
http://www.ncbi.nlm.nih.gov/pubmed/23281676.
https://www.nlm.nih.gov/medlineplus/ency/article/000920.htm.
http://www.psychforums.com/schizoid-personality/topic48750.html
https://www.verywell.com/overview-of-personality-disorders-2795449
http://www.webmd.com/mental-health/mental-health-schizoid-personality-disorder#1

FURTHER READING

American Psychiatric Association. (2013). Schizoid personality disorder. In *Diagnostic and statistical manual of mental disorders (DSM-5®)* (pp. 652-655). American Psychiatric Pub.

American Psychiatric Association. (2013). Schizotypal personality disorder. In *Diagnostic and statistical manual of mental disorders (DSM-5®)* (pp. 655-659). American Psychiatric Pub.

Blais, M.A., Smallwood, P., Groves, J.E., & Rivas-Vazquez, R.A. (2008). Personality and personality disorders. In T.A. Stern, J.F. Rosenbaum, M. Fava, J. Biederman, & S.L. Rauch (Eds.), *Massachusetts General Hospital comprehensive clinical psychiatry* (1st ed., chap 39). Philadelphia, PA: Elsevier Mosby.

-o0o-

SCHIZOTYPAL PERSONALITY DISORDER

Schizotypal personality disorder, a Cluster A eccentric and odd personality disorder, is characterized by an intense discomfort in social situations, decreased capacity to form close relationship, eccentric behavior, disorganized thinking, and distorted perception. Persons with this kind of disorder are loners, do not have close friends or confidants except for first-degree relatives, and are very uncomfortable relating to and socializing with other people. They become socially withdrawn because they are suspicious of others, and they sometimes resort to aggression due to their social discomfort and inability to control emotions. They can interact with people if they have to, but prefer not to do so because they feel that they do not belong, and because they think that their peers harbor negative thoughts and attitude towards them. They often dress oddly, strangely and inappropriately. Peculiar speech mannerisms are also symptoms of this disorder. They may react oddly in conversations, not responding, or talking to themselves. Some have a tendency to drift aimlessly and lead an idle, unproductive life. They often incorrectly interpret ordinary occurrences as having special meaning for them, although they are not delusional.

They may be superstitious and preoccupied with paranormal phenomena. They believe in clairvoyance, telepathy, or a sixth sense, and they cannot separate perception from reality. They are often suspicious and may think others are out to get them, although they are not delusional or out of touch with reality. They have unusual perceptional experiences, like hearing a voice whispering their name. Paranoid tendencies constitute one of the most common schizotypal personality disorder symptoms. The person experiences unusual bodily perceptions or mental illusions. Sometimes they have stereotypical thinking, and at other times, unrealistic beliefs. Their thinking is much more disorganized compared to other personality disorders. Their symptoms typically manifest during late adolescence or early adulthood, more often in males than in female

It is difficult to differentiate schizotypal personality disorder from major thought disorders such as schizophrenia, bipolar or depressive disorder with psychotic features, which typically have more severe, bizarre, and persistent manifestations and are accompanied by delusions and hallucinations. Also, it is different from paranoid or schizoid disorders because of its odd, disorganized thought and behavior, which are not present in the latter two disorders. There are many similarities between the schizotypal and schizoid personalities. Most notable of the similarities is the inability to initiate or maintain relationships (both friendly and romantic). The difference between the two appears to be that schizotypal individuals avoid social interaction because of a deep-seated fear of people, while schizoid individuals simply feel no desire to form relationships, because they see no point in sharing their time with others. In general, schizoid people are very withdrawn, live life joylessly, and seem to not be connected to others but they can be fairly functional and can maintain their jobs. People with schizotypal personality disorder are withdrawn too, but are much less functional because they tend to be paranoid, live in a fantasy world, and are more likely to be psychotic.

Schizotypal personality disorder should not be confused with schizophrenia. Although people with schizotypal personality disorder can have odd beliefs and behaviors, they are not disconnected from reality and usually do not hallucinate. While people with schizotypal personality disorder may experience brief psychotic episodes with delusions or hallucinations, the episodes are not as frequent, prolonged or intense as in schizophrenia. Another key distinction is that people with schizotypal personality disorder usually can be made aware of the difference between their distorted ideas and reality. Those with schizophrenia generally cannot be swayed away from their delusions. Schizotypal personality disorder is sometimes considered to be on a spectrum with schizophrenia, with schizotypal personality disorder viewed as less severe.

Many people with schizotypal personality disorder have subtle difficulties with memory, learning and attention. They usually do not have the more severe and disabling psychotic symptoms, such as delusions and hallucinations that appear in schizophrenia. However, people with schizotypal personality disorder do sometimes develop schizophrenia. The health-care professional will usually work toward ruling out other mental disorders, including screening for mood problems like depression and anxiety disorders, including anxiety attacks or generalized anxiety; other personality disorders like narcissistic personality disorder, antisocial personality disorder, schizoid personality disorder or histrionic personality disorder; or drug-abuse problems. There is a high rate of comorbidity with other personality disorders. This may be due to overlapping criteria with other personality disorders, such as avoidant personality disorder, paranoid personality disorder and borderline personality disorder.

Schizotypal personality disorder is thought to be part of a continuum of illnesses related to schizophrenia, and usually carries a dual diagnosis, combined with other personality disorders within the schizophrenia spectrum and other psychotic disorders. The main thing to understand is that schizophrenia is a psychotic disorder, whereas schizotypal personality disorder is not. The etiology of schizotypal personality disorder is thought to be primarily biologic because it shares many of the brain-based abnormalities characteristic of schizophrenia, and in rare case, may also develop schizophrenia. It is more common among first-degree relatives of people with schizophrenia or another psychotic disorder. Over half of the patients have had at least one episode of depression, and up to 50% have a major depressive disorder by the time they get diagnosed with schizotypal personality disorder. These patients also often have a substance abuse disorder. It is not clearly demarcated either from simple schizophrenia or from schizoid or paranoid personality disorders, or possibly autism and Asperger's syndrome as currently diagnosed.

Like most other mental disorders, a combination of genetics, biological, and environmental factors may play some role in the development of schizotypal personality disorder. People who have a close relative with schizotypal symptoms or schizophrenia can be as much as 50% more likely to develop the disorder, compared to people without that family history. Biologically, individuals with schizotypal personality disorder are also thought to have less brain matter in certain areas and abnormalities of the neurotransmitter dopamine in the brain, similar to individuals with schizophrenia. Inborn temperament, coupled with a person's unique reactions to life events, relationships in early life, and development of coping strategies likely together contribute significantly to the formation of personality during childhood and adolescence, and its abnormal development. Signs of schizotypal personality disorder, such as increased interest in solitary activities or a high level of social anxiety, may be seen in the teen years. The child may be an underperformer in school or appear socially out of step with peers, and as a result is often bullied or teased.

People who were born to a mother who smoked during pregnancy, had a lower birth weight, and had a smaller head circumference at the age of 12 months seem to have a risk for developing symptoms of schizotypal personality disorder. Children who use marijuana or methamphetamine for the first time before 14 years of age or have been prematurely placed in the role of an adult are also at risk. There is now evidence to suggest that parenting styles, early separation, and early childhood neglect can lead to the development of schizotypal traits. Those who are victims of childhood physical or sexual abuse, or those coming from a lower family socioeconomic status during childhood may also be predisposed to developing this illness. Preventing child abuse and substance abuse, encouraging good prenatal care, discouraging women from smoking during pregnancy, and providing emotional support to women during pregnancy and the postpartum period can help decrease the occurrence of schizotypal personality disorder.

People with schizotypal personality disorder rarely seek treatment for the disorder unless urged by friends or relatives. When they do seek treatment, it most often is due to a related disorder, such as depression or anxiety. If symptoms are present, a health care professional will begin an evaluation by performing a complete medical history and possibly, a physical exam, and other diagnostic tests to rule out physical illness. If no physical ailment is identified, the doctor might refer the person to a psychiatrist or psychologist, who is specially trained to diagnose and treat mental illnesses. Like other personality disorders, cognitive-behavioral therapy is the form of treatment most often used to manage patients with schizotypal personality disorder. It focuses on helping patients acquire social skills, managing their anxiety, and increasing their awareness of how their own behavior might be perceived by others. Supportive psychotherapy will enable the therapist to establish an emotional, encouraging, supportive relationship with patients, and help them develop healthy defense mechanisms, especially in interpersonal relationships. Psychotherapy is most effective when family members are involved and supportive.

Since people with a schizotypal personality disorder are at increased risk of also developing depression, medications that address that their symptoms may be of great benefit as well. *Fluoxetine (Prozac), sertraline (Zoloft), paroxetine (Paxil), citalopram (Celexa),* and *escitalopram (Lexapro)* are often prescribed because of their effectiveness and low incidence of side effects. Other often-prescribed antidepressant medications for the depression that can be associated with schizotypal personality disorder include *venlafaxine (Effexor), duloxetine (Cymbalta),* and *bupropion (Wellbutrin).* Schizotypal patients who appear to be almost schizophrenic in their beliefs and behaviors are usually treated with low doses of antipsychotic medications. For schizotypal patients who are more obsessive-compulsive in their beliefs and behaviors, SSRIs like *Sertraline* appear to be more effective. *Lamotrigine*, an anticonvulsant drug, appears to be helpful in dealing with social isolation. Drugs are usually not the main focus of treatment for personality disorders. However, some patients with this disorder do respond very well to treatment with medication. During times of crises or extreme stress, severe symptoms might develop, requiring a brief period of hospitalization.

The outlook for people with schizotypal personality disorder varies with its severity, and generally improves if a person is motivated to change, and seeks and complies with treatment. There is no specific definitive test, like a blood test or brain scan that can accurately assess whether a person has schizotypal personality disorder or not. People who are concerned that they may suffer from this diagnosis might explore the possibility by taking a self-test, either an online or printable test, like the Schizotypal Personality Questionnaire, the Oxford-Liverpool Inventory of Feelings and Experiences (O-LIFE), the Rust Inventory of Schizotypal Cognitions, the Community Assessment of Psychic Experiences, or the Schizotypal Personality Scale that can be found online.

-o0o-

PERSONS WITH SCHIZOTYPAL PERSONALITY DISORDER

People with schizoid and schizotypal personality disorders both live in their own world and are detached from society. It is often hard to differentiate one from the other, given that both of them belong to Cluster A personality disorder with odd and eccentric behavior. Both of them are loners who express little emotion and seem to take little pleasure in anything. Unless some public admission or health record exists with a definitive diagnosis, we can't know for sure whether anyone has the disorder. Between the two, individuals with schizotypal personality disorder are more dangerous. They are more distorted, they can become aggressive, and sometimes, they may even become schizophrenic.

-o0o-

TRAVIS BICKLE

Travis Bickle is a fictional character and the protagonist of the 1976 film "Taxi Driver" directed by Martin Scorsese, and portrayed by Robert De Niro, who received an Oscar nomination for his portrayal of the character. In the movie, he is depicted as a lonely and depressed young man a living in Manhattan. He becomes a night time taxi driver in order to cope with his chronic insomnia, He would read entries from his journals, expressing his inmost thoughts, looking for a purpose in his life. He is mad at everyone—disgusted by his passengers and by the violence he would witness on the streets. His own lack of social skills and his personal weirdness prevent him from realizing those connections. From his taxi, he keeps stopping to observe Betsy, a woman who works for the presidential candidate. He is able to invite her for a snack, and later makes a date to see a movie together. He takes her to a porno movie because he thinks that she will like it for a first date, the way he does. He is baffled when she walks out of the porno theatre and he goes into a rage, telling her to go to hell, when she refuses to talk to him. He becomes increasingly unstable, buys a full arsenal of guns, and begins talking to himself in front of the mirror, thinking that there is no one else in the world but him. He fantasizes about assassinating the presidential candidate and about freeing a 12-year-old prostitute who has tried to get into his cab before being dragged out by her pimp. He invites her for breakfast and urges her to leave her pimp and go back home. At one point in his progression, he commits an act of real violence and shoots a robber who is trying to stick up a convenience store. When he finally makes his move to kill the presidential candidate in a public rally, he shaves his head leaving a Mohawk on top—a symbol of his rebirth as an assassin. However, the Secret Service spots him and prevents him from shooting his target. He then decides to personally free the prostitute by killing her pimp, the brothel time keeper/clerk and a gangster who is visiting the girl. In the process, he gets wounded and shot multiple times—and he tries to kill himself too, but runs out of bullets. Instead of being sent to prison for murder, he is hailed as a hero by the newspapers, and the girl's parents warmly thank him for rescuing her. Ironically, if he had succeeded with his first idea of assassinating the candidate, everyone probably would have considered him a villain. Instead, having vented his rage in a more acceptable way, since everyone is so sick of New York's criminality and violence, he has become a hero. Even Betsy seeks out a ride with the now hailed vigilante. At the end of the movie, his eyes dart in his taxi's mirror, indicating that his mind is still that of a man with schizotypal personality disorder.

-o0o-

ADAM LANZA

Adam Lanza, the 20-year old young man who killed his mother, 20 children and 6 adults at Sandyhook Elementary School before taking his life, is speculated to have suffered from schizoid personality disorder, although this cannot be verified by a full psychological evaluation because he is dead. Neighbors have described him as odd, remote, and reclusive; schoolmates described him as a loner who was socially awkward; and a longtime family friend said that he was quiet, never said a word, and lacked the ability to feel pain. His brother, Ryan Lanza, claimed that he was autistic, or has Asperger syndrome, a 'personality disorder', and that he had not spoken to him in years His mother was reported to be strict and even harsh. Before the age of 6, Lanza had been diagnosed with a sensory disorder that was over-responsive to stimuli and find clothing, physical contact, light, sound or food unbearable, while also feeling little or no reaction to pain or extreme hot and cold. When he was six, he was raped by a catholic priest, which made Adam suffer in silence for years, and led to him being bullied and beaten at school. He reacted badly to the whole world and did not want to be part of it. He also exhibited repetitive behaviors and motor difficulties. Though his early elementary school years seemed relatively happy, he began avoiding eye contact and became increasingly fearful by the time he reached fifth grade. His anxiety and social-emotional problems worsened as he got older. When he was in eighth grade, his mother withdrew him from school, and he was placed on "homebound" status for the next year. He returned to school for a short time during 10th grade, but after some initial progress, he was described as withdrawing again. After graduating from high school, he went out less and less and eventually refused to come out of his room, covering his windows with black garbage bags and communicating with his mother via email. He was believed to have shot his mother in the head at her home, before taking her car and driving approximately five miles to the Sandy Hook Elementary School, where he shot and killed 20 students between the ages of 5 and 10, as well as six adult workers. After firing between 50 to 100 shots, he then turned the gun on himself, fatally shooting himself in the head as responders began arriving on scene. The attack on Sandy Hook Elementary appears to have been a purposefully thought-out and planned attack.

-o0o-

REFERENCES

http://www.merckmanuals.com/professional/psychiatric-disorders/personality-disorders/schizotypal-personality-disorder

http://www.webmd.com/mental-health/schizotypal-personality-disorder#1

https://www.psychologytoday.com/conditions/schizotypal-personality-disorder

https://psychcentral.com/blog/archives/2013/07/30/schizotypal-disorder-similar-to-other-disorders-yet-unique/

http://www.mayoclinic.org/diseases-conditions/schizotypal-personality-disorder/

https://psychcentral.com/disorders/schizotypal-personality-disorder-symptoms/

https://medlineplus.gov/ency/article/001525.htm

http://www.healthline.com/health/schizotypal-personality-disorder#Outlook6

https://www.drugs.com/health-guide/schizotypal-personality-disorder.html

http://www.nytimes.com/health/guides/disease/schizotypal-personality-disorder/overview.html

http://www.healthguideinfo.com/personality-disorders/p85166/

https://www.quora.com/What-is-the-difference-between-schizoid-and-schizotypal-personality-disorder

https://www.ncbi.nlm.nih.gov/pmc/articles/PMC2992453/

http://www.disorders.org/paranoid-schizoid-schizotypal/

https://www.sharecare.com/health/personality-disorders/schizotypal-personality-related-schizophrenia

https://en.wikipedia.org/wiki/Schizotypal_personality_disorder

http://www.emedmd.com/content/schizoaffective-and-schizotypal-disorders

http://www.minddisorders.com/Py-Z/Schizotypal-personality-disorder.html

https://www.mentalhelp.net/blogs/schizotypal-personality-disorder-and-schizophrenia/

http://www.newsmax.com/FastFeatures/schizotypal-personality-disorder-diagnosis/2010/10/04/id/372418/

https://www.reddit.com/r/askscience/comments/39s1aa/what_are_the_differences_between_schizotypal/

http://www.bipolarcentral.com/otherillnesses/schizotypal_personality_dis.php

http://www.healthyplace.com/personality-disorders/schizotypal-personality-disorder/famous-people-with-schizotypal-personality-disorder/

http://healthresearchfunding.org/famous-people-schizotypal-personality-disorder/

http://www.minddisorders.com/Py-Z/Schizotypal-personality-disorder.html#ixzz4az2cSQzO

http://villains.wikia.com/wiki/Travis_Bickle

https://en.wikipedia.org/wiki/Travis_Bickle

https://en.wikipedia.org/wiki/Taxi_Driver

http://www.shmoop.com/taxi-driver/robert-de-niro.html

https://www.theatlantic.com/health/archive/2012/12/diagnosing-adam-lanza/266322/

https://scienceofnaturalwellness.wordpress.com/2012/12/16/did-adam-lanza-have-a-personality-disorder/

http://abcnews.go.com/Health/newtown-shooter-adam-lanza-sensory-processing-disorder-controversial/story?id=18532645

http://real-life-villains.wikia.com/wiki/Adam_Lanza

FURTHER READING

American Psychiatric Association. (2013). *Diagnostic and statistical manual of mental disorders (DSM-5®)*. American Psychiatric Pub.

American Psychiatric Association. (2013). Schizotypal personality disorders. In *Diagnostic and statistical manual of mental disorders (DSM-5®* (pp. 655-659*)*. American Psychiatric Pub.

Comer, R. (2014). Schizotypal personality disorder. *Abnormal psychology* (p. 406). MacMillan Publishers.

Steel, C., Marzillier, S., Fearon, P., & Ruddle, A. (2009). Childhood abuse and schizotypal personality. *Soc Psychiatry Psychiatr Epidemiol, 44*, 917-923.

SCHIZOPHRENIA

Any disorder that is associated with bizarre behavior, mood, or thinking, like borderline personality disorder or another psychotic disorder, as well as dissociative identity disorder previously called multiple personality disorder, may be particularly challenging to distinguish from schizophrenia. Specifically, people should realize that schizophrenics are not always dangerous, and that schizophrenia is not the same as a bipolar disorder or a split personality.

-o0o-

Schizophrenia is a serious complex brain disorder wherein the person cannot tell what is real from what is imagined. It is the most chronic and extremely disabling form of the major mental illness that impairs functioning in society, at work, at school, and in relationships. It is a psychotic disorder characterized by extremely disordered thinking and behavior. To people with schizophrenia, the world may seem like a jumble of confusing thoughts, images, and sounds. Their sudden change of personality and behavior may be very strange, shocking, and frightening at times. Although symptoms can vary from person to person, schizophrenia is usually characterized by hallucinations (seeing of hearing things) and delusions (irrational or false beliefs). For example, a person may see demons sitting next to him at dinner or believe he is the Son of God. Schizophrenic individuals may think the others can read or control their mind, and say things that do not make sense. They also have disordered thinking, decreased attention span, and problems with focusing. They are likely to be very fearful, and may sit for hours without moving or talking. Typically, they withdraw socially, are inattentive, often speak with a flat voice, and have no facial expression. They are indecisive and may have thoughts of committing suicide or hurting others.

“Positive” symptoms, sometimes referred to as psychotic symptoms, are exaggerated forms of thinking and irrational behavior, delusions, hallucinations, catatonia (when the person becomes physically fixed in a single position for a very long time), and disorganized thinking like talking in sentences that do not make sense, using nonsense words that make it difficult for the person to communicate or engage in conversation. They have trouble focusing or paying attention, write excessively but without meaning, forget or lose things, and repeat movements or gestures like pacing or walking in circles.

“Negative” symptoms reflect the absence of certain normal behaviors in people with schizophrenia. These include a lack of emotion or a very limited range of emotions, reduced energy, reduced speech, lack of motivation, social withdrawal, poor hygiene and grooming habits, and loss of interest in pleasurable things in life.

Schizophrenia varies in severity from person to person. There are different forms of schizophrenia, based on predominant symptoms. The most common form is paranoid schizophrenia, or schizophrenia with paranoia as it is often called. People with paranoid schizophrenia have an altered perception of reality. They may see or hear things that don’t exist, speak in strange or confusing ways, believe that others are trying to harm them, that they are being persecuted, or being watched and spied on. Most people tend to associate hallucinations strictly with schizophrenia. However, hallucinations are often experienced by people with bipolar disorder when either depression or mania has psychotic features.

The clinical diagnosis of paranoia requires a more specific explanation than the usual behavior that is manifested by otherwise normal individuals. The key to true or clinical paranoia is that the person exhibits an unreasonable and/or exaggerated mistrust and suspicion of others, which is not based on fact and that attains the level of a delusion. While some people have passing thoughts or temporary feeling that others are speaking about them or making fun of them behind their back, people who are paranoid would avoid this feeling at all costs even to the point of changing their daily interactions to avoid it. Paranoia is a symptom that can be part of several syndromes, including delusional disorder, paranoid personality disorder, mood disorders including bipolar disorder, other conditions such as brain toxicity that may be caused by drug or alcohol abuse, and certain types of poisoning,

Catatonic schizophrenics can be physically immobile or unable to speak. Disorganized schizophrenics are confused and incoherent. Catatonia is primarily a symptom of schizophrenia and schizoaffective disorder, but it can appear -- though rarely -- as a psychotic symptom of bipolar disorder as well. When most people think of catatonia, they think of catatonic stupor, where the affected person sits absolutely still and doesn't respond to anything.

Some people experience only one psychotic episode. Others have many episodes during a lifetime but lead relatively normal lives between episodes. Still other individuals with this disorder may experience a decline in their functioning over time with little improvement between full blown psychotic episodes. When the illness first appears, symptoms usually are sudden and severe. The symptoms of schizophrenia worsen and improve in cycles known as relapses and remissions.

While there are no laboratory tests to specifically diagnose schizophrenia, the doctor may use various tests, and possibly blood tests or brain imaging studies, to rule out another physical illness or intoxication (substance-induced psychosis) as the cause of the symptoms. The most significant changes are typically in the amygdala, thalamus, caudate, hippocampus and cerebral cortex. If the doctor finds no other physical cause, the person may be referred to a psychiatrist or psychologist who can make the right diagnosis based on interviews, special assessment tools, personal and family history, and observation of the person’s behavior. A person is considered to have schizophrenia if he or she has characteristic symptoms that last for at least six months.

In asking questions about mental-health symptoms, mental-health professionals are often exploring if the individual suffers from hallucinations or delusions, depression and/or manic episode similar to those experienced by people with bipolar disorder or schizoaffective disorder, anxiety, substance abuse, schizotypal personality disorder, and autism spectrum disorders including the condition that was formerly called Asperger disorder.

Schizophrenia may be associated with high suicide risk, self-injury, depression, anxiety disorders, obsessive-compulsive disorder, alcohol or drug abuse, legal and financial problems, homelessness, and social isolation. Patients may show aggressive behavior, although this is uncommon. On the other hand, the prevalence of antisocial personality disorder is high among men and women with schizophrenia as compared to the general population. Some evidence suggests that paranoid schizophrenia may have a better prospect than other types of schizophrenia for independent living and occupational functioning. While there is no cure for schizophrenia, symptoms and the risk of relapse can be managed in most people with an appropriate treatment plan. They often have additional mental health problems such as anxiety disorders, major depressive illness, or substance use disorders. It may be inherited, but symptoms typically come on gradually, begin in young adulthood, and last a long time. Sometimes, symptoms do develop during childhood, but this is rare.

The exact cause of schizophrenia is not yet known. It is known, however, that schizophrenia, like cancer and diabetes, is a real illness with a biological basis. Anyone can get schizophrenia. It is diagnosed all over the world and in all races and cultures. It is not rare; the lifetime risk of developing schizophrenia is widely accepted to be around 1 in 100. More than 2 million Americans suffer from schizophrenia at any given time, and 100,000-200,000 people are newly diagnosed every year. It is not the result of bad parenting or personal weakness. Researchers have uncovered a number of factors that appear to play a role in the development of schizophrenia, including genetics, abnormal regulation of neurotransmitter circuits, specific structural differences in the volume of gray matter and cortical thickness, and environmental factors (viral infection, extensive exposure to toxins like marijuana, and high stressful situations or hormonal changes). Social problems, such as long-term unemployment, poverty, and homelessness are common. About 0.3–0.7% of people are affected by schizophrenia during their lifetimes. The disorder affects men and women equally, although symptoms generally appear earlier in men (in their teens or 20s) than in women (in their 20s or early 30s). Earlier onset of symptoms has been linked to a more severe course of illness. Those who go on to develop schizophrenia may experience transient or self-limiting psychotic symptoms and the non-specific symptoms of social withdrawal, irritability, and clumsiness.

Later age of onset, increased educational attainment, and established relationships tend to predict a better prognosis. A small number of people who develop schizophrenia may recover completely, but most have a chronic/lifelong course. Many of those affected are significantly impaired by the symptoms of schizophrenia and may not be able to hold down jobs. Some may be so incapacitated that they are unable to complete activities of daily living. With proper treatment, most people with schizophrenia can lead productive and fulfilling lives. Depending on the level of severity and the consistency of treatment received, they are able to live with their families or in community settings rather than in long-term psychiatric institutions. Early diagnosis and treatment can help avoid or reduce frequent relapses and hospitalizations, and help decrease the disruption to the person's life, family, and relationships. Schizophrenia is often episodic, so periods of remission are ideal times to employ self-help strategies to limit the length and frequency of any future episodes.

The mainstay of treatment is antipsychotic medication, along with counseling, job training, and social rehabilitation. Antipsychotics are the primary medications used to treat schizophrenia. These drugs do not cure schizophrenia but help relieve the most troubling symptoms, including delusions, hallucinations, and thinking problems. Older or "first generation" medications include: *chlorpromazine (Thorazine), fluphenazine (Prolixin), haloperidol (Haldol), loxapine (Loxapine), perphenazine (Trilafon), thioridazine (Mellaril), thiothixene (Navane)*, and *trifluoperazine (Stelazine)*. Newer or "atypical" generation drugs include: *aripiprazole (Abilify), aripiprazole lauroxil (Aristada), asenapine (Saphris), clozapine (Clozaril), iloperidone (Fanapt), lurasidone (Latuda), paliperidone (Invega Sustenna), paliperidone palmitate (Invega Trinza), quetiapine (Seroquel), risperidone (Risperdal), olanzapine (Zyprexa),* and *ziprasidone (Geodon).* Other, even newer atypical antipsychotics include *brexpiprazole (Rexulti)* and *cariprazine (Vraylar).* Each person responds differently to different antipsychotic medicines. Although medications cannot cure, they can treat the symptoms and help improve the patient's ability to function and cope with their illness.

While medication can help relieve symptoms of schizophrenia, various forms of psychotherapy can help the patients manage their symptoms, identify early warning signs of relapse, and develop a relapse prevention plan. Individual psychotherapy can help the person better understand his or her illness, and learn coping and problem-solving skills. Cognitive remediation involves learning techniques to compensate for problems with information processing, often through drills, coaching and computer-based exercises, to strengthen specific mental skills involving attention, memory and planning/organization. Rehabilitation focuses on social skills and job training to help people with schizophrenia function in the community and live as independently as possible. Family therapy can help families deal more effectively with a loved one who has schizophrenia, enabling them to better help their loved one. Group therapy or support groups can provide continuing mutual support.

Electroconvulsive therapy (ECT) is not well established for treating schizophrenia, and is therefore not used very often when mood symptoms are absent. It is sometimes helpful when medications fail or if severe depression or catatonia makes treating the illness difficult. ECT is a procedure in which electrodes are attached to the person's scalp and, while asleep under general anesthesia, a small electric shock is delivered to the brain. A course of ECT treatment usually involves 2-3 treatments per week for several weeks. Each shock treatment causes a controlled seizure, and a series of treatments over time leads to improvement in mood and thinking.

Many people with schizophrenia may be treated as outpatients, although involuntary hospitalization may be necessary to stabilize their condition when the symptoms get out of control, or when there is a risk of hurting themselves or others. People with schizophrenia may need housing, job training, and other community support programs. People with the most severe forms of this disorder may not be able to live alone, and may have to live in group homes or other long-term, structured residences.

Popular books and movies often depict people with schizophrenia and other mental illnesses as dangerous and violent. This is usually not true. Most people with schizophrenia are not violent. Many people with schizophrenia withdraw from the outside world, and act out in confusion and fear. They are at an increased risk of attempting suicide, especially during psychotic episodes, periods of depression, and in the first six months after starting treatment. In some cases, however, people with mental illness may engage in dangerous or violent behaviors to themselves or others, generally as a result of their psychosis and fear of being threatened in some way by their surroundings. On the other hand, people with schizophrenia can also be a danger to themselves. Suicide is the number one cause of premature death among people with schizophrenia

Many people confuse bipolar disorder with schizophrenia due to misinformation about both illnesses. This is not so surprising when we consider how much the two disorders have in common. They are both likely to run in families. Both bipolar disorder and schizophrenia appear to result from gene–environment interaction. During severe episodes of mania or depression people with bipolar disorder may have psychotic symptoms, such as hallucinations or delusions. People with either disorder may have delusions of grandeur in which they believe they are a famous person or historical figure. Other symptoms of schizophrenia, including lack of pleasure, difficulty making decisions, and difficulty focusing, are similar to some symptoms of depression seen in bipolar disorder. Substance abuse is a complicating factor for both conditions, making symptoms more difficult to recognize as a mental illness. Because of some similar symptoms, differentiating between the two can sometimes be difficult; indeed, there is an intermediate diagnosis schizoaffective disorder.

Bipolar and schizophrenia, though, are two completely different psychiatric disorders and are even in two different classes of mental illness. Schizophrenia is primarily a psychotic disorder, and bipolar disorder is primarily a mood disorder. In bipolar disorder, the symptoms surround mood swings of depression alternating with mania. On the other hand, schizophrenia's primary symptom is psychosis or the inability to tell reality from fantasy. While psychosis may be part of a manic or depressed episode, it is not the primary symptom of bipolar disorder. Schizophrenia is a less common disorder, and its symptoms are more severe than those of bipolar disorder. People with schizophrenia may appear to have a "flattened" mood (not happy or sad), whereas people with bipolar often appear moody. People with bipolar disorder may have psychotic symptoms that are related to mood, people with schizophrenia tend to have psychotic symptoms that are independent of their mood. Unlike schizophrenia, bipolar disorder shows very few differences in gray matter volume. Psychosis is a hallmark symptom of schizophrenia. People with bipolar I disorder can have psychotic symptoms, hallucinations and delusions, during mania and/or depression. Antipsychotics and atypical antipsychotics are the major classes of medications used to treat schizophrenia. Mood-stabilizers, such as lithium, are the primary medications used to treat bipolar disorder. Atypical antipsychotic medications may also be used for bipolar disorder, often in combination with antidepressant medications.

Bipolar disorder and schizophrenia can share a set of serious symptoms, but when distinguishing between the two disorders, doctors look at the differences between symptoms and also give a different weight to some of the symptoms that are shared. None of the symptoms of delusions, hallucinations, and disorganized speech and behavior have to be present in someone who is diagnosed with bipolar disorder, although they may be present. In fact, the only requirement for a diagnosis of bipolar I disorder is that the patient has had one manic episode; though depression is also common, it is not required for a diagnosis.

Schizophrenia and split personality or multiple personality disorder are often confused with each other. Contrary to popular belief, schizophrenia is not a split personality or multiple personality disorder. The two are distinctly different disorders. People with multiple personality disorder, also known as dissociative identity disorder, are not born with it. Rather, additional personalities are developed as a coping mechanism to handle a massive traumatic event, usually due to severe physical or sexual abuse during an early age. Personalities divide as a way for the child to deal with the stress and trauma, enabling him or her to pretend that the trauma was happening to someone else. The symptoms of multiple personality disorder typically start during early childhood—6 years old in average, while schizophrenics develop symptoms during adolescence or early adulthood. To be diagnosed with multiple personality disorder, a person must have at least one alter personality that controls the person's behavior at times. A person with multiple personality disorder may develop as many as 100 personalities, but the average is 10. They may take on alter personalities of the same sex, a different sex, or both sexes at the same time, and sometimes take on even the physical characteristics and behavior of their other personalities, such as their manner of walking and way of talking.

Although rare, there have been cases of childhood schizophrenia, occurring before age 18 (early onset) or before age 13 (very early onset). Affected children present symptoms similar to those seen among adult schizophrenics, including auditory and visual hallucinations, abnormal behavior, strange thoughts, delay in language and motor development, significantly and adversely impacting the child's ability to function and maintain normal interpersonal relationships. Some children may appear anxious or confused, with repetitive movements like rocking or fidgeting. Delusions and hallucinations, usually auditory, may be difficult to distinguish from normal child play or talking to an imaginary friend. Deterioration in school performance and self-care, diminished social skills, unusual or bizarre behavior, disorganized thinking, social withdrawal, lack of impulse control, hostility and aggression usually precede the psychotic symptoms. The criteria for diagnosis are similar to those of adult schizophrenia, and based on physical, laboratory and psychological evaluation, observed behavior, clinical history and reports from teachers, parents or caregivers. Schizophrenia has no definite cause although the condition may correlate with certain risk factors such as family history. An early- or very early onset schizophrenia carries a more severe prognosis than later-onset schizophrenia. Childhood schizophrenia is not curable, but can be controlled with the help of medications and behavioral therapy.

-o0o-

FAMOUS PERSONS WITH SCHIZOPHRENIC DISORDER

The following are five extraordinary people from different walks of life, who were affected by schizophrenia in different ways, but were able to deal with the loss of jobs, families, and their sanity. Their inspirational stories show how they persevered and won the hardest battle of their life. The fact that these famous people have had to deal with a severe debilitating mental illness such as schizophrenia shows that it can affect anyone—regardless of social standing or financial earnings. Some of them have gone public with their illness in an effort to reduce the stigma and shame attached to mental illness, and to instill the idea that people with severe mental illness can still attain tremendous benefits when given the right management and resources. Their courageous choice, to speak openly about the challenges they face with schizophrenia, can increase public awareness and help us realize that even with mental illness, we can still develop an optimistic outlook, explore our skills and talents, utilize our potential, and achieve success.

-o0o-

LIONEL ALDRIDGE

Lionel Aldridge was an All-Skyline tackle and co-captain of the Utah State Aggies, who enjoyed an 11-year career in the NFL playing for the Green Bay Packers and the San Diego Chargers. As a Packer, he played a role in three straight NFL Championships and in Packer vices in Super Bowls I and II. He played two seasons in San Diego before retiring from professional football in 1973. Upon his retirement he launched an impressive career in radio broadcasting and network TV, but he started hearing voices at the age of 33. He became suspicious of the people that he worked with, and he became very unhappy in his workplace. Later, he started having bouts of psychosis, with imaginary voices and hallucinations. While alone in his car, he overheard someone whispering that everyone knew he did not care about his job. The voices were very scary and confusing. He started talking back to the voices, shouting, bickering, pleading and cursing. He developed extreme paranoia and irritability, and it became difficult for him to get along with others. He was afraid to go home because he believed that his wife was a witch. Imaginary voices drove him from job to job in city after city. He felt that imaginary agents were controlling him and broadcasting his thoughts to others. Once, he ran barefoot through the snow looking for his psychotherapist. He was soon hospitalized. He stopped taking his medications after a couple of years because he felt like a zombie and could not work. The imaginary voices told him to quit his job and leave town. He had delusions that his station was underground, that nobody liked him, and that he had to watch out for himself. After his wife filed for divorce, he took a leave of absence from work and drove across the country. When he ran out of money, he sold his car and continued to travel by bus or by train. He found some jobs but the imaginary voices would not leave him alone. He soon became homeless, sleeping on the streets. Three years later, his friends convinced him to get himself admitted. He was finally diagnosed with paranoid schizophrenia and given the right medication. Later that year, he left the hospital and moved to a nursing home, and then moved to his own apartment. After getting help from professionals, he was able to make a recovery and started working at the post office. He later became an advocate for the homeless and the mentally ill and served as a board member for the Mental Health Association of Milwaukee. He died of congestive heart failure and obesity, at the age of 56.

-o0o-

NATHANIEL AYERS

Nathaniel Ayers was once such a talented musician that he became one of the first black teenagers to be accepted by the world-renowned Juilliard Music School in New York, but he dropped out before the end of his second year. Once he moved into an apartment to attend Juilliard, he became withdrawn from others, and began compulsively spelling his full name aloud to himself. He first experienced auditory hallucinations while playing the cello at a music rehearsal as a student in Juilliard, when he heard male, female, and youthful voices telling him different things such as "I'll protect you from the pain", "they can hear your thoughts", and "run away, Nathaniel." These hallucinations became frightening and derogatory, and began to impair his functioning in school. Terrified when the voices became seemingly impossible to ignore, he continued to experience auditory hallucinations, disorganized speech, a blunted affect and negative symptoms such as social withdrawal and loss of interest in things around him. At the early stage of his illness, he saw a rolling cart of fire by the window one evening, when he was playing cello. He suffered a mental breakdown during his third year and was institutionalized. He continued to experience auditory hallucinations, delusions, disorganized speech, a blunted affect and negative symptoms such as social withdrawal and loss of interest in things around him. For some years he lived with his mother in Cleveland, Ohio, where he received heavy doses of *Thorazine*, bodily restraints and electroconvulsive therapy for his illness. After his mother's death in 2000, he moved to Los Angeles, where he was reduced to playing and living on the streets, dragging his only possessions around in a shopping trolley. He was homeless with poor hygiene, dressed bizarrely in a construction vest with a visor, and a Hawaiian lei, playing one of Beethoven's pieces with his two-stringed violin, when he had a chance meeting with a Los Angeles Times reporter. Upon learning about his past and his estranged family, the reporter wrote several columns about his slow transition out of homelessness, attempting to bring him back to music and using a donated cello to persuade him to perform at various locations. He became the subject of numerous newspaper columns, a book, and a 2009 film adaptation, "The Soloist", based on the columns. He remained highly mistrustful of health-care providers and was adamantly opposed to forced medication. A foundation bearing his name was started in 2008 with an aim to support artistically gifted people with mental illness.

-o0o-

DR. JOHN FORBES NASH, JR.

Dr. John Forbes Nash, Jr. was an American mathematician who made fundamental contributions to game theory, differential geometry, and the study of partial differential equations. During his early childhood, he lost two friends when the homemade explosives that they were building together accidentally exploded. He received his PhD in 1950 at the age of 23. He started teaching at MIT, and in 1958 he was featured in Fortune magazine's new series as one of the brightest young math stars of the time. His symptoms seemed to have started in 1958 at the age of 31, when he showed up to a New Year's Eve party dressed as a baby, almost entirely naked except for a diaper and sash across his chest. He carried a milk bottle and spent much of his evening sitting on his wife's lap. He later claimed that he was receiving messages from aliens in outer space and from foreign governments via The New York Times. He wrote letters to the U.N., the pope, and the FBI, government officials, his colleagues and his friends, saying that he was going to found an international organization, and believing that aliens from outer space were ruining his career. During one of his lectures, he was disorganized, confused, and said things that made no sense to anyone. He claimed that he saw men in red ties walking around MIT campus, signaling for him to be part of "a crypto-communist party". He was diagnosed with paranoid schizophrenia in 1959. While in the hospital, he told visiting friends about his grandiose delusions. Two months after his release from the hospital, he quit his job at MIT right before he was supposed to receive tenure and then refused a job at the University of Chicago because he was "going to become the Emperor of Antarctica". He travelled to Europe, attempting to renounce his American citizenship and become the "first citizen of the world". He continued to develop more delusions revolving around God and religion. He believed that he was a religious or messianic figure of great and secret importance, and would often open up several bank accounts under false names across the world. He was deported back to the United States and he went to Princeton where he wandered and spent much of his time alone; quite aloof from others. Some of the students remembered him wearing what appeared to be a Russian peasant garment, carrying around a notebook, and talking to squirrels. He made a lot of phone calls, often full of nonsense, numerology, dates, and world affairs. He deteriorated when he went off of his medication, and he went back into his delusions. Eventually, during the second half of the height of his disorder, he began to have auditory hallucinations and heard persecutory voices of other "mathematicians" who opposed his ideas. When he was on his medication, he was able to function so well that he published scholarly papers. He was hospitalized again, but after his release in 1961, he began to get angry, restless, and obsessed over numerology and his time in the asylum, fearing that his food had been poisoned. He was hospitalized for a third time, and improved temporarily, only to again become delusional, haphazardly dressed with blank facial expression and wandering around, obsessed with numbers and mathematics in his delusions and hallucinations. He believed that Jewish people were the root of all of his personal problems and was afraid of death by Armageddon. He was hospitalized three more times in which he was given insulin coma therapy (ICT), *Stelazine*, and *Thorazine*. The ICT was administered to him for 6 weeks and seemed to be effective. After 1970, his condition slowly improved, allowing him to return to academic work by the mid-1980s. He was later given a Nobel Prize in 1994 for his contribution to game theory and what is known as Nash Equilibrium. He and his wife died from a vehicular accident in 2015, on their way home from the airport after a visit to Norway, where he had received the Abel Prize for his seminal work on partial differential equation.

-o0o-

ELYN SAKS

Elyn Saks is Associate Dean and Orrin B. Evans Professor of Law, Psychology, and Psychiatry and the Behavioral Sciences at the University of Southern California Gould Law School. She is an expert in mental health law and recipient of a $500,000 MacArthur Foundation Fellowship. She graduated summa cum laude from Vanderbilt University before earning her Master of Letters degree from Oxford University as a Marshall Scholar and her J.D. from Yale Law School, where she also edited the Yale Law Journal. She is a legal scholar and an outspoken advocate for schizophrenia and mental health awareness. She first started noticing that something was wrong when she was 16, when she suddenly left her classroom without any reason, and while walking home, believed all the houses in her neighborhood were transmitting hostile and insulting messages directly into her brain. Five years later, while attending law school at Oxford, she experienced her first complete schizophrenic break. When she broke down during her first semester at law school at the age of 21, she would tell her classmates words that were connected, but that didn't make any sense when put together. She had infrequent hallucinations, like watching a huge spider walk up her wall; and disorganized and confused thinking. She had delusions that she had killed hundreds of thousands of people with her thoughts, or that someone had set off a nuclear explosion in her brain. Another breakdown happened while Saks was a student at Yale Law School. She was found singing on the roof of the library at midnight. She was then taken to the emergency room, tied down to a hospital bed, and forced to take anti-psychotic medication. She spent the next five months in a psychiatric ward. Over the course of the next several years, she was in a state of debilitating psychosis. She refused to believe that she was suffering from a mental illness — a conviction that prevented her from taking her meds seriously. Prior to staying on her medication, she fantasized that everyone had the same "scary and weird thoughts," and that the only difference was that other people were better at hiding or managing it. Once, when her psychoanalyst announced his planned retirement, she fell apart. She barely ate for a week or more, and moved as though her legs were wooden. Her face looked and felt like a mask. She had pulled down all the shades, so the apartment was in near total darkness, and the place was a shambles. Her thoughts became disorganized, and she kept on saying that she was being pushed to the ground, that her situation was grave, that gravity was pulling her down, and that she was scared. It resulted in her involuntary hospitalization. She struggled over the course of the next decade, but she came through -- thanks to medication, therapy, and the support of her friends and family. She has managed to stay free of hospitals for more than 30 years. She writes extensively in the area of law and mental health, having published five books and more than fifty articles and book chapters. She is one of the few successful career people to come out and share their experiences about having been diagnosed with schizophrenia while they are still active in their jobs.

-o0o-

DANIEL PAUL SCHREBER

Daniel Paul Schreber was a German judge who developed a paranoid psychosis for which he was institutionalized on three separate occasions. He described his mental illness in his book, “Memoirs of My Nervous Illness”, which became an influential book in the history of psychiatry and psychoanalysis because of its value as a psychological memoir and its interpretation by Sigmund Freud. He was a successful and highly respected judge until middle age when he woke up alarmed one morning, because of his thinking that it would be pleasant to "succumb" to sexual intercourse as a woman. He felt that this thought had come from somewhere else, not from him. He hypothesized that a doctor, who had experimented with hypnosis on him; had telepathically invaded his mind, using a "nerve-language". He believed that hundreds of people's souls had taken special interest in him, and contacted his nerves by using "divine rays", telling him special information, or requesting things of him. At the age of 42 years, he had his first illness. He entered an asylum for about 6 months, was diagnosed with severe hypochondria, recovered, and returned to public office as a judge. Seven years later, at the age of 51, and while working as a presiding judge, he had a second episode that began with insomnia, forcing him to return to the clinic. There, his condition worsened rapidly and he had delusions that he had softening of the brain and the plague, that he was dead and decomposing, that he was being persecuted, and that his body was being handled, manipulated, and changed on behalf of a “holy purpose.” This state of total psychosis lasted for several years and he was readmitted to two asylums for 8 years. He felt tortured, longed for death, asked to be given cyanide, and tried drowning himself in his bath several times. The core of his delusion was that he had a mission to redeem the world and to restore mankind to their lost state of bliss. In order for this to happen, he had to be transformed bodily into a woman so that, as God's concubine, he could give birth to a new race of humanity. He experienced florid hallucinations in addition to bizarre and non-bizarre delusions. He was unable to care for himself and required long-term hospitalization. When he was not delusional, he had long periods of remission, sufficient enough to allow functioning outside of asylums. In the last 2 of these years, he wrote his memoirs and took legal action against his forced hospitalization and commitment to asylum where he would often sit motionless for hours. He won the case and was discharged a year before his memoirs were published. However, following his mother's death and his wife's stroke, he fell ill again and was admitted to asylum where he spent the remaining 4 years of his life. His older brother was likely to also have been psychotic, and committed suicide at the age of 38, which was ascribed to 'melancholia' as the cause of the event in obituaries. His nervous breakdown and his account of reading his own death notice in his memoirs may be an instance of identification with his deceased brother.

-o0o-

REFERENCES

http://aacap.org/page.ww?name=Schizophrenia+in+Children§ion=Facts+for+Families

http://abcnews.go.com/2020/MindMoodNews/paranoid schizophrenic-kid-urges-kill-mother/story? id=10073035#.

https://academic.oup.com/schizophreniabulletin/article/35/3/476/1873740/Psychosis-as-a-Disorder-of-Reduced-Cathectic

http://allpsych.com/disorders/mood/index.html

http://articles.latimes.com/1987-10-27/sports/sp-16847_1_lionel-aldridge

http://articles.latimes.com/2014/apr/22/local/la-me-0423-lopez-ayers-20140423

http://articles.nydailynews.com/2009-09-07/gossip/17931830_1_megan-fox-schizophrenia-mental

http://emedicine.medscape.com http://allpsych.com/disorders/psychotic/index.html /article/288259-overview

http://emedicine.medscape.com/article/286661-clinical

http://en.wikipedia.org/wiki/Atypical_antipsychotics

https://en.wikipedia.org/wiki/Daniel_Paul_Schreber

https://en.wikipedia.org/wiki/Elyn_Saks

https://en.wikipedia.org/wiki/John_Forbes_Nash_Jr.

http://en.wikipedia.org/wiki/History_of_schizophrenia

https://en.wikipedia.org/wiki/Lionel_Aldridge

https://en.wikipedia.org/wiki/Nathaniel_Ayers

https://en.wikipedia.org/wiki/Schizophrenia

http://en.wikipedia.org/wiki/Typical_antipsychotic

https://en.wikipedia.org/wiki/Vincent_van_Gogh

http://healthyplace.com/thought-disorders/schizophrenia-movies-and-people/famous-people-and-celebrities-with-schizophrenia/

https://hubpages.com/education/Daniel-Paul-Schreber-in-Discussion-of-Paranoid-Schizophrenia

http://infomory.com/famous/10-famous-people-with-schizophrenia/

http://io9.gizmodo.com/5983970/im-elyn-saks-and-this-is-what-its-like-to-live-with-schizophrenia

http://knowledgenuts.com/2014/10/27/difference-between-schizophrenia-and-split-personality-disorders/
http://mentalhealthdaily.com/2014/03/26/famous-people-with-schizophrenia-list-of-schizophrenic-celebrities/
http://mhc.cpnp.org/doi/full/10.9740/mhc.n164039?code=cpnp-site
http://mhk-rad.blogspot.com/2012/07/soloist-diagnostic-film-critique.html
https://news.google.com/newspapers?id=7fMtAAAAIBAJ&sjid=hNAFAAAAIBAJ&pg=6301%2C2161037
http://news.hjnews.com/sports/reflecting-on-aggie-great-lionel-aldridge/article_f493ceac-4918-11df-b231-001cc4c002e0.html
http://news.psu.edu/story/141375/2010/10/26/research/probing-question-how-do-schizophrenia-and-did-differ
http://news.sciencemag.org/sciencenow/2009/09/08-01.html
https://pediaview.com/openpedia/Daniel_Paul_Schreber
https://prezi.com/zkpgflzdbhnt/living-with-schizophrenia-lionel-aldridge/
https://psychcentral.com/lib/the-differences-between-bipolar-disorder-schizophrenia-and-multiple-personality-disorder/
http://psychcentral.com/lib/2011/schizophrenia-and-genetics-research-update/all/1/
http://psychology.wikia.com/wiki/Daniel_Paul_Schreber
http://pubs.niaaa.nih.gov/publications/arh26-2/99-102.pdf
http://ripleeforensicpsych.umwblogs.org/2012/08/02/overcoming-paranoid-schizophrenia-the-inspiring-case-of-john-forbes-nash-jr/
http://schizophrenia.about.com/od/schizophreniainsociety/a/highlights_hist.htm
http://schizophrenia.com/famous.htm#
http://support4hope.com/schizophrenia/schizophrenia_self_help.htm
http://weblaw.usc.edu/faculty/contactInfo.cfm?detailID=300
https://www.awesomestories.com/asset/view/schizophrenia-The-Soloist
http://www.camh.net/about_addiction_mental_health/mental_health_information/schizophrenia_partfam.html
http://www.cnn.com/2012/08/12/opinion/saks-mental-illness/index.html
http://www.dangerousbehaviour.com/Disturbing_News/Women%20and%20Schizophrenia.htm
http://www.dnalc.org/view/899-DSM-IV-Criteria-for-Schizophrenia.html
http://www.emedicinehealth.com/schizophrenia_health/article_em.htm
http://www.einstein-website.de/
http://www.encyclopedia.com/education/news-wires-white-papers-and-books/harrell-tom
http://www.healthyplace.com/blogs/dissociativeliving/2010/11/dissociative-identity-disorder-is-not
http://www.healthguidance.org/entry/14077/1/Debunking-Six-Myths-on-Schizophrenia.html
http://www.mademan.com/mm/10-best-songs-about-winning.html
http://www.mayoclinic.org/diseases-conditions/schizophrenia/home/ovc-20253194
http://www.mayoclinic.com/health/disorganized-schizophrenia/DS00864
http://www.mayoclinic.com/health/catatonic-schizophrenia/DS00863

http://www.mayoclinic.com/health/paranoid_shizophrenia862/DSECTION=symptoms
http://www.mayoclinic.com/health/schizophrenia/DS00196
http://www.mayoclinic.com/health/paranoid-schizophrenia/DS00862
http://www.mdjunction.com/forums/mental-health-discussions/general-support/326555-famous-people-with-mental-illness
http://www.medicinenet.com/script/main/art.asp?articlekey=50773
http://www.medicinenet.com/schizophrenia/article.htm
http://www.medicalnewstoday.com/articles/192621.php
https://melbournelacanian.wordpress.com/2013/05/25/biographical-and-historical-background-to-freuds-schreber-case/
http://www.mentalhealth.com/mag1/scz/sb-prod.html
http://www.mentalhealth.org.nz/page/680-2010-media-releases+lets-talk-about-it-schizophrenia-awareness-week
http://www.mentalhealthadvocacyinc.org/role-models
http://www.mentalhealthamerica.net/conditions/schizophrenia
http://www.mirror.co.uk/tv/tv-news/gifted-cellist-who-lived-on-skid-419898
http://www.mja.com.au/public/mentalhealth/articles/hustig/husbox1.html
http://www.ncbi.nlm.nih.gov/pubmed/22071584
http://www.ncbi.nlm.nih.gov/pubmed/19626210
http://www.ncbi.nlm.nih.gov/pubmed?term=12052573
http://www.ncbi.nlm.nih.gov/pubmed/20565524
http://www.ncbi.nlm.nih.gov/pmc/articles/PMC1914490/?tool=pubmed
http://www.nytimes.com/1998/02/14/sports/lionel-aldridge-56-stalwart-on-defense-for-packer-teams.html
http://www.nimh.nih.gov/health/publications/schizophrenia/complete-index.shtml#pub8
http://www.nimh.nih.gov/health/publications/schizophrenia/index.shtmlhttp://www.nimh.nih.gov/health/publicatios/bipolar-disorder/what-are-the-symptoms-of-bipolar-disorder.shtml
http://www.nimh.nih.gov/health/publications/schizophrenia/how-is-schizophrenia-treated.shtml
http://www.nimh.nih.gov/health/publications/schizophrenia/what-about-substance-abuse.shtml
http://www.nimh.nih.gov/health/publications/schizophrenia/what-causes-schizophrenia.shtml
http://www.nimh.nih.gov/health/publications/schizophrenia/what-is-schizophrenia.shtml
http://www.nimh.nih.gov/health/publications/schizophrenia/when-does-schizophrenia-start-and-who-gets-it.shtml
https://www.nimh.nih.gov/health/topics/schizophrenia/index.shtml
http://www.npr.org/programs/atc/features/2002/aug/schizophrenia/
http://www.online-psychology-degrees.org/20-famous-people-with-schizophrenia/
http://www.opposingviews.com/i/top-10-oscar-worthy-films-that-feature-mental-illness

http://www.peteearley.com/2014/04/23/nathaniel-ayers-of-soloist-fame-forced-medication/
http://www.quora.com/What-does-it-feel-like-to-have-schizophrenia
http://www.schizlife.com/famous-people-with-schizophrenia/
http://www.schizlife.com/john-nash-and-schizophrenia/
http://www.schizophrenia.com/disease.htm
http://www.schizophrenia.com/family/60tip.html
http://www.schizophrenia.com/research/hereditygen.htm
http://www.schizophrenia.com/research/szmen2000.htm
http://www.schizophrenia.com/stories/aldridge.htm
http://www.schizophrenia.com/suicide.html
http://www.schizophrenia.com/szfacts.htm
http://www.schizophrenic.com/articles/famous-schizophrenic-people
http://www.schizophrenic.com/articles/schizophrenia/schizophrenic-musicians
http://www.schizophrenic.com/content/schizophrenia/schizophrenia-statistics
http://www.schizophrenic.com/content/schizophrenia-related/split-personalityschizophrenia/
http://www.schizophrenic.com/content/schizophrenia/schizophrenia-statistics
http://www.schizophrenic.com/content/schizophrenia/symptoms/schizophrenia-delusions
http://www.schizophrenic.com/content/schizophrenia/schizophrenia-and-suicide
http://www.schizophrenic.com/content/schizophrenia/schizophrenia-risk-factors
http://www.sciencedaily.com/releases/2010/11/101109191750.htm
http://www.time.com/time/health/article/0,8599,2005559-1,00.html
http://www.webmd.com/schizophrenia/guide/mental-health-schizophrenia#1
http://www.wisegeek.org/what-is-the-difference-between-schizophrenia-and-multiple-personality-disorder.htm
http://www.wow.com/wiki/Daniel_Paul_Schreber
http://www.wow.com/wiki/Lionel_Aldridge?s_chn=90&s_pt=source2&s_gl=US&s_dto=d&v_t=content

FURTHER READING

American Psychiatric Association. (2013). *Diagnostic and statistical manual of mental disorders (DSM-5®).*

American Psychiatric Pub. American Psychiatric Association. (2013). Schizotypal personality disorders. In *Diagnostic and statistical manual of mental disorders (DSM-5®* (pp. 655-659*).*

American Psychiatric Pub. Comer, R. (2014). Schizotypal personality disorder. *Abnormal psychology* (p. 406). MacMillan Publishers.

Steel, C., Marzillier, S., Fearon, P., & Ruddle, A. (2009). Childhood abuse and schizotypal personality. *Soc Psychiatry Psychiatr Epidemiol, 44*, 917-923.

-o0o-

SCHIZOAFFECTIVE DISORDER

Even after following patients for many years, it may still be difficult to determine if they have schizophrenia or bipolar disorder, because they often present with a mixture or combination of symptoms. In such cases, they may receive a diagnostic label of schizoaffective disorder, bipolar type. It distorts the way a person thinks, acts, expresses emotions, perceives reality, and relates to others.

-oOo-

Schizoaffective disorder is a mental disorder characterized by abnormal thought processes and deregulated emotions, with both severe mood swings (mania and/or depression), and some of the psychotic symptoms of schizophrenia. Initially, people may be misdiagnosed with schizophrenia with prominent mood symptoms, or they may be misdiagnosed as having bipolar disorder with psychotic features, if their major manic and/or depressive episodes are accompanied by psychotic symptoms such as paranoia, catatonia, and hallucinations or others. However, if their mood stabilizes but they still experience symptoms of psychosis for at least two weeks, a new diagnosis of schizoaffective disorder is often given. Schizoaffective disorder symptoms may vary from person to person. The bipolar type includes episodes of mania and sometimes major depression, while the depressive type has only major depressive episodes.

Patients with schizoaffective disorder may have symptoms of mood disorder that are of sufficient severity and chronicity to exclude an uncomplicated diagnosis of schizophrenia, or they show features of schizophrenia that are sufficiently severe to exclude an uncomplicated diagnosis of a mood disorder. This cluster of symptoms may or may not occur simultaneously; that is, the clinical features mainly resemble those of schizophrenia in some cases, while features of affective or mood disorder predominates in other cases. In schizoaffective disorder the psychotic symptoms may be present during the times when the patient also experiences depression or mania. However, the diagnosis of schizoaffective disorder requires that the psychotic symptoms of hallucinations and delusions should be present for a long enough time (at least a couple of weeks) at times when the patient is not experiencing serious mood symptoms. Finally, the symptoms should not be attributable to either substance use or to a major medical condition. There are two subtypes of the disorder, including bipolar type and depressive type.

The occurrence of symptoms of schizoaffective disorder may vary greatly from one person to the next, and may be mild or severe. Symptoms of depression include loss of appetite, changes in sleeping patterns, agitation, lack of energy, loss of interest in usual activities, feelings of worthlessness, hopelessness or guilt, lack of concentration, and thoughts of suicide. Manic symptoms include rapid speech, unusual hyperactivity, racing thoughts, less need for sleep, agitation, being easily distracted, and self-destructive or dangerous behavior such as driving recklessly, gambling or going on spending sprees. Symptoms of schizophrenia include delusions, hallucinations disorganized thinking, odd or unusual behavior, slow movements, lack of emotion and facial expression, poor motivation, incoherent speech, and problems with communication. A core of psychotic symptoms, such as hallucinations, fixed delusional ideation, or disorganized thinking, are frequent and may come and go in patients diagnosed with schizoaffective disorder. At the same time, patients with schizoaffective disorder also experience frequent mood episodes such as depression and mania which may be brief or may be present for a significant period of time.

Schizoaffective disorder is often characterized by a rapid onset of symptoms, with a relatively high degree of remission and relapses. Some patients experience a severe onset of emotional disturbance, but "recover" and resume a relatively normal life after several weeks or months. The rate of death due to suicide or accident is comparable to those seen in schizophrenia and major affective disorder. Poor recovery or remission between episodes, persistent psychotic symptoms in the absence of affective features, and a greater number of schizophrenia-like symptoms are factors that may influence and result in poor clinical outcome among patients with schizoaffective disorder.

Schizoaffective disorder is thought to be less common than schizophrenia and mood disorders. It tends to be rare in children. In general, the disorder is more common in females than in males, and tends to be relatively younger than that seen in unipolar or bipolar disorder. The incidence of schizophrenia and bipolar disorder is higher among relatives of schizoaffective patients, compared to the normal population. Most of the patients diagnosed with schizophrenia have a more chronic and persistent course, while most patients diagnosed with schizoaffective disorder have a more episodic course, but it may be the other way around in some patients. Schizoaffective disorder also appears to have a better clinical outcome than schizophrenia, but has a worse outcome compared to bipolar disorder alone.

Diagnosis is difficult because the symptoms of schizoaffective disorder are similar to schizophrenia and bipolar disorder. People coming out of acute schizophrenic episodes are prone to depression (post-psychotic depression), while others who are severely depressed can sometimes suffer from hallucination. The symptoms of mania can easily be confused with the emotions, thoughts and behavior commonly experienced during a schizophrenic psychotic episode. It is only with extremely careful screening, testing and interviewing that a person can be diagnosed with schizoaffective disorder. Reassessing the diagnosis over the course of the illness may even be necessary to ensure that correct diagnosis has been made.

The diagnostic approach to schizoaffective disorder includes physical examination to rule out other problems, psychiatric evaluation, discussion of family and personal history, observed behavior, and ancillary procedures including MRI or CT scan to rule out abnormalities in brain structure. Laboratory tests should be performed to exclude psychosis associated with or caused by substance use, medications, toxins or poisons, surgical complications, or other medical illnesses. A long-term history of the person is necessary to confirm the diagnosis. Since general practitioners are not trained to exclude medical causes of psychosis, people experiencing psychosis should be referred to an emergency department or hospital.

Delirium should be ruled out, which can be distinguished by visual hallucinations, acute onset and fluctuating level of consciousness, indicating other underlying factors that include medical illnesses. Excluding medical illnesses associated with psychosis is performed by using blood tests to measure thyroid-stimulating hormone to exclude hypo- or hyperthyroidism, basic electrolytes and serum calcium to rule out a metabolic disturbance, full blood count including erythrocyte sedimentation rate (ESR) to rule out a systemic infection or chronic disease, and serology to exclude syphilis or HIV infection. Blood tests are not usually repeated for relapse in patients with an established diagnosis of schizoaffective disorder, unless there is a specific medical indication.

Amphetamine, cocaine, and to a lesser extent alcohol, can result in psychosis that presents clinically like psychosis in schizoaffective disorder. It is well understood that *methamphetamine* and cocaine use can result in *methamphetamine* or cocaine-induced psychosis that may persist even after the individual has stopped taking them. Alcohol-induced psychosis can also persist during withdrawal, although it appears to do so at a lower rate, than when it is being abused.

As with many mental illnesses, the cause of schizoaffective disorder is not clear but a combination of factors may contribute to its development. Genetics, neurobiology, early and current environment, behavioral, social, and experiential components appear to be important contributory factors. Some recreational and prescription drugs may cause or worsen symptoms. People with schizoaffective disorder are also likely to have co-occurring conditions, including anxiety disorders and substance use disorder. Social problems such as long-term unemployment, poverty and homelessness are common. There is a higher percentage of having a precipitating event, like a physical or interpersonal life stressor, with schizoaffective disorder compared to schizophrenia or bipolar disorder, or depression. People with schizoaffective disorder are at an increased risk of having suicide, suicide attempts or suicidal thoughts, family and interpersonal conflicts, social isolation, anxiety disorders, unemployment, poverty, and homelessness.

Although there is no cure, people with schizoaffective disorder generally respond best to a combination of medications, psychotherapy and life skills training. Treatment varies, depending on the type and severity of symptoms, and whether the disorder is the depressive or bipolar type. Atypical antipsychotic drug are given mostly during the times when the patient experiences severe psychotic symptoms, in addition to specific treatments for the mood symptoms. They include *risperidone (Risperdal), olanzapine (Zyprexa), quetiapine (Seroquel* and *Seroquel-XR), ziprasidone (Geodon), aripiprazole (Abilify), paliperidone (Invega), asenapine (Saphris), iloperidone (Fanapt), paliperidone (Invega), lurasidone (Latuda),* and *brexpiprazole (Rexulti)*. The use of these medications has allowed successful treatment and release back to their homes and the community for many people suffering from schizoaffective disorder. Some neuroleptic medications can either be injected into muscle (for example, *haloperidol, fluphenazine, risperidone,* and *aripiprazole)* or melt once placed under the tongue (for example, *asenapine*), and can further help the schizoaffective disorder patients to maintain critical compliance with their care. *Clozapine (Clozaril)* is not associated with movement disorder but it can produce other side effects, including a possible decrease in the number of white blood cells to the point of being dangerous, so the blood needs to be monitored every week during the first six months of treatment and then every two weeks to detect this side effect early if it occurs. In schizophrenic type schizoaffective disorder, antipsychotic medication may be augmented with lithium or antidepressant medication.

Mood-stabilizer medications like *lithium (Lithobid), valproic acid or divalproex (Stavzor or Depakote), carbamazepine (Tegretol, Tegretol XR, Equetro, Carbatrol),* and *lamotrigine (Lamictal)* can be useful in treating active (acute) symptoms of mania as well as in preventing return of such symptoms in schizoaffective disorder. *Lithium, divalproex,* and *carbamazepine* require monitoring of medication blood levels. Since people with schizoaffective disorder often have depression as part of the illness, medications that address that symptom may be of great benefit, as well. Serotonergic medications like *fluoxetine (Prozac), sertraline (Zoloft), paroxetine (Paxil), citalopram (Celexa), escitalopram (Lexapro), vilazodone (Viibryd),* and *vortioxetine (Brintellix)* are often prescribed because of their effectiveness and low incidence of side effects. Other often-prescribed antidepressant medications for treatment of schizoaffective disorder include *venlafaxine (Effexor), duloxetine (Cymbalta), desvenlafaxine (Pristiq),* and *bupropion (Wellbutrin).*

Most of these medications take several weeks to take effect. Patience is required if the dose needs to be adjusted, the specific medication changed, or another medication added. In order to determine whether an antipsychotic is effective or not, it should be tried for at least six to eight weeks (or even longer with *clozapine*).

In addition to medication, psychotherapy or talk therapy may help. Individual or one-on-one therapy focuses on real-life plans, problems and relationships. It may help them better understand their condition and learn to manage their symptoms. It helps normalize thought patterns and reduce symptoms. Cognitive behavioral therapy helps change the negative thinking and behavior associated with feelings of depression. The goal of this therapy is to help them recognize negative thoughts and to teach coping strategies. Building a trusting relationship is important for the psychotherapy to be effective. Family or group therapy can be more effective when people with schizoaffective disorder are able to discuss their real-life problems with others and decrease their social isolation. Social skills training is focused on improving communication and on enhancing one's ability to participate in daily activities. New skills and behaviors specific to settings such as the home or workplace can be practiced. Vocational rehabilitation and supported employment focuses on helping them prepare for, find, and keep jobs. Supportive psychotherapy and cognitive behavioral therapy are both helpful. Intensive case management has been shown to improve adherence to treatment, improve social functioning, and reduce hospitalization.

Psychiatric rehabilitation, psychotherapy, and vocational rehabilitation are very important for recovery of higher psychosocial function. As a group, people with schizoaffective disorder have a better outcome than people with schizophrenia, but have variable individual psychosocial functional outcomes compared to people with mood disorders. Electroconvulsive therapy may be considered for patients with schizoaffective disorder experiencing severe depression or severe psychotic symptoms that have not responded to treatment with antipsychotics and psychotherapy. It may also reduce mortality rates among schizoaffective patients.

During periods of crisis or times of severe symptoms, or when there is risk to self or others, hospitalization may be necessary to ensure their safety, proper nutrition, adequate sleep, and basic personal care and cleanliness. Long-term maintenance treatment can help to manage the symptoms, and is almost always with an antipsychotic, usually at lower doses than in schizophrenia, as well as an antidepressant or mood stabilizer.

-o0o-

PERSONS WITH SCHIZOAFFECTIVE DISORDER

The suggestion of a relationship between creativity and mental disorder has existed for centuries, particularly when it comes to music. There are only a few famous people with Schizoaffective Disorder that combines the symptoms of both schizophrenia and mood disorder, but they have flourished in spite of their disorder. The poignant narrative of artists who are recognized among the most creative figures in 20th century popular music more than proves that anyone can rise above the stigma of mental disorder.

-o0o-

TOM HARRELL

Tom Harrell is one of the finest jazz trumpeters in the world, and has been named jazz trumpeter of the year three times by Downbeat Magazine. Early on, he showed extraordinary talent in music and art. By the time he was eight, he was writing and illustrating his own children's books, which revealed the work of a precocious, original mind. In one book, young Tom told the story of a little boy who goes to a doctor for treatment of a mosquito bite and gets diagnosed with 'scissor-birds, dog-turtles' and other animal hybrids that he invented. He starting playing the trumpet at the age of eight. He began to play professionally by the time he was 13. He played both trumpet and piano with groups all over the San Francisco Bay area When he was 17, he became surly and aloof, a social misfit, and, at one very low point, he tried to kill himself. When he went off to college at 18, his sister received a call that he had tried to commit suicide. When he was in his 20s, he heard voices ordering him to walk through a window after he had some orange juice. He came in and saw blood all over the rug, so he had to break the window to get out. He got cut when the glass shattered, but it kept him inside. He was diagnosed with schizoaffective disorder, which combines the paranoia of schizophrenia with the wild mood swings of manic depression. For decades, he took *Stelazine,* an early antipsychotic that partially controlled his delusions and hallucinations but gave him unpredictable muscle contractions, obviously a terrible problem for a performer. Later, he switched to *Seroquel*, which had the common side effects of dizziness and sluggishness, but caused fewer tremors. The medication slowed his speech and gave him headaches, but he was able to carry on as a professional musician, working his way from band to band. He overcame his symptoms by playing music with his instrument, but once he stopped playing, voices materialize and threaten his sense of reality. He believed that people were out to get him - that they were targeting him in some way, and his behavior would change radically. As long as he took his medication, he was able to function, although his band members have all witnessed his paranoia. For no apparent reason, he would announce that he was hearing voices, that someone was whispering something and telling him to get off the stage because he sucked, or that people did not want to hear him play. Even though there were no buildings within sight of the apartment, he sometimes believed he was being watched. At other times, he believed his home had been bugged. Quite often, he heard voices that would make him deeply guilty and depressed. When the voices spoke, or when visual hallucinations beset him, his shaking worsened. But he was not always like that: he could be good-spirited, and could do things with and hang out with his friends. He would spend his days practicing and composing, with neat, logical, and orderly written notes. During interviews, he would be nervous, shaky, and reluctant or unable to communicate. He took three medications that staved off his depression, reduced his panic attacks, and sedated him. Without them, he turned psychotic. Once, when his wife of 11 years was researching a documentary for Japanese television on creativity and the brain, she held a tape to interview him. He started to talk, and then asked her to stop the tape because it was making him nervous. He started to get all flustered, and claimed that “I don’t belong in the music business. I better quit. I don’t have the personality to be in the music business.” He would have crises that included sudden disappearances, rapidly changing mood swings, and a suicide attempt. His medication, the only thing that kept him from being institutionalized, helped control his symptoms. Once, after his medicine caused a toxic reaction and nearly killed him, he stopped taking it. The results were fascinating and frightening. His moods changed more quickly and furiously than ever, from happy to sad, confident to insecure. His posture improved, his tremors vanished, and he became something close to affable. He would buy bags of groceries and leave them in front of his neighbors' doors as anonymous gifts. During one of his performances, he was seen doing crazy acts and shaking while playing the trumpet. He claimed that he was being told by a voice in the dark. He claimed that he did not always know how to approach social situation and he was not always able to fit into social groups, but the medicine helped in allaying his extreme fear from having his illness. He continued to produce and compose music, releasing his 24th album earlier in 2011. He now speaks openly about his struggles with the illness in hopes of helping others cope with their own challenges. He appears on more than 260 albums and has had his compositions published in a number of books. He has signed a contract with the RCA Victor label, and he has begun to gain recognition outside the hardcore group of fans who had previously followed his work.

-o0o-

DAVID HELFGOTT

David Helfgott is an Australian concert pianist whose life inspired the Oscar-Academy Award winning film "Shine", which portrayed him as an authentic example of someone who suffers from schizoaffective disorder. He was a delicate child who, early on, exhibited signs of agitation. In 1953, the year David started grade school, he began to develop frequent bladder control problems that might, even at the age of five years, have been related to stress in the family home. His father, a failed violinist for whom music was a great passion, prompted his son to develop his talent from an early age. His childhood years were often spent learning the difficult works of Russian and Hungarian composers and pianists, as well as preparing for, or performing in piano competitions. As a teenage prodigy during this period, he studied under a local teacher, and continued to compete in increasingly prominent piano competitions. In the film, he had his first severe mental breakdown around age 14 or 15, after his overbearing father forbade him to accept an invitation to study music in the United States. Acting against his father's wishes, he eventually left to study at the Royal College of Music in London. His father reportedly disowned him, exacerbating his emotional problems and precipitating what would eventually become full-fledged breakdowns that he later described as "fog" and a state of "being damaged." He was diagnosed with schizoaffective disorder by his psychiatrist following a breakdown. In 1971, he was discharged from his first stay at Charles Gairdner Hospital in Perth, married his first wife and got divorced after three years. His father's death in 1975 had little visible effect on him, and he was readmitted to a mental hospital in 1976. By 1977, he was unable to perform on consecutive days, and he expressed himself in a rapid-fire, unintelligible fashion that often gave the impression that his speech could not keep up with his thoughts. He had periods of anxiety, pressured speech and suicidal ideation. He began having hallucinations and was hyperactive, with little need for sleep, with racing thoughts, rapid talking and inflated self-esteem at times. He displayed extreme paranoia and excessive restlessness when practicing pieces for performances and during the entire film, he exhibited guilt or self-blame. He had disorganized speech and disordered thinking, even incoherent at times. He could not dress himself and his family members had to button his shirt and put on his shoes for his big performances. He was unable to fall asleep and would frantically scan the newspaper or chain smoke. He could not pay attention or concentrate. At times he showed difficulties with logical reasoning and impulse control, refusing to wear pants in public, and acting inappropriately to strangers by either kissing them or grabbing their breasts. Over the next ten years, he was in and out of mental institutions, where he underwent psychiatric treatment that included psychotropic medication and electroconvulsive therapy. He gradually recovered, first playing piano in a wine bar in his native Perth, then returning to concert halls in Australia with the help of his wife, and later embarking on a worldwide concert tour to sold-out audiences. His 2015 European tour was the subject of a documentary, "Hello I Am David!"

-o0o-

BRIAN WILSON

Brian Douglas Wilson is a composer, arranger, producer, vocalist and multi-instrumentalist, most famous for his work as bandleader of The Beach Boys. When he was a child, his father subjected him and his younger brothers to regular physical and mental abuse, and his mother was by all accounts an alcoholic. But as Wilson grew older, he increasingly turned to music as an escape from the pain of his home life. Along with his two younger brothers and their cousin, Wilson began performing at parties and small gatherings. His work with the Beach Boys helped raise pop music to the level of high art. As his fame and musical prowess progressed, he began to suff er from auditory hallucinations, various paranoid beliefs and delusions. He first reported hearing indistinct voices and screaming in his sleep in 1963 (at age 21), which he was able to stop as long as he kept working and producing music. By 1964, he would often become obsessed with tiny details (such counting the number of tiles on a floor, the number of peas on a plate, the number of stitches on an airplane seat), and by 1966 he would conduct important conversations only in his home swimming pool, as he believed his house was filled with hidden recording devices. More overtly psychotic symptoms gradually worsened as Wilson entered his mid-twenties, particularly his auditory hallucinations and the voices he heard grew more frightening, threatening to kill him and his family. He quit touring with the Beach Boys, due in part to a nervous breakdown he had suffered on the road. He began using marijuana recreationally in 1964, he had delusions that his band mate was having an affair with his wife, that his house was bugged, that recording a song about fire had caused a nearby building to burn down, and that a business associate's wife was a witch trying to control his mind. He also had periods of low mood and general disinterest in doing anything of his own volition, even growing bored of writing music. His appetite increased, and he started binge eating. He gained over 100 lbs. of weight, refused to groom himself, slept or stayed in bed for most of the day, and had suicidal ideation between 1973 and 1975. At other days, he would jump out of bed with all the energy and enthusiasm he had ever had. Sometimes, he would stay awake for prolonged periods of time, experience highly goal-motivated periods of activity and have flights of ideas. He also had mood swings, crying one minute and laughing hysterically the next minute, for no reason. In 1983, he was initially diagnosed as a paranoid schizophrenic by the controversial Dr. Eugene Landy, who put him under strict diet regimen, monitored his every move, and controlled his business affairs, relationships and contact with the outside world. Dr. Landy overdosed him with anti-psychotic drugs so much so that he developed involuntary movements of his tongue, face, lips and extremities (also known as tardive dyskinesia). Wilson went along with the Dr. Landy's program for fear that the doctor would have him committed to an institution. The shrewd psychologist controlled his life, took 25 per cent of his royalties, and made him sign a will leaving almost everything to his therapist. After breaking free from his psychologist a decade and a half later, psychiatric evaluations between 1992 and 1994 gave him the diagnosis of schizoaffective disorder, for which he was prescribed conventional medical treatment, including anti-depressants, and lower doses of antipsychotic. This appeared to have led to a greater lucidity and subjective sense of well-being .In the late 1990s, he revived his career, and began performing and recording consistently as a solo artist. In 1988 he and the Beach Boys were inducted into the Rock and Roll Hall of Fame and he remarried in 1995. In 2000, he was also inducted into the Songwriters Hall of Fame. He won the 2005 and 2011 Grammy Awards for Best Rock Instrumental, and in 2007 he received the prestigious Kennedy Center Honors for lifetime contribution to the performing arts.

-o0o-

REFERENCES

https://allpsych.com/disorders/psychotic/schizoaffective/
https://alumni.stanford.edu/get/page/magazine/article/?article_id=32012
http://emedicine.medscape.com/article/294763 overview
http://emedicine.medscape.com/article/294763-overview
https://en.wikipedia.org/wiki/Brian_Wilson
https://en.wikipedia.org/wiki/David_Helfgott
https://en.wikipedia.org/wiki/Kat_Bjelland
https://en.wikipedia.org/wiki/Michael_Hawkins (American_actor)
https://en.wikipedia.org/wiki/Nick_Blinko
https://en.wikipedia.org/wiki/Schizoaffective_disorder
https://en.wikipedia.org/wiki/Tom_Harrell
https://en.wikipedia.org/wiki/Vincent_van_Gogh
https://en.wikipedia.org/wiki/Wild_Man_Fischer

https://en.wikipedia.org/wiki/Aby_Warburg
http://healthyplace.com/thought-disorders/schizophrenia-movies-and-people/famous-people-and-celebrities-with-schizophrenia/
http://healthresearchfunding.org/famous-people-schizoaffective-disorder/
http://jazzprofiles.blogspot.com/2009/05/tom-harrell-part-1-interviews.htmL
http://nypost.com/2015/06/04/how-one-quack-doctor-almost-destroyed-brian-wilsons-career/
http://trialx.com/curetalk/2011/09/15/celebrities-famous-people-with-schizoaffective-disorder/
http://www.aifc.com.au/isaac-newton-schizophrenic/
http://www.abilitymagazine.com/past/brianW/brianw.html
http://www.browsebiography.com/bio-david_helfgott.html
http://www.cbsnews.com/news/a-beautiful-note/
http://www.dailymail.co.uk/news/article-3111278/Beach-Boys-singer-Brian-Wilson-misdiagnosed-paranoid-schizophrenic-drugged-weeks-end-therapist-stars-new-documentary-claims.html
https://www.drugs.com/cg/schizoaffective-disorder.html
http://www.healthline.com/health/schizoaffective-disorder#Outlook7
http://www.mayoclinic.org/diseases-conditions/schizoaffective-disorder/home/ovc-20258872
http://www.medicinenet.com/schizoaffective_disorder/article.htmhttps://medlineplus.gov/ency/article/000930.htm
http://www.mentalhealthamerica.net/conditions/schizoaffective-disorder
http://www.musicianguide.com/biographies/1608000385/David-Helfgott.html
https://www.myprivatesearch.com/search?q=schizoaffective%20disorder
https://www.nami.org/Learn-More/Mental-Health-Conditions/Schizoaffective-Disorder
http://www.nami.org/Learn-More/Mental-Health-Conditions/Schizoaffective-Disorder/Treatment
https://www.pastemagazine.com/blogs/lists/2011/05/brilliant-musicians-whove-battled-mental-illness.html
https://psychcentral.com/disorders/schizoaffective-disorder-symptoms/
https://www.researchgate.net/publication/223533269_A_psychobiographical_analysis_of_Brian_Douglas_Wilson_Creativity_drugs_and_models_of_schizophrenic_and_affective_disorders
http://www.biography.com/people/brian-wilson-586000#early-life
https://www.theguardian.com/music/2011/jun/24/brian-wilson-interview
https://www.ukessays.com/essays/psychology/symptoms-of-schizoaffective-disorder.php
https://www.verywell.com/what-is-schizoaffective-disorder-380507
https://www.verywell.com/how-is-schizophrenia-diagnosed-2953119
https://www.verywell.com/atypical-antipsychotics-treatment-for-schizophrenia-2330698
http://www.webmd.com/schizophrenia/guide/mental-health-schizoaffective-disorder#1

FURTHER READING

Goodwin, F.K., & Jamison, K.R. (2007). *Manic-depressive illness: Bipolar disorders and recurrent depression* (2nd ed.). New York, NY: Oxford University Press.

Goodwin, F.K., & Marneros, A. (2005). *Bipolar disorders: Mixed states, rapid cycling and atypical forms*. New York, NY: Cambridge University Press.

Malhi, G.S., Green, M., Fagiolini, A., Peselow, E.D., & Kumari, V. (2008). Schizoaffective disorder: Diagnostic issues and future recommendations. *Bipolar Disord, 10*(1 Pt. 2), 215–30.

Marneros, A., & Akiskal, H.S. (2007). *The overlap of schizophrenic and affective spectra*. New York, NY: Cambridge University Press. Murray, W.H. (2006). *Schizoaffective disorders: New research*. New York, NY: Nova Science Publishers, Inc.

-o0o-

PSYCHOSIS

While some bad people and serial killers have psychotic episodes, majority of psychotic individuals are not killers. In fact, many psychotic people contribute positively to society. Psychotic and psychopathic individuals have two separate, distinct disorders—and labeling everyone who falls under these categories as a "psycho" adds more to the confusion. Both conditions begin with the word "psycho", but they are very different, and they are distinct from each other. Psychotics cannot be cured, but they can be treated. Psychopaths cannot be cured and cannot be treated. Not all psychopaths are criminals, and not all criminals are psychopaths.

-o0o-

Mental illness is not the same as a personality disorder, although the two are often confused with each other. People tend to use the words psychopath and psychotic interchangeably because they are not aware of the difference between psychosis and psychopathy. Simply put, the psychotic mind is literally one that has stopped functioning normally, has lost contact with reality, and has lost the capacity to think and behave rationally. In contrast, psychopathy is an antisocial personality disorder characterized by impulsivity, recklessness, scrupulousness, callousness, a lack of empathy, and a desire to hurt others.

Psychotic disorders are a group of serious illnesses that affect the mind. They make it hard for someone to think clearly, make good judgments, respond emotionally, understand reality, communicate effectively, or behave appropriately. The most typical manifestations of psychosis are delusions (or bizarre and false beliefs) and hallucinations (or perceiving something that is not there). By far, auditory hallucinations (like "hearing voices") are the most frequently occurring, but psychotic individuals can also experience visual hallucinations (or "seeing things that aren't really there"), tactile hallucinations (such as, feeling like bugs are crawling on your skin when there is none present), and even olfactory hallucinations (or smelling something that is not there).

Delusional disorder is a type of psychotic disorder where people have “non-bizarre” beliefs that are not based in reality. For example, they may believe that a famous celebrity is in love with them, even though that celebrity has never met them. This is different from a “bizarre” belief, for example, that demons in the form of insects have fallen from heaven, are crawling under their skin, and are eating them alive.

Psychosis is a symptom of mental health disorder, not a diagnosis, per se. People experience psychosis in the course of psychotic-based disorders such as schizophrenia. A psychotic disorder not otherwise specified is a generalized disorder given to individuals who have experienced a psychotic episode but don’t meet any other criteria for other psychotic-based disorders such as schizophrenia. One cannot receive a diagnosis of psychosis but they could be diagnosed as having schizophrenia. Psychosis as a sign of a psychiatric disorder is a diagnosis of exclusion. That is, a new-onset episode of psychosis is not considered a symptom of a psychiatric disorder until other relevant and known causes of psychosis are properly excluded.

People can become psychotic due to a number of reasons. Certain substances such as alcohol, methamphetamine, LSD or “acid”, crack cocaine, and other drugs (including prescription drugs such as steroids, stimulants, and opiates) can induce a psychosis. Alzheimer’s disease and other types of dementia as well as brain tumors, complex partial seizures, infections or other physical abnormalities of the brain can also produce psychotic symptoms. Certain mental illnesses are commonly associated with psychosis, especially schizophrenia, and less frequently, bipolar disorder and deep depression. Persons with schizophrenia have paranoid delusions (believing that someone is poisoning them). Such delusions can be of the grandeur type (believing that they are God or that they have supernatural or magical powers), or of persecutory type, (believing that they are being pursued by the FBI or by extraterrestrial aliens). Similar delusions can also occur in individuals with bipolar disorder I. These individuals are simply not in their right mind, and have lost the capacity to correctly judge things or relate to others in a coherent, rational fashion. In layman's terms, a psychotic individual could be described as someone who is "insane."

On the other hand, psychopaths have an antisocial personality disorder characterized by an extreme lack of empathy, absence of guilty or remorse from abusing, hurting or exploiting of others. They may be superficially charming, but show little to no emotion or fear, are extremely manipulative, have no problem lying, and behave irresponsibly. They are in touch with reality, capable of rational thinking, and dangerous, because they are calculating and know how to victimize their targets. They see others as mere objects to possess, exploit, manipulate, abuse, or destroy. But not all psychopaths are openly antisocial. They can be heads of corporations, predators, pedophiles, con men or even your next door neighbor. They are good at coming across as deceptively normal, charming or even appealing, but they are definitely not insane.

It's important to remember that people afflicted with mental illnesses that can cause psychosis have essentially decent personalities except that brains have lost contact with reality. Psychotic individuals might also pose a danger at times, but they are not necessarily immoral serial killers. Psychotic individuals suffer from serious mental disorders that require proper care and treatment, and anti-psychotic medications as well as cognitive behavioral therapy can help mitigate these effects. Psychosis is not someone's fault, and neither does it mean that the person lacks a soul or empathy.

In contrast, psychopathy is a personality disorder that encompasses people who commit crimes and have no empathy for animals and other human beings. They begin exhibiting these qualities at a very young age; show no remorse or sensitivity, and have destructive impulses, like hurting animals or bullying other kids. They have no conscience and may range from being a predatory serial killer who gets aroused by hurting people to being a self-involved con man who uses others for his own benefit but who are not prone to violence. They are generally considered to be intelligent, manipulative, and charming — as well as being unable to learn from their mistakes or any form of punishment. Intelligent psychopaths may be successful CEO's and family men involved in white-collar crimes such as fraud, or they may simply be ruthless in business.

Psychosis is a mental illness that shouldn't be stigmatized. Just like any other form of physical or mental illness, psychotic individuals suffer from serious mental disorders that require proper care and treatment. Anti-psychotic medications as well as cognitive behavioral therapy can help control their symptoms, and most people will have a good recovery with treatment and close follow-up care. Basically, a psychotic person is not a danger to himself or society. Psychotic people might hurt themselves or others if their voices tell them to, or if they are responding to hallucinations (like when they see a person as a demon and try to attack them out of apparent self-defense), or if their delusions assure them it is the right thing to do. If that person thinks that he is being told to kill or harm others, then he will become a danger when he acts upon those delusions. In court, he (or she) will likely be found criminally insane and not responsible for his (or her) actions due to this delusional state.

Psychotic behavior can come and go. It can be a temporary or a permanent feature state of the mind. There is a big difference in the use of the terms "psychosis" and "insanity". The latter is used primarily in a legal setting to denote that a person cannot be held responsible for his or her actions in a court of law, due to psychological distress. Psychosis, on the other hand, is not a clinical diagnosis in and of itself, but a symptom common to several other mental illnesses. It can occur in both the chronically mentally ill and otherwise healthy individuals. It is treated by anti-psychotic medications, psychotherapy, and, in extreme cases, periods of hospitalization.

Psychopaths have a personality disorder, are distrustful, are cold-hearted and have no empathy or concern for others. They lie, steal, manipulate, torture, and kill. They are in touch with reality, but are unable to form meaningful relationships, and cannot control their emotions. They find satisfaction and get excited when they commit violent crimes, like serial murders. Early in life, they are prone to bullying, vandalism, torturing animals, and setting things on fire, not minding how their actions affect others. They are not "insane" nor are they mentally disabled. They know the difference between right and wrong, but don't give a damn. They show no emotion towards others, including love, guilt or hatred, and would happily destroy anything or anyone for personal pleasure and for the thrill of it.

Psychopaths hurt others because they know they can and because they want to, because they are focused on self-gratification, and often hurting others is what satisfies them. While people with psychosis can generally be treated with proper medication and therapy, most doctors and psychiatrists believe that psychopaths are not treatable, and the only way to stop many such people from further harming others is to put them behind bars.

-o0o-

PERSONS WITH PSYCHOSIS

Although people with schizophrenia can act unpredictably at times, most aren't violent, especially if they're getting treatment. When people with this brain disorder do commit violent acts, they usually have another condition, like childhood conduct problems or substance abuse. Each case of psychosis is different, and the exact cause is not always clear. A sense of personal threat and anger related to delusions are strongly linked with attempting to harm others.

-o0o-

PARVEEN BABI

Parveen Babi was the Indian actress who became a superstar most remembered for her glamorous roles alongside top heroes of the 1970s and early 1980s in blockbusters like "Deewar", "Namak Halaal", "Amar Akbar Anthony" and "Shaan". Many people regard her as one of the most beautiful actresses of all time in Indian cinema. There was even a movie created called "Woh Lamhe" which documents her struggles with the condition. When she travelled to California in 1984, she was suspected at John F. Kennedy International Airport after she failed to submit her identification papers. She was eventually handcuffed and ankle-cuffed by policemen and removed from the airport for hysteria. When she returned to Mumbai in 1989, she was rumored to have been diagnosed with paranoid schizophrenia, although she regularly denied this, stating that her being labeled as such was a conspiracy by the film industry and the media to malign her image and make her appear as insane, so that they can cover up their crimes. She broke relationships with most of her close dear ones including her own blood relatives. She had few contacts with known people and had become reclusive as she distrusted everyone. She created a stir when she filed a writ petition in the Bombay High Court, charging Indian film personalities as well as several dignitaries, Bill Clinton, Robert Redford, Prince Charles, Al Gore, US government, British government, French government, BJP government, Roman Catholic Church, CIA, CBI, KGB, and Mossad of conspiring to kill her, and when she was asked to show her evidences by the press, she showed some sort of scribbling on her notepad as her proof. During the early 1990s, whenever journalists or members of the press would come to her for an interview, she would often ask them to eat her food and drink her water first, so that she might be assured that her food was not poisoned. She assumed that her makeup was contaminated, and made her skin peel off. She claimed that the International Mafia had cut off her electricity to harass her. She resumed a career as an interior decorator in 1991, but in 2002, she again hit the headlines when she filed an affidavit in the special court hearing the 1993 serial bomb blasts case, claiming that she had gathered clinching evidence showing the involvement of an actor in the case, but she did not appear in court because she was afraid of being killed. In the last four years of her life, Babi recorded every phone call, always informing the caller about surveillance. She was found dead on 22 January 2005 from complications of diabetes at the age of 56.

-o0o-

DAVID BERKOWICH

David Berkowitz, also known as the "Son of Sam" and the ".44 Caliber Killer", was an American serial killer in the 1970s who killed six people and wounded seven others in New York, claiming that he was told to kill by a dog that was possessed by a demon. His crimes became legendary because of the bizarre content of the letters that he wrote to the police and the media, and his reasons for committing the attacks. As a child, he felt rejected and scorned because he was adopted. He displayed anti-social and aggressive behavior as a child, and had the reputation of being a loner and a bully. Although of above-average intelligence, he lost interest in learning at an early age and began an infatuation with petty larceny and pyromania. He grew up believing that his natural mother died while giving birth to him, and that his adoptive mother's death was a master plot designed to destroy him. While in the army, he had his one and only sexual experience with a prostitute and caught a venereal disease. His isolation, fantasies, and paranoid delusions were in full force when he briefly met his natural mother. In 1975, he claimed that his "demons" drove him to plunge his hunting knife in two women; one survived from six knife wounds. While staying in a two-family home, howling dogs in the neighborhood kept him from sleeping, which he interpreted as messages from demons that were ordering him to kill women. He said that he did what they asked just to quiet the demons. He killed a Labrador dog owned by his neighbor named Sam whom he thought was possessed by Satan himself. His killing spree began in 1976, with the shooting of two teenage women outside a Bronx apartment building. A handwritten letter addressed to the New York Police department was discovered while investigating one of the murders, written mostly in block capital letters with some lower-case letters with disorganized statements from a deranged person, who revealed the name "Son of Sam" for the first time. Several psychiatrists released a psychological profile, described him as neurotic and probably suffering from paranoid schizophrenia, and believed himself to be a victim of demonic possession. He later sent another letter taunting the police, signed by "Son of Sam". As the number of victims increased, he eluded the biggest police manhunt in the history of New York City while leaving letters that mocked the police and promised further crimes, which were highly publicized by the press. He was eventually caught and, during his trial in August 1978, he pled guilty to six murders for which he received six consecutive 25 years to life sentences. In the course of further police investigation, he was also implicated in many unsolved arsons in the city. When interviewed by an FBI veteran in 1979, he admitted that he invented the "Son of Sam" stories so that if caught he could convince the court that he was insane. He said the real reason he killed women was because he felt resentment toward his mother and his failures with women. He found killing them to be sexually arousing. On the same year, another inmate slashed his throat with a razor blade but he survived. During the mid-1990s, he amended his confession to claim that he had been a member of a violent satanic cult that orchestrated the incidents as ritual murder. He is currently serving a life sentence at a maximum-security correctional facility.

-o0o-

ED GEIN

Edward "Ed" Gein, also known as "The Butcher of Plainfield", was an American murderer and body snatcher, who gained widespread notoriety after authorities discovered that he had exhumed corpses from local graveyards and fashioned trophies and keepsakes from their bones and skin. He was the younger of two boys whose mother despised her husband, and an alcoholic who was unable to keep a job. Their mother took advantage of their home in an isolated 155-acre farm to turn away outsiders who could have influenced her sons. Ed spent most of his time doing chores on the farm, and his mother punished him whenever he tried to make friends. His mother preached to her boys about the innate immorality of the world, the evil of drinking, and the belief that all women were natural prostitutes and instruments of the devil. He was shy as a child, and classmates and teachers remembered him as having strange mannerisms, such as seemingly random laughter, as if he was laughing at his own personal jokes. A few years after his father's death, his brother died in a fire accident. His mother's death shortly thereafter left him devastated and all alone in a dark farm house at the age of 39. He boarded up the inside of the house, closing off his room and the upstairs. He held on to the farm and earned money from odd jobs. It was around this time that he became interested in reading death-cult magazines and adventure stories, particularly those involving cannibals or Nazi atrocities. He was obsessively devoted to his mother, a religious fanatic. After her death, he began robbing graves—keeping body parts as trophies, practicing necrophilia, and experimenting with human taxidermy. He then turned to murder, killing at least two women in 1957. When the police went to his farm home to investigate the disappearance of a local woman, they had no idea that they were about to discover some of the most grotesque crimes ever committed. Searching the house, authorities found whole human bones and fragments; wastebasket, chair seats, leggings, masks, made of human skin; skulls on his bedposts; bowls made of female skulls; nine vulvae in a shoe box, a belt made from human female nipples; his first victim's face mask in a paper bag and skull in a box; and his second victim's entire head in a burlap sack and heart in a plastic bag. When questioned, he told investigators that he had made as many as 40 nocturnal visits to three local graveyards to exhume recently buried bodies, dug up the graves of recently buried middle-aged women he thought resembled his mother, and took the corpses home, where he tanned their skins to make his paraphernalia. He was diagnosed with schizophrenia and was found mentally incompetent, unfit for trial. He was sent to the Central State Hospital for the Criminally Insane (now the Dodge Correctional Institution), a maximum-security facility, and later transferred to the Mendota State Hospital in Madison, Wisconsin. He died due from respiratory failure secondary to lung cancer in 1984, at the age of 77. In addition to "Psycho," films including "Texas Chainsaw Massacre" and "Silence of the Lambs" were said to be loosely based on Gein's crimes.

-o0o-

ADELE HUGO

Adèle Hugo was the youngest child of French poet, playwright, and politician Victor Hugo, known best for his novels *Les Misérables* and *The Hunchback of Notre Dame*. She is remembered for developing schizophrenia as a young woman, due to her romantic obsession with a British military officer. Raised in a cultured, affluent home in Paris, she enjoyed playing the piano, and was known for her beauty and long dark hair. After Victor Hugo was forced into political exile in 1851, the Hugo family moved to the island of Jersey, where she became romantically involved with a British army officer, Albert Pinson. After initially rejecting Pinson's proposal for marriage, she had a change of heart, but he refused to reconcile. Despite Pinson's rejection, she continued pursuing him, while her family worried for her well-being, and tried to track her whereabouts by letters. Much of what is known about her life and her pursuit of Pinson comes from her journal while she lived on Jersey and Guernsey. She stopped keeping a diary by the time she landed in Barbados, due to her mental deterioration. She was abandoned on Barbados, where she was known as "Madame Pinson", and found wandering the streets, talking to herself, detached from her surroundings. She devoted all her time seeking him and sent notes to him daily, but without effect. Gradually she drove herself insane, trying to return to the days when she had first met him, but the more she tried to regain his love, the more he spurned her. Her obsession was a manifestation of *erotomania*—a non-bizarre belief that Pinson was still in love with her. She had other symptoms of mental illness, including hallucinations. Although her letters to him were left unanswered, she wrote to her parents, telling them that she must be with her beloved and that they were planning to marry, but she would wait for their formal consent. She spent her evenings writing in her journal about her life and her love for him. She tried to persuade him, telling him that she's rejected another marriage proposal, threatened to expose him and ruin his military career, and even offered him money to pay for his gambling debts, but he remained unmoved. Convinced that she was his wife in spirit, she tried to conjure the ghost of her dead sister, and her behavior became more eccentric, fantasizing that she was married to him. Once, she followed him to a theater, where she was inspired to think that she could hypnotize him into loving her. She went mad with despair, and went to the father of his fiancé, claiming that he was married to her and that she was carrying his child. With his continued rebukes calling her ridiculous, she continued to deteriorate and wandered the streets in torn clothes talking to herself. Sometimes at night, she would disguise herself in male apparel, and would walk through the streets with a tall hat and a cane. She refused almost all food out of extreme unwillingness to spend money, would not allow a fire to be lit in her room, and bathed infrequently. She lived very nearly like an animal. Her hair became matted, dirty, and vermin-infested. Even more disturbing was her acquired habit of pacing almost continually back and forth in her room, often talking to herself in a loud voice, and shouting far into the night. She was ultimately sent to live in a mental institution for the affluent outside Paris, where she remained until her death at the age of 84.

-o0o-

ALEXANDER "SKIP" SPENCE

Alexander "Skip" Spence was a Canadian-born American musician, singer-songwriter, co-founder of the group Moby Grape, and the drummer for Jefferson Airplane on their debut album. He released one solo album, 1969's Oar, and then largely withdrew from the music industry. Once described on the Allmusic website as "one of psychedelia's brightest lights", his career was plagued by drug addictions coupled with mental health problems.

During the recording session of Moby Grape's second album, Wow, he attempted to break down a band mate's hotel room door with a fire axe, while under the influence of LSD. He thought he was the anti-Christ and tried to chop down the hotel room door with a fire axe to kill one of the band members to save him from himself. He went up to the 52nd floor of the CBS building where they had to wrestle him to the ground. He was confined to Bellevue where he was diagnosed with schizophrenia and given *Thorazine* for six months. On the day of his release, he rode a motorcycle, dressed in only his pajamas, and drove directly to Nashville to record his only solo album, the now-classic psychedelic/folk album Oar. Due to his deteriorating state and notwithstanding that he was no longer functioning in the band, he was supported by Moby Grape band members for extended periods. Voluminous consumption of heroin and cocaine resulted in a further involuntary committal for him. Once, he overdosed and sent to the morgue in San Jose with a tag on his toe, but he suddenly got up and asked for a glass of water. His mental illness worsened, and he spent much of the 1970s and 1980s in and out of mental hospitals. He would be pacing the room, describing axe murders and a little white rat named Oswald that would snort coke too. He was taken to the County Mental Health Hospital for trying to get little grammar school girls to go into the house with him. Mental illness, drug addiction and alcoholism thus prevented him from sustaining a career in the music industry. Much of his life was spent in third party care, as a ward of the State of California, and either homeless or in transient accommodations in his later years. His personal life and mental state worsened and he was forced to survive on welfare and handouts, living in a mobile home until his death from lung cancer at the age of 52.

-o0o-

REFERENCES

https://www.psychologytoday.com/blog/beautiful-minds/201103/psychotic-is-not-the-same-psychopathic

http://counsellingresource.com/features/2012/11/12/psychosis-psychopathy/

http://www.medicaldaily.com/what-it-really-means-be-psychotic-difference-between-psychosis-and-psychopathy-338712

http://yourselfseries.com/teens/topic/mental-disorders/what-is-the-difference-between-a-psychopath-and-a-psychotic/

http://www.diffen.com/difference/Psychopath_vs_Sociopath

http://www.differencebetween.net/science/health/difference-between-schizophrenia-and-psychosis/#ixzz4bdGyswgD

http://www.differencebetween.net/science/health/difference-between-schizophrenia-and-psychosis/

https://en.wikipedia.org/wiki/Psychosis

http://psychogendered.com/2015/06/are-psychopaths-psychotic/

http://www.whatisdifferencebetween.com/disease/what-is-the-difference-between-narcissist-psychotic-psychopath-and-sociopath.html

https://hubpages.com/health/The-Difference-Between-Psychopathy--Psychotic-Disorders

http://cycad.com/site/Brand/quotes/q15.html

http://www.webmd.com/schizophrenia/guide/mental-health-psychotic-disorders#1

http://www.webmd.com/schizophrenia/guide/mental-health-brief-psychotic-disorder#1

http://www.webmd.com/schizophrenia/guide/shared-psychotic-disorder#1

https://psychcentral.com/ask-the-therapist/2010/06/02/what-is-the-difference-between-psychosis-and-schizophrenia/

https://journalsonschizophrenia.wordpress.com/2015/05/04/psychotic-vs-psychopath/

http://thestrangestsituation.blogspot.com/2010/11/demystification-monday-psychotic-vs.html

http://www.remorselessfiction.com/psychotic-vs-psychopathic.html

http://paulrpurimd.com/psychotic-vs-psychopathic/

https://www.psychologytoday.com/blog/sacramento-street-psychiatry/201301/narcissists-psychopaths-and-other-bad-guys

http://characterassassinator-ruinyou.blogspot.com/2014/10/psychopath-vs-sociopath-vs-psychotic.html

https://www.healthtap.com/search/psychopath%20vs%20psychotic

http://www.urbandictionary.com/define.php?term=Psychopath

http://www.wisegeek.org/what-is-the-difference-between-neurotic-and-psychotic.htm

https://womensvoicesforchange.org/dr-ford-trying-to-understand-the-criminal-mind.htm

https://womensvoicesforchange.org/dr-ford-trying-to-understand-the-criminal-mind.htm

https://www.thoughtco.com/david-berkowitz-the-son-of-sam-972728

https://en.wikipedia.org/wiki/David_Berkowitz
http://www.biography.com/people/david-berkowitz-9209372#!
https://www.myprivatesearch.com/search?q=son+of+sam
http://www.history.com/this-day-in-history/son-of-sam-arrested
http://www.dailymail.co.uk/news/article-3176065/Man-slashed-throat-Son-Sam-murderer-prison-revealed-correctional-officer-says-miracle-serial-killer-survived-attack.html
https://en.wikipedia.org/wiki/Ed_Gein
http://www.wisconsinsickness.com/ed-gein/
http://www.biography.com/people/ed-gein-11291338#!
https://www.thoughtco.com/serial-killer-edward-gein-972713
http://serialkillersofwisconsin.weebly.com/ed-gein.html
http://www.history.com/this-day-in-history/real-life-psycho-ed-gein-dies
https://www.britannica.com/biography/Ed-Gein
https://simple.wikipedia.org/wiki/Ed_Gein
http://www.viralnova.com/ed-gein/
http://www.the-line-up.com/was-ed-gein-the-most-misunderstood-killer-in-american-history/
http://disturbinghorror.com/Serial-Killers/Serial-Killers-Bio/Ed-Gein.html
https://www.bizarrepedia.com/ed-gein/
http://mentalhealthdaily.com/2014/03/26/famous-people-with-schizophrenia-list-of-schizophrenic-celebrities/
https://en.wikipedia.org/wiki/Ad%C3%A8le_Hugo
https://en.wikipedia.org/wiki/The_Story_of_Adele_H.
http://www.blupete.com/Hist/BiosNS/1800-67/Hugo5.htm
http://www.blupete.com/Hist/BiosNS/1800-67/Hugo9.htm
https://en.wikipedia.org/wiki/Skip_Spence
https://www.last.fm/music/Alexander+%22Skip%22+Spence/+wiki
http://www.nytimes.com/1999/04/18/nyregion/skip-spence-psychedelic-musician-dies-at-52.html
http://www.oldies.com/artist-biography/Alexander-Skip-Spence.html
https://en.wikipedia.org/wiki/Parveen_Babi
http://www.imdb.com/name/nm0044916/bio
http://www.idiva.com/news-entertainment/the-myth-madness-of-the-late-parveen-babi/12285
http://sepiamutiny.com/blog/2005/01/22/parveen_babi_pa/
http://www.fashionlady.in/parveen-babi-illness-what-caused-her-death/36690
http://www.filmibeat.com/celebs/parveen-babi/biography.html
https://purepapertalk.quora.com/The-Rise-and-Fall-of-Parveen-Babi

FURTHER READING

Schultz, S.H., North, S.W., & Shields, C.G. (2007). Schizophrenia: A review. *Am Fam Physician, 75*(12), 1821–1929.

ANXIETY DISORDERS

People suffering from anxiety disorders, previously called "neurotics", are sometimes mislabeled as psychotic. Neurosis and psychosis are psychological terms that are often interchanged and used incorrectly in society. Because these two terms are both used to describe conditions that affect mental health, they are often misunderstood by friends and family. But there are differences between the two. Basically, the primary difference between neurosis and psychosis is the manner in which they affect mental health. The key feature of psychosis is a loss of perception of reality, associated with thought disorder, speech disorganization, delusions, and hallucinations. There are no delusions or hallucinations in neurosis. Neurotic persons may get panic attacks such as heart palpitations, numbness, fainting, chills and other symptoms, but they are aware and they are in touch with reality. Once believed to be a form of mental illness, neurosis is now looked upon as an unhealthy aspect of a certain spectrum of personalities.

-o0o-

Everyone gets worried or anxious sometimes. Most of us experience strong feelings of anxiety, sadness or panic at some period in our life and then we recover over time. We may worry about an upcoming routine medical screening, lie awake on the night before an airline flight, or have stage fright when speaking in front of large crowds. We experience anxiety in certain situations like taking exams, doing interviews and making presentations in public. But anxiety disorders involve more than temporary worry or fear. For a person with an anxiety disorder, the anxiety does not go away and can get worse over time. The feelings can interfere with daily activities that include job performance, school work, and relationships.

According to Sigmund Freud, often viewed as the "father" of modern psychology, the vast majority of neurotics would continue to function fairly normally in spite of increased emotional discomfort from time to time. Real neurosis, however, is a pattern of behavior characterized by obsessive worry and anxiety that can be emotionally crippling. The term “neurosis” is rarely used in today's psychological community. Rather, individuals with significant neurosis are now often diagnosed with Generalized Anxiety Disorder. More than normal everyday worries that can interfere with day-to-day activities may be a sign of generalized anxiety disorder.

Anxiety disorders are a group of related conditions, each with unique symptoms. Anxiety is a word that describes feelings of worry, nervousness, fear, apprehension, concern or restlessness. Normal feelings of anxiety often serve as an “alarm system,” alerting you to danger, like finding a burglar in your home, and hearing the fire alarm and seeing smoke coming out from the kitchen. But sometimes anxiety can be out of control, giving you a sense of dread and fear for no apparent reason. This kind of anxiety can disrupt your life. All anxiety disorders have one thing in common: persistent, excessive fear or worry in situations that are not threatening. Generalized anxiety disorder is an intense feeling of apprehension that causes sweating, rapid heart rate, and elevated blood pressure that may come spontaneously or be triggered by a certain stimulus. Its symptoms are similar to those of panic disorder, obsessive-compulsive disorder and other types of anxiety, but they’re all different conditions. They may manifest as individual disorders but may also be part of an underlying psychiatric condition.

People with generalized anxiety disorder are constant worriers. They get worried and stressed out about many things almost every day. They have a hard time controlling their worry. Adults with this problem often worry about money, family, health, or work. Children with this problem often worry about how well they can do an activity, such as in school or in sports. The worry, stress, and physical symptoms might make it hard for them to do normal activities such as going to work every day or doing grocery shopping. They can understand that they have a problem that hinders their life routine, but they can’t resolve it themselves.

Their symptoms must be consistent and ongoing, persisting at least six months, before a formal diagnosis of generalized anxiety disorder can be made. They cannot be better explained by another mental disorder such as panic attacks, social anxiety disorder, social phobia, contamination or other obsessions in obsessive-compulsive disorder. The symptoms may be due to separation from attachment figures in separation anxiety disorder, reminders of traumatic events in posttraumatic stress disorder, or gaining weight in anorexia nervosa. An organic mental disorder such hyperthyroidism, or a psychoactive substance-related disorder such as excess consumption of amphetamine-like substances, or withdrawal from benzodiazepines should also be ruled out.

People with generalized anxiety disorder display excessive anxiety or worry for months and face several anxiety-related symptoms. This excessive worry often interferes with daily functioning, as individuals with generalized anxiety disorder typically anticipate disaster, and are overly concerned about everyday matters such as health issues, money, death, family problems, friendship problems, interpersonal relationship problems, or work difficulties. Their symptoms include restlessness or feeling on edge; being easily fatigued; having difficulty with concentration; being lightheaded, twitching of the eyes, a mental block, irritability, muscle tension, problems with sleeping, and panic disorder. In addition to suffering from persistent worries and anxieties, people with generalized anxiety disorder may have low self-esteem or feel insecure. They may see people's intentions or events in negative terms, or they may experience them as intimidating or critical.

Anxiety disorders often occur along with depression. This is likely because of the considerable overlap of symptoms between the two disorders, and because the same environmental triggers can provoke symptoms in either condition. Sexual dysfunction also often accompanies anxiety disorders, although it is hard to determine whether anxiety causes the sexual dysfunction or whether the sexual dysfunction causes the anxiety. The most common manifestations among individuals with anxiety disorder are avoidance of intercourse, premature ejaculation or erectile dysfunction among men and pain during intercourse among women. Sexual dysfunction is particularly common among people affected by panic disorder and posttraumatic stress disorder.

Anyone can get generalized anxiety disorder at any age. But it usually starts during childhood or teenage years. Most people with generalized anxiety disorder have felt nervous or anxious as long as they can remember. In children, excessive worrying is centered on future events, past behaviors, social acceptance, family matters, personal abilities, and school performance. Unlike adults with general anxiety disorder, children and teens often don't realize that their anxiety is disproportionate to the situation, so adults need to recognize their symptoms. Along with many of the symptoms that appear in adults, some red flags for generalized anxiety disorder in children include perfectionism, excessive self-criticism, fear of making mistakes and feeling that they are to blame for any disaster. They may feel overly anxious to fit in, and constantly strive for approval or require a lot of reassurance about performances.

Separation anxiety disorder almost always occurs in children who are excessively anxious about separation from important family members or from home. Symptoms include extreme distress from either anticipating or actually being away from home or being separated from a parent or other loved one; intense worry about getting lost, being kidnapped, or otherwise being separated from loved ones; and frequent refusal to go to school or to sleep away from home. Children with separation anxiety disorder usually exhibit at least three of these symptoms for at least 4 weeks. Physical symptoms include headache, stomach ache, or even vomiting, when faced with separation from loved ones. Separation anxiety often disappears as the child grows older, but if not addressed, it may lead to panic disorder, agoraphobia, or combinations of anxiety disorders.

Anxiety disorders in children are often more challenging to identify than their adult counterparts owing to the difficulty many parents face in discerning them from normal childhood fears. Likewise, anxiety in children is sometimes misdiagnosed as an attention deficit disorder or, due to the tendency of children to interpret or convert their emotional distress into something physically wrong, anxiety disorders may initially be confused with physical ailments. Symptoms in children may be mistaken for behavioral problems (taking too long to do homework because of perfectionism, refusing to perform a chore because of fear of germs). Children do not usually recognize that their obsessions or compulsions are excessive.

Gifted children are also often more prone to excessive anxiety than non-gifted children. Other cases of anxiety arise from the child having experienced a traumatic event of some kind, and in some cases, the cause of the child's anxiety cannot be pinpointed. Anxiety in children tends to manifest along age-appropriate themes, such as fear of going to school (not related to bullying) or not performing well enough at school, fear of social rejection, or fear of something happening to loved ones. What separates disordered anxiety from normal childhood anxiety is the duration and intensity of the fears involved.

Genetic and environmental factors, frequently interacting with one another, are believed to be risk factors for anxiety disorders. Specific factors may also include shyness, or behavioral inhibition during childhood; being female; having low financial resources; being exposed to stressful events in the past; having close relatives with anxiety disorder; and having parents with history of mental disorder. Women are twice as likely as men to have the problem.

People with social anxiety disorder (sometimes called "social phobia") have a marked fear of social or public situations in which they expect to be embarrassed, rejected, or fearful of offending others. Basically, people with social phobia fear a negative evaluation of themselves and are intensely worried that they will do or say something that will make others think poorly of them. They tend to think that they are less socially competent than others. They often believe that everyone notices their smallest mistakes and may greatly exaggerate the severity of the comments about those mistakes. When an event such as a presentation or a party is unavoidable, they may worry for days or even weeks prior to that event.

Common things that make a social phobic anxious are public speaking, informal conversations in small or large groups, dating, interacting with authority figures, eating, writing, or other public performances. It is characterized by an intense fear of being judged negatively by others. Unlike shyness, this disorder causes intense fear, often driven by irrational worries about social humiliation– "saying something stupid," or "not knowing what to say." Someone with social anxiety disorder may not take part in conversations, contribute to class discussions, or offer their ideas, and may become isolated. They are highly anxious, self-conscious, and have a hard time talking in public for fear that they will be humiliated, embarrassed, or rejected, or that they might offend others. Other symptoms include blushing, sweating, trembling or feeling nauseous around other people; staying away from places where there are other people around; worrying for days or weeks before an event where other people will be there; and having a hard time making and keeping friends.

Everyone tries to avoid certain things or situations that make them uncomfortable or even fearful. Fear of various things is a common phenomenon but an excessive, persistent and irrational fear of certain things or situations that would not be frightening normally, is termed as phobia. Sometimes it is a result of a previous bad experience. The individual is often not able to find out the rationale behind this fear but he just cannot seem to face these or overcome these fears. Some common things that cause such phobias are fear of animals (spiders, lizards, cockroaches, rats, dogs, snakes, insects), environment (water, heights, fire, storms, darkness, elevators, closed places, crowded places, tunnels, bridges), and injections (pin pricks, or sight of blood). Hypochondriacs are people who have an excessive fear of having a serious disease.

When the feared object is easy to avoid, people with phobias may not feel they need treatment. In certain cases, however, specific phobias can become impairing or individuals may go to excessive lengths to avoid exposure to the feared object or situation. In these cases, treatment is recommended. This is particularly important, as individuals with a specific phobia are likely to develop additional phobias of similar objects or situations over a period of time. Specific phobias tend to run in families and, very often, family members have fear of similar objects or situations. In general, phobias appear in adolescence and adulthood. Adult-onset phobias tend to show a more stable course, with only a small percentage of these disappearing without treatment.

Agoraphobia is the excessive fear of venturing into open or crowded places. In extreme cases, they may become literally housebound due to fear of venturing away from the security of their home. The person experiences high levels of fear and physiological arousal when encountering the phobic object, manifests strong urges to avoid or escape the situation or avoid the feared stimulus. Agoraphobia may occur with or without panic disorder.

Panic attacks are characterized by sudden feelings of terror or intense fear—sometimes striking repeatedly and without warning. Often mistaken for a heart attack, a panic attack causes powerful, physical symptoms including chest pain, heart palpitations, increased heart rate, sweating, dizziness, shortness of breath, sensations of choking, trembling, stomach upset, and feeling of impending doom. However, for someone with a phobia, certain places, events or objects create powerful reactions of strong, irrational fear. Most people with specific phobias have several triggers. To avoid panicking, someone with specific phobias will work hard to avoid their triggers. Many people will go to desperate measures to avoid having an attack, including social isolation or avoiding going to specific places.

People can suffer from adjustment disorders or have difficulty adjusting to life stressors, such as business or marital problems, chronic illness, or bereavement over a loss. Acute stress disorder and posttraumatic stress disorder are two types of anxiety disorders that occur in response to traumatic events. Acute stress disorder is a maladaptive reaction that occurs during the initial month following the traumatic experience. It may occur in the context of combat or exposure to natural or physical disaster. Soldiers coming from combat, survivors from rape or childhood sexual abuse, victims of motor vehicle and other accidents, people who have witnessed their homes and communities destroyed by floods, earthquakes or tornadoes, or those who have experienced railroad or airplane crashes may feel numb and detached from the environment. They may walk around "in a daze" for days or weeks afterward; or feel that the world seems like an unreal place. They are bothered by intrusive images, flashbacks, and dreams about the disaster; or they may relive the experience as if it was happening again. They may also be unable to perform necessary tasks, such as obtaining needed medical or legal assistance.

Posttraumatic stress disorder, commonly known as PTSD, is a prolonged maladaptive reaction to a traumatic experience. In contrast to acute stress disorder, post-traumatic stress disorder may persist for months, years, or even decades and may not develop until many months or even years after the traumatic event. Many, if not all of those with acute stress disorder, end up developing post-traumatic stress disorder. In both acute and post-traumatic stress disorder, the traumatic event involves either actual or threatened death experience, serious physical injury, or threat to one's own or another's physical safety. The response to the threat involves feelings of intense fear, helplessness, or a sense of horror. Children with post-traumatic stress disorder may experience the threat differently, by showing confused or agitated behavior.

Post-traumatic stress disorder is often associated with psychological problems such as depression, anxiety, or alcohol or substance abuse that can make it difficult for people to function effectively and responsibly in their daily activities. They may be unusually tense or feel "on edge" much of the time. They may become hyper vigilant and complain of disturbed sleep, irritability, angry outbursts, and lack of concentration. They may show an exaggerated startle response, such as jumping at any sudden noise. They may feel "numb" inside and lose their ability to enjoy the things that used to give them pleasure.

Obsessive-compulsive disorder features an irresistible need to perform certain acts to take away the fear that may be caused by a persistent unwanted thought or belief. Obsessions are recurrent and persistent thoughts, impulses, or intrusive images that cause anxiety or distress. The patient makes attempts to ignore or suppress these thoughts or tries to neutralize them by thinking about or doing other things that will serve to distract them.

Compulsions are repetitive behaviors such as washing hands repeatedly, opening and closing doors, wiping doorknobs, or turning lights on and off. The patient feels driven to repeat these actions again and again in order to relieve their anxiety. The patient carries out other typical behavior or mental acts in order to reduce distress or anxiety. Compulsions are not realistically connected to the things which they are designed to neutralize. They are meant to reduce the anxiety or distress of the patient and not to provide any pleasure or gratification.

These obsessions and compulsions cause marked distress to the patient and marked interference in the patient's routine functioning. For example, a patient may be obsessed with cleanliness and may spend hours washing his hands because he feels that they get dirty even if he does not do anything that would catch germs. Fear of germs is an obsession and washing of hands is act of compulsion. The person is fully aware that this fear is irrational but cannot help from doing the act to get rid of anxiety caused by the obsessive thought. Obsessions and compulsions are unreasonable and excessive, and they cause marked distress to the patient. The disorder usually begins in adolescence or early adulthood, but it may begin in childhood. Generally, the onset is gradual, but occasionally acute onset has been noted in some cases. The majority of individuals have a chronic waxing and waning course, with stress-related exacerbation of symptoms.

When attempting to resist a compulsion, the patient may have a sense of increasing anxiety or tension that is often relieved by yielding to the compulsion. In the course of the disorder, after repeated failure to resist the obsessions and compulsions, the patient may give in to them; he no longer experiences a desire to resist them, and may incorporate the compulsions into his or her daily routines.

Obsessive-compulsive disorder should not be confused with obsessive-compulsive personality, which defines certain character traits (being a perfectionist, excessively conscientious, morally rigid, or preoccupied with rules and order). These traits do not necessarily occur in people with obsessive-compulsive disorder.

Eating disorders are also similar to obsessive disorders, but pertain specifically to the eating patterns and the anxiety that it causes. Anorexia nervosa is a neurotic disorder that causes people to stop eating for fear that they may become obese. Even if they eat, they try to get rid of the food in their stomach by taking laxatives and vomiting, before the body properly absorbs it. Bulimia is an eating disorder, in which the persons binge-eat and then induce vomiting, and starve themselves to “compensate”.

The physical symptoms of an anxiety disorder can be easily confused with other medical conditions like heart disease or hyperthyroidism. Therefore, a doctor will likely perform an evaluation involving a physical examination, an interview and lab tests. After ruling out a medical illness, the doctor may refer the person to a mental health professional who can identify the specific type of anxiety disorder causing the symptoms as well as any other possible disorders including depression, ADHD or substance abuse that may be involved.

Living with generalized anxiety disorder can be a long-term challenge. In many cases, it occurs along with other anxiety or mood disorders. In most cases, generalized anxiety disorder improves with medications or talk therapy (psychotherapy). To be effective, psychotherapy must be directed at the person's specific anxieties and tailored to his or her needs. A typical "side effect" of psychotherapy is temporary discomfort involved with thinking about confronting feared situations. Making lifestyle changes, learning coping skills and using relaxation techniques also can help.

People with anxiety disorder can benefit largely from counseling, behavior modification and suggestion therapy, although some drugs are prescribed to calm down anxiety and help induce sleep. The two kinds of therapy that are used to treat generalized anxiety disorder are called applied relaxation therapy and cognitive-behavioral therapy. In applied relaxation therapy, the therapist might ask them to meditate or imagine a calming situation to help them relax. Stress management techniques and meditation can help people with anxiety disorders calm themselves and may enhance the effects of therapy. Since caffeine, certain illicit drugs, and even some over-the-counter cold medications can aggravate the symptoms of anxiety disorders, avoiding them should be considered.

Cognitive-behavioral therapy is a type of psychotherapy that teaches different ways of thinking, behaving, and reacting to anxiety-producing and fearful situations. It can also help people learn and practice social skills, which are vital for treating social anxiety disorder. It focuses on identifying, challenging, and then neutralizing unhelpful thoughts underlying anxiety disorders. It may be conducted individually or with a group of people who have similar problems. Some people with anxiety disorders might benefit from joining a self-help or support group and sharing their problems and achievements with others. Group therapy is particularly effective for social anxiety disorder. Often, "homework" is assigned for participants to complete between sessions.

Internet chat rooms might also be useful, but any advice received over the Internet should be used with caution, as Internet acquaintances have usually never seen each other and false identities are common. Talking with a trusted friend or member of the clergy can also provide support, but it is not necessarily a sufficient alternative to care from an expert clinician.

Medication does not cure anxiety disorders but often relieves symptoms. Medication can only be prescribed by a medical doctor (such as a psychiatrist or a primary care provider), but a few States allow psychologists to prescribe psychiatric medications. Selective serotonin reuptake inhibitors (SSRIs), such as *fluoxetine (Prozac)* and *sertraline (Zoloft),* and serotonin and norepinephrine reuptake inhibitors (SNRIs), such as *duloxetine (Cymbalta)* and *venlafaxine (Effexor)* are the most common medications given to treat generalized anxiety disorder. These medicines usually take several weeks to a few months to work well. Other medications include benzodiazepines, such as *alprazolam (Xanax)* or *diazepam (Valium)*; tricyclic antidepressants such as *imipramine (Tofranil),* and antipsychotics such as *trifluoperazine (Stelazine).*

Some medicines work better for certain people than for others. Problems due to hyperthyroidism can cause generalized anxiety symptoms. Medicines like *amphetamines (Ritalin)* or too much caffeine can cause worry and stress, or make your stress worse. Illegal drugs such as cocaine can also cause these symptoms. Be sure to talk with your doctor about how the medicine is working for you. Sometimes they might need to try more than one type of medicine before they find the one that works best for them. Be sure to also talk with your doctor about other medicines that you are taking.

The effectiveness of treatment for generalized anxiety disorder varies from one person to another. Some people might feel less worried and stressed out after a couple months of treatment. And some people might not feel better until after a year or more. It is common for patients treated with a combination of psychotherapy and medication to have better outcomes than those treated with only one or the other.

Taking medicines for anxiety during pregnancy may increase the risk of birth defects. Women who are pregnant, or thinking of becoming pregnant should talk to their doctor who can help them weigh the risks of treatment against the risk of harm to their pregnancy.

-o0o-

PERSONS WITH ANXIETY DISORDER

Anxiety does not discriminate. Anyone from all walks of life can suffer from anxiety disorders. It affects the poor, the rich, the young, the old, the healthy, the sick, and common people as well as celebrities. Some people may be more prone to anxiety than others, and it can come in different forms. Severe generalized anxiety disorder is incredibly stressful and requires treatment, but people can go on with their lives without admitting to others that their anxiety exists. Many people are unwilling to do anything about their anxiety disorder because they are too embarrassed. The most famous, rich, and successful people in the world suffer from anxiety just like everyone else. And many of them have sought help. Many celebrities today have started to discuss their own experiences with these conditions, making the public aware and helping others to find ways to deal with the symptoms and causes of their disorder. Although they have struggled with anxiety, they still continue to pursue their chosen career and be in the public spotlight. Their stories can inspire those who live with social anxiety disorder.

-o0o-

JESSICA ALBA

Jessica Alba is the American television star and movie actress of Fantastic Four movies. Her interest in acting started at the tender age of 5, and she got the first break at the age of 13. Her early life was marked by a number of physical maladies. During childhood, she suffered from partially collapsed lungs twice, had pneumonia four to five times a year, as well as a ruptured appendix and a tonsillar cyst. Her physical illnesses and her family's frequent moving contributed to her isolation from her peers. She has acknowledged that she suffered from obsessive-compulsive disorder during her childhood. She has won various awards for her acting, including the Choice Actress Teen Choice Award and Saturn Award for Best Actress on Television, and a Golden Globe nomination for her lead role in the television series Dark Angel. In 2012, she launched a company known as “The Honest Company” which provides a wide array of toxin-free household goods, diapers, and body products. During an interview, she confessed that she is battling with an eating disorder, and has also struggled with obsessive-compulsive behavior, anxiety attacks and insomnia. She told a British newspaper that the problem started when she was at school but worsened after she filmed Dark Angel in 2002, when she stopped eating and started a three-hour-a-day exercise regime. When she lost so much weight that she couldn't stop shivering, she sought help. Her obsessive-compulsive disorder peaked on her 25th birthday, while staying at an expensive hotel in New York City, when her boyfriend filled her hotel room with candles and balloons. She was initially thrilled with her gift, but romance quickly turned into anxiety when two hours later she still had 200 balloons everywhere, and it took housekeeping half an hour to clean them up. Her obsessive-compulsive disorder (OCD) now causes her anxiety if she does not repeat activities such as constantly combing her hair or washing her hands. She also used to unplug every single appliance in her house. Or she would double-check every door in her house to make sure it was locked at night. She has become germ-o-phobic, and she admits to using antibacterial *Febreze* liberally when she has to stay in hotels. She is so obsessed with germs that she carries the disinfectant spray with her and drenches hotel beddings with the chemical, because she is disgusted by the thought of someone else having slept in her bed. She has said her OCD came out of a need to have control over her life.

-o0o-

KIM BASINGER

Kimila Ann "Kim" Basinger is a well-known American actress, singer and former fashion model who had struggled with anxiety throughout her life and career. Her shyness and anxiety during her childhood were so severe that she would faint if asked to speak in class. Growing up, her worst fear was reading aloud in class, to the point that teachers believed she was having a nervous breakdown. She was so withdrawn as a child that her parents had her tested for autism and other psychiatric disorders. The tests did not reveal any issues, and her condition was not diagnosed. By her mid-teens, she became more confident, and successfully auditioned for the school cheerleading team. She was subsequently offered a modeling contract with the Ford Modeling Agency. Despite earning $1,000 a day, she never enjoyed modeling, because she could not stand always having to deal with the way she looked. She felt herself choking, and while other models relished looking in the mirror before appearing, she abhorred it and would avoid mirrors out of insecurity. After five years as a cover girl, she quit modeling and moved to Los Angeles where she began her acting career on television in 1976. She became famous when she appeared in the 1983 James Bond movie film "Never Say Never Again". In 1980, she married makeup artist Ron Snyder-Britton (born Ronald Snyder) on the film Hard Country, and in the same year, she developed agoraphobia following an episode where she had a panic attack in a grocery store. She recalled that her hands were shaking, she was sweating so profusely, and she could not move. She made it to her car and remembered getting the keys in the ignition, cranking the car up, taking the back roads to her home and parking. She didn't leave the house for six months. In 1997, after a three-year hiatus from acting, she made a comeback as the femme fatale in L.A. Confidential, which she initially turned down twice, because of her insecurity at returning to the screen and enjoying motherhood. The role earned her an Academy Award for Best Supporting Actress, as well as the Golden Globe and Screen Actors Guild Award. When she took the podium to accept her Oscar in 1997 for "LA Confidential," she couldn't find the words to speak, even though she had practiced for days. She married makeup artist Ron Snyder in 1980, suffered a miscarriage in 1981 and had an affair with Richard Gere while filming No Mercy in 1986. She left her husband for Batman producer Jon Peters, and was divorced in 1989. She married her second husband, Alec Baldwin, in 1993, separated in 2000, and divorced in 2002. She and Alec have a daughter together (Ireland Eliesse) who was born in 1995. She has spoken publicly about her struggles with panic disorder, agoraphobia, and social anxiety, and she appeared in the documentary "Panic: A Film about Coping" produced by HBO, hoping to raise awareness for the spectrum of these disorders. She said she has lived with fear of being in public places her entire life, which led to anxiety or panic attacks. She would stay in her house and would literally cry every day. She received psychotherapy for her anxiety but still remains shy and susceptible to panic and agoraphobia.

-o0o-

WHOOPI GOLDBERG

Whoopi Goldberg is an award-winning comedian, actress and human rights advocate, as well as longtime host of the daytime talk show "The View". She is best known for her skillful portrayals in both comedic and dramatic roles, as well as her groundbreaking work in the Hollywood film industry as an African-American woman. She unknowingly suffered from dyslexia when she was young, which affected her studies and ultimately caused her to drop out of high school at the age of 17. She starred in a popular one-woman production in 1983, and in 1985, she won a Grammy Award for Best Comedy Recording. That year, Goldberg's success with "The Color Purple" launched a highly visible acting career. She won an Academy Award in 1991 for her performance in "Ghost", and in 2007 she embarked on a lengthy run as moderator of the TV talk show "The View". Her need to travel was always complicated for many years because of her deep fear of flying, a type of fear that is often also called aerophobia. She would be sweating a lot and her mind would "do bad stuff" to her. She said her fear was instilled nearly 30 years ago when she witnessed a mid-air collision while standing on a balcony in San Diego. She was working at a cafe as a waitress in San Diego in 1978 when she saw a commercial airliner collide with a Cessna killing 144 people. The actress said that what frightened her so much was that "the people on the plane were aware that they were in some danger." She said she particularly fears for people "who see something that they're not sure they're going to be able to live through." Before her recent treatment, she would travel only by bus, train, or car in order to get from one end of the country to the other. For decades, she traveled back and forth from New York to Los Angeles via private bus. With two drivers, she was able to arrive on the other coast in 23 hours. Another one of her quirks is her self-proclaimed refusal to eat "anything that could be hiding something." When Whoopi agreed to appear at a London theater performance of "Sister Act," she knew she'd have to face her fears and fly overseas. With the help of anesthesia and a program designed by British Virgin Airlines to help people overcome their fear of flying, Whoopi was able to make the trip overseas and appear in London. Her own treatment was a type of exposure therapy in which she enrolled in a flying without fear program. The program uses education, practical experience and the special psychological techniques of Thought Field Therapy (TFT) to provide rapid relief from the panic, anxiety, claustrophobia and turbulence of fear of flying in just a single day. However, the next couple of times she flew, she was confronted with aggressive passengers, pilots and stewardesses, and she felt that she had too many new, stressful elements to navigate. Though she'll fly today if she absolutely must, she prefers her signature rock bus for travel.

-o0o-

DONNY OSMOND

Donald Clark "Donny" Osmond is an American singer, actor, radio personality, and former teen idol. He has also been a talk and game show host, record producer and author. He has been performing in public since he was 5 years old, and has enjoyed a lifetime of success as an entertainer both as a solo artist and with his brothers and sister, Marie. But he has had stage fright and experienced panic attacks during his performances. The panic attacks prevented him from singing and made him believe he was going to black out. He first began feeling anxious when he was 11. He thought that he had to be perfect because at least somebody in that audience was looking at him all the time. For him, performing in front of millions of people as a young child seemed like a nightmare. During one of his first performances on the Andy Williams Show, he recalls running offstage after his song, afraid of the audience applause and flashing lights. When the musical talents of Donny and his brothers were discovered at an early age by Andy Williams, his anxiety from being a celebrity resulted in severe panic attacks that would send him to the corner of the room, curled up into the fetal position and unable to handle any situation. At age 6, he felt like a failure because he could not do an Ella Fitzgerald song when he was put on the spot and asked to perform. He felt even more stressed out and pressured to be perfect when he became an adult star. He became paralyzed by fear while playing the lead character in the Andrew Lloyd Webber musical onstage. The only thing he recalled of the night the show premiered, were those of the curtains being opened and closed. He was constantly worried that he would not be successful in show business, letting not just himself down but also negatively impacting his family. He was crippled with low self-esteem and confidence issues when his pop career fizzled out in the 1980s and he felt so ill before big shows that he was convinced he would die onstage. The fear of performing affected other areas of his life. He soon found himself afraid to go into stores and shopping centers, worried about what people were thinking of him, and fearing that they might gather around to ridicule him. The pressure once triggered a full-blown panic attack. He thought that he was actually going crazy and that he was having a nervous breakdown. He could not stop shaking, and he couldn't get out of bed. He knew something was wrong, and his wife took him to the hospital. He sought the help of mental health professionals, was diagnosed with social anxiety disorder, and took medication to control and fight the symptoms of his anxiety and panic attacks. He engaged himself in cognitive behavioral therapy. Through hard work, he has learned how to recognize and control negative thought patterns, so that he is now able to manage the disorder without medication. He is currently an honorary member of the board of directors for the Anxiety Disorders Association of America (ADAA).

-o0o-

BARBRA STREISAND

Barbra Streisand is an American singer, songwriter, actress, director, producer and one of the most successful personalities in show business. She was raised in a middle-class family and grew up dreaming of becoming an actress. She has described her childhood as painful. She was shy as a child, and often felt rejected by other children because her looks were unusual. Additionally, she saw her stepfather as emotionally abusive. She also found no support from her mother, who thought she was too unattractive to pursue her dreams in show business. After a period of working as a nightclub singer and off-Broadway performer in New York City, she began to attract interest and a fan base. She debuted on Broadway in a 1962 musical comedy and received a Tony Award nomination for Best Supporting Actress and a New York Drama Critics Poll award. In a career spanning six decades, she has become an icon in multiple fields of entertainment, which earned her recognition as Mother of All Contemporary Pop Divas or Queen of The Divas. She has been recognized with two Academy Awards, ten Grammy Awards including the Grammy Lifetime Achievement Award and the Grammy Legend Award, five Emmy Awards including one Daytime Emmy, a Special Tony Award, an American Film Institute award, a

Kennedy Center Honors prize, four Peabody Awards, the Presidential Medal of Freedom, and nine Golden Globes. She was known in the music industry for being such a reclusive singer. She acquired generalized anxiety disorder right after her 1967 concert in New York City when she blanked out and unexpectedly forgot lyrics of the song that she was singing. After the concert, her fear and anxiety kept building up as she kept thinking about those songs, playing those moments over and over in her mind. Because of this, she developed great anxiety and a fear of facing people as well. She was worried that it might happen again, and it made her uncomfortable. Her self-confidence waged war with her self- doubt. She was infamous for having avoided live performances for nearly three decades due to a debilitating bout of stage fright. She became so fearful of making such a mistake again that she chose not to be seen by the public for almost 30 years. But since she was determined to gain back her musical career, she sought the assistance of experts on how she could deal with her condition. She claims that she learned how to cover her insecurity on stage by studying the flamboyance of the drag queens she met during this time. In 1994, Barbra faced her fears by performing live—but with a teleprompter, just in case. She has defended her choice in using a teleprompter to display lyrics during their live performances. She eventually faced her fear and finally agreed to sing at a large public event, then on a national tour, and eventually in front of a large television audience. She gave concerts for the first time in continental Europe. She is now one of the most successful entertainers in history.

-o0o-

REFERENCES

http://behavenet.com/node/21591
https://campus.aynrand.org/lexicon/neurosis-vs-psychosis
http://emedicine.medscape.com/article/286227-overview
https://en.wikipedia.org/wiki/Alfred,_Lord_Tennyson
https://en.wikipedia.org/wiki/Anxiety_disorder
https://en.wikipedia.org/wiki/Barbra_Streisand
https://en.wikipedia.org/wiki/Donny_Osmond
https://en.wikipedia.org/wiki/Generalized_anxiety_disorder

https://en.wikipedia.org/wiki/Jessica_Alba
https://en.wikipedia.org/wiki/Kim_Basinger
https://en.wikipedia.org/wiki/Neurosis
https://familydoctor.org/condition/generalized-anxiety-disorder/#everyday-life
https://flowpsychology.com/neurotic-vs-psychotic/
http://fox.klte.hu/~keresofi/psyth/guide/neurosis_psychosis_borderline_and_acting_out.html
http://healthresearchfunding.org/famous-people-generalized-anxiety-disorder/
http://healthyplace.com/anxiety-panic/articles/famous-people-who-have-experienced-an-anxiety-disorder/
http://hellogiggles.com/social-anxiety-celebs/
https://hubpages.com/education/Psychosis_Vs_Neurosis
https://medlineplus.gov/ency/article/000917.htm
http://nypost.com/2007/05/06/life-of-drama-for-basinger/
https://psychcentral.com/disorders/anxiety/generalized-anxiety-disorder-symptoms/
http://theydiffer.com/difference-between-neurosis-and-psychosis/
http://whatis.thedifferencebetween.com/compare/neurosis-and-psychosis/
https://www.academia.edu/8353030/psychotic_vs_neurotic
https://www.adaa.org/donny-osmond
https://www.anxietybc.com/parenting/generalized-anxiety-disorder
https://www.askdrshah.com/app/anxiety-neurosis/anxiety-neurosis-types.aspx
http://www.biography.com/people/barbra-streisand-9497402
http://www.biography.com/people/donny-osmond-342932
http://www.biography.com/people/jessica-alba-299896#!
http://www.biography.com/people/whoopi-goldberg-9314384
http://www.brown.edu/Courses/BI_278/Other/Clerkship/Didactics/Readings/gad.pdf
http://www.calmclinic.com/anxiety/famous-people-with-anxiety-disorder
http://www.calmclinic.com/anxiety/types/neurosis
http://www.cbsnews.com/news/donny-osmond-confronts-panic/
http://www.cbsnews.com/news/barbra-streisands-encore/
http://www.celebitchy.com/1022/jessica_alba_has_ocd_wheres_he/
http://www.contactmusic.net/barbra-streisand/news/streisand-overcomes-stagefright-with-anti-anxiety-pills_1009549
http://www.contactmusic.com/donny-osmond/news/osmond-conquers-stagefright-fears-with-wifes-help_1009306
http://www.csun.edu/~hcpsy002/Nevid_ch06.pdf
http://www.dailymail.co.uk/tvshowbiz/article-485982/I-hated-says-teen-idol-Donny-Osmond.html
http://www.dailymail.co.uk/tvshowbiz/article-357338/Jessicas-battle-eating-disorder.html
http://www.depression-guide.com/anxiety-neuroses.htm
http://www.depression-guide.com/celebrities/jessica-alba.htm
http://www.differencebetween.com/difference-between-psychosis-and-neurosis/
https://www.disabled-world.com/artman/publish/famous-ocd.shtml

https://www.drugs.com/health-guide/generalized-anxiety-disorder.html
http://www.femalefirst.co.uk/music/musicnews/Jessica+Alba-18659.html
http://www.healthaim.com/jessica-alba-ocd-dual-psychotherapies-can-ease-condition/36875
http://www.healthline.com/health/anxiety/generalized-anxiety-disorder#Outlook7
https://www.helpguide.org/articles/anxiety/generalized-anxiety-disorder-gad.htm
http://www.huffingtonpost.com/jonathan-alpert/overcome-fear_b_1807807.html
http://www.huffingtonpost.com/2014/03/06/my-fear-of-flying-from-wh_n_4914434.html
http://www.imdb.com/name/nm0000659/bio?ref_=nm_ov_bio_sm
http://www.imdb.com/name/nm0004695/bio?ref_=nm_ov_bio_sm
http://www.livescience.com/45781-generalized-anxiety-disorder.html
http://www.livestrong.com/article/129929-anxiety-neurosis-symptoms/
http://www.mayoclinic.org/diseases-conditions/generalized-anxiety-disorder/basics/definition/CON-20024562
http://www.medindia.net/patients/patientinfo/mental-health-neurosis-vs-psychosis.htm
http://www.mentalhealthamerica.net/conditions/generalized-anxiety-disorder-gad
https://www.myprivatesearch.com/search?q=jessica%20alba%20ocd
https://www.nami.org/Learn-More/Mental-Health-Conditions/Anxiety-Disorders
http://www.news.com.au/things-you-never-knew-about-whoopi-goldberg/news-story/9d76894131ae6f2572c4322b319326ef
https://www.nimh.nih.gov/health/topics/anxiety-disorders/index.shtml
http://www.nopanic.org.uk/neurosis-or-psychosis/
https://www.psychologytoday.com/blog/evil-deeds/201003/normalcy-neurosis-and-psychosis-what-is-mental-disorder
http://www.prweb.com/releases/2009/04/prweb2291284.htm
https://www.reference.com/world-view/differences-between-neurosis-psychosis-e8ac69b2b5c6a194
http://www.rightdiagnosis.com/n/neurosis/basics.htm
http://www.cnn.com/2011/SHOWBIZ/04/12/whoopi.goldberg.piers.morgan/
http://www.socialworkdegreeguide.com/10-famous-people-with-anxiety-disorders/
http://umm.edu/health/medical/reports/articles/anxiety-disorders
https://www.verywell.com/donny-osmond-social-anxiety-disorder-3024261
https://www.verywell.com/how-to-cope-with-generalized-anxiety-disorder-1393164
https://www.verywell.com/what-is-kim-basingers-experience-with-social-anxiety-3024264
https://www.verywell.com/which-celebrities-suffer-with-social-anxiety-3024283
http://www.webmd.com/anxiety-panic/default.htm
http://www.wisegeek.org/what-is-the-difference-between-neurotic-and-psychotic.htm
http://www.yourarticlelibrary.com/psychology/12-major-difference-between-neuroses-and-psychoses-psychology/12494/

FURTHER READING

American Psychiatric Association. (2013*). Diagnostic and statistical manual of mental disorders (DSM-5®).* American Psychiatric Pub.

Calkins, A.W., Bui, E., Taylor, C.T., Pollack, M.H., LeBeau, R.T., & Simon, N.M. (2016). *Anxiety disorders.* In T.A. Stern, M. Fava, T.E. Wilens, & J.F. Rosenbaum (Eds.), *Massachusetts General Hospital comprehensive clinical psychiatry* (2nd ed., chap 32). Philadelphia, PA: Elsevier Mosby.

Ebell, M.H. (2008). Diagnosis of anxiety disorders in primary care. *Am Fam Physician, 78*(4), 501-502.

Schneier, F.R. (2006). Clinical practice. Social anxiety disorder. *N Engl J Med, 355*(10), 1029-1036.

Stein, M.B., & Stein, D.J. (2008). Social anxiety disorder. *Lancet, 371*(9618):1115-1125.

-o0o-

OBSESSIVE-COMPULSIVE PERSONALITY DISORDER

While Obsessive-Compulsive Personality Disorder (OCPD) may sound like Obsessive-Compulsive Disorder (OCD), they are not the same and they should not be confused with each other.

-o0o-

Obsessive-Compulsive Personality Disorder (OCPD) is a Cluster C anxious or fearful personality disorder. It is characterized by an extensive pattern of preoccupation with perfectionism, orderliness, and interpersonal and mental control, at the cost of efficiency and flexibility. Because it is a personality disorder, people with OCPD are comfortable with their high standards and rigid mindset, considering it as a virtue even though more often than not it hampers success. People with OCPD will justify actions instead of admitting any sort of problem, because in their mind, they are always right.

People with OCPD are preoccupied with details, lists, order, organization, or schedules, and may impose all sorts of rules to maintain "efficiency," but instead only succeed in making the task more difficult. Their perfectionism interferes with their ability to complete a project when their own overly strict standards are not met. They are excessively devoted to work and productivity at the expense of their leisurely activities and friendships. They are overly conscientious, scrupulous, and inflexible when it comes to their moral and ethical values. Hoarding is one of the criteria for OCPD because of their inability to discard worn-out or worthless objects even when they have no sentimental value. They are very stringent with money, which they consider necessary, in case something unavoidably catastrophic occurs. They are reluctant to delegate tasks or to work with others. They will stubbornly and unreasonably insist that everything be done their way and that others conform to their way of doing things. They will give very detailed instructions about how things should be done, and will be surprised and irritated when someone suggests other creative alternatives.

People with OCPD find it difficult to relax, and are often workaholics who always feel that their time and effort are not enough to achieve their goals. They plan their activities down to greatest detail, and hate unpredictable things that they cannot control. They spend an excessive amount of time and effort planning an event, but are then unable to enjoy it or spend time with others, especially if it does not go as planned. Individuals who suffer from this disorder often have trouble relaxing because they are preoccupied with details, rules, and productivity. They tend to be upset or angry over a seemingly minor matter or in situations where they are not able to maintain control of their physical or interpersonal environment. They are often unable to form meaningful relationships; they resent authority and they feel uneasy in emotional situations. If they do find long-term relationships, they may be too demanding toward their partner and children, holding them to the same unrealistic standards they impose on themselves. They are less likely to engage in substance abuse, which is common in other mental disorders.

To some extent, OCD and OCPD may have similar characteristics, including rigid and ritualistic behaviors, but their attitude towards them are different. Most people with OCPD do not have OCD and, likewise, most people with OCD do not have OCPD. The main difference is that someone with OCD is focused on particular distressing obsessions such as repeated hand-washing or abnormal fears of danger. In general, people with OCPD do not generally feel the need to repeatedly perform ritualistic actions, which is a common symptom of OCD. They usually find pleasure in their drive to perfection, whereas people with OCD are often more distressed after their actions. People with OCD consider their compulsive rituals to be unhealthy and unwanted, caused by their anxiety and obsessive thoughts. People with OCPD believe that their strong adherence to routines, cautiousness, and drive for perfection are rational and desirable qualities to achieve success. They are rigid and inflexible, preoccupied with minute details and facts, and strictly adhere to rules, regulations and schedules, to the point of interfering with their occupational and social functioning. Interpersonal relationships are difficult because of the excessive demands placed on friends, romantic partners, and children. People with OCPD are usually pessimistic and have problems with social relationships, which can lead to clinical depression and anxiety.

There are certain similarities in the symptoms of OCD and OCPD that can make it difficult to distinguish them clinically. For example, perfectionism is one of the criteria for the diagnosis of OCPD, while it can be a symptom of OCD if it involves the need for tidiness and order. Hoarding is also considered both a compulsion found in OCD and a criterion for OCPD. Regardless of their similarities, there are discrete qualitative dissimilarities between these two disorders. Unlike OCPD, the compulsive habits of OCD are aimed at reducing the obsession-related mental anxiety.

People with OCD usually seek help for the psychological stress caused by having to carry out their compulsive behavior due to their obsessive thoughts or beliefs. In contrast, people with OCPD will usually seek treatment because of the conflict caused between them and their family or friends related to their need to have others conform to their way of doing things. While the severity of OCD symptoms will often fluctuate over time, OCPD is chronic in nature, with little change in personality style. Sometimes a person can be affected by both OCD and OCPD. Family physicians and general practitioners are generally not trained or well equipped to make this type of psychological diagnosis. In these complex cases, the clinical experience of a qualified psychiatrist or psychologist is often needed to make a proper diagnosis and ensure proper treatment.

Eating disorders, especially Anorexia Nervosa and bulimia, have been linked with OCPD. People with OCPD have more severe anorexic symptoms, worse remission rates, and aggravating behaviors such as compulsive exercising. Anorexic individuals are usually rigid and hyperconscious about their appearance, and tend to be perfectionists. The obsessive compulsive personality traits of over-attention to details and inflexibility have also been found in anorexics.

OCPD is approximately twice as common in males compared to females, and occurs in between 2.1 and 7.9 percent of the general population. It is most often diagnosed in adulthood. However, if it is diagnosed in a child or teen, the features must have been present for at least 1 year. As with other personality disorders, OCPD is likely due to biological, genetic and environmental factors, which shape the individual's personality, temperament, and coping skills to deal with stress. OCPD tends to occur in families, so genes may be involved. But genetic concomitants may lie dormant until triggered by events in the lives of those who are predisposed to OCPD. Because OCPD is a learned behavior, it can be triggered by adverse factors including trauma faced during childhood, such as physical, emotional, or sexual abuse, or other psychological trauma. It is possible that people with OCPD may have been raised by parents who were unavailable and either overly controlling or overly protective. They may have been consistently punished for negative behavior, failure, and rule-breaking, while receiving no praise for success and compliance. They may have developed a habit of rigidly following rules that lasts into adulthood as a sort of coping mechanism to be "perfect", and thus, avoid punishment.

People with OCPD do not often seek out treatment until the disorder starts to significantly interfere or otherwise impact their life. This most often happens when a person's coping resources are stretched too thin to deal with their stress or other life events. Treatment becomes complicated if these individuals do not admit having OCPD, or believe that there is no reason to change behaviors that they think are rational and correct. When they do seek the help of a mental health professional, the treatment will include psychotherapy, cognitive behavioral therapy, behavior therapy or self-help. People with OCPD are three times more likely to receive individual psychotherapy than people with major depressive disorder. The goal in psychodynamic therapy is to help the patients identify their feelings towards a situation, accept that they are human who are just as prone to error as anyone else, and that making a mistake is not as bad as they may believe. The goal of Cognitive/Behavioral Therapy is to help the patients realize the effect that their attempts to exert control have on their feelings, and change their extreme belief that they are a failure if they make a mistake. In behavior therapy, a person with OCPD discusses with a psychotherapist ways of changing compulsions into healthier, productive behaviors. Medication alone is generally not indicated for this type of personality disorder. Serotonin reuptake inhibitor (SSRI) antidepressants, such as *Prozac, Zoloft,* or *Paxil*, may help to reduce anxiety and depression, but they are just partial remedies to improve the patient's ability to cope.

-o0o

PERSONS WITH OBSESSIVE-COMPULSIVE PERSONALITY DISORDER

There is a lot of speculation about celebrities and famous people with obsessive-compulsive disorder (OCD), but not much about famous people with obsessive-compulsive personality disorder (OCPD). Individuals who suffer from this personality disorder often have an overwhelming preoccupation with orderliness, perfectionism and control of their lives and relationships. The celebrities and famous people who reportedly have OCD probably also have OCPD, because creativity and productivity can go hand in hand with obsessive-compulsive personality traits. Many of them seem excessively devoted to work at the expense of their friends and family. This could explain why many famous people end up isolated and lonely.

-o0o-

DAVID BECKHAM

David Robert Joseph Beckham is an English former professional footballer. He played for Manchester United, Preston North End,

Real Madrid, Milan, LA Galaxy, Paris Saint-Germain, and the England national team. He has received praises from his managers for his discipline to spend hours practicing his free kicks, and achieve an accuracy that other players would not care about. Renowned for his perfectionism on the pitch, it seems everything has to be just right for David Beckham at home as well. He suffers from OCD and it manifests itself through constant cleanliness and perfection of all that is around him. Anything out of order is enough to cause a conflict and must be attended to immediately. Before he can relax in his hotel room, he has to move all the leaflets and all the books and put them in a drawer. "Everything has to be perfect". Everything has to be in line, and everything has to be in pairs, if there are three books on a table one must be added, or one must be removed. He discussed his need to rearrange hotel furniture and line up soda can labels, which he said was "tiring", but justified it by saying that it's more tiring if it's not done the right way. He has three fridges—food in one, salad in another and drinks in the third. In the drinks, everything has to be symmetrical. If there are three cans, he'll throw one away because it has to be an even number. In a television interview, he confessed to counting the Pepsi cans that he keeps in his fridge. His wife has said: "Everything has to match in the house. If there are three cans of Diet Pepsi, he'd throw one away because it's uneven." He said the condition leads him to count clothes and place magazines in straight lines and symmetrical patterns. He reportedly spends hours straightening the furniture, apparently buys exactly 20 packets of Super Noodles on each visit to the supermarket and wears a new pair of football boots for every match. He had kept the condition secret, but his battle with OCD was common knowledge amongst teammates at his previous club, Manchester United. He was quoted, telling Esquire Magazine that "It's not something I worry about. I've accepted it. I'm just very obsessive with certain things. Everything has to be in order. That's the way it is." He has 20 tattoos including the names of his sons, and says he keeps having tattoos because he is addicted to the pain of the needle.

-o0o-

HOWARD HUGHES

Howard Hughes was an American aviator, engineer, industrialist, film producer and director, and one of the wealthiest people in the world. When he was four years old, his father patented and commercialized a rotary drill bit able to penetrate thick rock, which revolutionized oil drilling, and which created start-up capital for his subsequent vast empire. His early life was shaped by his mother who doted on him with excessive concern about his health, constantly worried about her son's exposure to germs, and terrified that he would catch polio. When his father died two years after his mother's death, he took control of his father's company at age 18. He got divorced 2 years after marrying a Houston socialite, whom he kept at home, isolated for weeks at a time. He then became romantically linked to a number of celebrities. During the production of his movie film "The Outlaw", he became obsessed with a minor flaw in one of Russell's blouses, and wrote a detailed memorandum on how to fix the problem. In 1952 he purchased RKO Studios and immediately cut the staff there from 2,500 to 600, shut down productions for weeks at a time to try to control dust, or to check the staff's credentials to sift out communists, eventually leading to the studio's downfall. He was fixated on trivial details and was alternately indecisive and obstinate. His unpredictable mood swings made his director wonder if his film would ever be completed. While screening some movies at a film studio near his home, he stayed in the studio's darkened screening room for more than four months, never leaving. He ate only chocolate bars and chicken and drank only milk, and was surrounded by dozens of Kleenex boxes that he continuously stacked and re-arranged. He wrote detailed memos to his aides giving them explicit instructions not to look at him nor speak to him unless spoken to. He wrote a staff manual on how to open a can of peaches--including directions for removing the label, scrubbing the can down until it was bare metal, washing it again and pouring the contents into a bowl without touching the can to the bowl. He used a special fork to obsessively sort his peas by size. He insisted on using tissues to pick up objects to insulate him from germs. He would also notice dust, stains or other imperfections on people's clothes and demand that they take care of them. He even forced his compulsions on those around him, ordering staff to wash their hands multiple times and layer their hands with paper towels when serving his food. Before handing a spoon to Hughes, servants were required to wrap the utensil in tissue paper and cellophane tape. When removing his hearing aid cord from the bathroom, the staff was required to use six to eight tissues to turn the bathroom door knob. Up to fifteen tissues were required before opening cabinet doors in the bathroom. Ironically, he ended up neglecting his own hygiene later in his life, rarely bathing or brushing his teeth. He spent most of his life trying to avoid germs. Toward the end of his life, he lay naked in bed in darkened hotel rooms in what he considered a germ-free zone. He wore tissue boxes on his feet to protect them. And he burned his clothing if someone near him became ill. When Howard Hughes died, he was severely malnourished, he weighed 40 kg. (or 88 lbs.) and his hair, beard, fingernails and toenails had grown grossly long. X-rays revealed broken-off hypodermic needles still embedded in his arms.

-o0o-

NIKOLA TESLA

Nikola Tesla was an inventor, physicist, mechanical engineer, and electrical engineer. He is best known for his many revolutionary contributions to the discipline of electricity and magnetism in the late 19th and early 20th century. As a five year-old child, he demonstrated the ability to sustain his attention for unusually long time spans, spending hours at a time on his projects and inventions. He was an elegant, stylish figure in New York City, meticulous in his grooming, clothing, and regimented in his daily activities. Throughout his life, he suffered from phobias and compulsions. He had a phobia of germs and washed his hands obsessively. He would eat only boiled food. He hated touching round objects, disliked hair other than his own, found jewelry repulsive, and tended to do things that were either in 3's or in numbers divisible by 3. For meals, he insisted on estimating the mass of everything he was about to consume, always used 18 napkins, and refused to eat alone with a woman. When leaving a building, he had to turn right only, and walk around the entire block before becoming “free” and being able to leave. After walking around a block once, he would feel compelled to do so two more times. For exercise, he walked between 8 and 10 miles per day. He curled his toes one hundred times for each foot every night, saying that it stimulated his brain cells. When taking his daily swim at the public pool, he always swam 33 laps, but if he lost count he said he couldn’t leave, and instead had to start over from zero. He also preferred to dine alone, due to his meticulous compulsion to clean his plates and silverware with 18 (divisible by 3) napkins before a meal. When eating, he found he couldn't enjoy food unless he first mentally calculated its volume. He counted his jaw movements when chewing food and habitually surprised dinner guests by estimating the weight of his meal before taking the first bite. At one point a friend gifted him a special bowl which internally was a perfect hemisphere; meant to ease his task in calculating soup volume. His university tried to kick him out for fear of his ruining his health by exhaustion and collapse. They caught him attempting to read the entire university library, by remaining awake 20 hours a day for months. He claimed to never sleep more than two hours per night. He spent much of his life working obsessively and in solitude; interacting with ordinary humans seemed difficult for him. He had particular difficulties interacting with authority figures, especially his employers. He preferred to work alone because he could not slow down to wait for “lesser men” (including Thomas Edison who was his previous employer). He could be harsh at times and openly expressed disgust for overweight people, such as when he fired a secretary because of her weight. He was quick to criticize clothing. On several occasions, Tesla directed a subordinate to go home and change her dress. Although he was close to his family, he had very few intimate relationships as an adult. He never married or had children. He chose to never pursue or engage in any known relationships, instead finding all the stimulation he needed in his work. Although he seemed capable of developing friendships, he rarely sought or cultivated them. In his later years, Tesla became even more socially isolated. In 1943, he died alone and broke in a New York City hotel at the age of 86. Despite his eccentricities, or possibly because of them, he was able to use his mind to improve the lives of billions of human beings.

-o0o-

REFERENCES

http://bandofartists.org/famous-people-with-neurological-disorders/david-beckham/

http://www.brainphysics.com/lifestyle/ocd/an-inventive-genius-with-ocd-nikola-tesla

http://cognitivebehaviortherapycenter.com/ocpd-vs-ocd/

https://en.wikipedia.org/wiki/David_Beckham

https://en.wikipedia.org/wiki/Howard_Hughes

https://en.wikipedia.org/wiki/Nikola_Tesla

https://en.wikipedia.org/wiki/Obsessive%E2%80%93compulsive_disorder

https://en.wikipedia.org/wiki/Obsessive%E2%80%93compulsive_personality_disorder

https://flowpsychology.com/ocpd-vs-ocd/

http://frontierpsychiatrist.co.uk/psychiatric-disorders-of-the-rich-and-famous-1-howard-hughes/

https://iocdf.org/wp-content/uploads/2014/10/OCPD-Fact-Sheet.pdf

http://io9.gizmodo.com/5648455/the-mad-scientist-hall-of-fame-nikola-tesla

https://medlineplus.gov/ency/article/000942.htm

http://mentalhealth.com/home/dx/obsessivepersonality.html

https://nobullying.com/howard-hughes/

http://outofthefog.website/personality-disorders-1/2015/12/6/obsessive-compulsive-personality-disorder-ocpd

http://pediatrics.med.nyu.edu/conditions-we-treat/conditions/obsessive-compulsive-personality-disorder

https://psychcentral.com/disorders/obsessive-compulsive-personality-disorder-symptoms/

http://science.howstuffworks.com/innovation/famous-inventors/nikola-tesla5.htm

http://youhaveocd.com/2010/07/18/david-beckham-talks-about-his-ocd/

ohttps://www.allaboutcounseling.com/library/obsessive-compulsive-personality-disorder/

http://www.amhc.org/6-obsessive-compulsive-spectrum-disorders/advice/204-ocd-vs-ocpd

http://www.anxietyhouse.com.au/ocd-or-ocpd-whats-the-difference

http://www.apa.org/monitor/julaug05/hughes.aspx

http://www.biography.com/people/david-beckham-9204321#!

http://www.brainphysics.com/articles/ocd/ocd-vs-ocpd

http://www.brainphysics.com/oc-personality.php

http://www.brainphysics.com/news/ocd/beckham-talks-about-his-ocd
http://www.celebrityfunfacts.com/david-beckham/f5675/
http://www.dailymail.co.uk/tvshowbiz/article-381802/The-obsessive-disorder-haunts-life.html
http://www.differencebetween.com/difference-between-ocd-and-vs-ocpd/
https://www.disabled-world.com/artman/publish/famous-ocd.shtml
http://www.empowher.com/media/reference/obsessive-compulsive-disorder-and-obsessive-compulsive-personality-disorder-theyre-n.
http://www.eonline.com/news/394118/lena-dunham-julianne-moore-and-jessica-alba-what-ocd-has-to-do-with-it
http://www.greatgenius.com/the-life-and-personality-of-nikola-tesla
http://www.healthyplace.com/personality-disorders/obsessive-compulsive-personality-disorder/famous-people-with-obsessive-compulsive-personality-disorder/
http://www.healthguideinfo.com/living-with-ocd/p86849/
http://www.healthyplace.com/personality-disorders/obsessive-compulsive-personality-disorder/what-is-obsessive-compulsive-personality-disorder/
http://www.huffingtonpost.com/carol-w-berman-md/obsessive-compulsive-personality-disorder_b_5816816.html
http://www.minddisorders.com/Ob-Ps/Obsessive-compulsive-personality-disorder.html
http://www.minddisorders.com/Ob-Ps/Obsessive-compulsive-personality-disorder.html
http://www.mayoclinic.org/diseases-conditions/obsessive-compulsive-disorder/home/ovc-20245947
http://www.mayoclinic.org/diseases-conditions/personality-disorders/symptoms-causes/dxc-20247656
http://www.medindia.net/news/soccer-star-david-beckham-admits-his-ocd-is-tiring-105080-1.htm
https://www.mentalhelp.net/articles/obsessive-compulsive-disorder-versus-obsessive-compulsive-personality-disorder/
https://www.mentalhelp.net/blogs/david-beckham-has-ocd/
http://www.mentalhelp.net/poc/view_doc.php?type=advice&id=204&at=2&cn=6
http://www.metropolitanorganizing.com/mindfullness/ocd-vs-ocpd/
http://www.minddisorders.com/Ob-Ps/Obsessive-compulsive-personality-disorder.htmlhttp://www.minddisorders.com/Ob-Ps/Obsessive-compulsive-personality-disorder.html
http://www.ncbi.nlm.nih.gov/pubmed/23865406.
https://www.nimh.nih.gov/health/topics/obsessive-compulsive-disorder-ocd/index.shtml
http://www.nlm.nih.gov/medlineplus/ency/article/000942.htm
http://www.nlm.nih.gov/medlineplus/ency/article/000942.htm
http://www.ocdonline.com/articlephillipson6.php
http://www.ocfoundation.org/uploadedfiles/maincontent/find_help/ocpd%20fact%20sheet.pdf
http://www.psychforums.com/obsessive-compulsive-personality/topic36628.html

https://www.psychologytoday.com/blog/the-truisms-wellness/201612/perfectionism-vs-obsessive-compulsive-disorder

http://www.quickanddirtytips.com/health-fitness/mental-health/ocd-vs-ocpd-5-differences

https://www.quora.com/What-mental-disorders-did-Tesla-have

https://www.sciencedaily.com/releases/2011/04/110401121344.htm

http://www.sciencedaily.com/articles/o/obsessive-compulsive_personality_disorder.htm

https://www.sciencedaily.com/terms/obsessive-compulsive_personality_disorder.htm

http://www.telegraph.co.uk/news/health/news/8306947/OCD-David-Beckham-has-it-as-do-over-a-million-other-Britons.html

http://www.thehealthcenter.info/adult-ocd/ocpd.htm.

https://www.verywell.com/obsessive-compulsive-disorders-2330640

https://www.verywell.com/ocd-vs-obsessive-compulsive-personality-disorder-2510584

http://www.webmd.com/mental-health/obsessive-compulsive-disorder#1

http://www.webmd.com/mental-health/tc/obsessive-compulsive-disorder-ocd-topic-overview#1

FURTHER READING

Gordon. O.M., Salkovskis, P.M., Oldfield, V.B., & Carter, N. (2013). The association between obsessive compulsive disorder and obsessive compulsive personality disorder: Prevalence and clinical presentation. *Br J Clin Psychol, 52*(3), 300-315.

Mancebo, M.C., Eisen, J.L., Grant, J.E., & Rasmussen, S.A. (2005). Obsessive compulsive personality disorder and obsessive compulsive disorder: Clinical characteristics, diagnostic difficulties and treatment. *Ann Clin Psychol, 17*, 197-204.

AVOIDANT PERSONALITY DISORDER

Because avoidant personality disorder shares many symptoms with generalized social phobia, the two disorders can be easily confused. It is still controversial whether avoidant personality disorder is really distinct from generalized social anxiety disorder or not. Both have similar diagnostic criteria and may have similar causes, subjective experience, course, treatment and identical underlying personality features, such as shyness.

-o0o-

Avoidant personality disorder is a Cluster C "anxious" personality disorder characterized by a lifelong pattern of extreme shyness, social inhibition, feelings of inadequacy and inferiority, extreme sensitivity to criticisms, and avoidance of social interaction despite a strong desire to be close to others for fear of rejection. More than simply being shy or socially awkward, they have significant problems that affect their ability to interact with others and maintain relationships in day-to-day life. Those with this disorder may often choose jobs where they do not have to interact with the public, due to their anxiety and fear of embarrassing themselves in front of others. They are described by others as being "shy," "timid," "lonely," and "isolated."

People with symptoms of avoidant personality disorder avoid occupational, social or school activities that involve significant interpersonal contact, because they are afraid to be criticized, disapproved, or rejected. Because they are sensitive to rejection and criticism, they may misinterpret neutral comments or actions as negative. They feel unwelcome in social situations, even when that is not the case. This is because they have a low self-esteem, and often imagine themselves to be inferior to others. They may be afraid to speak up for fear of saying the wrong thing, blushing, stammering, or otherwise getting embarrassed. They are aware of being uncomfortable in social situations and often feel socially inept. Their fear of rejection often makes it difficult to connect with other people. They may be hesitant to seek out friendships, unless they are certain that the other person will like them. They hold back in relationships because they are afraid that they will be ridiculed or humiliated.

As with other types of personality disorder, it may be influenced by a combination of social, genetic, and psychological factors, and may be related to temperamental factors that are inherited. It is usually first noticed in early adulthood. Both childhood emotional neglect (in particular, the rejection of a child by one or both parents) and peer group rejection may the risk of developing the disorder. This avoidant behavior often starts in infancy or childhood with shyness, isolation, and fear of strangers and new situations. Unfortunately, for some, this avoidant behavior persists and intensifies into adulthood; thus they become diagnosed with this disorder. As with most personality disorders, avoidant personality disorder usually is not diagnosed in people younger than 18 years of age. There is no way to know who will develop avoidant personality disorder. People who have the disorder are typically very shy as children. However, not every child who is shy will develop the disorder. Likewise, not every adult who is shy has the disorder. Like most personality disorders, avoidant personality disorder typically will decrease in intensity with age, with many people experiencing few of the most extreme symptoms by the time they are in the 40s or 50s.

Avoidant personality disorder is only diagnosed if the symptoms begin no later than early adulthood; if the avoidant behaviors occur at home, work, and community; and if these behaviors cause significant distress or impairment in social and occupational functioning. It should not be diagnosed if the symptoms can be better explained by another mental disorder, substance use, or other medical conditions. When shyness, unfounded fear of rejection, hypersensitivity to criticism, and a pattern of social avoidance persist and intensify through adolescence and young adulthood, a diagnosis of avoidant personality disorder is often indicated.

People with avoidant personality disorder tend to be good candidates for treatment because their disorder causes them significant distress, and most of them want to develop relationships. Treatments vary; psychodynamic psychotherapy or cognitive behavioral therapy is most effective. Psychodynamic therapy helps them become aware of their unconscious thoughts, and can help them understand how past experiences influence their current behavior, and can help them resolve past emotional pains and conflicts. Cognitive behavioral therapy helps them recognize and replace unhealthy beliefs and thought processes with healthier ones. A key issue in treatment is gaining and keeping the patient's trust, since people with avoidant personality disorder will often start to avoid treatment sessions if they distrust the therapist or fear that they are being rejected.

Anti-anxiety agents and antidepressants may be prescribed for avoidant personality disorder only when another psychiatric problem (e.g., anxiety or depression) co-occurs. But these should be given with caution. Because anxieties among patients with avoidant personality disorder are situationally related, the medication may actually interfere with effective psychotherapeutic treatment.

-o0o-

PERSONS WITH AVOIDANT PERSONALITY DISORDER

Famous people with avoidant personality disorder experience the same level of shyness, fear of rejection, and feelings of inadequacy as the typical person who suffers from the condition. It is difficult to identify celebrities and famous persons with avoidant personality disorder because very few, if ever, have publicly revealed that they suffer from it. There are many actors that suffer from anxiety and most of them do not show it because they are portraying someone else other than themselves when they act. But a number of them have admitted being "shy" or "timid" or "a loner".

-o0o-

JOHNNY DEPP

John Christopher "Johnny" Depp II is an American actor, producer, and musician. He has won the Golden Globe Award and Screen Actors Guild Award for Best Actor. Although one of the biggest celebrities today, he also suffers from anxiety that affects his everyday life. He can take on a broad range of characters and change the way he looks dramatically. This acting ability allows him to be free of his anxiety without having to worry about people seeing him the way he really is. He has admitted that he hates interviews, and that he was the nerdy guy in high school who never got any attention from the opposite sex. One cannot tell that he is anxious while he's acting, but he is very shy and sometimes doesn't speak a lot when he's doing interviews on various talk shows. He is uncomfortable and even panics when he's in front of a crowd or when he is off the cameras. As a child, he had a troublesome life. His family moved around a lot, living in motels, shifting from place to place, while his father was continually searching for a secure work in order to support his family. When he was 8, he was considered a bright and curious boy, but paid no attention to school rules. He was rebellious, and even was suspended once for "mooning" his gym teacher. By 12, he started smoking, which later led to drinking and taking illegal drugs. He lost his virginity at 13 and had various misdemeanors such as petty theft and vandalism. He rose to prominence in the 1980s television series 21 Jump Street, when he became a teen pin-up and was obsessed by teenage girls everywhere. He hated being a teen idol so intensely that he shaved his eyebrows just to make himself uglier and less photogenic for teen-adoring magazines. In order to destroy this teen idol status, he embarked on a journey through underground filmmaking, taking on eccentric, dark and just plain weird roles. Slowly, he became part of the elite, was nominated for Oscars, and had top billing for some of the biggest "money-makers" in movie history. Rising to fame in 1984's "A Nightmare on Elm Street". He finds it strange when people call him a "celebrity". He does not think he is famous, ambitious, or driven, and he prefers to hide away from the public spotlight, which was why he moved to France. He insists that he never sought fame and that he became successful by chance. He claims that, in a sense, he lives like a fugitive. He does not like to be in social situations, and it is fine for him, in a strange way -- to run and hide. He has admitted that it's tough for him to disassociate himself from the character of Jack Sparrow, in "Pirates of the Caribbean", which he plays in the franchise. He has also been quoted as saying, "I'm shy, paranoid, whatever word you want to use. I hate fame. I've done everything I can to avoid it." He has access to therapists at all times, including on movie sets, to help talk to him and advise him on how to control anxiety when it strikes. They also help him change his way of thinking so he is able to get through the day doing what he loves the most. He is a great role model for anxiety sufferers because of what he has been able to achieve and how he deals with his disorder on a regular basis.

-o0o-

REFERENCES

https://blogs.psychcentral.com/caregivers/2015/07/understanding-avoidant-attachment-disorder/

http://emedicine.medscape.com/article/913360-overview#a6

http://emedicine.medscape.com/article/913360-overview#a6 Updated Oct. 7, 2015. Accessed June 11, 2016.

https://en.wikipedia.org/wiki/Avoidant_personality_disorder

https://medlineplus.gov/ency/article/000940.htm

http://mentalhealth.com/home/dx/avoidantpersonality.html

http://my.clevelandclinic.org/health/articles/avoidant-personality-disorder

http://outofthefog.website/personality-disorders-1/2015/12/6/avoidant-personality-disorder-avpd

https://psychcentral.com/disorders/avoidant-personality-disorder-symptoms/

https://simple.wikipedia.org/wiki/Avoidant_personality_disorder

http://absoluteconfidence.com/53-shy-celebrtities-shocking-to-see-whos-on-the-list

http://www.answers.com/Q/What_is_Avoidant_Personality_disorder_symptoms

http://www.4degreez.com/disorder/avoidant.html

https://www.brainyquote.com/quotes/quotes/j/johnnydepp169416.html

http://www.contactmusic.net/johnny-depp/news/publicity-shy-johnny-depp_1107842

http://www.disorders.org/avoidant-personality-disorder/

http://www.gurl.com/2015/03/04/celebrities-who-are-shy-you-never-knew/#1
http://www.healmylife.com/articles/counselling/avoidant%20personality.html
http://www.healthline.com/health/avoidant-personality-disorder#Outlook7
http://www.huffingtonpost.com/2014/01/23/famous-people-quiet_n_4597823.html
http://www.huffingtonpost.com/2012/12/06/shy-celebrities-celebrity-introverts-photos_n_2239122.html
http://www.jiposhy.com/2014/01/why-is-johnny-depp-so-shy.html
https://www.lucidatreatment.com/resources/mental-health-resources/avoidant-personality-disorder/
http://www.newsmax.com/FastFeatures/Avoidant-Personality-Disorder-symptoms/2011/01/03/id/381683/
http://www.nowrunning.com/johnny-depp-feels-he-is-a-shy-person-in-real-life/104439/story.htm
http://www.nytimes.com/health/guides/disease/avoidant-personality-disorder/overview.html
http://www.peopleskillsdecoded.com/avoidant-personality-disorder/
http://psychcentral.com/disorders/avoidant-personality-disorder-symptoms/
http://www.psychiatrictimes.com/personality-disorders/avoidant-personality-disorder-boundaries-diagnosis
https://www.psychologytoday.com/conditions/avoidant-personality-disorder
https://www.psychologytoday.com/blog/sideways-view/201703/avoidant-personality-disorder
https://www.quora.com/What-is-Johnny-Depps-personality-like
http://www.teen.com/2014/08/31/celebrities/celebrities-who-admit-to-being-shy-quotes/#3
http://www.therichest.com/buzz/21-shy-celebrities-who-hate-the-spotlight/
https://www.verywell.com/avoidant-personality-disorder-2795442
https://www.verywell.com/avoidant-personality-social-anxiety-disorder-difference-3024444
https://www.verywell.com/shy-comedians-3024275
http://www.webmd.com/mental-health/avoidant-personality-disorders#1
http://www.wikihow.com/Overcome-an-Avoidant-Personality-Disorder

FURTHER READING

American Psychiatric Association. (2013). Avoidant personality disorder. In *Diagnostic and statistical manual of mental disorders (DSM-5®)* (pp. 672-675). American Psychiatric Pub.

Hales, R.E., & Yudofsky, S.C. (Eds.). (2003). *The American psychiatric publishing textbook of clinical Psychiatry* (4th ed.). Arlington, VA: American Psychiatric Pub.

Hummelen, B, Wilberg, T., Pedersen, G., & Karterud, S. (2007). The relationship between avoidant personality disorder and social phobia. *Compr Psychiatry, 48*(4), 348-356.

Millon, T., Grossman, S.. Millon, C., Meagher, S., & Ramnath, R. (2004). The avoidant personality. In *Personality Disorders in Modern Life* (2nd ed.). Hoboken, NJ: John Wiley & Sons, Inc.

Reich, J. (2009). Avoidant personality disorder and its relationship to social phobia. *Curr Psychiatry Rep, 2009*(11), 89-93.

Sanislow, C.A., Da Cruz, K., Gianoli, M.O., & Reagan, E.R. (2012). *The Oxford handbook for personality disorders* (pp. 549-565). New York, NY: Oxford University Press.

-o0o-

DEPENDENT PERSONALITY AND CODEPENDENCY

Dependent personality disorder is a “Cluster C” anxious personality disorder characterized by a pervasive psychological dependence on other people, and an inability to be alone. People with dependent personality disorder have a long-standing need to be taken care of. This leads the person to engage in dependent and submissive behaviors in order to elicit caregiving behaviors in others. People with dependent personality disorder become emotionally dependent on other people and spend great effort trying to please others. They tend to belittle their abilities and assets, and may constantly refer to themselves as “stupid.” They take criticism and disapproval as proof of their worthlessness and lose faith in themselves. They avoid adult responsibilities and are unable to make even everyday decisions, without the advice and reassurance of others. They are passive, helpless, and dependent on others, especially their spouse or friend. They have an intense fear of abandonment and become devastated when relationship is severed, often causing them to move right into a similar relationship for fear of abandonment. They are pessimistic, oversensitive to criticism, afraid to be alone, and avoid disagreeing with others for fear of losing approval or support. They are unable to start projects because they lack self-confidence. They are also at risk for being abused because they may find themselves willing to do virtually anything to maintain the relationship with a dominant partner or person of authority. These individuals feel so unable to function alone that they will agree with things that they feel are wrong rather than risk losing the help of those to whom they look for guidance and support.

Dependent personality disorder is most likely caused by a combination of biological, developmental, temperamental, and psychological factors. Some risk factors that might contribute to the development of this disorder include a history of neglect, abusive upbringing or long-term abusive relationship, overprotective or authoritarian parents, and family history of anxiety disorders. It occurs equally in men and women, although it is diagnosed more often in females than males, largely due to behavioral differences in interviews and self-reporting rather than a difference in prevalence between the sexes. It usually becomes apparent in young adulthood or later as important adult relationships form. There is significant evidence that this disorder runs in families. Similar to issues found in authoritarian parenting, overprotective parenting makes children believe that they cannot function on their own without the help, guidance, and support of others. Children and adolescents with a history of anxiety disorders and physical illnesses are more susceptible to acquiring this disorder. Chronic physical illness or separation anxiety disorder in childhood or adolescence may also predispose an individual to the development of dependent personality disorder.

Dependency and separation anxiety are developmentally appropriate in children and pre-adolescents. Most adolescents grow out of their dependency and separation anxiety. If this dependency and separation anxiety becomes very pervasive and persistent by early adulthood, the person possibly has Dependent Personality Disorder. However, an experienced mental health professional, not self-made, should confirm the diagnosis. This diagnosis should be used with great caution, if at all, in children and adolescents, for whom dependent behavior may be age appropriate. Dependent Personality Disorder should not be diagnosed if its symptoms can be better explained as being due to another mental disorder, substance use disorder, or another medical condition.

Dependent personality disorder has symptoms in common with borderline personality disorder, but should be distinguished from it. People with borderline personality disorder respond to fears of abandonment with rage and a feeling of emptiness, while people with dependent personality respond to their fear by being submissive, and seeking another relationship to maintain their dependency. People with dependent personality disorder may also develop depression, phobias, substance abuse and anxiety disorders (such as panic disorder, obsessive compulsive personality disorder and avoidant personality disorder).

As with other personality disorders, many people are ashamed to seek help for their symptoms. They are likely to seek help only when their problem becomes overwhelming, they are no longer able to cope, or they are going to depression or anxiety.

Psychotherapy is the main treatment for dependent personality disorder and will allow those who are prone to this disorder to learn more productive ways of dealing with situations. The main goal is to help them become more active and independent, so they can form healthy relationships. Specific strategies might include assertiveness training to help them develop self-confidence and cognitive-behavioral therapy to help them develop new attitudes and perspectives about themselves relative to other people and experiences. People with dependent personality disorder may improve with short-term psychotherapy.

Long-term therapy, while ideal for many personality disorders, is contraindicated in this instance since it reinforces a dependent relationship on the therapist. Termination of therapy should always be a joint decision between the clinician and the patient. As the end of therapy approaches, the patient is likely to re-experience feelings of insecurity, anxiety and perhaps even depression, which should be treated appropriately. However, the therapist should not allow the patient to use these new symptoms as a way of prolonging the current therapy. Suggesting a support group later in treatment, where they can share their common experiences and feelings, and help put some of their new skill sets to use, may be helpful.

Medication may be used to relieve them from depression or anxiety, but will not treat disorder, per se. In addition, medications are only used as a last resort, and should be carefully monitored, because people with dependent personality could use them inappropriately or abuse certain prescription drugs. Sedative drug abuse and overdose is common in this population so medication should be prescribed with extreme caution.

Living with a person who suffers from dependent personality disorder can be a frustrating, frightening, and destructive experience. Yet despite being so common, few people have even heard of it. You may find yourself with an ever growing sense of anger and injustice when a capable adult acts like a helpless child, and you may be doing more harm than good if you continue to provide the kind of care that a person with dependent personality is seeking.

If you suspect that a loved one might have dependent personality disorder, it is important to encourage him or her to seek treatment before the condition worsens. This can be a sensitive matter, since people with dependent personality disorder may see this as a form of criticism or rejection. People with dependent personality seek constant approval and don't want to disappoint their loved ones. When suggesting that they see a therapist, you should focus on the positive aspects to let them know that they're not being rejected.

-o0o-

CODEPENDENCY

While not an actual diagnosis, the term "codependency" was first used to describe how family members of individuals with substance abuse issues might actually interfere with recovery by over-helping. Codependency often affects a spouse, a parent, sibling, friend, or co-worker of a person afflicted with alcohol or drug dependence. Similar patterns have been seen in relationships with chronically or mentally ill individuals. Today, however, the term has broadened to describe any co-dependent person from any dysfunctional family. This condition appears to run in different degrees, whereby the intensity of symptoms is on a spectrum of severity, as opposed to an all or nothing scale.

Being codependent is hardly the same thing as simply being dependent. Codependency does not refer to all caring behavior or feelings. Rather, it represents caring that is excessive to an unhealthy degree; that is, codependents are primarily dependent on the other person's dependence on them to satisfy their own emotional needs.

In a codependent relationship, the codependent's sense of purpose is based on making extreme sacrifices to satisfy their partner's needs. Some codependents often find themselves in relationships where their primary role is that of rescuer, supporter, and confidante.

Codependency is clearly maladaptive and dysfunctional. To some degree, we all need to be needed. We all want to feel useful and able to give. Having some degree of dependency also is not by itself unhealthy, when such relationship contributes to both individuals' resilience, resourcefulness, and inner strength. In a healthy interdependent relationship, each party is able to comfortably rely on the other for help, understanding, and support, while at the same time remaining self-sufficient and quite able to stand on their own two feet.

On the other hand, a codependent relationship is one where both parties become over-dependent on each other. As opposed to healthy inter-dependency, the codependent individual needs to be needed if they are to feel okay about themselves. Without being depended upon, they feel alone, inadequate, insecure, and unworthy. One key sign of codependency is when your sense of purpose in life wraps around making extreme sacrifices to satisfy your partner's needs.

During childhood, most codependents are conditioned to think and believe that to be "good enough" to be accepted by their parents, they had to deny themselves or repress many of their thoughts, feelings, and impulses. Their self-esteem depends on the validation of others, so that asserting their own needs in a relationship is highly constrained. Their behavior is largely dictated by an underlying fear of being alone, and feeling abandoned, spurned, or rejected. Their sense of responsibility depends more on satisfying the other person's feelings, needs, wants, and desires than on their own. Yet, outwardly, they may not appear dependent. They can hide their reliance on others to confirm their own worth, but saying and doing things to them appear that they are in control. They become professional "volunteers," routinely going beyond the call of duty to demonstrate their worth. They repeatedly do favors for, give gifts to, or anticipate the needs of others; encourage others to let them be their indispensable caretaker or confidante; and take on the role of problem-solver, decision-maker, support person, savior or rescuer. To them, such actions are necessary to address their own self-doubts and self-perceived deficiencies.

If you spend all of your energy in meeting your partner's needs, feel trapped in your relationship, or notice that you are the one who is constantly making sacrifices in your relationship, then you may be in a codependent relationship. Sometimes you can delude yourself into thinking that you are helping your dependent partner by continuing to cater to his or her needs. But giving up your own needs and identity to meet the needs of your partner can have unhealthy short-term and long-term consequences. You can get burned out, exhausted, and begin to neglect other important relationships. Codependency can create stress and lead to feelings of anger and resentment, depression, hopelessness, and despair. When the feelings are too much, you can feel numb.

But breaking up is not necessarily the best or only solution to change or improve your codependent relationship. To repair a codependent relationship, it's important to set boundaries. Talk about and set relationship goals that satisfy both of you. Spend time with relatives, friends, and family to broaden your circle of support. Get involved in hobbies of your own. Try separating from each other for certain periods of time. Work on becoming more assertive and building your self-esteem. And when things go out of hand, you feel overwhelmed or have trouble coping, do not hesitate to seek help, support and counseling from a mental health professional. The more you understand codependency, the better you can cope with its effects. Reaching out for information and assistance can help someone live a healthier, more fulfilling life.

Because codependency is usually rooted in a person's childhood, treatment often involves exploration into early childhood issues and their relationship to current destructive behavior patterns. The treatment focuses on helping patients to get in touch with their feelings that may have been buried during childhood. It includes individual, family and group therapy to help codependents rediscover themselves and identify self-defeating behavior patterns. It is important for patients and their family members to educate themselves about the course and cycle of addiction and codependency.

-o0o-

Although well-known personalities can suffer from dependent personality disorder or codependence, there aren't any valid media outlets or authoritative sources documenting famous people and celebrities with dependent personality disorder. This is because famous people rarely exhibit behaviors in public that indicate they might have dependent or codependent personalities.

-o0o-

REFERENCES

https://en.wikipedia.org/wiki/Dependent_personality_disorder
http://healthresearchfunding.org/famous-people-dependent-personality-disorder/
http://illnessquiz.com/dependent-personality-disorder-test/
http://www.mdedge.com/currentpsychiatry/article/62499/dependent-personality-disorder-effective-time-limited-therapy/
https://medlineplus.gov/ency/article/000941.htm
http://mentalhealth.com/home/dx/dependentpersonality.html
http://outofthefog.website/personality-disorders-1/2015/12/6/dependent-personality-disorder-dpd
https://psychcentral.com/disorders/dependent-personality-disorder-symptoms/
http://samvak.tripod.com/personalitydisorders22.html
http://umm.edu/health/medical/ency/articles/dependent-personality-disorder
https://www.allaboutcounseling.com/codependency.htm
http://www.disorders.org/dependent-personality-disorder/
http://www.goodtherapy.org/learn about therapy/issues/codependency
http://www.healthline.com/health/dependent-personality-disorder#CaregivingandSupport8
http://www.healthyplace.com/personality-disorders/personality-disorders-information/personality-disorder-references/#Dependent
http://www.healthyplace.com/personality-disorders/dependent-personality-disorder/famous-people-with-dependent-personality-disorder/
http://www.imdb.com/title/tt0367279/

http://www.mayoclinic.org/diseases-conditions/personality-disorders/symptoms-causes/dxc-20247656

https://medlineplus.gov/ency/article/000941.htm

http://www.mentalhealth.com/home/dx/dependentpersonality.html

http://www.mentalhealthamerica.net/co-dependency

http://www.mountsinai.org/health-library/diseases-conditions/dependent-personality-disorder

http://my.clevelandclinic.org/health/articles/dependent-personality-disorder

http://my.clevelandclinic.org/services/neurological_institute/center-for-behavorial-health/disease-conditions/hic-dependent-personality-disorder

http://www.nlm.nih.gov/medlineplus/ency/article/000941.htm

http://www.nytimes.com/health/guides/disease/dependent-personality-disorder/overview.html

https://psychcentral.com/lib/symptoms-of-codependency/https://www.psychologytoday.com/conditions/dependent-personality-disorder

https://www.psychologytoday.com/blog/evolution-the-self/201412/codependent-or-simply-dependent-what-s-the-big-difference

https://www.psychologytoday.com/blog/presence-mind/201604/six-hallmarks-codependence

http://www.psyweb.com/mdisord/jsp/depd.jsp

https://www.theravive.com/therapedia/Dependent-Personality-Disorder-DSM--5-301.6-(F60.7)

http://www.trustineducation.org/resources/life-as-an-afghan-woman/

http://www.webmd.com/anxiety-panic/guide/dependent-personality-disorder#1

http://www.webmd.com/anxiety-panic/guide/dependent-personality-disorder

http://www.webmd.com/anxiety-panic/guide/dependent-personality-disorder

http://www.wikihow.com/Know-if-Someone-Has-a-Dependent-Personality-Disorder

http://www.webmd.com/sex-relationships/features/signs-of-a-codependent-relationship#1

http://www.wikihow.com/Tell-if-You-Are-Codependent

https://www.psychologytoday.com/blog/evolution-the-self/201412/codependent-or-simply-dependent-what-s-the-big-difference

FURTHER READING

Benjamin, L.S. (1996). Dependent personality disorder. *Interpersonal Diagnosis and Treatment of Personality Disorders* (pp. 221-239). New York, NY: The Guilford Press.

Blais, M.A., Smallwood, P., Groves, J.E., & Rivas-Vazquez, R.A. (2008). Personality and personality disorders. In T.A. Stern, J.F. Rosenbaum, M. Fava, J. Biederman, & S.L. Rauch (Eds.), *Massachusetts General Hospital comprehensive clinical psychiatry* (1st ed., chap 39). Philadelphia, PA: Elsevier Mosby.

Blais, M.A., Smallwood, P., Groves, J.E., & Rivas-Vazquez, R.A. (2008). Dependent personality disorder. In T.A. Stern, J.F. Rosenbaum, M. Fava, J. Biederman, & S.L. Rauch (Eds.), *Massachusetts General Hospital comprehensive clinical psychiatry* (1st ed., chap 39). Philadelphia, PA: Elsevier Mosby.

-o0o-

ASPERGER'S and AUTISM SPECTRUM DISORDER

The diagnostic criteria for Autism Spectrum Disorder or Asperger's do not include mood disorders such as anxiety, depression, or obsessive-compulsive disorder. But many people with Asperger's are overwhelmed by these mood disorders -- perhaps even more than by the symptoms of autism itself. Adult individuals with Asperger's can be difficult to differentiate from bipolar and other co-morbid behavioral or personality disorders. While the hypothesis that individuals with Asperger's are predisposed to violent or criminal behavior is not supported by data, a number of reported violent criminals with Asperger's do have coexisting psychiatric disorders such as schizoaffective disorder.

-o0o-

Until 2013, Asperger syndrome, often just called "Asperger's", was a distinct diagnosis which described a person of average or higher-than-average intelligence and age appropriate language skills who also had significant social and communication challenges. Asperger's was a diagnostic category that existed only for a short period of time, from 1994, when it was added to the Diagnostic and Statistical Manual of Mental Disorders (DSM) to 2013, when it was removed. Unofficially, however, many people, including clinicians, will continue to use the term Asperger's for the foreseeable future. While the American Psychiatric Association no longer finds the term useful, almost everyone else still does. People who are brilliant, quirky, anxious, creative, and socially awkward have been diagnosed with Asperger's. These people are very different from those diagnosed with more severe forms of autism, but are grouped together under the autism spectrum.

Both autism and Asperger's are known as "Autism Spectrum Disorders" -- a spectrum of developmental disorders or psychological conditions characterized by a shared pattern of symptoms that range from very severely disabled to a highly functioning disorder. Autism is a spectrum disorder characterized by difficulty with social interaction and communication, as well as repetitive and restrictive behaviors and interests. People who have classic autism and Asperger's both suffer from poor communication skills. Many children with high functioning autism or Asperger's would rather talk to adults than kids their own age. They resist changes in their routine, are hyper or hyposensitivity to pain and touch, and have problems with gross and fine motor skills. Both classic autism and Asperger's have poor eye contact and may develop obsessions to a specific subject of interest. Individuals with Asperger's appear to have normal life expectancy, but have an increased prevalence of comorbid psychiatric conditions, such as major depressive disorder and anxiety disorder.

The two disorders also have differences. Signs of autism usually begin before three years old and typically last for a person's entire life, while Asperger's is usually detected later, when children are typically diagnosed between the ages of 6 and 11. The main difference between Asperger's and classic autism is that language acquisition is not delayed in Asperger's and there is no significant delay in cognitive development. Asperger's is different from other disorders on the autism spectrum, in part because it is often diagnosed in older children and adults, as opposed to very young children. Young children with Asperger's reach most developmental milestones within a typical timeframe, with normal to above average intelligence and language development, although their verbal IQ is higher than their performance IQ. In autism, children's IQ is usually below average, and communication delays are always present. Many autistic children are very late at developing verbal, and sometimes, nonverbal language. Children with Asperger's express a desire to fit in socially, while autistic kids gravitate toward complete exclusion and seclusion. To some degree, autistic individuals are oblivious to the need for social interactions, while those with Asperger's tend to know that they have social challenges, which is why anxiety and depression is more common, compared those with autism. The grammar of individuals with Asperger's is usually very good, even though their speech is sometimes repetitive.

Asperger's and high functioning autism are often considered as the same diagnosis. While they currently exist as two separate diagnoses, there is an ongoing debate about whether that is necessary. Individuals with high functioning autism and Asperger's both have average or above average intelligence but may struggle with issues related to social interaction and communication. It is important to remember that both Asperger's and high functioning autism do present themselves largely the same way, and as a result may be treated in a similar way. The primary difference is that a diagnosis of high function autism requires that, early in development, the child has delayed language whereas in Asperger's, there is no significant delay in language development during early childhood. Also, people with high functioning autism have no problem with basic speech, are not lacking in emotions, and may be very intelligent and capable. In some cases they may be creative and innovative. However, they may also prefer to talk and think about only a few topics of special interest. They have difficulty with changes in routines, and have a tough time imagining what other people are thinking or feeling. People with symptoms of the disorder once called Asperger's are now officially diagnosed with "Level 1" (meaning in need of relatively little support) on the Autism Spectrum Disorder.

During the 1990s, Asperger's was famously dubbed "The Geek Syndrome" and "The Little Professor Syndrome" because people with Asperger's tend to be very intelligent and articulate, but socially clueless. The official diagnosis has now been discontinued because it was so difficult for practitioners to tell the difference between Asperger's and high functioning autism spectrum disorder. Individuals with "lower functioning" autism spectrum disorder (classic autism) might spend most of their day in a supported setting where the possibility of dangerous interactions is almost zero. Meanwhile, individuals with "high functioning" autism (like

Asperger's) may need to navigate a world of complex and hazardous situations.

Individuals with Asperger's often have difficulty in social settings, which ranges from awkwardness to anxiety, lack of empathy to preoccupation with a narrow subject, and one-sided verbosity. However, as the children grow up, they are able to better cope because their cognitive abilities are intact, and often, even superior. They have no problem with verbal communication but they have impaired nonverbal behaviors such as eye contact, facial expression, posture, and gesture. They may choose to only talk to people they like, may come across as insensitive to other people's feelings, and may not be interested in making friends, developing relationships or sharing experiences with others. They are more likely to have sleep problems, including difficulty in falling asleep, frequent nocturnal awakenings, and early morning awakenings. Children with Asperger's may have an unusually sophisticated vocabulary at a young age, but have difficulty understanding figurative language and tend to use language literally. They have difficulty in understanding humor, irony, teasing, and sarcasm. Most young adults with Asperger's remain at home, although some do marry and can work independently.

They may be poorly coordinated, or have an odd or bouncy gait or posture, poor handwriting, or problems with visual-motor integration. They may be unusually sensitive or insensitive to sound, light, and other stimuli. Pursuit of specific and narrow areas of interest is one of their most striking features. Children with Asperger's may be delayed in acquiring skills that require motor dexterity, such as riding a bicycle or opening a jar, and may seem to move awkwardly. Most children improve as they grow up, but social and communication difficulties usually persist. Although many attend regular education classes, some children with Asperger's may need special education services because of their social and behavioral difficulties.

They may show problems with proprioception (sensation of body position), balance, tandem gait, and finger-thumb apposition. Stereotyped behaviors include hand movements such as flapping or twisting, and complex whole-body movements. They are typically repeated in longer bursts and look more voluntary or ritualistic than tics, which are usually faster, less rhythmical and less often symmetrical. They may be able to approach others, even if awkwardly, and may engage in a one-sided, long-winded speech about a favorite topic, while misunderstanding or not recognizing the listener's feelings or reactions. Even though they have great expressive language skills, they will have problems communicating due to trouble interpreting other people's social cues. They also have difficulty in identifying and showing their emotions. Depression is often the result of chronic frustration from repeated failure to engage others socially, and mood disorders requiring treatment may develop. There are legal implications for individuals with Asperger's who run the risk of being exploited by others and being unable to comprehend the implications and consequences of their actions.

Diagnosis is based on neurological and genetic assessment as well as tests for cognition, psychomotor function, verbal and nonverbal strengths and weaknesses, style of learning, and skills for independent living. Under-diagnosis and over-diagnosis may be problems, and the cost and difficulty of screening and assessment can delay diagnosis. It can be difficult to diagnose bipolar disorder or other psychiatric illnesses in someone who has Asperger's, because doctors may attribute their symptoms to the developmental disability and not consider that there could be another, undiagnosed disorder. Many children with Asperger's are initially misdiagnosed with attention deficit hyperactivity disorder (ADHD). Diagnosing adults is more challenging, as standard diagnostic criteria are designed for children and the expression of Asperger's changes with age. Conditions that must be considered in a differential diagnosis include other autism spectrum disorders, the schizophrenia spectrum, ADHD, obsessive–compulsive disorder, major depressive disorder, bipolar disorder, and social-cognitive deficits due to brain damage from alcohol abuse.

Both Asperger's and attention deficit hyperactivity disorder (ADHD) develop early in a child's life, and can lead to difficulty in socializing, communicating, and learning, and developing. Both have difficulty sitting still, social awkwardness, frequent episodes of non-stop talking, an inability to focus on things that don't interest them, and impulsivity. But people with Asperger's have all-absorbing interest in a specific, focused topic; are unable to practice nonverbal communication, such as eye contact, facial expressions, or body gestures; do not understand another person's feelings, have monotone pitch when speaking, and are slow with motor skill development milestones. They tend to be very focused and attentive. They may be physically clumsy and will not develop many friends as they lack the typical social instinct. Many of them will display selective mutism and will not talk to specific people at all. On the other hand, patients with ADHD are easily distracted and forgetful, impatient, have learning difficulties, react without restraint when upset or bothered, and are compelled to touch or play with everything, especially in a new environment. Their tremendous restlessness and hyperactive behavior are unintended and purposeless. They tend to constantly move about from one place to another and have great difficulty in concentrating, playing with one toy or sitting down for a while for studies. They have a very short span of attention and tend to lose interest in activities very quickly. They need to be occupied with multiple games and activities one after the other continuously. They will always be demanding and desire constant activity.

Asperger's is sometimes confused with obsessive-compulsive disorder (OCD) because of considerable similarities and overlap between the two, including intensely repetitive thoughts and behaviors. But people with Asperger's may be distinguished from the latter because they also have a range of other social, language, and cognitive differences not seen in people with the latter. People with obsessive compulsive disorder usually feel uncomfortable with their symptoms, and would like to be rid of them, whereas people with Asperger's usually are not bothered by their obsessions, and in fact may even embrace them.

Asperger's can be misdiagnosed with childhood bipolar disorder because they have similar symptoms. Both disorders tend to lack behavioral and anger issues. Those with Asperger's can get very frustrated sometimes—which could look like mood instability, without complete history. Bipolar disorder is a mood disorder -- the person may cycle between depression and mania, interspersed with normal mood. Features of Asperger's that are not present in Bipolar disorder include problems with social skills, eccentric or repetitive behaviors, unusual preoccupations or rituals, difficulty with communication, and problems with coordination.

In contrast with Asperger's, schizoid personality disorder does not involve impairments in nonverbal communication and a pattern of restricted interests or repetitive behaviors. Schizoid personality disorder is characterized by prominent conduct disorder, better adult adjustment, less severely impaired social interaction and a slightly increased risk of schizophrenia, compared to Asperger's.

Although the cause of social impairment in Asperger's and schizoid affective disorder may be different, they share many of the symptoms related to social skills deficits, including problems with eye contact, body postures, gestures and speech qualities, such as tone, volume and rate. People with both conditions probably also have trouble building and maintaining friendships. However, for people with schizoid affective disorder, anxiety is the driving force behind the difficulties that are experienced in social and performance situations. Their ability to function is limited by their anxiety in those situations. A diagnosis of Asperger's, on the other hand, does not require the presence of anxiety. Behavior in social situations is instead impaired because of trouble reading and understanding social and emotional cues.

Treatment is usually aimed at addressing the core symptoms of the disorder, including poor communication skills, obsessive or repetitive routines, and physical clumsiness. Interventions may include social skills training, cognitive behavioral therapy, physical therapy, speech therapy, parent training, and medications for associated problems such as mood or anxiety. A positive behavior support includes training and support of parents, doctors, teachers, and mental health counselors to help build social and learning skills. School programs, job training, and counseling can also help in behavior management strategies to use in the home and school. Cognitive behavioral therapy aims to improve stress management relating to anxiety or explosive emotions, and to cut back on obsessive interests and repetitive routines. Specialized speech therapy can help improve communication and carry on a normal conversation. Vocational training is important to teach job interview etiquette and workplace behavior to older children and adults with Asperger's. Education is critical in helping the family cope and develop strategies for understanding the strengths and weaknesses of people with Asperger's.

Medications do not cure, but can be effectively combined with behavioral interventions and environmental accommodations when treating coexisting conditions such as anxiety disorder, major depressive disorder, inattention and aggression. The atypical antipsychotic medications *risperidone (Risperdal)* and *olanzapine (Zyprexa)*, and selective serotonin reuptake inhibitors (SSRIs) *fluoxetine (Prozac)*, and *sertraline (Zoloft)* have been shown to reduce repetitive and self-injurious behaviors, aggressive outbursts and impulsivity, and improve stereotypical patterns of behavior and social relatedness. Care must be taken with medications, as side effects may be more common and harder to evaluate in individuals with Asperger's. Abnormalities in metabolism, cardiac conduction times, and an increased risk of type 2 diabetes have been raised as concerns with these medications, along with serious long-term neurological side effects. SSRIs can sometimes cause increased impulsivity, aggression, and sleep disturbance. Weight gain and fatigue are the commonly reported side effects of *risperidone*, which may also lead to increased risk for extrapyramidal symptoms such as restlessness and dystonia or involuntary muscle contractions. With effective treatment, children with Asperger's can learn to cope with their disabilities, but they may still find social situations and personal relationships challenging. Many adults are able to work successfully in mainstream jobs, although they may continue to need encouragement and moral support to maintain an independent life.

-o0o-

PERSONS WITH ASPERGER'S

Asperger's is nothing to be ashamed of. It is not a death sentence, nor is it a character defect. People with Asperger's may stick out in a crowd because they are different, and they are usually the ones who suffer the most from peer abuse while growing up. But there are many celebrities and famous people with Asperger's, whose unique personality traits, interests, or talents have led to some of the greatest contributions to society. They just perceive the world through a slightly different lens than others.

-o0o-

DAN AYKROYD

Daniel Edward "Dan" Ackroyd is a Canadian-American actor, comedian, producer, screenwriter, musician and businessman. He gained fame on the American late-night comedy show "Saturday Night Live" and brought a unique sensibility to the show, combining youth, unusual interests, talent as an impersonator and an almost lunatic intensity. He was known for his impersonations of celebrities like Jimmy Carter, Vincent Price, Richard Nixon, Rod Serling, Tom Snyder, Julia Child, and others. He conceived and starred in Ghostbusters, which spawned a sequel (Ghostbusters II) and eventually an entire media franchise. In 1990, he was nominated for the Academy Award for Best Supporting Actor for his work in the 1989 film Driving Miss Daisy. He is also a successful businessman, having co-founded the House of Blues chain of music venues and the Crystal Head Vodka brand. He was diagnosed with Tourette's at 12. He had physical tics, nervousness and made grunting noises and it affected how outgoing he was. He had therapy that really worked and by 14, his symptoms eased. He also has Asperger's that wasn't diagnosed until the early 80s when his wife persuaded him to see a doctor. One of his symptoms included his obsession with the supernatural, ghosts and law enforcement. He became obsessed with Hans Holzer, the greatest ghost hunter ever. That's when the idea of his film Ghostbusters was born. Nowadays, both are controllable and manageable, and he has been able to channel them creatively.

-o0o-

SUSAN BOYLE

Susan Boyle wowed the world when she auditioned for Britain's "Got Talent" in 2009 with her rendition of "I Dreamed a Dream." She finished second place in the competition, but has since become a multi-millionaire because of her musical records. She came from a large Catholic family of nine children, and the most important relationship of her life has been with her mother who died just before she became famous. She lives alone. She once had a boyfriend when she was in her 20s, but her protective father ended the relationship because he did not want her to get hurt. Her mother's death left her emotionally distraught, and she didn't know what to do. She could not cope and had to get social services in. She had learning difficulties as a child, which she was told were the result of brain damage from oxygen deprivation at birth. She struggled in school and was bullied by other children. For most of her life, Susan was told she had "brain damage." It was only in 2013 that she discovered she actually had Asperger's, a high-functioning form of autism that mainly affects people's social interaction and communication skills. Her warmth, kindness and empathy in conversation are sometimes lost in articles about her, which refer variously to "learning difficulties" or "slowness" caused by complications at birth. She exhibits delayed eye contact and a slightly offbeat laughter in the middle of conversation. She used to be called Susie Simple, when she was in school. She suffered from depression when she was younger, though she says her life is better now. Mood swings are part of her. She has visible anxiety in the presence of a stranger that is not at least superficially familiar to her, and an obvious emotional withdrawal if she feels uncomfortable with a particular subject. She does not like to criticize anyone, and one can almost see her anxiety levels rising during an interview. She now has a personal assistant who lives locally; a PR from London who flies up especially for interviews, a manager, and someone who helps with housework. Sometimes she gets frustrated when press articles say that she has brain damage, because she says that she has always known she has had an unfair label put upon her. Her diagnosis of Asperger's, that made her different before, now explains why her childhood was marred by feelings of being an outsider. She admits that the isolation, and the attempts to prove herself to people who didn't always understand, left her with inner anger and frustration. Security seems a key concept for her. She struggles with relationships, loses her train of thought during a sentence, and has difficulties in communicating, which lead to a lot of frustration. Asperger’s is a condition that she has to live with and work through, but she feels more relaxed about herself. She hopes that people will have a greater understanding of who she is and why she does the things she does.

-o0o-

TEMPLE GRANDIN

Mary Temple Grandin is an American author, professor of animal science at Colorado State University, world-renowned autism spokesperson and consultant to the livestock industry on animal behavior. Considered to be the most well-known autistic individual in the world, she has appeared on the Today Show, Larry King Live, 48 hours, ABC’s Primetime Live, and 20/20. She has been featured in publications such as Time Magazine, People Magazine, Forbes, U.S. News and World Report, and the New York Times. In 2010, she was included in the Time 100 list of the one hundred most influential people in the world in the “Heroes” category. Her outspoken activism makes her a prominent voice in the autistic community. Her life is the focus of a 2010 HBO biopic, Temple Grandin, which was nominated for 15 Emmys and won five awards. She was the eldest of four siblings, and displayed many of what are now recognized as the classic early symptoms of autism—she hated to be touched, would dissolve into temper tantrums, and was, for the large part, silent. When she was very young, she had no speech, attention span or eye contact at all. She would just hum to herself and dribble sand through her hands. The expert opinion at that time was that she was brain-damaged and should be confined to an institution to receive long-term care. She was never formally diagnosed with autism in childhood or in youth. When she was in her mid-teens, her mother hypothesized that her symptoms were best explained by autism after completing a checklist on autism. However, she was not formally diagnosed with autism disorder spectrum until she was in her 40s. She did not begin talking until she was three and a half years, and would play educational games for hours. She has described herself as the "nerdy kid" whom everyone ridiculed, and there were occasions when she walked down the hallways and her fellow students would taunt her by saying "tape recorder" because of her habit of repetitive speech. She was expelled at the age of 14 for throwing a book at a schoolmate who had taunted her. Like many autistic people, while she may lack natural verbal and emotional reactions, she is gifted with the ability to recall and perfectly re-create anything she has seen. She can visualize highly detailed systems in her mind, and translate them into complex designs. High school may have been hard, but she persisted and earned a degree in psychology at Franklin Pierce University in New Hampshire. She finally found her voice, researching animal behavior, in graduate school at Arizona State University.

-o0o-

MICHELANGELO

Michelangelo was an Italian sculptor, painter, architect, and poet of the High Renaissance who exerted an unparalleled influence on the development of Western art. Considered to be the greatest living artist during his lifetime, he has since been described as one of the greatest artists of all time. Two of his best-known works, the Pietà and David, were sculpted before he turned thirty. Despite his low opinion of painting, Michelangelo also created two of the most influential works in fresco in the history of Western art: the scenes from Genesis on the ceiling and The Last Judgment on the altar wall of the Sistine Chapel in Rome. He was the second oldest of five boys, but did not get along with his family and suffered physical abuse from his fathers and uncles. The men in Michelangelo's family "displayed autistic traits" and mood disturbances. He was "erratic" and "had trouble applying himself to anything". He was very insecure, aloof, self-absorbed, and a loner. As a boy he was unsure about himself outside of his talent as an artist. He was indifferent to food and drink, eating "more out of necessity than of pleasure" and he often slept in his clothes and boots. He had few friends, found it difficult to maintain relationships, and did not attend his brother's funeral, which underscored his inability to show emotion. Michelangelo was not a great public speaker and had difficulty maintaining a conversation, often walking away in the middle of it. He had a short temper, a sarcastic wit, and was paranoid at times. He was bad-tempered and had angry outbursts. He always preferred to work independently even when he needed help on a project, and gave his undivided attention to his masterpieces, obsessed with nudity and was focused so much on his work that he toiled eight years over to complete. Loss of control caused him great frustration. He was able to generate, in a short time, many hundreds of sketches for the Sistine ceiling -- no two alike, nor any pose similar. He had a single-minded work routine, unusual lifestyle, limited interests, and poor social and communication skills. He died in Rome in 1564, at the age of 88 (three weeks before his 89th birthday). His body was taken from Rome for interment at the

Basilica of Santa Croce, fulfilling the maestro's last request to be buried in his beloved Florence.

-o0o-

REFERENCES

http://aspennj.org/what-is-asperger-syndrome
http://emedicine.medscape.com/article/912296-overview
https://en.wikipedia.org/wiki/Category:People_with_Asperger_syndrome
https://en.wikipedia.org/wiki/Dan_Aykroyd
https://en.wikipedia.org/wiki/Diagnosis_of_Asperger_syndrome
https://en.wikipedia.org/wiki/Michelangelo
https://en.wikipedia.org/wiki/Temple_Grandin
https://everydayaspergers.com/2014/08/20/bipolar-or-aspergers/
https://iancommunity.org/cs/about_asds/aspergers_syndrome
http://kidshealth.org/en/parents/asperger.html
https://psychcentral.com/lib/aspergers-syndrome/
http://wrongplanet.net/interview-with-temple-grandin/
http://www.activebeat.com/your-health/10-symptoms-of-aspergers-syndrome
http://www.aspergers.com/aspbib.html
http://www.aspergerssyndrome.net/
http://www.autism.org.uk/about/what-is/asperger.aspx
https://www.autismspeaks.org/family-services/tool-kits/asperger-syndrome-and-high-functioning-autism-tool-kit/how-are-and-hfa-dif
https://www.autismspeaks.org/news/news-item/dan-aykroyd-talks-about-his-autism-diagnosis
http://www.autism-society.org/what-is/aspergers-syndrome/
https://www.betterhealth.vic.gov.au/health/conditionsandtreatments/asperger-syndrome
http://www.cdc.gov/ncbddd/features/counting-autism.html
https://www.cigna.com/healthwellness/hw/medical-topics/aspergers-syndrome-zq1008
https://www.disabled-world.com/artman/publish/article_2086.shtml
http://www.dailymail.co.uk/femail/article-2828626/The-truth-Asperger-s-Susan-Boyle-reveals-just-difficult-living-condition-makes-behaviour-unpredictable.html
http://www.dailymail.co.uk/home/you/article-1368868/Temple-Grandin-Autistic-woman-leading-animal-behaviour-expert.html
http://www.emedicinehealth.com/aspergers_syndrome-health/article_em.htm
http://www.healthguideinfo.com/aspergers-syndrome/p31859/
http://www.healthline.com/health/adhd/aspergers#Differences5
http://www.healthline.com/health/asperger-syndrome
http://www.lifescript.com/health/a-z/conditions_a-z/conditions/a/asperger_syndrome.aspx
http://www.medicalnewstoday.com/articles/7601.php

http://www.medicinenet.com/asperger_syndrome/
http://www.myaspergerschild.com/2010/10/aspergers-and-comorbid-bipolar.html
https://www.ncbi.nlm.nih.gov/pubmedhealth/PMHT0024670/
http://www.news-medical.net/news/2004/05/26/1931.aspx
https://www.psychologytoday.com/basics/aspergers-syndrome
https://www.sharecare.com/health/aspersers-syndrome/what-difference-aspergers-syndrome-ocd
https://www.theguardian.com/fashion/2013/dec/08/susan-boyle-i-have-aspergers
http://www.usatoday.com/story/life/people/2013/12/08/susan-boyle-aspergers-syndrome/3908299/
https://www.verywell.com/autism-vs-obsessive-compulsive-disorder-260344
http://www.webmd.com/brain/autism/mental-health-aspergers-syndrome#1
http://www.webmd.com/brain/autism/news/20131209/susan-boyle-aspergers#1
http://www.webmd.com/mental-health/news/20040526/did-michelangelo-have-autism#1

FURTHER READING

Fitzgerald, M., & Corvin, A. (2001). Diagnosis and differential diagnosis of Asperger syndrome. *Adv Psychiatr Treat, 7*(4), 310–318.

Szatmari, P., Bremner, R., & Nagy, J. (1989). Asperger's syndrome: A review of clinical features. *Can J Psychiatry, 34*(6), 554–560.

U.S. Department of Health and Human Services, National Institutes of Health, National Institute of Neurological Disorders and Stroke. (2008). What is Asperger's syndrome? Retrieved from http://www.schoolbehavior.com/Files/NINDS_AspFactSheet_2005.pdf

U.S. Department of Health and Human Services, National Institutes of Health, National Institute of Mental Health. (2016). *Autism spectrum disorder.* Retrieved from*https://www.nimh.nih.gov/health/topics/autism-spectrum-disorders-asd/index.shtml*

-o0o-

WE ARE NOT ALONE

I used to be afraid of my own shadow. Every time I looked back to the milestones of my past, I saw nothing but darkness -- a lingering depression and emptiness – feeling and thinking that I had never done anything good in my life, and probably never would. I often wondered why.

At times, I would be riding high, smiling and singing like there was no tomorrow. Then, at a moment's notice and more often than not, I would be going deep into the abyss – crying and moaning like there was no tomorrow.

I was in constant turmoil – but I had no one to turn to, because I was afraid that no one would understand. I wore a mask to hide my face, so no one would know who and what I truly was. For years, I pretended that everything was fine. I was afraid of the stigma.

When I could cope no more, I knew I had to seek help – and I did. I was told that I had a mood disorder.

It opened my eyes. I finally understood why I was feeling and acting the way I was – for a very long time. It took a while before I was able to control my moods, but I finally did – thanks to my family and my friends who accepted me for what I am. Still, that was not enough. I feel that I have to know more, and understand why I am the way I am, and why all the others are the same, and yet different.

That is the reason for this book -- so the public may know that mental illness has many faces, and that it comes in many forms.

It's not our fault that we are what we are. Mental illness can happen to anyone – celebrities and commoners alike. It's refreshing to hear and learn about famous people who were and are also vulnerable like the rest of us. Many of them have struggled and yet, were able to accomplish much in spite of their illness. Some have even achieved greatness and helped shape the very world that we live in. When celebrities go public, they help reduce and erase the stigma that all too often has been attached to our condition. Like most of them, we can get over the hurdle. Like most of them, we can lead a normal and satisfying life.

We are not alone…

EPILOGUE

Fear and shame have touched
The deepest recesses of our hearts and minds
Fearing rejection
Shamed by no fault of ours
We look around and see
Faceless beings behind the mask
Hiding from stigma
Haunting
Laughing
The sun shines
Enlightens them and shows the way
Take off that mask
And find others who are like us
We're not alone.

-o0o-

It Lies Within

It lies within
Our heart
The power to change
Someone's soul.
But would it be right
To be the ghost,
Or somebody's spirit.
I, alone cannot do that,
For I am who I am.
And you are you.
It's up to us
To live within
Our own realm.
But be different
Than other souls.
Our own ghosts
Will last
Through eternity,
And our spirit
Will live forever,
When we reach
Our unknown
Destination.

Ross Bruce

I wish…

I wish
I could cry
So tears can drown
The sorrow and the pain
Of losing someone
So dear and lovable

I wish
I could forget
That wonderful smile
Of someone I care for
Who now is gone
Perhaps forever

I wish
I could erase
This awful loneliness
Creeping from inside me
Disturbing my peace
And my sanity

I wish
I could smile
And think only of good
That I hope will come out
Of these trying moments
So I can be strong

-oOo-

Stigma

I think I am lost
In the wilderness of life
The road is dark and lonely
I turn around
Hoping to see your face
But you are gone
I feel alone
Afraid of what the future holds
I do not know
Which way to go
Diverging paths that lead nowhere
I close my eyes
Hoping to ease my mind
I tell myself
That all is well
I must find light
Somewhere along the road
To see me through
These trying times
Till then
I will be lost

-oOo-

Sometimes
I wonder
What life is all about
Smiling faces
With tearful eyes
Wounded souls
Weeping
Hoping
Searching for love
Lonely beings
Wandering
Without purpose
Looking for peace
I heave a sigh
And ask myself
What is life all about?

-oOo-

Stigma

I see that you are moving
To a new horizon
Hoping to find yourself
Wanting to be free
I see you smiling
I feel the gladness
Emanating from your being
For this is a new day
Full of hope
You are on to a new life
To a new beginning
The tears will flow
Out of loneliness
But I should let go
So you can be free
To pursue your goals
You will survive
And so will I
Someday perhaps
We'll meet again
When you have lived
A fuller life
Then perhaps
I can smile
And say that parting
Was not that bad
After all.

-oOo-

The storm is gone
Beneath the clouds I see the sun
Upon your face
I see your smile
I heave a sigh
Not out of pain
But out of joy
For all is well
The storm is gone.

Be not afraid
You'll see the best is yet to come
Do not lose sight
Of all the good that lies ahead
For love is life
And life is love
Follow your dreams
Be not afraid
For all is well
The storm is gone.

-oOo-

I will be there
To guide you through the rocky road
To give you light
And lift you up when you are down
So just be glad
You'll have a friend
If you need one
I will be there.

-oOo-

Guilt is painful
Not to be chastised
But to be forgotten
Love is beauty
Not to be forsaken
But to be cherished
Life is short
Not to be wasted
But to be enjoyed.

-oOo-

Time
Will pass away
Unnoticed
Just relax and enjoy
For today
Will soon be yesterday
And tomorrow
Will soon be today.

Distance
Is nothing but space
Which the mind can reach
Anytime
Just close your eyes
And feel
The tender care
That comes within.

Love
Will conquer
Time
And distance
If it's real.

-oOo-

Joy Bruce, M.D.

Sometimes I wander aimlessly
Through the maze of this thing called life
Knowing nothing
Seeing nothing
Feeling nothing
I close my eyes
And search my mind
What is life all about?

Useless efforts that always fail
Shattered memories that hurt
Faceless beings
Unfounded doubts
Words without meaning
I shake my head
And look around
What is life all about?

Suddenly a light comes through
Shining brightly along the way
Leading me
Guiding me
Helping me
I stretch my hand
And grasp the truth
About what life is all about.

All that I am and all that I want
Really mean nothing, I realize
The past is gone
Start anew
Live for tomorrow
For it means nothing
That life is nothing
This is what life is all about

-oOo-

Stigma

What right have I
To crush a flower
And then complain
That its crimson extract
Has stained my cruel hand?

What right have I
To stir the silence
And then complain
That the noise I hear
Is deafening my senseless mind?

What right have I
To stab my heart
And then complain
That the wound I've made
Is ruining my ruthless life?

What right have I
To complain and cry
When it was I
Who made them happen
After all?

-oOo-

I close my eyes
And feel the warmth of the sun
Piercing through me
Yellow and red
Merging with blue
Creating a vision
What a beautiful sight!

My mind wanders
Beyond the boundless sea
Spanning the horizon
Soaring up high
Dreaming of dreams
That never used to be
What a beautiful life!

-oOo-

Yesterday is gone
And will never be
What I want it to be
For time flies onward
And never looks back
So why should I?

-oOo-

Open the door
And let the future
Dispel the shadows

Open your eyes
And see the beauty
Beneath your tears

Open your heart
And feel the warmth
That comes from nowhere

Open your mind
And find the meaning
Of emptiness

-oOo-

Stigma

The sea
Peaceful and blue
Rippling waves
Forever moving
Yet so calm

Mirage
Images formed beyond
White clouds hovering
Shadows forming
Out of nowhere

Life
Powerful yet powerless
Arising from nothing
Beings existing
But not really moving

-oOo-

Where will I go?
Two roads lie before me
Which one should I take?
The familiar path
That goes to places I have seen and been
That leads to joy and pain I've known so well
That I can cross without even thinking?
Or the winding road
Of the great unknown
Where everything is possible
Where jewels are yet to be found
With crosses that I have yet to bear?
Where will I go?

-oOo-

Stigma

Out of nothing comes everything
The little laughter
The tender smile
The warm hello
The sweet goodbye

Out of everything comes nothing
The piercing pain
The cruel words
The evil thought
The iron hand

Nothing means everything
Everything means nothing
Life is real
Yet life is not
And so be it.

-oOo-

I am confused
I think I know
Yet I know not
Pretend to be not what I am
And be what I am not

I am lost
In this world of make believe
Where everything is nothing
And nothing is everything
Oblivious of the past
Unmindful of the future

What should I be
Other than what I am?
Where should I stand?

-oOo-

Stigma

I'd like to be
A little flower
Beaming and blooming
So I can have
Petals that heal
The grieving soul
That cries for love

I'd like to be
A little bird
Flying above the sky
So I can see
The vastness of space
And the universe
Where I exist

I'd like to be
A human being
Discerning of truth
So I can create
Something from nothing
And be the reality
That I hope to be

-o0o-

The Colors of My Mind

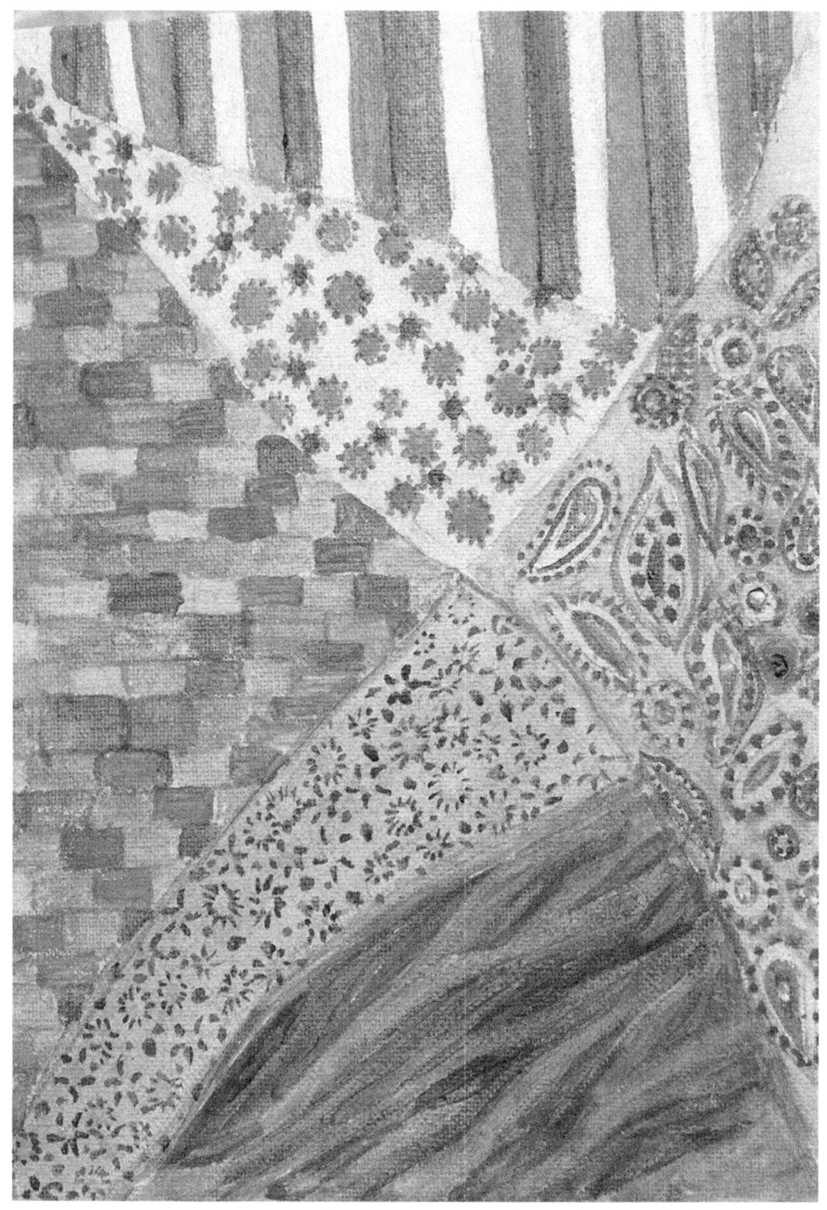

The Many Faces of Illness

Yellow Roses for You

The Sea

The Cabin

The Rock

The Path

The Crooked Road

The Journey

A Family United by Love, Faith and Hope

Starry Night Publishing

Everyone has a story...

Don't spend your life trying to get published! Don't tolerate rejection! Don't do all the work and allow the publishing companies reap the rewards!

Millions of independent authors like you, are making money, publishing their stories now. Our technological know-how will take the headaches out of getting published. Let "Starry Night Publishing.Com" take care of the hard parts, so you can focus on writing. You simply send us your Word Document and we do the rest. It really is that simple!

The big companies want to publish only "celebrity authors," not the average book-writer. It's almost impossible for first-time authors to get published today. This has led many authors to go the self-publishing route. Until recently, this was considered "vanity-publishing." You spent large sums of your money, to get twenty copies of your book, to give to relatives at Christmas, just so you could see your name on the cover. Now, however, the self-publishing industry allows authors to get published in a timely fashion, retain the rights to your work, keeping up to ninety-percent of your royalties, instead of the traditional five-percent.

We've opened up the gates, allowing you inside the world of publishing. While others charge you as much as fifteen-thousand dollars for a publishing package, we charge less than five-hundred dollars to cover copyright, ISBN, and distribution costs. Do you really want to spend all your time formatting, converting, designing a cover, and then promoting your book, because no one else will?

Our editors are professionals, able to create a top-notch book that you will be proud of. Becoming a published author is supposed to be fun, not a hassle.

At Starry Night Publishing, you submit your work, we create a professional-looking cover, a table of contents, compile your text and images into the appropriate format, convert your files for eReaders, take care of copyright information, assign an ISBN, allow you to keep one-hundred-percent of your rights, distribute your story worldwide on Amazon, Barnes & Noble and many other retailers, and write you a check for your royalties. There are no other hidden fees involved! You don't pay extra for a cover, or to keep your book in print. We promise! Everything is included! You even get a free copy of your book and unlimited half-price copies.

In four short years, we've published more than fifteen-hundred books, compared to the major publishing houses which only add an average of six new titles per year. We will publish your fiction, or non-fiction books about anything, and look forward to reading your stories and sharing them with the world.

We sincerely hope that you will join the growing Starry Night Publishing family, become a published author and gain the world-wide exposure that you deserve. You deserve to succeed. Success comes to those who make opportunities happen, not those who wait for opportunities to happen. You just have to try. Thanks for joining us on our journey.

www.starrynightpublishing.com

www.facebook.com/starrynightpublishing/

Made in the USA
Middletown, DE
04 October 2023

40203697R00235